The Fourth K

THE FOURTH K

MARIO PUZO

HEINEMANN : LONDON

William Heinemann Ltd
Michelin House, 81 Fulham Road, London SW3 6RB
LONDON   MELBOURNE   AUCKLAND

First published 1991
Copyright © Mario Puzo 1991
ISBN 0 434 60495 X
A CIP catalogue record for this book
is available from the British Library

Printed and bound in Great Britain
by Clays Ltd, St Ives plc

BOOK I

1

In Rome, on the Good Friday before Easter, seven terrorists made their final preparations to assassinate the Pope of the Roman Catholic Church. This band of four men and three women believed they were liberators of mankind. They called themselves the 'Christs of Violence'.

The leader of this particular band was an Italian youth well seasoned in the technique of terror. For this particular operation he had assumed the code name 'Romeo'; it pleased his youthful sense of irony, and its sentimentality sweetened his intellectual love of mankind.

On the late afternoon of Good Friday, Romeo rested in a 'safe' house provided by the International One Hundred. Lying on rumpled bedsheets stained with cigarette ash and night sweat he read a paperback edition of *The Brothers Karamazov*. His leg muscles cramped with tension, perhaps fear, it didn't matter. It would pass as it always did. But this mission was so different, so complex, involved so much danger of the body and the spirit. On this mission he would be truly a Christ of Violence, that name so Jesuitical it always moved him to laughter.

Romeo had been born Armando Giangi, to rich, high society parents who subjected him to a drowsy, luxurious, religious upbringing, a combination that so offended his ascetic nature that at the age of sixteen he renounced worldly goods and the Catholic Church. So now, at twenty-three, what greater rebellion could there be for him than the killing of the Pope? And yet there was still, for Romeo, a superstitious dread. As a child he had received Holy Confirmation

3

from a red-hatted cardinal. Romeo remembered always that ominous red hat painted in the very fires of hell.

So, confirmed by God in every ritual, Romeo prepared himself to commit a crime so terrible that hundreds of millions would curse his name, for his true name would become known. He would be captured. That was part of the plan. And then what happened depended on Yabril. But in time he, Romeo, would be acclaimed a hero who helped change this cruel social order. What was infamy in one century grew saintly in the next. And vice versa, he thought with a smile. The very first Pope to take the name of Innocent, centuries ago, had published a Papal Bull authorizing torture, and had been hailed for propagating the true Faith, rescuing heretic souls.

It also appealed to Romeo's youthful irony that the Church would canonize the Pope he was planning to kill. He would create a new saint. And how he hated them. All these Popes. Pope Innocent IV, Pope Pius, Pope Benedict, oh they sanctified too much, these amassers of wealth, these suppressors of the true faith of human freedom, these pompous wizards who smothered the wretched of the earth with their magic of ignorance, their hot insults to credulity.

He, Romeo, one of the 'First Hundred' of the Christs of Violence, would help erase that crude magic. The First Hundred, vulgarly called terrorists, were spread over Japan, Germany, Italy, Spain and even the tulipy Dutch. It was worth noting that there were none of the First Hundred in America. That democracy, that birthplace of freedom, had only intellectual revolutionaries who fainted at the sight of blood. Who exploded their bombs in empty buildings after warning people to leave; who thought public fornication on the steps of houses of state an act of idealistic rebellion. How contemptible they were. It was not surprising that America had never given one man to the Revolutionary Hundred.

Romeo put a halt to his day-dreaming. What the hell, he

4

didn't know if there were a hundred. There might be fifty or sixty, it was just a symbolic number. But such symbols rallied the masses and seduced the media. The only fact he really knew was that he, Romeo, was one of the First Hundred, and so was his friend and fellow conspirator, Yabril.

One of the many churches of Rome chimed its bells. It was nearly six in the evening of this Good Friday. In another hour Yabril would arrive to review all the mechanics of the complicated operation. The killing of the Pope would be the opening move of a brilliantly conceived chess game; a series of daring acts that delighted Romeo's romantic soul.

Yabril was the only man who had ever awed Romeo, physically and mentally. Yabril knew the treacheries of governments, the hypocrisies of legal authority, the dangerous optimism of idealists, the surprising deceptions in loyalty of even the most dedicated terrorists. But most of all Yabril was a genius of revolutionary warfare. He was contemptuous of the small mercies and infantile pity that affect most men. Yabril had but one aim, to free the future.

And Yabril was more merciless than Romeo could ever be. Romeo had murdered innocent people, betrayed his parents and his friends, assassinated a judge who had once protected him. Romeo understood that political killing might be a kind of insanity, he was willing to pay that price. But when Yabril said to him, 'If you cannot throw a bomb into a kindergarten, then you are not a true revolutionary,' Romeo told him, 'That I could never do.'

But he could kill a Pope.

Yet in the dark Roman nights, horrible little monsters, only the fetuses of dreams, covered Romeo's body with sweat distilled from ice.

Romeo sighed, rolled off his filthy bed to shower and shave before Yabril arrived. He knew that Yabril would judge his cleanliness a good sign, morale high for the coming mission. Yabril, like many sensualists, believed in a certain

5

amount of spit and polish. Romeo, a true ascetic, could live in shit.

On the Roman streets, on his walk to visit Romeo, Yabril took the usual precautions. But in fact everything really depended on internal security, the loyalty of the fighting cadres, the integrity of the First Hundred. But not they, not even Romeo knew the full extent of the mission.

Yabril was an Arab who easily passed for a Sicilian, as indeed many could. He had the thin dark face but the lower part, the chin and jaw, were surprisingly heavier, coarser, as if with an extra layer of bone. In his leisure time he grew a silky fur of a beard to hide the coarseness. But when he was part of an operation, he shaved himself clean. As the Angel of Death he showed his true face to the enemy.

Yabril's eyes were a pale tan, his hair had only isolated lines of gray and that heaviness of the jaw was repeated in the thickness of his chest and shoulders. His legs were long for the shortness of his body and masked the physical power he could generate. But nothing could hide the alert intelligence of his eyes.

Yabril detested the whole idea of the First Hundred. He thought it a fashionable public relations gimmick, despised its formal renunciation of the material world. These university-trained revolutionaries, like Romeo, were too romantic in their idealism, too contemptuous of compromise. Yabril understood that a little corruption in the rising bread of revolution was necessary.

Yabril had long ago given up all moral vanity. He had the clear conscience of those who believe and know that they are devoted with all their souls to the betterment of mankind. But he never reproached himself for his acts of self-interest. There had been his personal contracts with oil sheiks to kill political rivals. Odd jobs of murder for those new African heads of state, who, educated at Oxford, had learned to

6

delegate; then the random acts of terror for sundry respectable political chiefs. All those men in the world, who control everything except the power of life and death.

These acts were never known to the First Hundred, and certainly never confided to Romeo. Yabril received funds from the Dutch, English and American oil companies, money from Russian Communist fronts, and even long ago in his career, payment from the American CIA for a very special secret execution. But all that was in the early days.

Now, he lived well, he was not ascetic, after all he had been poor, though not born so. He was fond of good wine and gourmet food, preferred luxury hotels, enjoyed gambling, and often succumbed to the ecstasy of a woman's flesh. Always paying for that ecstasy with money, gifts and exerting his personal charm. He had a dread of romantic love.

Despite these 'revolutionary' weaknesses, Yabril was famous in his circles for the power of his will. He had absolutely no fear of death, not so extraordinary, but more uniquely he had no fear of pain. And it was, perhaps, because of this that he could be so ruthless.

Yabril had proved himself over the years. He was absolutely unbreakable under any kind of physical or psychological persuasion. He had survived imprisonment in Greece, France, Russia and two months of interrogation by Israeli Security whose expertness inspired his admiration. He had defeated them, perhaps because his body had the trick of losing feeling under duress. At last everyone understood. Yabril was granite under pain.

When he was the captor, he often charmed his victims. That he recognized a certain insanity in himself was part of his charm and part of the fear he inspired. Or perhaps that there was no malice in his cruelties. Yet all in all he savored life, he was a light-hearted terrorist. Even now he thoroughly enjoyed the fragrant streets of Rome, the twilight of Good

7

Friday filled with the chimes of countless holy bells, though he was preparing the most dangerous operation of his life.

Everything was in place. Romeo's cadre was in place. Yabril's own cadre would arrive in Rome the next day. The two cadres would be in separate safe houses, their only link the two leaders. Yabril knew that this was a great moment. This coming Easter Sunday and the days after would be a brilliant creation.

He, Yabril, would direct nations down roads they abhorred to tread. He would throw off all his shadowy masters, they would be his pawns and he would sacrifice them all, even poor Romeo. Only death could defeat his plans, or failure of nerve. Or to be truthful, one of a hundred errors in timing. But the operation was so complicated, so ingenious, it gave him pleasure. Yabril stopped in the street to enjoy the spires of cathedrals, the happy faces of the citizens of Rome, his melodramatic speculation of the future.

But like all men who think they can change the course of history by their own will, their own intelligence, their own strength, Yabril did not give due weight to the accidents and coincidences of history, nor to the possibility that there could be men more terrible than himself. Men bred in the strict structure of society, wearing the mask of benign law givers, could be far more ruthless and cruel.

Watching the devout and joyful pilgrims in the streets of Rome, believers in an omnipotent God, he was filled with a sense of his own invincibility. Proudly he would go beyond their God's forgiveness, for at the uttermost reach of evil, good must necessarily begin.

Yabril was now in one of the poorer districts of Rome where people could more easily be intimidated and bribed. He came to Romeo's safe house as darkness fell. The ancient four-storey apartment building had a large courtyard half encircled by a stone wall, all the apartments controlled by the underground revolutionary movement. Yabril was admitted by one of the three females in Romeo's cadre. She

8

was a thin woman in jeans and a blue denim shirt that was unbuttoned almost down to her waist. She wore no bra, there was no roundness of breasts visible. She had been on one of Yabril's operations before. He did not like her but he admired her ferocity. They had quarreled once and she had not backed down.

The woman's name was Annee. She wore her jet black hair in a Prince Valiant cut that did not flatter her strong blunt face, but drew notice to her blazing eyes that measured everyone with a sort of fury, even Romeo and Yabril. She had not yet been fully briefed on the mission but the appearance of Yabril told her it was of the utmost importance. She smiled briefly, without speaking, then closed the door after Yabril stepped inside.

Yabril noted with disgust how filthy the interior of the house had become. There were dirty dishes and glasses and remnants of food scattered over the living room, the floor littered with newspapers. Romeo's cadre was composed of four men and three women, all Italian. The women refused to clean up, it was contrary to their revolutionary belief to do domestic chores on an operation unless the men did their share. The men, all university students, still young, had the same belief in the rights of women, but they were the conditioned darlings of Italian mothers, and also knew that a back-up cadre would clean the house of all incriminating marks after they left. The unspoken compromise was that the squalor would be ignored. A compromise that irritated only Yabril.

He said to Annee, 'What pigs you are.'

Annee measured him with a cool contempt. 'I'm not a housekeeper,' she said.

And Yabril recognized her quality immediately. She was not afraid of him or any man or woman. She was a true believer. She was quite willing to burn at the stake. Alarm bells went off in his mind.

Romeo, so handsome, so vital that Annee lowered her

eyes, came racing down the stairs from the apartment above and embraced Yabril with real affection, then led him out into the courtyard where they sat on a small stone bench. The night air was filled with the scent of spring flowers, and with that scent there was a faint hum, the sound of countless thousands of pilgrims shouting and talking in the streets of Lenten Rome. Above it all the ascending and descending tolls of hundreds of church bells acclaimed the approaching Easter Sunday.

Romeo lit a cigarette and said, 'Our time has finally come, Yabril. No matter what happens, our names will be known to mankind for ever.'

Yabril laughed at the stilted romanticism, felt a little contempt for this desire for personal glory. 'Infamous,' he said. 'We compete with a long history of terror.' Yabril was thinking of their embrace. An embrace of professional love on his part, but shot through with remembered terror like parricides standing over a father they had murdered together.

There were dim electric lights along the courtyard walls but their faces were in darkness. Romeo said, 'They will know everything in time. But will they give us credit for our motives? Or will they paint us as lunatics? What the hell, the poets of the future will understand us.'

Yabril said, 'We can't worry about that now.' It embarrassed him when Romeo became theatrical, it made him question the man's efficiency though it had been proved many times. Romeo, despite delicate good looks, his fuzziness of concept, was a truly dangerous man. Romeo was too fearless, Yabril perhaps too cunning.

Just a year before, they had walked the streets of Beirut together. Bravely in their path was a brown paper sack, seemingly empty, greased with the food it had contained. Yabril walked around it. Romeo kicked and sailed the sack into the gutter. Different instincts. Yabril believed that

10

everything on this earth was dangerous. Romeo had a certain innocent trust.

There were other differences. Yabril was ugly with his small marbled tan eyes, Romeo was almost beautiful. Yabril was proud of his ugliness, Romeo was ashamed of his beauty. Yabril had always understood that when an innocent man commits absolutely to political change it must lead to murder. Romeo had come to that belief late, and reluctantly. His conversion had been an intellectual one.

Romeo had won sexual victories with the accident of physical beauty and his family money protected him from economic humiliations. Romeo was intelligent enough to know his good fortune was not morally correct, and so the very 'goodness' of his life disgusted him. He drowned himself in literature and his studies, which confirmed his belief. It was inevitable that his radical professors convinced him that he should help make the world a better place.

He did not want to be like his father, an Italian who spent more time in barber shops than courtesans at their hairdresser's. Did not want to spend his life in the pursuit of beautiful women. Above all he would never spend money reeking with the sweat of the poor. The poor must be made free and happy and then he too could taste happiness. And so he reached out, for a Second Communion, to the books of Karl Marx.

Yabril's conversion was more visceral. As a child in Palestine he had lived in a Garden of Eden. He had been a happy boy, extremely intelligent, devotedly obedient to his parents. Especially to his father who spent an hour each day reading to him from the Koran.

The family lived in large villas with many servants, on extended grounds which were magically green in that desert land. But one day, when Yabril was five years old, he was cast out of this Paradise. His beloved parents vanished, the villa and gardens dissolved into a cloud of purple smoke.

11

And suddenly he was living in a small dirty village on the bottom of a mountain, an orphan living on the charity of blood kin. His only treasure was his father's Koran printed on vellum, with illuminated figures of gold, startling calligraphy of a rich blue. And he always remembered his father reading it aloud, exactly from the text, according to Muslim custom. Those orders of God given to the Prophet Mohammed, words that could never be discussed or argued. As a grown man Yabril had remarked to a Jewish friend, 'The Koran is not a Torah', and they both laughed.

The truth exile from the Garden of Eden had been revealed to him almost at once but he did not fully understand it until a few years later. His father had been a secret supporter of Palestine liberation from the state of Israel, a leader of the underground. His father had been betrayed, gunned down in a police raid, and his mother had committed suicide when the villa and grounds were blown up by the Israelis.

It was most natural for Yabril to become a terrorist. His blood kin and his teachers in the local school taught him to hate all Jews but did not fully succeed. He did hate his God for banishing him from his childhood Paradise. When he was eighteen he sold his father's Koran for an enormous sum of money and enrolled in the University of Beirut. There he spent most of his fortune on women and, finally, after two years, became a member of the Palestinian underground. And over the years he became a deadly weapon in that cause. But his people's freedom was not his final aim. In some way his work was a search for inner peace.

Now, together in the courtyard of the safe house, it took Romeo and Yabril a little over two hours to go over every detail of their mission. Romeo smoked cigarettes constantly. He was nervous about one thing. 'Are you sure they will give me up?' he asked.

Yabril said softly, 'How can they not with the hostage I

12

will be holding? Believe me, you will be safer in their hands than I will be in Sherhaben.'

They gave each other a final embrace in the darkness, not knowing that after Easter Sunday they would never see each other again.

After Yabril left, Romeo smoked a final cigarette in the darkness of the courtyard. Beyond the stone walls he could see the peaks of the great cathedrals of Rome. Then he went inside. It was time to brief his cadre.

The woman, Annee, served as the cadre's armorer and she unlocked a huge trunk to give out the weapons and ammunition. One of the men spread a dirty bedsheet on the floor of the living room and Annee put gun oil and rags on to it. They would clean and oil their weapons as they listened to the briefing. For hours they listened and asked questions, they rehearsed their movements. Annee distributed the operational clothing and they made jokes about that. Finally they all sat down to a meal together that Romeo and the men had prepared. They toasted the success of their mission with new spring wine and then some of them played cards for an hour before they retired to their rooms. There was no need for a guard, they had locked themselves in securely and they had their weapons beside their beds. Still they all had trouble falling asleep.

It was after midnight when the armament woman, Annee, knocked on Romeo's door. Romeo was reading. He let her in and she quickly threw his copy of The Brothers Karamazov on the floor. She said almost contemptuously, 'You're reading that shit again?' Romeo shrugged and smiled and said, 'He amuses me, his characters strike me as Italians trying hard to be serious.'

They undressed quickly and lay down on the soiled sheets, both on their backs. Their bodies were tense not with the excitement of sex but with a mysterious terror. Romeo stared straight up at the ceiling and the woman Annee closed

13

her eyes. She was on his left and used her right hand to slowly and gently masturbate him. Their shoulders barely touched, the rest of their bodies were apart. When she felt Romeo erect she continued the strokes with her right hand and at the same time masturbated herself with her left hand. It was a continuous slow rhythm during which Romeo once reached out tentatively to touch her small breast but she made a grimace like a child, her eyes tightly shut. Now her pulling became tighter and stronger, the stroking frantic and unrhythmical and Romeo came to orgasm. As the semen flowed over Annee's hand she too came to orgasm, her eyes flew open and her slight body seemed to hurl itself into the air, lifting and turning to Romeo as if to kiss him, but she ducked her head and buried it in his chest for a moment until her body shuddered to a stop. Then, very matter of factly, she sat up and wiped her hand on the soiled sheet of the bed. She took Romeo's cigarettes and lighter from the marble night table and started to smoke. 'I feel better,' she said.

Romeo went into the bathroom and wet a towel. He came back and washed her hands and then wiped himself. Then he gave her the towel and she rubbed it between her legs.

They had done this on another mission and Romeo understood that this was the only kind of affection she could permit. She was so fierce in her independence, for whatever reason, that she could not bear that a man she did not love would penetrate her. And as for fellatio and cunnilingus, which he had suggested, they were also another form of surrender. What she had done was the only way she could satisfy her need without betraying her ideals of independence.

Romeo watched her face. It was not so stern now, the eyes not so fierce. She was so young, he thought, how did she become so deadly in so short a time? 'Do you want to sleep with me tonight, just for company?' he said.

Annee stubbed out the cigarette. 'Oh no,' she said. 'Why

14

would I want to do that? We've both got what we need.' She started to dress.

Romeo said jokingly, 'At least you could say something tender before you leave.'

She stood in the doorway for a moment and then turned. For a moment he thought she would return to the bed. She was smiling, and for the first time he saw her as a young girl he could love. But then she seemed to stand up on tiptoe, and said, 'Romeo, Romeo! wherefore art thou Romeo?' She thumbed her nose at him and disappeared behind the door she closed.

At Brigham Young University in Provo, Utah, two students, David Jatney and Cryder Cole, prepared their kits for the traditional once-a-term assassination hunt. This game had again come back into favor with the election of Francis Xavier Kennedy to the Presidency of the United States. By the rules of the game a student team had twenty-four hours to commit the assassination, that is, fire their toy pistols at a cardboard effigy of the President of the United States from no more than five paces away. To prevent this there was a Law and Order fraternity defense team of more than a hundred students. The 'Money Prize Bet' was used to pay for the Victory Banquet at the conclusion of the hunt.

The college faculty and administration, influenced by the Mormon Church, disapproved of these games but they had become popular on campuses all over the United States, one of the vexations of a free society. Poor taste, an appetite for the grossness in life, was part of the very high spirits of the young. And it was an outlet for the resentment of authority, a protest by those who had not yet achieved anything against those who had already become successful. It was a symbolic protest, and certainly preferable to political demonstrations, random violence and sit-ins. The hunting game was a safety valve for rioting hormones.

The two hunters, David Jatney and Cryder Cole, strolled

the campus arm in arm. Jatney was the planner and Cole the actor so it was Cole who did the talking as they made their way towards the fraternity brothers guarding the effigy of the President. The cardboard figure of Francis Kennedy was a recognizable likeness but extravagantly colored to show him wearing a blue suit, a green tie, red socks and no shoes. Where the shoes should have been was the Roman numeral IV.

The Law and Order gang threatened Jatney and Cole with their toy pistols and the two hunters veered off. Cole shouted a cheerful insult but Jatney was grim-faced. He took his mission very seriously. Jatney was reviewing his master plan and already feeling a savage satisfaction over its assured success. This walk in view of the enemy was to establish that they were wearing ski gear, to establish a visual identity and so prepare for a later surprise. Also to plant the idea that they were leaving the campus for the weekend.

Part of the hunting game required the itinerary of the Presidential effigy be published. The effigy would be at the victory banquet that was scheduled for that evening before midnight. Jatney and Cole planned to make their strike before the midnight deadline.

Everything worked out as planned. Jatney and Cole reunited at six p.m. in the designated restaurant. The proprietor had no knowledge of their plans. They were just two young students who had been working for him for the past two weeks. They were very good waiters, especially Cole, and the proprietor was delighted with them.

At nine that evening when the Law and Order guards, a hundred strong, entered with their Presidential effigy, guards were posted at all the entries to the restaurant. The effigy was placed in the center of the circle of tables. The proprietor was rubbing his hand at this influx of business. It was only when he went into the kitchen and saw his two young waiters hiding their toy pistols in the soup tureens that he caught on. 'Oh for Christ's sake,' he said, 'that means you

16

two guys are quitting tonight.' Cole grinned at him but David Jatney gave him a menacing scowl and they marched into the dining room, soup tureens lifted high to shield their faces.

The guards were already drinking victory toasts when Jatney and Cole placed the tureens on the center table, whipped off the covers and lifted out the toy pistols. They held their weapons against the garishly colored effigy and fired the little pops of the mechanism. Cole fired one shot and burst out laughing. Jatney fired three shots very deliberately then threw his pistol on the floor. He did not move, he did not smile until the guards mobbed him with congratulatory curses and all of them sat down to dinner. Jatney gave the effigy a kick so that it slid down to the floor where it could not be seen.

This had been one of the more simple hunts. In other colleges across the country the game was more serious. Elaborate security structures were set up, effigies squirted synthetic blood. In the more liberal colleges the effigy was sometimes black.

But in Washington DC, the Attorney General of the United States, Christian Klee, had his own file of all these playful assassins. And it was the photograph and memo on Jatney that caught his interest. He made a note to assign a case team to the life of David Jatney.

On this same Good Friday before Easter, two far more serious-minded young men with far more idealistic beliefs than Jatney and Cole, far more concerned about the future of their world, drove from the Massachusetts Institute of Technology to New York, and deposited a small suitcase in a baggage locker of the Port Authority Building. They picked their way fastidiously through the drunken homeless bums, the sharp-eyed pimps, the incipient whores who thronged the halls of the building. The two were prodigies, at age twenty professors of physics, part of an advanced program

17

at the University. The suitcase held a tiny atom bomb they had constructed using stolen lab materials and the necessary plutonium oxide. It had taken them two years to steal these materials from their programs, bit by bit, falsifying their reports and experiments so that it would not be noticed.

Their names were Adam Gresse and Henry Tibbot and they had been classified as geniuses since they were twelve. Their parents had brought them up to be aware of their responsibilities to humankind. They had no vices except knowledge. The brilliance of their intelligence made them disdain those appetites that were lice on the hide of humanity, such as alcohol, gambling, women, gluttony and drugs.

But they succumbed to the powerful drug of clear thinking. They had a social conscience and saw all the evil in the world. They knew that the making of atomic weapons was wrong, that the fate of humanity hung in the balance, and they decided to do what they could to avert an eternal disaster. So after a year of boyish talk they decided to scare the government. They would show how easy it was for a crazed individual to inflict grave punishment on mankind. They built the tiny atom bomb, only half a kiloton in power, would plant it, and then warn the authorities of its existence. They thought themselves and their deed unique, Godlike. They did not know that this precise situation had been predicted by the psychological reports of a prestigious 'think tank', funded by the government, as one of the possibilities of the atomic age of mankind.

While they were still in New York, Adam Gresse and Henry Tibbot mailed their warning letter to the *New York Times* explaining their motivations and asking that the letter be published before being sent to the authorities. The composing of the letter had been a long process, not only because it had to be worded so precisely to show no malice but because they used scissored printed words and letters lifted out of old newspapers which they pasted on to blank sheets of paper.

The bomb would not go off till the following Thursday. By that time the letter would be in the hands of the authorities and the bomb surely found. It would be a warning to the rulers of the world.

Oliver Ollifant was one hundred years old and his mind was as clear as a bell. Unfortunately for him.

It was a mind so clear, yet so subtle, that, while breaking a great many moral laws, it had washed his conscience clean. A mind so cunning that Oliver Ollifant had never fallen into the almost inevitable traps of everyday life; he had never married, never run for political office and never had a friend he trusted absolutely.

On a huge, secluded, heavily guarded estate only ten miles from the White House, Oliver Ollifant, the richest man in the America and possibly the most powerful private citizen, awaited the arrival of his godson, the Attorney General of the United States, Christian Klee.

Oliver Ollifant's charm equaled his brilliance, his power rested on both. Even at the advanced age of one hundred his advice was still sought by great men who relied on his analytic powers to such an extent that he had been nick-named the 'Oracle'.

As advisor to presidents the Oracle had predicted economic crises. Wall Street crashes, the fall of the dollar, the flight of foreign capital, the fantasies of oil prices. He had predicted the political moves of the Soviet Union, the unexpected embraces of rivals in the Democratic and Republican parties. But above all he amassed ten billion dollars. It was natural that advice from such a rich man be valued, even when wrong. The Oracle was nearly always right.

Now on this Good Friday the Oracle was worried about one thing. The birthday party to celebrate his one hundred years on this earth. A party to be held on Easter Sunday in

19

the Rose Garden of the White House, the host none other than the President of the United States, Francis Xavier Kennedy.

It was a permissible vanity for the Oracle to take great pleasure in this spectacular affair. The world would again remember him for one brief moment. It would be, he thought sadly, his last appearance on the stage.

And in Rome on that Good Friday, Theresa Catherine Kennedy, daughter of the President of the United States, prepared to end her European exile and return to live with her father in the White House.

Her Secret Service security detail had already made all the travel arrangements. Obeying her instructions they had booked passage on the Easter Sunday flight from Rome to New York.

Theresa Kennedy was twenty-three years old and was studying in Europe, first at the Sorbonne in Paris and then in Rome where she had just ended a serious affair with a radical Italian student, to their mutual relief.

She loved her father but hated his being President because she was too loyal to publicly voice her own views. She was a believer in socialism, in the brotherhood of man, the sisterhood of women. She was a feminist in the American style; economic independence was the foundation of freedom and so she had no guilt about the trust funds that guaranteed her freedom.

With a curious but very human morality she rejected the idea of privilege and rarely visited her father in the White House. And perhaps she unconsciously judged her father for her mother's death, that he had struggled for political power while her mother was dying. Later she had wanted to lose herself in Europe but by law she had to be protected by the Secret Service as a member of the immediate Presidential family. She had tried to 'sign off' on that security protection but her father had begged her not to. Francis Kennedy told her he could not bear it if something were to happen to her.

A detail of twenty men, spread over three shifts a day guarded Theresa Kennedy. When she went to a restaurant, if she went to a movie with her boyfriend, they were there. They rented apartments in the same building, used a command van in the street. She was never alone. And she had to tell her schedule to the chief of the security detail, every single day.

Her guards were two-headed monsters, half-servant, half-master. With advanced electronic equipment they could hear the love-making when she brought a male friend back to her apartment. And they were frightening, they moved like wolves, with silent glides, their heads tilted alertly to catch a scent on the wind, but really straining to listen to their ear-plug radios.

Theresa Kennedy had refused a 'net' security, that is, a close, live-in, drive-in, security. She drove her own car, refused to let the security team take an adjoining apartment, refused to walk with guards alongside her. She had insisted that the security be a 'perimeter' security, that they could erect a wall around her as if she were a large garden. In this way she could lead a personal life. This led to some embarrassing moments. One day she went shopping and needed change for a telephone call. She had seen one of her security detail pretending to shop nearby. She had gone up to him and said, 'Could you give me a quarter?' The man had looked at her with shocked bewilderment and she realized suddenly that she had made a mistake, that he was not her security guard. She had burst out laughing and apologized. The man was amused and delighted as he gave her the quarter. 'Anything for a Kennedy,' he said jokingly.

Like so many of the young, Theresa Kennedy believed, on no particular evidence, that people were 'good'; as she believed herself to be good. She marched for freedom, spoke out for the right and against the wrong. She tried never to commit petty mean acts of everyday life. As a child she gave her piggy bank to the American Indians.

In her position as daughter of the President of the United States it was awkward for her when she spoke out for abortion, lent her name to radical and left-wing organizations. She endured the abuse of the media and the insults of political opponents. Innocently, she was scrupulously fair in her love affairs, she believed in absolute frankness, she abhorred deceit.

She should have learned some valuable lessons. In Paris a group of tramps living under one of the bridges tried to rape her when she roamed the city in search of local color. In Rome two beggars tried to snatch her purse as she was giving them money and in both cases she had to be rescued by her patient, vigilant Secret Service detail. But this made no impression on her general faith, that man was good. Every human being had the immortal seed of goodness in his soul, no one was beyond redemption. She had, of course, as a feminist learned of the tyranny of men over women, but did not really comprehend the brutal force men used when dealing with their world. She had no sense of how one human being could betray another human being in the most false and cruel ways.

The chief of her security detail, a man too old to guard the more important people in government, was horrified by her innocence and tried to educate her. He told her horror stories about men in general, stories taken from his long experience in the service, more frank than he would ordinarily be since this was his last assignment before retiring.

'You're too young to understand this world,' he said. 'And in your position you have to be very careful. You think because you do good for someone they will do good to you.' He was telling her this particular story because just the day before she had picked up a male hitchhiker, who assumed that this was an invitation. The security chief had acted immediately, the two security cars forced Theresa's car to the edge of the road just as the hitchhiker put his hand in Theresa's lap.

'Let me tell you a story,' the chief said. 'I once worked for the smartest and nicest man in the government service. In clandestine operations. Just once he got outsmarted, caught in a trap and this bad guy had him at his mercy. Could just blow him away. And this guy was a real bad guy. But for some reason he let my boss off the hook and said, "Remember, you owe me one."

'Well, we spent six months tracking this guy down and we nailed him. And my boss blew him away, never gave him a chance to surrender or turn double. And you know why? He told me himself. This bad guy once had the power of God and therefore was too dangerous to be allowed to live. And my boss didn't have a feeling of gratitude, he said the guy's mercy was just a whim and you can't count on whims the next time around.' The chief did not tell Theresa Kennedy his boss had been a man named Christian Klee.

All these events converged on one man. The President of the United States, Francis Xavier Kennedy.

President Francis Xavier Kennedy and his election were a miracle of American politics. He had been elected to the Presidency on the magic of his name and his extraordinary physical and intellectual gifts, despite the fact that he had only served one term in the Senate before his election to the Presidency.

He was the 'nephew' of John F. Kennedy, the President who had been assassinated in 1963, but was outside the organized Kennedy clan still active in American politics. He was in reality, a cousin, and the only one of the far-flung family who had inherited the charisma of his two famous 'uncles', John and Robert Kennedy.

Francis Kennedy had been a boy genius in the law, a Professor at Harvard at the age of twenty-four. Later he had organized his own law firm which crusaded for broad liberal

23

reforms in the government and the private business sector. His law firm did not make a great deal of money, which was not important to him since he had inherited considerable wealth but it did not bring him a great deal of national fame. He crusaded for the rights of minorities, the welfare of the economically disabled, he defended the helpless.

All these good deeds would have availed him nothing politically except for his other gifts. He was extraordinarily handsome with the satiny blue eyes of his two dead uncles, pale white skin, and jet black hair. He had a wit that was cutting, yet full of such good humor that it destroyed his opponents without a hint of petty malice. He was never pompous and never overbearing. He was well read in the sciences and in the literary arts and above all he cherished humanitarian values.

But most importantly he was extraordinarily effective on television. On that screen he was mesmerizing. That and the Kennedy name carried him to the Presidency. Four of his closest friends orchestrated his election. Christian Klee, Arthur Wix, Eugene Dazzy and Oddblood Gray. They were appointed his personal Senior Staff.

When he was nominated as the Democratic candidate for the Presidency, Francis Kennedy did an extraordinary thing. Instead of putting his inherited wealth in blind trusts, he donated it to charity. His wife and daughter had trusts that would take care of their needs. He himself was talented enough to earn a rich living by his own efforts. It was no great sacrifice, he claimed, as indeed did some of his opponents. But he wanted to set some sort of example. It was one of his strongest beliefs that no individual citizen should accrue extraordinary wealth. Not that he was a communist, every man should be allowed to provide for wife and children and family, but why should one man have billions of dollars? His action and words aroused the admiration of millions and the hatred of thousands.

Great things were expected, but unfortunately the Democratic Congress elected with Kennedy failed to pass his ambitious social programs. On television Francis Kennedy had promised that every family would be well housed, he had announced extraordinary plans for education, guaranteed equal medical care for every citizen, that a rich America would construct an economic safety net that would catch unfortunates who tumbled to the bottom of society. On television, with his magnetic voice, his handsome physical presence, these promises were electrifying. And when elected, he tried to fulfil them. Congress defeated him.

On this Good Friday he met his Senior Staff of top advisors and his Vice President to give them news that he knew would make them unhappy.

He met with them in the Yellow Oval Room of the White House, his favorite room, larger and more comfortable than the more famous Oval Office. The Yellow Oval Room was more a living room and they could be comfortable while being served an English tea.

They were all waiting for him and they rose when his Secret Service bodyguards ushered him into the room. Kennedy motioned his staff to sit down while telling his bodyguards to wait outside the room. Two things irritated him in this little scene. The first was that he had to personally order the Secret Service men out of the room according to the protocols, and the second was that the Vice President had to stand in respect for the Presidency. What annoyed him about this was that the Vice President was a woman; political courtesy overruled social courtesy. This was compounded by the fact that Vice President Helen DuPray was ten years older than him, was still quite a beautiful woman, and had extraordinary political and social intelligence. Which was, of course, why he had picked her as his running mate, despite the opposition of the heavyweights in the Democratic Party.

'Damn it, Helen,' Francis Kennedy said. 'Stop standing up

25

when I come into a room. Now I have to pour tea for everybody to show my humility.'

'I wanted to express my gratitude,' Helen DuPray said. 'When the Vice President gets summoned to your staff meeting it's usually to get orders on how to wash the dishes.' They both laughed. The staff did not.

Francis Kennedy waited until everyone had been served their tea and then said, 'I have decided not to run for a second term. Which is why you are invited to this meeting, Helen,' he said to the Vice President. 'I want you to prepare to make your run for the Presidency. You will have my full support. Whatever it's worth.'

They were all struck dumb then Helen DuPray smiled at him. All the men in the room noted that she had a lovely smile and also noted that this smile was one of her great political weapons. She said, 'Francis, I think a decision not to run requires a full length review by your staff without my presence. But before I leave let me say this. At this particular point of time I know how discouraged you are by Congress. But I won't be able to do any better, assuming I could be elected. I think you should be more patient. Your second term could be more effective.'

President Kennedy said impatiently, 'Helen, you know as well as I do that a President of the United States has more clout in his first term than in his second.'

'True in most cases,' Helen DuPray said. 'But maybe we could get a different House of Representatives for your second term. And let me speak of my own self interest. As Vice President for only one term I am in a weaker position than if I served for two terms. Also your support would be more valuable as a two-term President and not a President who's been chased out of office by his own Democratic Congress.'

As she picked up her memorandum file and prepared to leave, Francis Kennedy said, 'You don't have to go.'

Helen DuPray gave everybody the same sweet smile. 'I'm

sure your staff can speak far more freely if I'm not present,' she said and she left the Yellow Oval Room.

The four men around Kennedy were silent as she left. When the door was safely closed there was a small flurry of movement as they fluffed their folders of memoranda sheets and reached for tea and sandwiches. The President's Chief of Staff said casually, 'Helen may be the smartest person in this administration.' This was Eugene Dazzy but he was known to have a weakness for beautiful women.

Francis Kennedy smiled at him. 'And what do you think, Euge?' he said. 'Do you think I should be more patient and run again?'

All the men shifted uneasily in their seats. Helen DuPray, smart as she was, did not know Francis Kennedy as well as they did. All four men had a far closer personal relationship with the President. They had been with him since the beginning of his political career and even before. They knew that his easy and bantering statement, his announcement that he would support DuPray masked an almost irreversible decision. They also knew that it meant the end of their power. They got along well with the Vice President but they had no illusions about what she would do if she became President. She would have her own hand-picked staff.

Kennedy's Chief of Staff, Eugene Dazzy was a large affable man whose great art was to avoid making enemies of people whose important wishes and special requests the President denied. Dazzy bowed his balding head over his notes, his tubby upper body straining the wall of his well tailored jacket. He spoke in a casual voice.

'Why not run?' Dazzy said. 'You'll have a nice goof off job. Congress will tell you what to do and refuse to do what you want done. Everything will stay the same. Except in foreign policy, there you can have some fun. You might even do some good. Sure, the world is falling apart and the other countries sort of shit on us, even the small fry – helped as we know by big American companies with their international affiliates. Our army is fifty per cent under quota, we've educated our kids so well they're too smart to be patriotic. Of course we have our technology but then who buys our goods? Our balance of payments is hopeless. Japan outsells us, Israel has a more effective army. You can only go up. I say go get re-elected and relax and have a good time for four years. What the hell, it's not a bad job and you can use the money.' Dazzy smiled and waved a hand to show that he was at least half kidding.

The four men of the staff watched Kennedy closely, despite their seemingly casual attitudes. None of them felt Dazzy was being disrespectful; the playfulness of his remarks was an attitude that Kennedy had encouraged over the past three years.

Arthur Wix, the National Security Advisor, a burly man with a big city face, that is, ethnic, born of a Jewish father and Italian mother, could be savagely witty, but a little in awe of the Presidential office and Kennedy. He did not indulge himself now. Also as the National Security Advisor, he felt that his responsibilities obliged him to be more serious in tone than the others. He spoke in a quiet persuasive tone that still had a New York buzz. 'Euge,' he said, motioning to Dazzy, 'may think he's kidding, but you can make a valuable contribution in our country's foreign policy. We have far more leverage than Europe or Asia believes. I think it's imperative you run for another term. After all in foreign policy, the President of the United States has the power of a king.'

Again the other men of the staff watched Kennedy for his reaction but he simply turned to the man who was closest to him, even closer than Dazzy.

'What do you feel about this, Chris?' Kennedy said.

Christian Klee was Attorney General of the United States. And in an extraordinary move by Kennedy, he was also appointed the head of the FBI and the Chief of the Secret

Service that guarded the Presidency. Essentially he controlled the whole internal security system of the United States. Kennedy had paid a heavy political price for this. He had traded Congress the appointment of two justices of the Supreme Court, three Cabinet posts and the ambassadorship to Britain.

'Francis, you have to make up your mind about two things,' Christian Klee said. 'First, do you really want to run again for President? You can win just with your voice and smile on TV. Certainly your administration hasn't done shit for this country. So. Do you really want it? The second question is: do you still want to do something for this country? Do you want to fight all its enemies, internal and external? Do you really want to set this country on its true course? Because I think this country is dying, I think it's a dinosaur that will be wiped out. Or do you just want to enjoy a four-year vacation and use the White House as your private country club?' Christian paused for a moment and said with a smile, 'Three questions.'

Christian Klee and Francis Kennedy had first met in college. Christian had been one of the important young men at Harvard, Kennedy had only had his own inner circle of admirers, but Christian became one of them.

Now President Kennedy looked at Christian Klee. He said dryly, 'The answer to all three of your questions is no.' Then he turned to his chief political advisor and liaison with Congress. This was Oddblood Gray, the youngest man on his staff, only ten years out of college.

Oddblood Gray had come out of the black left-wing movement, via Harvard and a Rhodes Scholarship. His youthful idealism had been perhaps corrupted by his instinctive political genius. He knew how government worked, where leverage could be applied, when to use the brute force of patronage, when to skip in place, when to surrender gracefully. Kennedy had ignored his warning against trying

29

to push his new programs through Congress. Gray had foretold the massive defeats.

Kennedy said to him, 'Otto, give us the word.'

'Quit,' Oddblood Gray said. 'While you're only just losing.' Kennedy smiled and the other men laughed. Oddblood Gray went on. 'Congress shits on you, the press kicks your ass. The lobbyists and big business have strangled your programs. The working people are disappointed in you, the intellectuals feel you've betrayed them. The right wing and left wing in this country agree on one thing. That you're a dishrag. You're driving this damn big Cadillac of a country and the steering wheel doesn't work. And to boot, every damn maniac in this country gets another four years to knock you off. The hat trick. Let's all of us get out of this damn White House.'

'Do you think I could be re-elected?' Kennedy asked, smiling.

Oddblood Gray faked a look of astonishment. 'Of course,' he said. 'This country always re-elects useless Presidents. Even your worst enemies want you re-elected.'

Kennedy smiled. They were trying to goad him into running again by appealing to his pride. None of them wanted to leave this center of power, this Washington, this White House. It was better to be this clawless lion than not to be a lion at all.

Then Oddblood Gray spoke again. 'We might do some good if we work differently. If you really put your heart into it.'

Eugene Dazzy said, 'You're really the only hope, Francis. The rich are too rich, the poor are too poor. This country is becoming a feeding ground for the big industries, for Wall Street. They're running wild, with no thought for the future. It may be decades down the road but trouble, big trouble is on the way. There's a chance for you to reverse the whole thing in the next four years.'

They all waited for his answer and with different

emotions. It was unusual for political advisors to have such strong personal attachments to their President but all these men held him in some kind of awe.

Francis Kennedy had an overpowering charisma. It was not only that he was imposing in body, indeed had a kind of physical beauty that echoed his two famous uncles, but that he had intellectual brilliance that was rare, even exotic in a politician. He had been a successful lawyer, a writer on the sciences, had a knowledge of physics and an impeccable taste in literature. He even understood economic theory without the help of financial ghosts. And he had a sympathy for the ordinary man that was unusual in a man who had been born to wealth and had never suffered any kind of economic stress.

Eugene Dazzy broke the silence. 'You have to think about it more, Francis. Helen is right.' But it was clear to all of them that Kennedy had made up his mind. He would not run again. This was the end of the road for all of them.

Kennedy shrugged. 'After the Easter vacation, I'll make a formal announcement. Eugene, start your staff doing the paperwork. My advice to you guys is to start looking for jobs with the big law firms and the defense industries.'

They took this as a dismissal and left, except for Christian Klee.

Christian said casually, 'Will Theresa be home for the holidays?'

Francis Kennedy shrugged. 'She's in Rome with a new boyfriend. She'll be flying in on Easter Sunday. She makes a point of ignoring religious holidays.'

Christian said, 'I'm glad she's getting the hell out. I really can't protect her in Europe. And she thinks she can shoot her mouth off there and it won't be reported here.' He paused a moment. 'If you do run again, you'll have to keep your daughter out of sight or disown her.'

Kennedy laughed. 'It doesn't matter, Christian, I won't run again. Make other plans.'

'OK,' Christian said. 'Now about the birthday party for the Oracle. He's really looking forward to it.'

'Don't worry,' Kennedy said. 'I'll give him the full treatment. My God, a hundred years old and he still looks forward to his birthday party.'

'He was and is a great man,' Christian said.

Kennedy gave him a sharp look. 'You were always fonder of him than I ever was. He had his faults, he made his mistakes.'

'Sure,' Christian said. 'But I never saw a man control his life better. He changed my life with his advice, his guidance.' Christian paused for a moment. 'I'm having dinner with him tonight so I'll just tell him the party is definitely on.'

Kennedy smiled dryly. 'You can safely tell him that,' he said.

At the end of the day Kennedy signed some papers in the Oval Office, then sat at his desk and gazed through the windows. He could see the tops of the gates that surrounded the White House grounds, black iron tipped with white electrified thorns. As always he felt uneasy by his proximity to the streets and to the public, though he knew that the seeming vulnerability to attack was an illusion. He was extraordinarily protected. There were seven perimeters guarding the White House. For two miles away every building had a Security team on the roofs and in apartments. All the streets leading to the White House were commanded by concealed rapid fire and heavy weapons. The tourists who came mornings to visit the ground floor of the White House in their many hundreds were heavily infiltrated with Secret Service agents who circulated constantly, and took part in the small talk, their eyes alert. Every inch of the White House that these tourists were permitted to visit behind the walling off ropes was covered by TV monitors and special audio equipment that could pick up secret whispers. Armed guards manned special computer desks

32

that could serve as barricades at every turn in the corridors. And during these visits by the public Kennedy would always be up in the new specially built fourth floor that served as his living quarters. Living quarters guarded by specially reinforced floors and walls and ceilings.

Now in the famous Oval Office that he rarely used except to sign official documents in special ceremonies, Francis Kennedy relaxed to enjoy one of the few minutes he was completely alone. He took a long thin Cuban cigar from the humidor on his desk, felt the oiliness of the leafy wrapper on his fingers. He cut the end, lit it carefully, took the first rich puff and looked out through the bullet-proof windows.

He could see himself as a child walking across the vast green lawn, the faraway white-painted guard post, then running to greet his Uncle Jack and Uncle Robert. How he had loved them. Uncle Jack so full of charm, so childlike, and yet so powerful, to give hope that a child could wield power over the world. And Uncle Robert, so serious and earnest and yet so gentle and playful. And here Francis Kennedy thought, no, we called him Uncle Bobby, not Robert, or did we sometimes? He could not remember.

But he did remember one day more than forty years ago when he had run to meet both his uncles on that very same lawn and how they had each taken one of his arms and swung him so that his feet never touched the ground as they walked him with them into the White House.

And now he stood in their place. The power that had awed him as a child was now his. It was a pity that memory could evoke so much pain and so much beauty, and so much disappointment. What they had died for, he was giving up.

On this Good Friday Francis Xavier Kennedy did not know that all this could be changed by two insignificant revolutionaries in Rome.

2

On Easter Sunday morning, Romeo and his cadre of four men and three women, in full operational gear, disembarked from their van. They billowed into the Roman streets outside St Peter's Square, mingling with the crowds attired in Easter finery; the women glorious in the pastel colors of spring, operatic in worshipping hats, the men handsome in silky creamy suits, yellow palm crosses stitched into their lapels. The children were even more dazzling, little girls with gloves and frilly frocks, the boys in navy blue suits of Confirmation with red ties bisecting snowy shirts. Scattered throughout were priests smiling approving benedictions to the faithful.

But Romeo was a more sober pilgrim, a serious witness to the Resurrection that this Easter morning celebrated. He was dressed in a dead black suit, a white shirt heavily starched, and a pure white tie almost invisible against it. His shoes were black but rubber-soled. And now he buttoned the camelhair coat to conceal the rifle that hung in its special sling. He had practised with this rifle for the past three months until his accuracy was deadly.

The four men in his cadre were dressed as monks of the Capuchin order; long flowing robes of dingy brown, girdled by fat cloth belts. Their heads were tonsured but covered with skull caps. Concealed inside the loose robes were grenades and handguns.

The three women, one of them Annee, were dressed as nuns and they too had weapons beneath their loose-fitting clothing. Annee and the other two nuns walked ahead, people made way for them, and Romeo followed easily in their black and white wake. After Romeo came the four monks of the cadre, observing everything, ready to interdict if Romeo was stopped by Papal police.

And so Romeo's band made their way to St Peter's Square, invisible in the huge crowd that was assembling. Finally like dark corks bobbing on an ocean of flowery silk, they came to rest on the far side of the square, their backs protected by marble columns and stone walls. Romeo stood a little apart. He was watching for a signal from the other side of the square, where Yabril and his cadre were busy attaching holy figurines to the walls.

Yabril and his cadre of three men and three women were in casual attire with loose-fitting jackets. The men carried concealed handguns and the women were working with the religious figurines. These figurines, small statues of Christ, were loaded with explosives designed to go off by radio signal. The backs had adhesive glue so strong that they could not be detached by any of the curious in the crowd. Also the figurines were beautifully designed and made of an expensive looking white-painted terracotta formed around a wired skeleton. They appeared to be part of the Easter decorations and as such inviolate.

When this was done, Yabril led his cadre through the crowd and out of St Peter's Square to his own waiting van. He sent one of his men in the cadre to Romeo to give him the radio signal device for the setting off of the figurines. Then Yabril and his cadre got into their van and started the drive to Rome airport. Pope Innocent would not appear on the balcony until three hours later. They were on schedule.

In the van, closed off from the Easter world of Rome, Yabril thought about how this whole exercise had begun . . .

On a mission together a few years ago, Romeo had mentioned that the Pope had the heaviest security guard of

35

any ruler in Europe. Yabril had laughed and said, 'Who would want to kill a pope? Like killing a snake that has no poison. A useless old figurehead and with a dozen useless old men ready to replace him. Bridegrooms of Christ, a set of a dozen red-capped dummies. What would change in the world with the death of a pope? I can see kidnapping him, he's the richest man in the world. But killing him would be like killing a lizard sleeping in the sun.'

Romeo had argued his case and intrigued Yabril. The Pope was revered by hundreds of millions of Catholics all over the world. And certainly the Pope was a symbol of capitalism; the bourgeois Western Christian States propped him up. The Pope was one of the great stones of authority in the edifice of that society. And so it followed that if the Pope were assassinated it would be a shocking psychological blow to the enemy world. And killing the representative of that God on earth in which they did not believe. The royalty of Russia and France had been murdered because they too ruled from divine right, and those murders had advanced humanity. God was the fraud of the rich, the swindler of the poor, the Pope an earthly wielder of that evil power. But still it was only half an idea. Yabril expanded the concept. Now the operation had a grandeur that awed Romeo and filled Yabril with self-admiration.

Romeo for all his talk and sacrifices was not what Yabril considered a true revolutionary. Yabril had studied the history of Italian terrorists. They were very good at assassinating heads of state, they had studied at the feet of the Russians who had killed their Czar finally after many attempts, indeed they had borrowed from the Russians that name Yabril detested, 'the Christs of Violence'.

Yabril had met Romeo's parents once. The father, a useless man, a parasite on humanity. Complete with chauffeur, valet, and a great big lamb-like dog that he used as bait to snare women on the boulevards. But a man with beautiful

36

manners. It was impossible not to like him if you were not his son.

And the mother, another beauty of the capitalistic system, voracious for money and jewels, a devout Catholic. Beautifully dressed, maids in tow, she walked to mass every morning. That penance accomplished, she devoted the rest of her day to pleasure. Like her husband she was self-indulgent, unfaithful, and devoted to their only son, Romeo.

So now, this happy family finally would be punished. The father a Knight of Malta, the mother a daily communicant with Christ and their son the murderer of the Pope. What a betrayal, Yabril thought. Poor Romeo, you will spend a bad week when I betray you.

Except for the final twist that Yabril had added, Romeo knew the whole plan. 'Just like chess,' Romeo said. 'Check to the king, check to the king, and the checkmate. Beautiful.'

Yabril looked at his watch, it would be another fifteen minutes. The van was going at moderate speed along the highway to the airport.

It was time to begin. He collected all the weapons and grenades from his cadre and put them in a suitcase. When the van stopped in front of the airport terminal Yabril got out first. The van went on to discharge the rest of the cadre at another entrance. Yabril walked through the terminal slowly, carrying the suitcase, his eyes searching for undercover security police. Just short of the checkpoint, he walked into a gift and flower shop. A 'Closed' sign in bright red and green letters hung on a peg inside the door. This was a signal that it was safe to enter and also kept the shop clear of customers.

The woman in the shop was a dyed blonde with heavy make-up, quite ordinary looks, but with a warm inviting voice and a lush body shown to advantage in a plain woollen dress belted severely at the waist.

'I'm sorry,' she said to Yabril, 'but you can see by the sign that we are closed. It is Easter Sunday after all.' But her voice was friendly, not rejecting. She smiled warmly.

Yabril gave her the code sentence, designed merely for recognition. 'Christ is risen but I must still travel on business.' She reached out and took the suitcase from his hand.

'Is the plane on time?' Yabril asked.

'Yes,' the woman said. 'You have an hour. Are there any changes?'

'No,' Yabril said. 'But remember, everything depends on you.' Then he went out. He had never seen the woman before and would never see her again and she knew only about this phase of the operation. He checked the schedules on the departure board. Yes, the plane would leave on time.

The woman was one of the few female members of the First Hundred. She had been planted in the shop three years ago as owner and during that time she had carefully and seductively built up relationships with airline terminal personnel and security guards. Her practice of bypassing the scanners at the checkpoints to deliver parcels to people on planes was cleverly established. She had done it not too often but just often enough. In the third year she began an affair with one of the armed guards who could wave her through the unscanned entry. Her lover was on guard duty this day, she had promised him lunch and a siesta in the back room of her shop. And so he had volunteered for the Easter Sunday duty.

The lunch was already laid out on the table in the back room when she emptied the suitcase to pack the weapons in gaily wrapped Gucci gift boxes. She put the boxes into mauve-colored paper shopping bags and waited until twenty minutes before departure time. Then cradling the bag in her arms because it was so heavy and she was afraid the paper might break, she ran awkwardly toward the unscanned entry corridor. Her lover on guard duty waved her through

38

gallantly. She gave him a brilliantly affectionate and apologizing smile. As she boarded the plane the stewardess recognized her and said with a laugh, 'Again, Livia.' The woman walked through to the tourist section until she saw Yabril seated with three men and three women of his cadre beside him. One of the women raised her arms to accept the heavy package.

The woman known as Livia dropped the bag into those waiting arms and then turned and ran out of the plane. She went back to the shop and finished preparing lunch in the back room.

This security guard, Faenzi, was one of those magnificent specimens of Italian manhood who seem deliberately created to delight womanhood. That he was handsome was the least of his virtues. More importantly he was one of those sweet-tempered men who are extraordinarily satisfied with the range of their talents and the scope of their ambition. The woman, Livia, had spotted him almost immediately on his first day of duty as a security guard in the airport.

Faenzi wore his airport uniform as grandly as a Napoleonic Field Marshal, his mustache was as neat and pretty as the tilted nose of a soubrette. You could see he believed that he had a significant job, an important duty to the state. He viewed passing women fondly and benevolently, they were under his protection. Livia immediately marked him as her own. At first he had treated her with an exquisitely filial courtliness, but she had soon put an end to that with a torrent of flattery, a few charming gifts that hinted at hidden wealth, and then evening snacks in her boutique at night. Now he loved her or was at least as devoted to her as a dog to an indulgent master. She was a source of treats.

And Livia enjoyed him. He was a wonderful and cheerful lover without a serious thought in his head. She much preferred him in bed to those gloomy young revolutionaries consumed with guilt, belabored by conscience, that she bedded because they were her political comrades.

39

He became her pet and she fondly called him Zonzi. When he entered the shop and locked the door, she went to him with the utmost affection and desire; she had a bad conscience. Poor Zonzi, the Italian Anti-Terrorist Branch would track everything down, and note her disappearance from the scene. Zonzi had undoubtedly boasted of his conquest, after all she was an older and experienced woman, her honor need not be protected. Their connections would be uncovered. Poor Zonzi, this lunch would be his last hour of happiness.

Quickly and expertly on her side, enthusiastically and joyfully on his, they made love. Livia pondered the irony that here was an act that she thoroughly enjoyed and yet served her purposes as a revolutionary woman. Zonzi would be punished for his pride and his presumption, his condescending love for an older woman, she would achieve a tactical and strategic victory. And yet poor Zonzi. How beautiful he was naked, the olive skin, the large doelike eyes and jet black hair, the pretty mustache, the penis and balls firm as bronze. 'Ah, Zonzi, Zonzi,' she whispered into his thighs, 'always remember that I love you.' Which was not true but might repair his broken ego as he served his time in prison.

She fed him a marvelous meal, they drank a superior bottle of wine and then they made love again. Zonzi dressed, kissed her goodbye, and glowed with the belief that he deserved such good fortune. After he left she took a long look around the shop. She gathered all her belongings together with some extra clothes and used Yabril's suitcase to carry them. That had been part of the instructions. There should be no trace of Yabril. Her last task was to erase all the obvious fingerprints she might have left in the shop but that was just a token task. She would probably not get all of them. Then, carrying the suitcase, she went out, locked up the shop, and walked out of the terminal. Outside in the brilliant sunshine, a woman of her own cadre was waiting

40

with a car. She got into it, gave the driver a brief kiss of greeting and said almost regretfully, 'Thank God that's the end of that.' The other woman said, 'It wasn't so bad. We made money on the shop.'

Yabril and his cadre were in the tourist cabin because Theresa Kennedy, daughter of the President of the United States, was travelling First Class with her six-man Secret Service security detail. Yabril did not want the handover of the gift-wrapped weapons to be seen by them. He also knew that Theresa Kennedy would not get on the plane until just before take off, that the security guards would not be on the plane beforehand, because they never knew when Theresa Kennedy would change her mind and, Yabril thought, because they had become lazy and careless.

The plane, a jumbo jet, was sparsely occupied. Not many people in Italy choose to travel on Easter Sunday and Yabril wondered why the President's daughter was doing so. After all she was a Roman Catholic, though lapsed into the new religion of the liberal left, that most despicable political division. But the sparsity of passengers suited his plans, a hundred hostages, easier to control.

An hour later, the plane in the air, Yabril slumped down in his seat as the women began tearing the Gucci paper off the packages. The three men of the cadre used their bodies as shields, leaning over the seats and talking to the women. There were no passengers seated near them, they had a small circle of privacy. The women handed Yabril the grenades wrapped in gift paper and he adorned his body with them quickly. The three men accepted the small handguns and hid them inside their jackets. Yabril also accepted a small handgun and the three women armed themselves.

When all was ready, Yabril intercepted a stewardess going down the aisle. She saw the grenades and the gun even before Yabril whispered his commands and took her by the hand. The look of shock, then amazement, then fear was

41

familiar to him. He held her clammy hand and smiled. Two of his men positioned themselves to command the tourist section. Yabril still held the stewardess by the hand as they entered First Class. The Secret Service bodyguards saw him immediately, recognized the grenades and saw the guns. Yabril smiled at them. 'Remain seated, gentlemen,' he said. The President's daughter slowly turned her head and gazed into Yabril's eyes. Her face became taut but not frightened. She was brave, Yabril thought, and handsome. It was really a pity. He waited until the three women of the cadre took their positions in the First Class cabin and then had the stewardess open the door leading to the pilot's cockpit. Yabril felt he was entering the brain of a huge whale, and making the rest of the body helpless.

When Theresa Kennedy first saw Yabril her body suddenly shook with a nausea of unconscious recognition. He was the demon she had been warned against. There was a ferocity on his slim dark face. Its brutal, massive lower jaw gave it the quality of a face in a nightmare. The grenades strung over his jacket and in his hand looked like squat green toads. Then she saw the three women dressed in dark trousers and white jackets with the large steel-colored guns in their hands. After the first animal fear, Theresa Kennedy's second reaction was that of a guilty child. Shit, she had gotten her father into trouble, she would never ever be able to get rid of her Secret Service security detail. She watched Yabril go to the door of the pilot cabin holding the stewardess by the hand. She turned her head to look at the chief of her security detail, but he was watching the armed women very intently.

At that moment one of Yabril's men came into the First Class cabin holding a grenade in his hand. One of the cadre women made another stewardess pick up the intercom. The voice came over the phone. It only quavered slightly. 'All passengers fasten your seat belts. The plane has been commandeered by a revolutionary group. Please remain calm

42

and await further instructions. Do not stand up. Do not touch your hand luggage. Do not leave your seats for any reason. Please remain calm. Remain calm.'

In the cockpit the pilot saw the stewardess enter and said to her excitedly, 'Hey, the radio just said somebody shot at the Pope.' Then he saw Yabril enter behind the stewardess and his mouth opened into a silent 'O' of surprise, words frozen there. Just like in a cartoon, Yabril thought, as he raised the hand which held the grenade. But the pilot had said 'shot at the Pope'. Did that mean Romeo had missed? Had the mission already failed? In any case Yabril had no alternative. He gave his orders to the pilot to change their course to the Arab state of Sherhaben.

On the sea of humanity in St Peter's Square, Romeo and his cadre floated to a corner backed by a stone wall and formed their own murderous island. Annee in her nun's habit stood directly in front of Romeo, gun ready beneath her habit. She was responsible for protecting him, giving him time for his shot. The other members of the cadre, in their religious disguises, formed a circle, a perimeter to give him space. They had three hours to wait before the Pope appeared.

Romeo leaned back against the stone wall, shuttered his eyes against the Easter morning sun and quickly ran his mind over the rehearsed moves of the operation. When the Pope appeared he would tap the shoulder of the cadre man on his left. That man would then set off the radio signal device that would explode the holy figurines on the opposite wall of the square. In that moment of the explosions he would have his rifle out and fire. The time had to be exact so that his shot would be a reverberation of the other explosions. Then he would drop the rifle, his monks and nuns would form a circle around him and they would flee with the others. The figurines were also smoke bombs and St Peter's Square would be enveloped with dense clouds. There would be enormous confusion and there would be

43

panic. With all this he should be able to make his escape. Those spectators near him in the crowd might be dangerous, they would be aware, but the motions of the multitude in flight would soon separate them. Those who were foolhardy enough to persist would be gunned down.

Romeo could feel the cold sweat on his chest. The vast multitude waving flowers aloft became a sea of white and purple, pink and red. He wondered at their joy, their belief in the resurrection, their ecstasy of hope against death. He wiped his hands against the outside of his coat, felt the weight of his rifle in its sling. He could feel his legs begin to ache and go numb. He sent his mind outside his body to pass the long hours he would have to wait for the Pope to appear on his balcony.

Lost scenes from his childhood formed again. Tutored for confirmation by a romantic priest, he knew that a red-hatted senior cardinal always certified the death of a pope by tapping him on the forehead with a silver mallet. Was that still really done? It would be a very bloody mallet this time. But how big would such a mallet be? Toy-sized? Heavy and big enough to drive a nail? But of course it would be a precious relic from the Renaissance, crusty with jewels, a work of art. No matter, there would be very little of the Pope's head left to tap, the rifle under his coat held explosive bullets. And Romeo was sure he would not miss. He believed in his left-handedness, to be *sinistra* was to be successful, in sports, love, and certainly by every superstition, in murder.

As he waited, Romeo wondered that he had no sense of sacrilege, after all he had been brought up a strict Catholic in a city whose every street and building reminded one of the beginnings of Christianity. Even now he could see the domed roofs on holy buildings like marble disks against the sky, hear deep, consoling yet intimidating bells of churches. In this great hallowed square he could see the statues of martyrs, smell the very air choked with the countless spring flowers offered by true believers in Christ.

44

The overpowering fragrance of the multitudinous flowers washed over him and he was reminded of his mother and father and the heavy scents they always wore to mask the odor of their plush and pampered Mediterranean flesh.

And then the vast crowd in their Easter finery began shouting, 'Papa, Papa, Papa.' Standing in the lemon light of early spring, stone angels above their heads, the crowd chanted incessantly for the blessing of their Pope. Finally two red-robed cardinals appeared and stretched out their arms in benediction. Then Pope Innocent was on the balcony.

He was a very old man dressed in a cloak of glittering white; on it a cross of gold, the woolly pallium embroidered with crosses. On his head was a white skullcap and on his feet the traditional low, open red shoes, gold crosses embroidered on their fronts. On one of the hands raised to greet the crowd was the pontifical fisherman's ring of St Peter.

The multitude sent their flowers up into the sky, the voices roared, a great motor of ecstasy, the balcony shimmered in the sun as if to fall with the descending flowers.

At that moment Romeo felt the dread these symbols had always inspired in his youth, the red-hatted cardinal of his first confirmation pockmarked like the Devil, and then he felt an elation that lifted his whole being into bliss, ultimate pride. Romeo tapped his cadre man's shoulder to send the radio signal.

The Pope raised his white-sleeved arms to answer the cries of 'Papa, Papa', to bless them all, to praise the Eastertide, the resurrection of Christ, to salute the stone angels that rode around the walls. Romeo slid his rifle out from beneath his coat, two monks of his cadre in front of him knelt to give him a clear shot. Annee placed herself so that he could lay his rifle across her shoulder. The cadre man behind him flashed the radio signal that set off the mined figurines on the other side of the square.

The explosions rocked the foundations of the square, a cloud of pink floated in the air, the fragrance of the flowers turned rotten with the stench of burnt flesh. And at that moment Romeo, rifle sighted, pulled the trigger. The explosions on the other side of the square changed the welcoming roar of the crowd to the shrieking of countless gulls.

On the balcony the body of the Pope seemed to rise up off the ground, the white skullcap flew into the air above it, swirled in violent whirlwinds of compressed air and then drifted down into the crowd, a bloody rag. A frightening wail of horror, of terror and animal rage filled the square as the body of the Pope slumped over the balcony rail. His cross of gold dangled free, the pallium drenched red.

Clouds of dust rolled over the square. Marble fragments of shattered angels and saints fell. There was a terrible silence, the crowd frozen by the sight of the murdered Pope. They could see his head blown apart. Then the panic began. The people fled from the square, trampling the Swiss Guards who were trying to seal off the exits. The gaudy Renaissance uniforms were buried by the mass of terror-stricken worshippers.

Romeo let his rifle drop to the ground. Surrounded by his cadre of armed monks and nuns, he let himself be swept out of the square into the streets of Rome. He seemed to have lost his vision, he staggered blindly, and Annee grasped him by the arm and thrust him into the waiting van. Romeo held his hands over his ears to shut out the screams; he was shaking with shock, and then a sense of exaltation and wonder, as if the murder had been a dream.

On the jumbo jet plane scheduled from Rome to New York, Yabril and his cadre were in full control, the First Class section cleared of all passengers except Theresa Kennedy.

Theresa Kennedy was now more interested than frightened. She was fascinated that the hijackers so easily cowed her Secret Service detail by simply showing detonation

46

devices all over their bodies, any bullet fired would send the plane flying into bits through the skies. She noted that the three men and three women terrorists were very slender with faces screwed up in the tension of great athletes, various expressions of emotion changing their features. A male hijacker gave one of her Secret Service agents a violent push out of the First Class cabin and kept pushing him down the open aisle of the tourist section. One of the female hijackers kept her distance, her gun ready. When a Secret Service agent showed some reluctance to leave Theresa Kennedy's side, the woman raised her gun and pressed the barrel to his head. And her eyes showed plainly she was about to shoot. The eyes squinted, facial lines creased, her teeth showed from the extreme compression of the muscles around her mouth which parted the lips slightly to relieve pressure. At that moment Theresa Kennedy pushed her guard away and put her own body in front of the woman hijacker, who smiled with relief and waved her into the seat.

Theresa Kennedy watched Yabril rule the operation. He seemed almost distant as if he were a director watching his actors perform, not seeming to give orders but only hints, suggestions. She noted that he used his cadre as a noose to cut off the tourist body of the plane from its head. With a slight reassuring smile he motioned that she should keep to her seat. It was the action of a man looking after someone who had been put in his special care. Then he went into the pilot's cabin. One of the male hijackers guarded the entry into First Class from the tourist cabin. Two women hijackers stood back to back in the section with her, guns at the ready. There was a stewardess manning the intercom phone that relayed messages to the passengers under the direction of the male hijacker. They all looked too small to cause such terror.

In the cockpit Yabril gave the pilot permission to radio that his plane was hijacked and relay the new flight plan to Sherhaben. The American authorities would think their only problem would be to negotiate the usual Arab terrorist

47

demands. Yabril stayed in the cabin to listen to the radio traffic.

As the plane flew through the air there was nothing to do but wait. Yabril dreamed of Palestine, as it was when he was a child, his home a green oasis in the desert, his father and mother angels of light, the beautiful Koran as it rested on his father's desk, always ready to renew faith. And how it had all finished in dead gray rolls of smoke, fire and the brimstone of bombs falling from the air. And the Israelis came and it seemed as if his whole childhood had been spent in some great prison camp of ramshackle huts, a vast settlement united in only one thing, their hatred of the Jews. Those very same Jews that the Koran praised.

He remembered even at the University, how some of the teachers spoke of a botched job as 'Arab work'. Yabril himself had used the phrase to a gunmaker who had given him defective weapons. Ah, but they would not call this day's business 'Arab work'.

He had always hated the Jews, no not the Jews, the Israelis. He remembered when he was a child of four, maybe five, not later, the soldiers of Israel had raided the settlement camp in which he went to school. They had received false information, 'Arab work', that the settlement was hiding terrorists. All the inhabitants had been ordered out of their houses and into the streets with their hands up. Including the children in the long yellow-painted tin hut that was the school and lay just a little outside the settlement. Yabril with other small boys and girls his age had clustered together wailing, their little arms and tiny hands high in the air, screaming their surrender, screaming in terror. And Yabril had always remembered one of the young Israeli soldiers, the new breed of Jew, blond as a Nazi, looking at the children with a sort of horror, and then the fair skin of that alien Semite's face was streaming with tears. The Israeli lowered his gun and shouted at the children to stop, to put down their hands. They had nothing to fear, he said, little children had nothing to fear. The Israeli soldier spoke almost perfect Arabic and when the children still stood with their arms held high, the soldier strode among them trying to pull down their arms, weeping all the while. Yabril had never forgotten the soldier, had resolved, later in life, never to be like him, never to let pity destroy him.

Now below the plane he could see the deserts of Arabia. Soon the flight would come to an end and he would be in the Sultanate of Sherhaben.

Sherhaben was one of the smallest countries in the world but had such a richness of oil that its camel riding Sultan begot hundreds of children and grandchildren who drove Mercedes and were educated in the finest universities abroad. The original Sultan owned huge industrial companies in Germany and the United States and had died the single most wealthy person in the world. Only one of these grandchildren had endured the murderous intrigues of half-brothers and became the present Sultan – Maurobi.

The Sultan Maurobi was a militant and fanatically devout Muslim and the citizens of Sherhaben, now rich, were equally devout. No woman could go without a veil, no money could be loaned for interest, there was not a drop of liquor in that thirsty desert land except at the foreign embassies.

Long ago Yabril had helped the Sultan establish and consolidate power by assassinating four of the Sultan's more dangerous half-brothers. The Sultan, because of these debts of gratitude, and because of his own hatred of the great powers, had agreed to help Yabril in this operation.

The plane carrying Yabril and his hostages landed and rolled slowly toward the small glass-encircled terminal, pale yellow in the desert sun. Beyond the airfield was an endless stretch of sand studded with oil rigs. When the plane came to a stop Yabril could see that the airfield was surrounded by at least a thousand of Sultan Maurobi's troops.

Now the most intricate and satisfying part of the operation

49

would begin, and the most dangerous. He would have to be careful until Romeo was finally in place. And he would be gambling on the Sultan's reaction to his secret and final checkmate. No, this was not Arab work.

Because of the European time difference, Francis Kennedy received the first report of the shooting of the Pope at six a.m. Easter Sunday. It was given to him by Press Secretary Matthew Gladyce who had the White House watch for the holiday. Eugene Dazzy and Christian Klee had already been informed and were in the White House.

Francis Kennedy came down the stairs from his living quarters and entered the Oval Office to find Dazzy and Christian waiting for him. They both looked very grim. Far away on the streets of Washington there were long screams of sirens. Kennedy sat down behind his desk. He looked at Eugene Dazzy who, as Chief of Staff, would do the briefing. But to Kennedy's surprise it was Christian who spoke first.

He said, 'Francis, the Pope is dead. But we've received news just as bad. The plane Theresa is on has been hijacked and is now on its way to Sherhaben.'

Francis Kennedy felt the wave of nausea hit him. Then he heard Eugene Dazzy say, 'The hijackers have everything under control, there are no incidents on the plane. As soon as it lands we'll negotiate, we'll call in all our favours, it will come out OK. I don't think they even knew Theresa was on the plane.'

Christian said, 'Arthur Wix and Otto Gray are on their way in. So are CIA, Defense, and the Vice President. They will all be waiting for you in the Cabinet Room within the half hour.'

'OK,' Kennedy said. He forced himself to smile at the two men. 'Is there any connection?' he said.

He saw that Christian was not surprised but that Dazzy didn't get it. 'Between the Pope and the hijacking,' Kennedy said. When neither of them answered, he said, 'Wait for me

in the Cabinet Room. I want a few moments by myself.'
They left.

Francis Kennedy was almost invulnerable to assassins but he had always known he could never fully protect his daughter. She was too independent, she would not permit him to restrict her life. And it had not seemed a serious danger. He could not recall that the daughter of the head of a nation had ever been attacked. It was a bad political and public relations move for any terrorist or revolutionary organization.

After her father's inauguration Theresa went her own way, lending her name to radical and feminist political groups. Stating her own position in life as distinct from her father. He had never tried to persuade her to act differently, to present to the public an image false to herself. It was enough that he loved her. And whenever she visited the White House for a brief stay, they had a good time together arguing politics, dissecting the uses of power.

The conservative, Republican press, the disreputable tabloids, had taken their shot, hoping to damage the Presidency. Theresa was photographed marching with feminists, demonstrating against nuclear weapons and once even marching for a home state for Palestinians. Which would now inspire ironic columns in the paper.

Oddly enough the American public responded to Theresa Kennedy with affection, even when it became known she was living with a radical Italian in Rome. There were pictures of them strolling the ancient streets of stone, kissing and holding hands, pictures of the balcony of the flat they shared. The young Italian lover was handsome, Theresa Kennedy was pretty in her blondness and her pale milky Irish skin, the Kennedy satiny blue eyes. And her almost lanky Kennedy frame draped in casual Italian clothes made her so appealing that the text beneath the photographs was drained of poison.

A news photo of her shielding her young Italian lover

from Italian police clubs brought back atavistic feelings in older Americans, memories of that long-ago terrible day in Dallas.

She was a witty heroine. During the campaign she had been cornered by TV reporters and asked, 'So you agree with your father politically?' If she answered 'yes' she would appear a hypocrite or a child commanded by a power-hungry father. If she answered 'no' the headlines would indicate that she did not support her father in his race for the Presidency. But she showed the Kennedy political genius. 'Sure, he's my Dad,' she said, hugging her father, 'and I know he's a good guy. But if he does something I don't like I'll yell at him just like you reporters do.' It came off great on the tube. Her father loved her for it. And now she was in mortal danger.

Pacing the Oval Office, Francis Kennedy knew that he would give the hijackers anything they demanded. That was the message he would send no matter what his advisors said. The hell with world political balance or any of the other arguments. This was one time he would use all his power, no matter what the cost. Suddenly he felt a little faint and leaned against the desk in fearful anguish. But then to his surprise he knew that what he was feeling was rage against his daughter.

If only she had remained close to him, if only she had been more of a loving daughter and lived with him at the White House, if only she had been less radical, none of this would be happening. And why did she have to have a foreign lover, a student radical who perhaps had given the hijacker crucial information? And then he laughed at himself. He was feeling the exasperation of a parent who wanted his child to be as little trouble as possible. He loved her, and he would save her. At least this was something he could fight against, not like the terrible, long and painful death of his wife.

Now, Eugene Dazzy appeared and told him it was time. They were waiting for him in the Cabinet Room.

*

When Kennedy entered, everyone rose from their chairs. He quickly motioned for them to be seated, but they surged around him to offer their sympathy. Kennedy made way to the head of the long oval table and sat in the chair near the fireplace.

Two pure white light chandeliers bleached the rich brown of the table, glistened the black of the leather chairs, six to each side of the table, and more chairs along the back of the far wall. And there were other sconces of white light that burned from the walls. Next to the two windows that opened to the Rose Garden were two flags, the striped flag of the United States and the flag of the President, a field of deep blue filled with pale stars.

Kennedy's staff took the seats next to him, resting their information logs and memoranda sheets on the oval table. Further down were the Cabinet Secretaries and the head of the CIA. And at the other end of the table, the Chairman of the Joint Chiefs of Staff, an Army General in full uniform, a gaudy color cut-out in the funeral-dressed crowd. The Vice President, Helen DuPray sat at the far side of the table, away from Kennedy, the only woman in the room. She wore a fashionable dark blue suit with a pure white silk blouse. Her handsome face was stern. The smell of the Rose Garden filled the room, seeping through the heavy curtains and drapes that covered glass paneled doors. Underneath those drapes the aquamarine rug reflected green light into the room.

It was the CIA Chief, Theodore Tappey, who gave the briefing. Tappey had once been head of the FBI, was not flamboyant or politically ambitious. And had never exceeded the CIA charter with risky, illegal, or empire building schemes. He had a great deal of credit with Kennedy's personal staff, especially Christian Klee.

'In the few hours we had, we've come up with some hard information,' Theodore Tappey said. 'The killing of the Pope was carried out by an all-Italian cadre. The hijacking of

53

Theresa's plane was done by a mixed team led by an Arab who goes by the name of Yabril. The fact that both incidents happened on the same day and originated in the same city seems to be coincidence. Which of course we must always mistrust.'

Francis Kennedy said softly, 'At this moment the killing of the Pope is not primary. Our main concern is to handle the hijacking problem. Have they made any demands yet?'

Tappey said quickly and firmly, 'No. That's an odd circumstance in itself.'

Kennedy said, 'Get your contacts on negotiation and report to me personally at every step.' He turned to the Secretary of State and asked, 'What countries will help us?'

The Secretary said, 'Everyone, the other Arab states are horrified, they despise the idea of your daughter being held hostage. It offends their sense of honor and also they think of their own customs of blood feud. They believe they cannot achieve any good from this. France has a good relationship with the Sultan. They offered to send in observers for us. Britain and Israel can't help, they are not trusted. But until the hijackers make their demands we're sort of in limbo.'

Francis Kennedy turned to Christian. 'Chris how do you figure it, they're not making demands?'

Christian said, 'It may be too early. Or they have another card to play.'

The Cabinet room was eerie in silence, in the blackness of the many high heavy chairs the white sconces of light on the walls turned the skin of the people in the room into a very light gray. Kennedy waited for them to speak, all of them, and he closed down his mind when they spoke of options, the threat of sanctions, the threat of a naval blockade, the freezing of Sherhaben assets in the United States. The expectation that the hijackers would extend the negotiation interminably to milk the TV time and news reports all over the world.

After a time Francis Kennedy turned to Oddblood Gray and said abruptly, 'Schedule a meeting with the Congressional leaders and the relevant Committee Chairmen for me and my staff.' Then he turned to Arthur Wix. 'Get your National Security working on plans if this thing turns into something wider.' Kennedy stood up to leave. He addressed them all. 'Gentlemen,' he said, 'I must tell you I don't believe in coincidence. I don't believe the Pope of the Roman Catholic Church can be murdered on the same day, in the same city, that the daughter of the President of the United States is kidnapped.'

It was a long Easter Sunday. The White House was filling up with staff personnel of the different action committees set up by the CIA, the Army and Navy, and the State Department. They all agreed the most baffling fact was that the terrorists had not yet made their demands for the release of the hostages.

Outside, the streets were congested with traffic. Newspaper and TV reporters were flocking into Washington. Government staff workers had been called to their desks despite the holiday. And Christian Klee had ordered a thousand extra men from the Secret Service and the FBI to provide additional protection for the White House.

The telephone traffic in the White House increased in volume. There was bedlam, people rushing to and fro from the White House to the Executive Office Building. Eugene Dazzy tried to bring everything under control.

The rest of that Sunday in the White House consisted of Kennedy receiving reports from the Situation Room, long solemn conferences on what options were open, telephone conversations between heads of foreign countries and the Cabinet members of the United States.

Late Sunday night the President's staff had dinner with him and prepared for the next day. They monitored the TV news reports, which were continuous.

Finally, Kennedy decided to go to bed. A Secret Service man led the way as Kennedy went up the small stairway that led to the living quarters on the fourth floor of the White House. Another Secret Service man trailed behind. They both knew that the President hated to take the elevators in the White House.

The top of the stairs opened into a lounge which held a communications desk and two more Secret Service men. When he passed through that lounge Kennedy was in his personal living quarters with only his personal servants: a maid, a butler and a valet whose duty it was to keep track of the extensive Presidential wardrobe.

What Kennedy did not know was that even these personal servants were members of the Secret Service. Christian Klee had invented this set-up. It was part of his overall plan to keep the President free from all personal harm, part of the intricate shield Christian had woven around Francis Kennedy.

When Christian had put this wrinkle into the security system he had briefed the special platoon of Secret Service men and women. 'You're going to be the best goddamn personal servants in the world and you can go straight from here and get a job in Buckingham Palace. Remember, your first duty is to take any bullets thrown at the President. But it will be as much your duty to make the personal life of the President comfortable.'

The chief of the special platoon was the manservant on duty this night. Ostensibly he was a black naval steward named Jefferson with the rank of Chief Petty Officer. Actually he had top rank in the Secret Service and was exceptionally well trained in hand-to-hand combat. He was a natural athlete and had been a college All American in football. And his IQ was 160. He also had a sense of humor which made him take an especial delight in becoming the perfect servant.

Now he helped Kennedy take off his jacket and hung it up

56

carefully. He handed Kennedy a silk dressing-gown but had learned that the President did not like to be helped putting it on. When Kennedy went to the small bar in the living room of the suite, Jefferson was there before him mixing a vodka with tonic and ice. Then Jefferson said, 'Mr President, your bath is drawn.'

Kennedy looked at him with a little smile on his face. Jefferson was a little too good to be true. Kennedy said, 'Please turn off all the phones. You can wake me personally if I'm needed.'

He soaked in the hot bath for nearly a half-hour. The tub had jet streams which pounded his back and thighs and soothed the weariness out of his muscles. The bathwater had a pleasant masculine scent and the ledge around the tub was filled with an assortment of soaps, liniments and magazines. There was even a plastic basket that held a pile of memos.

When Kennedy came out of the bath he put on a white terry cloth robe that had a monogram in red, white and blue lettering that said, 'THE BOSS'. This was a gift from Jefferson himself who thought it part of the character he was playing to give such a present. Francis Kennedy rubbed his white almost hairless body with the robe to get himself dry and thought he had to get south and get a sun tan. He had always been dissatisfied with the paleness of his skin and his lack of body hair.

In the bedroom, Jefferson had pulled the curtains closed and switched on the reading light. He had also turned down the bed covers. There was a small marble-topped table with specially attached wheels near the bed and a comfortable armchair nearby. The table was dressed with a beautifully embroidered pale rose cloth and on the cloth was a dark blue pitcher which held the hot chocolate. Chocolate had already been poured into a cup of lighter cerulean blue. There was an intricately painted dish which held six varieties of biscuit. The silver accompanying them was so polished it looked like heavy ivory. Comfortingly there was a pure white crock of pale saltless butter and four colored crocks of different jams, green for apple, blue spotted white for raspberry, yellow for marmalade and red for strawberry.

Francis Kennedy said, 'That looks great,' and Jefferson left the room. For some reason these little attentions comforted Kennedy more than they should, he felt. He sat in the armchair and drank the chocolate, ate a biscuit but could not finish it. He rolled the table away and got into bed. He started to read from a pile of memos but he was too tired. He turned off the light and tried to sleep.

But through the muffling of the drapes he could very faintly hear a tiny residue of the immense noise that was building up outside the White House. The media of the whole world was assembling to keep a twenty-four-hour-a-day watch. Hundreds of communications vehicles, the TV cameras and crews, the setting up of a Marine Battalion as extra security.

Francis Kennedy felt that deep sense of foreboding that had only come to him once before in his life. He let himself think directly about his daughter Theresa. She was sleeping on that plane, surrounded by murderous men. And it was not bad luck. Fate had given him many warnings. His two uncles had been killed when he was a boy. And then just over three years ago his wife, Catherine, had died of cancer.

The first great defeat in Francis Kennedy's life was when Catherine Kennedy discovered the lump in her breast six months before her husband won the nomination for President. After the diagnosis of cancer, Francis Kennedy offered to withdraw from the political process, but she forbade him. She wanted to live in the White House she said. She would get well, she said, and her husband never doubted her. At first they worried about her losing her breast and Francis Kennedy consulted cancer experts all over the world about a lumpectomy which could remove the cancer and leave the breast. He and Catherine finally wound up going to one of the greatest cancer specialists available in the United States. The doctor looked at Catherine's medical file and encouraged removal of the breast. He said, and Francis Kennedy forever remembered the words, 'It is a very aggressive strain of cancer.'

She was on chemotherapy when he won the Democratic nomination for the Presidency in July, and her doctors sent her home. She was in remission. She put on weight, her skeleton hid again behind a wall of flesh.

She rested a great deal, she could not leave the house, but she was always on her feet to greet him when he came home. Theresa went back to school, Francis Kennedy went on the political trail, campaigning for the Presidency. But he arranged his schedule so that he could fly home every few days to be with her. Each time he returned she seemed to be stronger and these days were sweet, they never loved each other more. He brought her gifts, she knitted him mufflers and gloves and one time she gave the day off to the nurses and servants so that she and her husband could be alone in the house, to eat the simple supper she prepared. She was getting well.

It was the happiest moment in his life, nothing could be measured against it. Francis Kennedy wept tears of pure joy, relieved of anguish, of dread. The next morning they went for a walk in the green hills around their house, her arm around his waist. When they returned he cooked her breakfast and she ate heartily, more than he had ever remembered her eating. She had always been vain about her appearance, anxious about how she fitted into her new dresses, her bathing suits, the extra fold of flesh beneath her chin. But now she tried to put on weight. He felt each bone in her body when they walked entwined.

Her remission gave Francis Kennedy the energy to rise to the peak of his powers as he continued his campaign for the Presidency. He swept everything before him; he was witty, he was charming, he was sincere, he established a rapport

59

with the voters and the polls showed him far ahead. He bested his opponents in debate, destroyed them with his strategies, skillfully escaped the media traps, won over his enemies, cemented his allies. Everything was malleable, to be shaped to his fortunate destiny. His body generated enormous energy, his mind worked with a precision that was extraordinary.

And then on one of his trips home he was plunged into the netherworld. Catherine was ill again, she was not there to greet him. And all his gifts and strength were powerless.

Catherine had been the perfect wife for him. Not that she had been an extraordinary woman but she had been one of those women who seemed to be almost genetically gifted in the art of love. She had what seemed to be a natural sweetness of disposition and character that was extraordinary. He had never heard her say a mean word about anyone, she forgave other people's faults, never felt herself slighted or done an injury. She never harbored resentments.

She was in all ways pleasing. She had a willowy body and her face had a tranquil beauty that inspired affection in nearly everyone. She had a weakness of course, she loved beautiful clothes and was a little vain. But she could be teased about that. She was witty without being insulting or mordant and she was never depressed. She was well educated and had made her living as a journalist before she married. She had other skills, too: she was a skilled if amateur pianist, she painted as a hobby. She had brought up her daughter well and they loved each other; she was understanding of her husband and never jealous of his achievements. She was one of those rare accidents, a contented and happy human being. She was, therefore, most precious in his life.

The day came when the doctor met Francis Kennedy in the corridor of the hospital and quite brutally and frankly told him that his wife must die. That there was no appeal to a higher court, there could be no retrial, no mitigating

60

circumstances. She was condemned more fiercely than any murderer.

The doctor explained. There were holes in the bones of Catherine Kennedy's body, her skeleton would collapse. There were tumors in her brain, tiny now but that would inevitably expand. And her blood ruthlessly manufactured poisons to put her to death.

Francis Kennedy could not tell his wife this. He could not tell her because he could not believe it. He mustered all his resources, contacted all his powerful friends, even consulted the Oracle. There was one hope. At different research centers in different medical centers all around the United States there were programs with new and dangerous drugs, experimental programs available only to those who had been decreed doomed. Since these new drugs were dangerously toxic, they were used only on volunteers. And there were so many doomed people that there were a hundred volunteers for each spot in the programs.

So Francis Kennedy committed what he would have ordinarily thought an immoral act. He used all his power to get his wife into these research programs, he pulled every string so that his wife could receive these lethal but life-preserving poisons into her body. And he succeeded. He felt a new confidence. A few people had been cured in these research centers. Why not his wife? Why could he not save her? He had triumphed all his life, he would triumph now.

And then began a reign of darkness. At first it was a research program in Houston. He entered her into a hospital there. Stayed with her for the treatment which weakened her so that she was helplessly bedridden. She made him leave her there so that he could continue campaigning for the Presidency. He flew from Houston to Los Angeles to make his campaign speeches, confident, witty, cheerful. Then late at night he flew to Houston to spend a few hours with his wife. Then he flew to his next campaign stop to play the part of lawgiver.

61

The treatment in Houston failed. In Boston they cut the tumor from her brain and the operation was a success though the tumor tested malignant. Malignant, too, the new tumors in her lungs. The holes in her bones on X-ray were larger and even more gracefully sculpted. In another Boston hospital new drugs and protocols worked a miracle. The new tumor in her brain stopped growing, the tumors in her remaining breast shrivelled. Every night Francis Kennedy flew from his campaign cities to spend a few hours with her, to read to her, to joke with her. Sometimes Theresa Kennedy flew from her school in Los Angeles to visit her mother. Father and daughter dined together and then visited the patient in her hospital room to sit in the darkness with her. Theresa told funny stories of her adventures in school, Francis Kennedy related his adventures on the campaign trail. Catherine Kennedy would laugh.

Of course Francis Kennedy again offered to drop out of the campaign to be with his wife. Of course Theresa Kennedy wanted to leave school to be with her mother constantly. But Catherine Kennedy told them she would not, could not bear for them to do so. She might be ill for a long time. They must continue their lives. Only that could give her hope, only that could give her the strength to bear her torture. On this she could not be moved. She threatened to check out of the hospital and return home if they did not continue as if things were normal.

Francis Kennedy on long trips through the night to her bedside could only marvel at her tenacity. Catherine Kennedy, her body filled with chemical poison fighting the poisons of her body, clung fiercely to her belief that she would be well and that the two people she loved most in the world would not be dragged down with her.

Finally the nightmare seemed to end. Again she was in remission. Francis Kennedy could take her home. They had been all over the United States, she had been in seven different hospitals with their protocols of experimental treatments, and the great flood of chemicals seemed to have worked, and Francis Kennedy felt an exultation that he had succeeded once again. He took his wife home to Los Angeles and then one night he, Catherine and Theresa went out to dinner before he resumed the campaign trail. It was a lovely summer night, the soft balmy California air caressed their skins. There was one strange moment. A waiter had spilled just a tiny drop of sauce from a dish on the sleeve of Catherine Kennedy's new dress. She burst into tears and when the waiter left she asked weeping, 'Why did he have to do that to me?' This was so uncharacteristic of her – in former times she would have laughed such an incident away – that Francis Kennedy felt a strange foreboding. She had gone through the torture of all those operations, the removal of her breast, the excision from her brain, the pain of those growing tumors and had never wept or complained. And now obviously this stain seemed to sink into her heart beneath. She was inconsolable.

The next day Francis Kennedy had to fly to New York to campaign. In the morning Catherine made him his breakfast. She was radiant and her beauty seemed even greater, the lovely bones of her face sculpted only by skin. All the newspapers had polls that showed Francis Kennedy was in the lead, that he would win the Presidency. Catherine Kennedy read them aloud. 'Oh, Francis,' she said, 'we'll live in the White House and I'll have my own staff. And Theresa can bring her friends to stay for weekends and on vacations. Think how happy we'll be. And I won't get sick again. I promise. You'll do great things, Francis, I know you will.' She put her arms around him and wept with happiness and love. 'I'll help,' Catherine said. 'We'll walk through all those lovely rooms together and I'll help you make your plans. You'll be the greatest President. I'm going to be all right, darling, and I'll have so much to do. We'll be so happy. We'll be so good. We're so lucky. Aren't we lucky?'

*

63

She died in autumn, October light became her shroud. Francis Kennedy stood amongst fading green hills and wept. Silver trees veiled the horizon and in dumb agony he closed his eyes with his own hands to shut out the world. And in that moment without light, he felt the spine of his mind break.

And some priceless cell of energy fled. It was the first time in his life that his extraordinary intelligence was worth nothing. His wealth meant nothing. His political power, his position in the world meant nothing. He could not save his wife from death. And therefore it all became nothing.

He took his hands away from his eyes and with a supreme effort of his will fought against the nothingness. He reassembled what was left of the world, summoned power to fight against grief. There was less than a month to go before the election and he made the final effort.

He entered the White House without his wife, with only his daughter Theresa, Theresa who had tried to be happy but who had wept all that first night because her mother could not be with them.

And now, three years after his wife's death, Francis Kennedy, President of the United States, one of the most powerful men on earth, was alone in his bed, fearful for his daughter's life, and unable to command sleep. The lament of the powerful, that they could never find such sweet sanctuary.

Sleep forbidden, he tried to stave off the terror that kept him from sleep. He told himself the hijackers would not dare to harm Theresa, that his daughter would come safely home. In this he was not powerless, he did not have to rely on the weak, fallible gods of medicine, he did not have to fight those terrible invincible cancerous cells. No. He could save his daughter's life. He could bend the power of his country, spend its authority. It all rested in his hands and thank God he had no political scruples. His daughter was the only thing he had left on this earth that he really loved. He would save her.

But then anxiety, a wave of such fear it seemed to stop his heart, made him put on the light above his head. He rose and sat in the armchair. He pulled the marble table close and sipped the residue of cold chocolate from his cup.

He believed the plane had been hijacked because his daughter was on it. The hijacking was possible because of the vulnerability of established authority to a few determined, ruthless and possibly high-minded terrorists. And it had been inspired by the fact that he, Francis Kennedy, President of the United States was the prominent symbol of that established authority. So by his desire to be President of the United States, he, Francis Kennedy, was responsible for placing his daughter in danger.

Again he heard the doctor's words. 'It is a very aggressive strain of cancer.' But now he understood. Everything was more dangerous than it appeared. This was a night to plan, to defend, he had the power to turn fate aside. Sleep would never come to the chambers of his brain so sown with mines.

What had been his wish? To work out the destiny of the Kennedy name? But he had been only a cousin. He remembered Great-Uncle Joseph Kennedy, legendary womanizer, a maker of gold, a mind so sharp for the instant, but so blind to the future. He remembered Old Joe fondly, though he would have been Francis Kennedy's opposite right wall politically if he were alive today. But Great-Uncle Joe had given Francis Kennedy gold pieces for his toddler birthdays and set up a trust fund for him though he was just a poor relation. What a selfish life the man had led, screwing Hollywood stars, lifting his sons high. Never mind that he had been a political dinosaur. And what a tragic end. A lucky life until the last chapter. Then the murders of his sons, so young, so high and the old man defeated. A final stroke exploding his brain.

Making your son President, could a father have such joy?

And had the old king-maker sacrificed his sons for nothing? Had the gods punished him not so much for his pride but for his pleasure? Or was it all accident? His sons Jack and Robert, so rich, so handsome, so gifted, killed by those powerless nobodies who wrote themselves into history with the murder of their betters. No, there could be no purpose, it was all accident. So many little things could turn fate aside, tiny precautions reverse tragedy into little grazings of destiny.

So now, Francis Kennedy thought, he would leave nothing to fate. He would bring home his daughter safe with his own sense of terror. He would give the hijackers everything, and surely that must satisfy them, though the United States would be humiliated in the eyes of the world. A small price to pay for Theresa.

And yet – and yet there was the odd feeling of doom. Why the binding of the Pope's killer and the hijacking of the President's daughter? Why the delay before stating their demands? What other strings were there in the labyrinth to be played out? And all this from a man he had never heard of, a mysterious Arab named Yabril, and an Italian youth, named in scornful irony, Romeo.

In the darkness he was terrified at how it all might end. He felt the familiar, always contained rage, the dread. He remembered the terrible day when as a child playing on the White House lawn with his little cousins, he had heard the first whisper that his Uncle John was dead, and from the interior of the White House the long terrible scream of a woman in agony.

Then mercifully, the chambers of his brain unlocked, his memories fled. He fell asleep in his armchair.

3

The member of the President's staff with the most influence on Kennedy was the Attorney General. Christian Klee had been born into a wealthy family stretching back into the first days of the Republic. His trust funds were now worth over a hundred million dollars, due to the guidance and advice of his godfather, the Oracle, Oliver Ollifant. He had never wanted for anything and there had come a time when he wanted nothing. He had too much intelligence, too much energy to become another of the idle rich who invest in movies, chase women, abuse drugs and booze or descend into a religious viciousness. Two men, the Oracle and Francis Xavier Kennedy led him finally into politics.

Christian first met Kennedy at Harvard, not as fellow undergraduates but as teacher and student. Kennedy had been the youngest professor to teach law at Harvard. In his twenties, he had been a prodigy. Christian still remembered that opening lecture. Kennedy had begun with the words, 'Everybody knows or has heard of the majesty of the law. It is the power of the state to control the existing political organization that permits civilization to exist. That is true. Without the rule of law, we are all lost. But remember this, the law is also full of shit.'

Then he had smiled at his student audience. 'I can get around any law you may write. The law can be twisted out of shape to serve a wicked civilization. The rich can escape the law and sometimes even the poor get lucky. Some lawyers treat the law like pimps treat their women. Judges sell the law, courts betray it. All true. But remember this, we have nothing better that works. There is no other way we can make a social contract with our fellow human beings.'

When Christian Klee graduated from Harvard Law School he had not the faintest idea of what to do with his life. Nothing interested him. He was worth over a hundred million dollars, but he had no interest in money, nor did he have a real interest in the law. He had the usual romanticism of a young man. He liked women, had brief affairs but could not summon up that feeling of true belief in love that leads to a passionate attachment. He desperately was looking for something to commit his life to. He was interested in the arts, but had no creative drive, no talent for painting, music, writing. He was paralyzed by his security in society. He was not so much unhappy as bewildered.

He had, of course, tried drugs for a brief period – it was after all as integral a part of American culture as it had once been of the Chinese Empire. And for the first time he discovered a startling thing about himself. He could not bear the loss of control that drugs caused. He did not mind being unhappy as long as he had control of his mind and body. Loss of that control was the ultimate in despair. And the drugs did not even make him feel the ecstasy that other people felt. So at the age of twenty-two, with everything in the world at his feet, he could not feel that anything was worth doing. He did not even feel, what every young man felt, a desire to improve the world he lived in.

He consulted his godfather, the Oracle, then a 'young' man of seventy-five, who still had an inordinate appetite for life, who kept three mistresses busy, who had a finger in every business pie and who conferred with the President of the United States at least once a week. The Oracle had the secret of life.

The Oracle said, 'Pick out the most useless thing for you to do and do it for the next few years. Something that you would never consider doing, that you have no desire to do.

But something that will improve you at least physically and mentally. Learn a part of the world that you think you will never make part of your life. Don't squander your time. Learn. That's how I got into politics originally. And this would surprise my friends, I really had no interest in money. Do something you hate. In three or four years more things will be possible and what is possible becomes more attractive.'

The next day Christian applied for an appointment to West Point and spent the next four years becoming an officer in the United States Army. The Oracle had been astounded, then delighted. 'The very thing,' he said. 'You will never be a soldier. And you will develop a taste for denial.'

Christian, after four years at West Point remained another four years in the Army training in Special Assault Brigades and becoming proficient in armed and unarmed combat. The feeling that his body could perform any task he demanded of it gave him a sense of immortality.

At the age of thirty he resigned his commision and took a post in the operations divisions of the CIA. He became an officer in clandestine operations and spent the next four years in the European theater. From there he went to the Middle East for six years and rose high in the operational division of the Agency until a bomb took off his foot. This was another challenge. He learned to use and manage a prosthetic device, an artificial foot, so that he did not even limp. But that ended his career in the field and he returned home to enter a prestigious law firm.

Then for the first time he fell in love and married a girl he thought was the answer to all his youthful dreams. She was intelligent, she was witty, she was very good-looking and very passionate. For the next five years he was happy in marriage, happy in the fatherhood of two young children and found satisfaction in the political maze through which the Oracle was guiding him. He was, finally, he thought, a man who had found his place in life. Then misfortune. His wife fell in love with another man and sued for divorce.

Christian Klee had been dumbstruck, then furious. He was happy, how could his wife not be? And what had changed her? He had been loving and courteous to her every wish. Of course he had been busy in his work, to build a career. But he was rich and she lacked for nothing. In his rage he was determined to resist her every demand, to fight for custody of the children, deny her the house she wanted so badly, restrict all monetary rewards that come to a divorced woman. Above all he was astounded that she planned to live their house with her new husband. True, it was a palatial mansion but what about the sacred memories they had shared in that house? And he had been a faithful husband.

He had gone again to the Oracle and poured out his grief and pain. To his surprise the Oracle was completely unsympathetic. 'You were faithful so that makes you think your wife should be faithful? How does that follow, if you no longer interest her? Infidelity is the precaution of a prudent man who knows that his wife can unilaterally deprive him of his house and children without moral cause. You accepted that deal when you married, now you must abide by it.' Then the Oracle had laughed in his face. 'Your wife was quite right to leave you,' he said. 'She saw through you though I must say you gave quite a performance. She knew you were never truly happy. But believe me it's the best thing. You are now a man ready to assume his real station in life. You've got everything out of the way, a wife and children would only be a hindrance. You are essentially a man who has to live alone to do great things. I know because I was that way. Wives can be dangerous to men with real ambition, children are the very breeding grounds for tragedy. Use your common sense, use your training as a lawyer. Give her everything she wants, it will make only a small dent in

70

your fortune. Your children are very young, they will forget you. Think of it this way. Now you are free. Your life will be directed by yourself.'

And so it had been.

So late on Easter Sunday night Attorney General Christian Klee left the White House to visit Oliver Ollifant, to ask his advice and also to inform him that his one hundredth birthday party had been postponed by President Kennedy.

The Oracle lived on a fenced estate that was expensively guarded, its security system had bagged five enterprising burglars in the last year. His large staff of servants, well paid and well pensioned, included a barber, a valet, a cook, and maids. For there were still many important men who came to the Oracle for advice, and had to be fed elaborate dinners and sometimes provided with a bedroom.

Christian looked forward to his visit with the Oracle. He enjoyed the old man's company, the stories he told of terrible wars on the battlefields of money, the strategies of men dealing with fathers, mothers, wives and lovers. How to defend against the government, its strength so prodigious, its justice so blind, its laws so treacherous, its free elections so corrupting. Not thet the Oracle was a professional cynic, merely clear-sighted. And he insisted that one could lead a happy successful life, yet observe the ethical values on which true civilization endures. The Oracle could be dazzling.

The Oracle received Christian in his second-storey suite of rooms which consisted of a narrow bedroom, an enormous bathroom tiled blue which held a jacuzzi and a shower with a marble bench and handholds sculptured into its walls. There was also a den with an impressive fireplace, a library and a cozy sitting room with brightly colored sofa and armchairs.

The Oracle was in this sitting room resting in a specially built motorized wheelchair. Beside him was a table. Facing him was an armchair and a table set for an English tea.

Christian took his place in the armchair opposite the

71

Oracle and helped himself to tea and one of the little sandwiches. As always Christian was delighted by the appearance of the Oracle, the intensity of the man's gaze so remarkable in one who had lived for one hundred years. And it seemed logical to Christian that the Oracle had evolved from a homely sixty-five-year-old to a striking ancientness. The skin was shell-like as was his bald pate which showed liver spots dark as nicotine. Leopardskin hands protruded from his exquisitely cut suit; extreme age had not vanquished his sartorial vanity. The neck encircled loosely by the silk tie was scaly and ridged, the back broad, curved like glass. The front of the body fell away to a tiny chest, his waist you could encircle with your fingers, his legs no more than strands in a spider's web. But the facial features were not yet crenelated by approaching death.

For the first few minutes they smiled at each other, drinking tea; Christian poured the Oracle his cup.

The Oracle spoke first. 'You've come to cancel my birthday party, I assume. I've been watching the TV with my secretaries. I told them the party would be postponed.' His voice had the low growl of a worn larynx.

'Yes,' Christian said. 'But only for a month. Think you can hold out that long?' He was smiling.

'I sure do,' the Oracle said. 'That shit is on every TV station. Take my advice, my boy, buy stock in the TV companies. They will make a fortune out of this tragedy and all the forthcoming tragedies. They are the crocodiles of our society.' He paused for a moment and said more softly, 'How is your beloved President taking all this?'

'I admire that man more than ever,' Christian said. 'I have never seen someone in his position more composed over a dreadful tragedy. He is much stronger now than after his wife died.'

The Oracle said dryly, 'When the worst that can happen to you actually happens and you bear it, then you are the

72

strongest of men in the world. Which, actually, may not be a very good thing.'

He paused for a moment to sip his tea, his colorless lips closed into a pale white line like a scratch on the seamed nicotine-colored skin of his face. Then he said, 'If you feel it's not breaking your oath of office or your loyalty to the President, why don't you tell me what action is being taken.'

Christian knew that this was what the old man lived for. To be inside the skin of power. 'Francis is very concerned that the hijackers have not yet made any demands. It's been ten hours,' Christian said. 'He thinks that's sinister.'

'So it is,' the Oracle said.

They were both silent for a long time. The Oracle's eyes had lost their vibrancy, seemed extinguished by the pouches of dying skin beneath them.

Christian said, 'I'm really worried about Francis. He can't take much more. Right now he'll give up everything to get his daughter back. But if something happens to her . . . He might blow up the whole of Sherhaben.'

The Oracle said, 'They won't let him do it. There will be a very dangerous confrontation. You know, I remember Francis Kennedy as a little boy when he used to play with his cousins on the White House grounds. Even then I was struck at how he dominated the other children.'

The Oracle paused and Christian poured him some hot tea though the cup was still more than half full. He knew the old man could not taste anything unless it was very hot or very cold.

'Who won't let him do it?' Christian asked.

'The Cabinet, the Congress, even some members of the President's staff,' the Oracle said. 'Maybe even the joint Chiefs of Staff. All of them will get together.'

Christian said, 'If the President tells me to stop them, I'll stop them.'

The Oracle's eyes were suddenly very bright and visible. He said musingly, 'You've become a very dangerous man in

73

these past years, Christian. But not terribly original. All through history there have been men, some considered "great", who have had to choose between God and country. And some very religious men have chosen country over God, believing they would go to everlasting hell, thinking it noble. But Christian, we have come to a time when we must decide whether to give our lives to our country or to help mankind continue to exist. We live in a nuclear age. That is the new and interesting question, a question never before posed to individual men. Think in those terms. If you side with your President do you endanger mankind? It's not so simple as rejecting God.'

'It doesn't matter,' Christian said, 'I know Francis is better than Congress, the Socrates Club and the terrorists.'

The Oracle said, 'I've always wondered about your overwhelming loyalty to Francis Kennedy. There are some vulgar gossips who say it's a very faggy business. On your part. Not his. Which is odd since you have women and he does not, not since the death of his wife. But why do the people around Kennedy hold him in a peculiar veneration, though he's recognized as a political dunderhead? All those reformist and regulatory laws he tried to shove down that dinosaur Congress. I thought that you were smarter than that, but I presume you were overruled. Still your inordinate affection for Kennedy is a mystery to me.'

'He's the man I always wished I could be,' Christian said. 'It's as simple as that.'

'Then you and I would not be such longtime friends,' the Oracle said. 'I never cared for Francis Kennedy.'

'He's just better than anybody else,' Christian said. 'I've known him for over twenty years and he's the only politician who has been honest with the public, he doesn't lie to them. And he is religious, not really I think out of true faith, but as a form of humility.'

The Oracle said dryly, 'The man you describe could never

be elected President of the United States.' He seemed to puff out his insect body, his shiny-skinned hands tapped the controls of his wheelchair. The Oracle leaned back. In the dark suit, the ivory shirt and simple blue streak of his tie, the glazed face looked like a piece of mahogany wood. He said, 'His charm escapes me, but we never got on. Now I must warn you. Every man in his lifetime makes many mistakes. That is human, and unavoidable. The trick is never to make the mistake that destroys you. Beware of your friend Kennedy who is so good, remember that evil often springs from the desire to do good. The next few days will be terribly dangerous. Be careful.'

'Character doesn't change,' Christian said confidently.

The Oracle fluttered his arms like bird wings. 'Yes, it does,' he said. 'Pain changes character. Sorrow changes character. Love and money certainly. And time erodes character. Let me tell you a little story. When I was a man of fifty, I had a mistress thirty years younger than myself. She had a brother who was ten years older then her, about thirty. I was her mentor, as I was with all my young women. I had their interests at heart. Her brother was a Wall Street hotshot and a careless man, which later got him into big trouble. Now I was never jealous, she went out with young men. But on her twenty-first birthday, her brother gave her a party and as a joke hired a male stripper to perform before her and her friends. It was all above board, they made no secret of it. But I was always conscious of my homeliness, my lack of physical appeal to women. And so I was affronted, and that was unworthy of me. We all remained friends and she went on to marriage and a career. I went on to younger mistressess. Ten years later her brother gets into financial trouble as many of those Wall Street types do. Inside tips, finagling with money entrusted to him. Very serious trouble that landed him a couple of years in prison and of course the end of his career.

'By this time I was sixty years old, still friends with both of them. They never asked for my help, they really didn't know the extent of what I could do. I could have saved him but I never lifted a finger. I let him go down the drain. And ten years later it came to me that I didn't help him because of that foolish little trick of his, letting his sister see the body of a man so much younger than myself. And it wasn't sexual jealousy, it was the affront to my power, or the power I thought I had. I've thought of that often. It is one of the few things in my life that shames me. I would never have been guilty of such an act at thirty or at seventy. Why at sixty? Character does change. That is man's triumph and his tragedy.'

Christian switched to the brandy that the Oracle had provided. It was delicious and very expensive. The Oracle always served the best. Christian enjoyed it though he would never buy it; born rich he never felt he deserved to treat himself so well. He said, 'I've known you all my life, over forty-five years, and you haven't changed. You are going to be a hundred next week. And you're still the great man I always thought you were.'

The Oracle shook his head. 'You know me only in my old age, from sixty to a hundred. That means nothing. The venom is gone then and the strength to enforce it. It's no trick to be virtuous in old age, as that humbug Tolstoy knew.' He paused and sighed. 'Now how about this great birthday party of mine? Your friend Kennedy never really liked me and I knew you pushed the idea of the White House Rose Garden and a big media event. Is he using this crisis situation to get out of it?'

Christian said, 'No, no, he values your life's work, he wants to do it. Oliver, you were and are a great man. Just hang on. Hell, what's a few months after a hundred years?' He paused. 'But if you prefer, since you don't like Francis, we can forget about his big plans for your birthday party, mass coverage by the media, your name and picture in all the papers and on TV. I can always throw you a little private party right away and get the whole thing over with.' He smiled at the Oracle to show that he was joking. Sometimes the old man took him too literally.

'Thank you, but no,' the Oracle said. 'I want to have something to live for. Namely, a birthday party given by the President of the United States. But let me tell you, your Kennedy is shrewd. He knows my name still means something. The publicity will enhance his image. Your Francis Xavier Kennedy is as crafty as was his Uncle Jack. Now Bobby would have shown me the back of his hand.'

Christian said. 'None of your contemporaries are left. But your protégés are some of the great men and women in the country, and they look forward to doing you this honor. Including the President. He doesn't forget that you helped him on his way. He's even inviting your buddies in the Socrates Club and he hates them. It will be your best birthday party.'

'And my last,' the Oracle said. 'I'm hanging on by my fucking fingernails.'

Christian laughed. The Oracle had never used bad language until he was ninety, so now he used it as innocently as a child.

'That's settled,' the Oracle said. 'Now let me tell you something about great men, Kennedy and myself included. They finally consume themselves and the people around them. Not that I concede your Kennedy is a great man. After all what has he done so noteworthy except become President of the United States? And that is an illusionist's trick. Do you know, by the way, that in show business the magician is considered to be completely without artistic talent?' Here the Oracle cocked his head, he astonishingly resembled an owl.

'I will concede that Kennedy is not your typical politician,' the Oracle said. 'He is an idealist, he is far more intelligent and he has morals, though I wonder whether sexual rigidity is healthy. But, all these virtues are a handicap to political

77

greatness. A man without a vice? A sailing ship without a sail!'

Christian asked. 'You disapprove of his actions. What course would you take?'

'That is not relevant,' the Oracle said. 'His whole three years, he's got his dick half in, half out, and that's always trouble.' Now the Oracle's eyes became cloudy. 'I hope it doesn't interfere with my birthday party too long. What a life I had, eh? Who had a better life than me? Poor at birth so that I could appreciate the wealth I earned later. A homely man who learned to captivate and enjoy beautiful women. A good brain, a learned compassion so much better than genetic. Enormous energy, enough to power me past old age. A good constitution, I've never been sick really in my life, and long! And that's the trouble, maybe a little too long. I can't bear to look at myself in the mirror now but as I said, I was never handsome.' He paused for a time and then said abruptly to Christian, 'Leave government service. Disassociate yourself from everything that is happening now.'

'I can't do that,' Christian said. 'It's too late.' He studied the old man's head, freckled with the chromosomes of death, and marveled at the brain still so alive. Christian stared into those aged eyes, shrouded like a never-ending misty sea. Would he ever be so old with his body shriveling like some dead insect?

And the Oracle, watching him, thought, how transparent they all are, as guileless as little children to parents. It was obvious to the Oracle that his advice had been given too late, that Christian would commit a treachery to himself, and was in some way exhilarated by it.

Christian finished his brandy and rose to leave. He tucked the blankets around the old man and rang for the nurses to come into the room. Then he whispered into the Oracle's glazed skin ear, 'Tell me the truth about Helen DuPray, she was one of your protégées before she got married. I know you arranged for her first entry into politics. Did you ever screw her, or were you too old?'

The Oracle shook his head. 'I was never too old until after ninety. And let me tell you that when your cock leaves you, that is real loneliness. But to answer your question. She didn't fancy me, I was no beauty. I must say I was disappointed, she was very beautiful and very intelligent, my favorite combination. I could never love intelligent homely women, they were too much like myself. I could love beautiful, dumb women but when they were intelligent then I was in heaven. Helen DuPray, ah, I knew she would go far, she was very strong, a strong will. Yes I tried but never succeeded, a rare failure I must say. But we always remained good friends. That was a talent she had, to refuse a man sexually and yet be an intimate friend. Very rare. That was when I knew she was a seriously ambitious woman.'

Christian touched his hand, it felt like a scar. 'I'll phone or drop in to see you every day,' he said. 'I'll keep you up to date.'

The Oracle was very busy after Christian left. He had to pass on the information Klee had given him to the Socrates Club, whose members were important figures in the structure of America. He did not consider this a betrayal of Christian whom he dearly loved. Love was always secondary.

And he had to take action, his country was sailing dangerous waters. It was his duty to help guide it to safety. And what else could a man his age do to make life worth living. And to tell the truth he had always despised the Kennedy legend. Here was a chance to destroy it for ever.

Finally the Oracle let the nurse fuss over him and prepare his bed. He remembered Helen DuPray with affection, and now without disappointment. She had been very young, early twenties, her beauty enhanced by a tremendous vitality. He had often lectured her on power, its acquisition and uses, and more importantly to abstain from its use. And she had listened with the patience that is necessary to acquire power.

He told her that one of the great mysteries of mankind was how people acted against their own self-interests. Points of pride ruined their lives. Envy and self-delusion led them down paths that led to nothingness. Why was it so important for people to maintain self-images? There were those who would never truckle, never flatter, never lie, never back down, never betray, never deceive. There were those who lived in envy and jealousy of the happier fate of others.

It had all been a special sort of pleading and she had seen through it. She rejected him and went on without his help, to achieve her own dream of power.

One of the problems of having a mind as clear as a bell when you are a hundred years old, is that you can see the hatching of unconscious villainy in yourself, and ferret it out in past history. He had been mortified when Helen DuPray had refused to make love with him. He knew she had other lovers, she was not prissy. But at seventy he, amazingly, had still been vain.

He had gone to the rejuvenation center in Switzerland, submitted to surgical erasing of wrinkles, the sanding of his skin, the injection of animal fetus pulp into his own veins. But nothing could be done for the shrinking of his skeleton, the freezing of his joints, the very turning of his blood into water.

Though it no longer did him any good, the Oracle believed he understood men and women in love. Even past his sixtieth year young mistresses adored him. The whole secret was never to impose any rules on their behavior, never to be jealous, never hurt their feelings. They took young men as their true loves and treated the Oracle with careless cruelty, it didn't matter. He showered them with expensive gifts, paintings, jewelry in the best of taste. He let them call on his power to get unearned favors from society, and the use of his money in generous but not lavish amounts. But he was a

80

prudent man and would always have three or four mistresses
at one time. For they had their own lives to lead. They would
fall in love and neglect him, they would take trips, they
would be working hard at their careers. He could not make
too many demands on their time. But when he needed female
company (not only for sex but for the sweet music of their
voices, the innocent deviousness of their wiles), one of the
four would be available. And of course to be seen at
important functions in his company gave them entrée into
circles it would be difficult for them to penetrate on their
own. That was one of his assets of power.

He made no secrets, they all knew about each other. He
believed that in their hearts women disliked monogamous
men.

How cruel that he remembered bad things he had done
more often than good. His money had built medical centers,
churches, rest homes for the elderly, he had done many good
things. But his memories of himself were not good. Fortu-
nately he thought about love often. In an interesting and
peculiar way, it had been the most commercial thing in his
life. And he had owned Wall Street firms, banks, airlines.

Anointed with money he had been invited to share in
world-shaking events, been advisor to the powerful. He had
helped shape the very world people lived in. A fascinating,
important, valuable life. And yet the managing of his countless mistresses was far more valid in his hundred-year-old
brain. Ah those intelligent headstrong beauties, how delightful they had been, and how they had vindicated his judgment, most of them. Now they were judges, heads of
magazines, powers in Wall Street, TV news queens. How
cunning they had been in their love affairs with him and
how he had outwitted them. But without cheating them of
their due. He had no guilts, only regrets. If one of them had
truly loved him, he would have raised her to the skies. But
then his mind reminded him that he had not deserved to be

so loved. They had recognized his love, it was a hollow drum that made his body thump.

It was at the age of eighty that his skeleton began to contract inside its envelope of flesh. Physical desire receded and a vast ocean of youthful and lost images drowned his brain. And it was at this time he found it necessary to employ young women to lie innocently in his bed just so that he could look at them. Oh that perversity so scorned in literature, so mocked by the young who must grow old. And yet what a peace it gave his crumbling body to see the beauty he could no longer devour. How pure it was. The rolling mound of breast, satiny white skin crowned with its tiny red rose. The mysterious thighs, their rounded flesh giving off a golden glow, the surprising triangle of hair, a choice of colors, and then on the other side the heartbreak of buttocks divided into two exquisite haunches. So much beauty, to his bodily senses dead and lost, but sparking the flickering billions of cells in his brain. And their faces, the mysterious shells of ears spiraling into some inner sea, the hollowed eyes with their banked fires of blue and gray and brown and green looking out from their private eternal cells, the planes of their faces descending into unshielded lips, so open to pleasure and to wounds. He would look upon them before he went to sleep. He would reach out and touch the warm flesh; the satin of thigh and buttock, touch the burning lips, and oh so rarely smooth the crinkled vulva hair to feel the throbbing pulse beneath. There was so much comfort there that he would fall asleep and the pulse softened the terror of his dreams. In his dreams he hated the very young and would devour them. He dreamed of the bodies of young men piled high in trenches, sailors by the thousands floating fathoms deep beneath the sea, vast skies clouded by the space-suited bodies of celestial explorers spinning endlessly into black holes of the universe.

Awake he dreamed. But awake he recognized his dreams

as a form of senile madness, his disgust of his own body. He hated his skin that gleamed like scar tissue, the brown spots on his hands and bald pate, those deadly freckles of death, his failing sight, the feebleness of his limbs, the spinning heart, the evilness tumoring his brain clear as a bell.

Oh, what a pity that fairy godmothers came to the cradle of newborn infants to bestow their three magical wishes! Those infants had no need, old men like himself should receive such gifts. Especially those with minds clear as a bell.

BOOK II

4

Romeo's escape from Italy had been meticulously planned. From St Peter's Square the van took his cadre to a safe house where he changed clothes, was furnished with an almost foolproof passport, picked up an already packed suitcase and was taken by underground routes over the border into Southern France. There in the city of Nice he boarded the flight to Paris that continued on to New York. Though he had gone without sleep for the past thirty hours, Romeo remained alert. This was all tricky detail, the easy portion of an operation that sometimes went wrong because of some crazy fluke or hitch in planning.

The dinner and wine on Air France planes was always good and Romeo gradually relaxed. He gazed down at endless pale green oceans and horizons of white and blue sky. He took two strong sleeping pills. But still some nerve of fear in his body kept him awake. He thought of passing through United States Customs, would something go wrong there? But even if he was caught at that time and place, it would not make any difference to Yabril's scheme. A treacherous survival instinct kept him awake. Romeo had no illusions about the suffering he would have to endure. He had agreed to commit an immolating act of sacrifice for the sins of his family, his class and his country but now that mysterious nerve of fear tautened his body.

Finally the pills worked and he fell asleep. In his dreams he fired the shot and ran out of St Peter's Square, and now still running, he came awake. The plane was landing at

87

Kennedy Airport in New York. The stewardess handed him his jacket, and he reached for his carry-on case from the overhead bin. When he passed through Customs, he acted his part perfectly, and carried his bag outside to the central plaza of the airport terminal.

He spotted his contacts immediately. The girl wore a green ski cap with white stripes. The young man pulled out a red billed cap and put it on his head so that the blue stencil reading 'Yankees' was visible. Romeo himself wore no signal markers, he had wanted to keep his options open. He bent down and fiddled with his bags, opening one and rummaging through it as he studied the two contacts. He could observe nothing that was suspicious. Not that it really mattered.

The girl was skinny and blonde and too angular for Romeo's taste, but her face had a feminine sternness that some serious-minded girls have and he liked that in a woman. He wondered how she would be in bed and hoped he would remain free long enough to seduce her. It shouldn't be too difficult. He had always been attractive to women. In that way he was a better man than Yabril. She would guess that he was connected to the killing of the Pope, and to a serious-minded revolutionary girl, sharing his bed might be the fulfillment of a romantic dream. He noticed that she did not lean toward or touch the man who was with her.

That young man had such a warm, open face, he radiated such American kindliness, that Romeo immediately disliked him. Americans are such worthless shits, they had too comfortable a life. Imagine, in over two hundred years they had never come close to having a revolutionary party. And this in a country that had come into existence through revolution. The young man sent to greet him was typical of such softness. Romeo picked up his bags and walked directly to them.

'Excuse me,' Romeo said smiling, his English heavily accented. 'Could you tell me where the bus leaves for Long Island?'

The girl turned her face toward him. She was much prettier up close. He saw a tiny scar on her chin and that aroused his desire. She said, 'Do you want the North Shore or the South Shore?'

'East Hampton,' Romeo said.

The young girl smiled, it was a warm smile, even a smile of admiration. The young man took one of Romeo's bags and said, 'Follow us.'

They led the way out of the terminal. Romeo followed. The noise of traffic, the density of people, almost stunned him. A car was waiting with a driver who wore another red billed baseball cap. The two young men sat in the front, the girl got into the back seat with Romeo. As the car rolled into traffic, the girl extended her hand and said, 'My name is Dorothea. Please don't worry.' The two young men up front also murmured their names. Then the girl said, 'You will be very comfortable and very safe.' And in that moment Romeo felt the agony of a Judas.

That night the young American couple took great pains to cook Romeo a good dinner. He had a comfortable room overlooking the ocean, and although the bed was lumpy it made little difference since Romeo knew he would sleep in it one night, if he slept at all. The house was expensively furnished but it had no real taste, it was modern, beach America. The three of them spent a quiet evening talking in a mixture of Italian and English.

The girl Dorothea was a surprise. She was extremely intelligent as well as pretty. She also turned out not to be flirtatious, which destroyed Romeo's hopes of spending his last night of freedom playing sexual fun games. The young man, Richard, was quite serious. It was evident that they had guessed he was involved in the murder of the Pope, but they did not ask specific questions. They simply treated him with the frightening respect that people show to someone slowly dying of a terminal illness. Romeo was impressed by them. They had such lithe bodies when they moved. They talked intelligently, they had compassion for the unfortunate and they radiated confidence in their beliefs and their abilities.

Spending that quiet evening with the two young people, so sincere in their beliefs, so innocent in the necessities of true revolution, Romeo felt a little sick of his whole life. Was it necessary that these two be betrayed along with himself? He would be released eventually, he believed in Yabril's plan, he thought it so simple, so elegant. And he had volunteered to place himself in the noose. But this young man and woman were also true believers, people on their side. And they would be in handcuffs, they would know the sufferings of revolutionaries. For a moment he thought of warning them. But it was necessary that the world know that there were Americans involved in the plot, these two were sacrificial lambs. And then he was angry with himself, he was too softhearted. True he could never throw a bomb into a kindergarten, like Yabril, but surely he could sacrifice a few adults. He had killed a pope, after all.

And what real harm would come to them? They would serve a few years in prison. America was so soft from top to bottom that they might even go free. America was a land of lawyers who were fearsome as the knights of the Round Table. They could get anybody off.

And so he tried to go to sleep. But all the terrors of the past few days came over the ocean air blowing through the open window. Again he raised his rifle, again he saw the Pope fall, again he was rushing through the Square, and heard the celebrating pilgrims screaming in horror.

Early the next morning, Monday morning, twenty-four hours after he had killed the Pope, Romeo decided he would walk along the American ocean and get his last whiff of freedom. The house was silent as he came down the stairs but he found Dorothea and Richard sleeping on the two couches in the living room, as if they were standing guard. The poison of his treachery drove him out of the door into the salt breeze of the beach. On sight, he hated this foreign beach, the barbaric gray shrubs, the tall wild yellow weeds, the flashing sunlight off silver-red soda cans. Even the sunshine was watery, early spring colder in this strange land. But he was glad to be out in the open while treachery was being done. A helicopter sailed overhead and then out of sight, there were two boats motionless in the water with not a sign of life aboard. The sun rose the color of a blood orange then yellowed into gold as it rose higher in the sky. He walked for a long time, rounded a corner of the bay, and lost sight of his house. For some reason this panicked him or perhaps it was the sight of a vast forest of thin high mottled gray weeds that came almost to water's edge. He turned back.

It was then he heard the sirens of police cars. Far down the beach he saw the flashing lights and he walked rapidly toward them. He felt no fear, no doubt in Yabril, though he could still flee. He felt contempt for this American society that could not even organize his capture properly, how stupid they were. But then the helicopter reappeared in the sky, the two ships that had seemed so still and deserted were racing in to shore. He felt the fear and panic. Now that there was no chance of escape he wanted to run and run and run. But he steeled himself and walked toward the house surrounded with men and guns. The helicopter hovered over its roof. There were more men coming up the beach and down the beach. Romeo prepared his charade of guilt and fright, he started to run out into the ocean but men rose out of the water in masks. Romeo turned and ran back toward the house and then he saw Richard and Dorothea.

They were chained, in handcuffs, ropes of iron rooted their bodies to the earth. And they were weeping. Romeo knew how they felt, so he had stood once long ago. They were weeping in shame, in humiliation, stripped of their sense of power, bewilderingly defeated. And filled with the unutterably nightmarish terror of being completely helpless. Their fate no longer in the laps of the whimsical perhaps merciful gods but in the hands of their implacable fellow man.

Romeo gave them both a smile of helpless pity. He knew he would be free in a matter of days, he knew he had betrayed these true believers in his own faith, but after all, it had been a tactical decision, not an evil or malicious one. Then he was swarmed over by armed men and linked in steel and heavy iron.

Far across the world, that world whose roof of sky was riddled with spying satellites, its ozone patrolled by voodoo radar, across the seas filled with American warships sweeping toward Sherhaben, across continents spaced with missile silos and stationary armies rooted to the earth to act as lightning rods for death, Yabril had breakfast in the palace with the Sultan of Sherhaben.

The Sultan of Sherhaben was a believer in Arab Freedom, in the Palestinian right to a homeland. He regarded the United States as the bulwark of Israel, Israel could not stand without American support. Therefore America was the ultimate enemy. And Yabril's plot to destabilize America's authority had appealed to his subtle mind. The humiliation of a great power by Sherhaben, militarily so helpless, delighted him.

The Sultan had absolute power in Sherhaben. He had vast wealth, every pleasure in life was his for the asking. Quite simply this had all become unsatisfying. The Sultan had no perculiar vices to spice up his life. He observed Muslim law, he lived a virtuous life. The standard of living in Sherhaben, with its vast revenues of oil, was one of the highest in the world, because the Sultan built new schools, new hospitals. Indeed his dream was to make Sherhaben the Switzerland of the Arab world. His only eccentricity was his mania for cleanliness, on his person and in his state.

92

The Sultan had taken part in this conspiracy because he missed the sense of adventure, the gambling for high stakes, the striving for high ideals. So this action of Yabril's had appealed to him. And there was little personal risk to himself and to his country, since he had a magic shield, billions of barrels of oil safely locked beneath his desert land.

Another strong motive was his love and sense of gratitude to Yabril. When the Sultan had been a minor prince, there had been a fierce struggle for power in Sherhaben, especially after the oil fields proved so vast. The American oil companies supported the Sultan's opponents who would naturally favor the American cause. The Sultan, educated abroad, understood the true value of the oil fields, and fought for their value. Civil war broke out. It had been the then very young Yabril who helped the Sultan achieve power by killing off the Sultan's opponents. For the Sultan, though a man of personal virtue, recognized that political struggle had its own rules.

After his assumption of power, the Sultan gave Yabril sanctuary when needed. Indeed Yabril had spent more time in Sherhaben in the last ten years than in any other place. He established a separate identity with a home and servants and a wife and children. He was also, in that identity, employed as a special government minor official. This identity was never penetrated by any foreign intelligence service. During the next ten years he and the Sultan became close. They were both students of the Koran, educated by foreign teachers and they were united in their hatred of Israel. And here they made an especial distinction, they did not hate the Jews as Jews, they hated the official state of the Jews.

The Sultan of Sherhaben had a secret dream, one so bizarre he did not dare to share it with anyone, not even Yabril. That one day Israel would be destroyed and the Jews dispersed again all over the world. And then he, the Sultan,

93

would lure Jewish scientists and scholars to Sherhaben. He would establish a great university that would collect the Jewish brain. For had not history proved that this race owned the genes to greatness of the mind? Einstein and other Jewish scientists had given the world the atom bomb. What other mysteries of God and nature could they not solve? And were they not fellow Semites? Time erodes hatred, Jew and Arab could live in peace together and make Sherhaben great. Oh, he would lure them with riches and sweet civility, he would respect all their stubborn whims of culture, he would create them a paradise of the brain. Who knew what would happen? Sherhaben could be another Athens. The thought made the Sultan smile at his own foolishness, but still what was the harm in a dream?

But now Yabril was perhaps a nightmare. The Sultan had summoned him to the palace, spirited him from the plane, to make sure that Yabril's ferocity would be controlled. Yabril had a history of adding his own little twists to his operations.

The Sultan insisted that Yabril be bathed and shaved and enjoy a beautiful dancing girl of the palace. Then they sat in the glassed air-conditioned terraced room, Yabril refreshed and in the Sultan's minor debt.

The Sultan felt he could speak frankly. 'I must congratulate you,' he said to Yabril. 'Your timing has been perfect, and I must say lucky. Allah watches over you without a doubt.' Here he smiled affectionately at Yabril. Then he went on. 'I have received advance notice that the United States will meet any demands you make. Be content. You have humiliated the greatest country in the world. You have killed the world's greatest religious leader. You will achieve the release of your killer of the Pope and that will be like pissing in their face. But go no further. Give thought to what happens afterwards. You will be the most hunted man in the history of this century.'

Yabril knew what was coming, the probing for more

information on how to handle the negotiations. For a moment he wondered of the Sultan would try to take over the operation. 'I will be safe here in Sherhaben,' Yabril said. 'As always.'

The Sultan shook his head. 'You know as well as I do, that they will concentrate on Sherhaben after this is over. You will have to find another refuge.'

Yabril laughed. 'I will be a begger in Jerusalem. But you should worry about yourself. They will know you have been a part of it.'

'Not probable,' the Sultan said. 'And I sit on the greatest and cheapest ocean of oil in the world. Also the Americans have fifty billion dollars invested here, the cost of the oil city of Dak and even more. Then I have the Russian Army who will resist any American attempt to control the Gulf. No, I think I will be forgiven much more quickly than you and your Romeo. Now, Yabril, my friend, I know you well, you have gone far enough this time, really a magnificent performance. Please, do not ruin everything with one of your little flourishes at the end of the game.' He paused for a moment. 'When do I present your demands?'

Yabril said softly, 'Romeo is in place. Give the ultimatum this afternoon. They must agree by eleven Tuesday morning, Washington time. I will not negotiate.'

The Sultan said, 'Be very careful, Yabril. Give them more time.'

They embraced before Yabril was taken back to the plane, which was now held by the three men of his cadre and four other men who had come aboard in Sherhaben. The hostages were all in the tourist section of the plane, including the crew. The plane was sitting isolated in midfield, the crowds of spectators, the TV people with their camera equipment vehicles from all over the world pushed back five hundred yards from the aircraft, where the Sultan's army had established a picket line.

Yabril was smuggled back on to the plane as a member of

95

the crew of a provisioning truck that was bringing food supplies and water for the hostages.

In Washington DC it was very early Monday morning. The last thing that Yabril had said to the Sultan of Sherhaben was, 'Now we will see what this Kennedy is made of.'

5

It is often dangerous to all concerned when a man rejects the pleasures of this world and devotes his life to helping his fellow man. The President of the United States, Francis Xavier Kennedy, was such a man.

Francis Xavier Kennedy first showed specialness after entry into Havard University. There it became evident that people were attracted to him. It helped that he was a good athlete. Physical grace, unlike intellectual force, is one of the very few traits that is universally admired. It helped that he was a brilliant student, it helped, especially with the unworldly, that he was virtuous.

The friendships he made and the followers he won, were due to his charisma, his generosity of spirit. He was never critical in a personal fashion but he was never the professional good guy. He argued politics vigorously but with humor. Though he was somewhat grave in temperament, the part of him that was Irish sparked a high-spiritedness that was irresistible. Above all he was a good listener who made a real effort to understand completely what someone was trying to say, and then took great care to make an appropriate answer. He had a cheerful wit that he used mainly to prick general hypocrisies.

But above all this he had a natural honesty and sincerity. The young with their keen, if somewhat unfair nose for hypocrisy, could find none in him. True he was a practising Catholic but never discussed his religion. He said simply that it was a matter of faith. This was his only unreasonableness.

No man can hide his villainy over a period of time, Iago is a conceit. No man can hide his faults but faults are easily forgiven or explained. True virtue, especially to the young, can be so dazzling that it blinds common sense. It was not remarked that Francis Kennedy was subject to depression when he was defeated in some endeavor. After all, what could be more natural? It was not remarked that he could be extraordinarily single-minded, not ruthless exactly, but perhaps reckless.

Francis Kennedy, from the very beginning of his political career, posed a simplistic question that was to be his motif. How was it, he said, that after every war that consumed trillions of dollars in goods, there was a period of economic prosperity? He compared it to a bank being looted of its billions and then becoming more profitable.

What if those trillions of dollars were spent building homes for the people, what if those billions and trillions were spent on medical care, on education? What if this money was spent to help the people? What a glorious country this would be and indeed a far better world.

When he was elected to the Presidency, his administration, he said, would declare an internal war, on all the miseries of people who could not afford lobbyists and other pressure groups.

All this in ordinary circumstances would have been far too radical for the voting populace of America if it were not for Kennedy's magical presence on the TV screen. He was handsomer than his two famous uncles and a far better actor. He also had a better brain than his two uncles and was far superior in education, a true scholar. He could back up his rhetoric with figures, eonomic rules. He could present the skeleton of plans that had been prepared by eminent men in the different fields with dazzling elegance. And a somewhat caustic wit.

'With a good education,' Francis Kennedy said, 'any burglar, stick-up man, any mugger, will know enough to steal without hurting anyone. They'll know how to steal like the people on Wall Street, learn how to evade their taxes, like respectable people in our society. We may create more white-collar crime but at least nobody will get hurt.'

Francis Xavier Kennedy had won his election to the Presidency by a landslide on the Democratic ticket, and with a Democratic Congress.

But from the very first, the Presidency and the Legislative branch were enemies. Kennedy lost the extreme right wing in Congress because he was for abortion. He lost the extreme left wing because he supported the death penalty for certain crimes. He claimed he was consistent. He often pointed out that the left who were for abortion were usually against the death penalty. And the right who were against abortion as a form of murder usually were avidly in favor of the death penalty.

Kennedy also made enemies of Congress because he proposed severe restrictions on the huge corporations of America, the oil industry, the grain industry, the medical industry, and also proposed the TV stations, newspapers and magazines should not be held by one company. This last was attacked as an attempt to destroy the freedom of the press. The First Amendment was brandished in all its holiness.

Now in the last year of his Presidency, on the Monday after Easter, at seven in the morning, the members of President Francis Kennedy's staff, his cabinet and Vice President Helen DuPray assembled in the Cabinet Room of the White House. And on this Monday morning they were fearful of what action he would take.

In the Cabinet Room, the CIA Chief, Theodore Tappey, waited for a signal from Kennedy and then opened the session. 'Let me say first that Theresa is OK,' he said. 'No one has been injured. As yet no specific demands have been made. But demands will be made by evening and we have been warned that they must be met immediately, without negotiation. But that's standard. The hijacker leader, Yabril, is a name famous in terrorist circles and indeed known in our files. He is a maverick and usually does his own operations with help from some of the organized terror groups, like the mythical First Hundred.'

Klee cut in. 'Why mythical, Theo?'

Theodore Tappey said, 'It's not like Ali Baba and the forty thieves. Just liaison actions between terrorists of different countries.'

Francis Kennedy said curtly, 'Go on.'

Theodore Tappey consulted his notes. 'There is no doubt that the Sultan of Sherhaben is co-operating with Yabril. His army is protecting the airfield to prevent any rescue attempt. Meanwhile the Sultan pretends to be our friend and volunteers his services as a negotiator. What his purpose is in this no one can guess, but it is to our interest. The Sultan is reasonable and vulnerable to pressure. Yabril is a wild card.'

The CIA Chief hesitated, then at a nod from Kennedy, went on reluctantly. 'Yabril is trying to brainwash your daughter, Mr President. They have had several long conversations. He seems to think she's a potential revolutionary and that it would be a great coup if she gave out some sort of sympathetic statement. She doesn't seem afraid of him.'

The others in the room remained silent. They knew better than to ask Tappey how he had gotten such information.

The hall outside the Cabinet Room hummed with voices, they could hear the excited shouts of the TV camera crews waiting on the White House lawn. Then one of Eugene Dazzy's assistants was let into the room and handed Dazzy a handwritten memo. Kennedy's Chief of Staff read it at a glance.

'This has all been confirmed?' he asked the aide.

'Yes, sir,' the aide said.

Dazzy stared directly at Francis Kennedy. 'Mr President,' he said. 'I have the most extraordinary news. The assassin of the Pope has been captured here in the United States. The prisoner confirms that he is the assassin of the Pope, that his code name is Romeo. He refuses to give his real name. It has been checked with the Italian Security people and the prisoner gives details that confirm his guilt.'

Arthur Wix exploded, as if an uninvited guest had arrived at some intimate party, 'What the hell is he doing here? I don't believe it.'

Eugene Dazzy patiently explained the verification. Italian Security had already captured some of Romeo's cadre and they had confessed and identified Romeo as their leader. The Chief of the Italian Security, Franco Sebbediccio, was famous for his ability to get confessions. But he could not learn why Romeo had fled to America and how he had been so easily captured.

Francis Kennedy went to the french doors overlooking the Rose Garden. He watched the military detachments patrolling the White House grounds and adjoining Washington streets. He felt a familiar sense of dread. Nothing in his life was an accident, life was a deadly conspiracy, not only between fellow humans but between faith and death. In one instant of paranoid divination he comprehended the whole plan that Yabril had created with such pride and cunning. Now for the first time he truly feared for his daughter's safety.

Francis Kennedy turned back from the window and returned to the conference table. He surveyed the room filled with the highest ranking people in the country, the most clever, the most intelligent, the schemers, the planners. None of them knew. He said, almost jokingly, 'What do you guys want to bet, that today we get a set of demands from the hijacker? And one of the demands will be that we release this killer of the Pope.'

The others stared at Kennedy in amazement. Otto Gray said, 'Mr President, that's an awful big stretch. That is an outrageous demand, it would be non-negotiable.'

Theodore Tappey said carefully, 'Intelligence shows no

101

connection between the two acts. Indeed it would be inconceivable for any terrorist group to launch two such important operations in the same city on the same day.' He paused for a moment and turned to Christian Klee. 'Mr Attorney General,' he asked, 'just how did you capture this man?' and then added with distaste, 'Romeo.'

Christian Klee said, 'An informer we've been using for years. We thought it impossible but my deputy, Peter Cloot, followed through with a full-scale operation, which seems to have succeeded. I must say I'm surprised. It just doesn't make any sense.'

Francis Kennedy said quietly, 'Let's adjourn this meeting until the hijackers make their demands. But here are my preliminary instructions. We will give them what they want. The Secretary of State and the Attorney General will stall off the Italians when they request Romeo's extradition. Wix, you and Defense and State get ready to lean on Israel if the demands include release of Arab prisoners they have. And Otto, prepare Congress and any of our friends there for what our opponents will call our complete capitulation.'

Kennedy spoke directly to his Chief of Staff. 'Euge, tell the Press Secretary that I will have no contact personally with the media until this crisis is over. And that every press release has to be cleared by me, not through you.'

Eugene Dazzy said, 'Yes, sir.'

Francis Kennedy now addressed the room full of people almost sternly. 'There will be no comments directly from you to the media. And I hope no leaks. That is all, gentlemen. Please remain on call.'

Yabril's demands came through the White House Communications Center late Monday afternoon, relayed through the seemingly helpful Sultan of Sherhaben. The first demand was ransom of fifty million dollars for the aircraft. The second, the freeing of six hundred Arab prisoners in Israeli jails. The third was for the release of the newly captured assassin of the Pope, Romeo, and his transport to Sherhaben. Also, that if the demands were not met in twenty-four hours, one hostage would be shot.

The President, his staff, his Cabinet, his special advisors met immediately to discuss Yabril's demands. Francis Kennedy put himself in the minds of the terrorists, he had always had this gift of empathy. Their primary aim was to humiliate the United States, to destroy its mantle of power in the eyes of the world, even in the eyes of friendly nations. And Kennedy thought it a master psychological stroke. Who could ever take America seriously again, after its nose was rubbed in dirt by a few armed men and a small oil Sultanate? But Kennedy knew he must allow this to happen to bring his daughter safely home. Yet in his empathy he divined that the scenario was not complete, that there were more surprises to come. But he did not speak. He let the others in the Cabinet Room continue their briefings.

The Secretary of State gave his Departmental Staff's recommendations. That they ship the Pope's assassin back to Rome and let the Italian authorities deal with the situation. The hijackers would have to route their demand for Romeo's release to the Italian government. They all noticed that Francis Kennedy turned his head away at this suggestion.

The threat by the hijackers that they would execute one of the hostages if the demands were not met in twenty-four hours was discounted by all the advisors. Time could be stretched, the threat was an accustomed ploy.

One of the Congressional leaders present suggested that President Kennedy remove himself from all the decisions in this affair because his daughter was involved and he might not be able, emotionally, to make the most effective decisions.

The Congressman who made this suggestion was a Republican veteran with twenty years of service in the House. His name was Alfred Jintz and in three years of Kennedy's administration he had been one of the most effective blockers of social welfare laws proposed by the White House. Like most Congressmen who got through the first few terms and did what was necessary for big business firms, Jintz was automatically re-elected term after term.

Kennedy did not hide his distaste for the suggestion and the Congressman. In his three years as President, Francis Kennedy had acquired a disdain for the legislative branch of the government. Both branches, the House and the Senate, had become self-perpetuating. In the House, even though Congressmen had to run every two years, the power of their positions, especially as heads of Committees, effectively gave them lifelong tenure. Once a Congressman made it clear that he was a believer in the virtue and importance of big business, millions of dollars poured into his campaign, millions to buy lifeblood TV time to be re-elected. And in the 435-member House there was not one working man. As for the Senate with its six-year terms, it would be a very stupid or a very idealistic Senator who did not get re-elected for two or three terms. Kennedy thought this traitorous to democracy.

At this moment Francis Kennedy felt a cold rage, at Jintz, at all the members of the House and Senate.

When Alfred Jintz made his suggestion that Kennedy remove himself from the negotiations, he did so with the utmost courtesy and tact. The New York Senator, Thomas Lambertino, stated that the Senate also thought the President should remove himself.

Kennedy stood up again. He addressed the room in general. 'I thank you for your help and your suggestions. My staff and I will meet later on and you will all be notified of the decisions made. I especially thank Congressman Jintz and Senator Lambertino for their suggestion. I will consider it. But for now I must tell you that all instructions and orders will come from me personally. Nothing in this matter will be delegated. That will be all gentlemen. Please remain on call.'

Vice President Helen DuPray observed everything silently. She knew that this was not the time to oppose the President, even privately.

Francis Kennedy had dinner with his personal staff in the large northwest dining room on the second floor of the White House. The antique table was set for Otto Gray, Arthur Wix, Eugene Dazzy and Christian Klee. Kennedy's place was at one end of the table and set so that he had more space than the others. Kennedy remained standing while the others sat down. He smiled at them grimly. 'Forget all the bullshit you heard today. Dazzy, you tell the Sultan that we will comply with all the hijacker's demands before the expiration of the twenty-four-hour limit. We do not return the Pope's killer to Italy, we send him to Sherhaben. And Wix, you lean hard on Israel. They turn those prisoners loose or they will never see an American gun as long as I'm in office. Tell the Secretary of State, no diplomatic talk, just lay it on the line.'

He sat finally and allowed the stewards to serve him. Then he spoke again. 'I want all of you here to know, that no matter what I have to say at all these meetings, there is only one priority; to get Theresa home safely. No giving them any excuse to commit another crime.'

Arthur Wix kept his hand in his lap as if he planned to refuse his dinner. He said, 'You're leaving yourself very vulnerable. There should be some bargaining, it's mandatory in all hostage cases. You have to go through some of the motions before you do what you want to do, then we can whitewash it.'

'I know that,' Kennedy said. 'I just don't want to take the chance. And besides I only have another year in office and you know I won't run again. So what the hell can they do to me? Otto, you sweet-talk the Congressional leaders. Don't

105

waste time on Jintz. That son of a bitch has been against me on everything for the past three years.'

They all started eating quietly, all thinking that Kennedy was putting the Administration into a difficult position.

As they were drinking their coffee the White House duty officer was ushered into the room. He handed a message slip to Christian Klee. Christian read it and then said to Kennedy, 'Francis, I have to get back to my office. This message has the highest classification, it can't be done by phone. As soon as I get briefed, I'll come back to you. Obviously it's something that must have your immediate attention.'

Francis Kennedy said harshly to him, 'Then why the hell didn't they come and brief us both?'

Christian smiled at him. 'I don't know, but there must be a reason. Maybe they didn't want to bother you with it until I give the OK.' He was lying. His system was set up so that the President could never be briefed before Christian himself had been briefed. What Christian did know was that this message was the first he had ever received from his office that bore the ultra secrecy code. It had to be devastating news.

Francis Kennedy waved him away with an impatient gesture. He knew that there was something not quite right about Christian's answer, that he was being deceived in some way, but he was always careful not to be critical of the people working for him or even of his friends. Kennedy knew that the power of his office gave his words and actions too much weight, he could not indulge his minor irritations.

Shortly after being elected President, he had one of his usual friendly political disagreements with his daughter Theresa. He had delighted in parrying her arguments with his superior skill and then delivering a lightening slash of his own at her radical friends. He had been surprised when she burst into tears and fled. It was then he realized that because of the public weight of his office he could not indulge in natural verbal swordplay with close friends and relatives. He even had to be careful with Christian. In the old days he would have told Christian he was full of shit and demanded the truth.

It was Oddblood Gray who broke into his thoughts. He said, 'Mr President, why don't you try to get some sleep? We'll hold the watch and wake you if anything needs your attention.'

Kennedy saw the look of concern on their faces. During dinner they had done all they could to reassure him about the safety of his daughter, that she was in no real danger. And they had been more formal with him than usual, as people are with each other going through periods of danger or tragedy.

Kennedy said, 'I'll do that, Otto, and thank you all.'

He left them.

When Christian Klee left the White House, he went directly to FBI Headquarters. By protocol, two security vehicles preceded him and another tailed closely behind. In his office he found his Deputy Director waiting for him, the man who actually did the administrative job of running the FBI.

Peter Cloot was a man that Christian understood but could not bring himself to really like. Cloot was part of the trade-off Kennedy had negotiated with Congress when Christian Klee was made Attorney General, FBI Director and head of the Secret Service. Cloot was the man Congress designated to keep an eye on Klee. Cloot was very spare, his body a flat slate of muscles. He had a tiny mustache which did nothing to soften the bony face. As deputy commanding the FBI Cloot had his faults. He was too unbending in the discharge of responsibilities, too fierce in the discharge of his duties, and believed too much in internal security. He lobbied for stricter laws, Draconian punishment for drug dealers and spies. When he could, he dodged the civil liberties sections of the law. But he always exercised good judgment. And certainly he had never spooked before. He had never sent such a message in the last three years he had worked with Christian in running the FBI.

Over three years ago when Christian had interviewed Peter Cloot for the job of Deputy Director of the FBI (Congress had given him three candidates), it was obvious that Cloot did not give a damn if he got the job or not. He had been extraordinarily frank.

'I'm a reactionary to the left and a terror to the right,' Cloot said. 'When a man commits what is called a criminal act, I feel it is a sin. Law enforcement is my theology. A man who commits a criminal act exercises the power of God over another human being. Then it becomes the decision of the victim whether to accept this other god in his life. When the victim and society accepts the criminal act in any way, we destroy our society's will to survive.' He went on. 'Society and even the individual has no right to forgive or ameliorate punishment. Why impose the tyranny of the criminal over a law-abiding populace that adheres to the social contract. In terrible cases of murder and armed robbery and rapes, the criminal proclaims his godhead.'

Christian said smilingly, 'Put them all in jail?'

Peter Cloot said grimly, 'We haven't got enough jails.'

Christian had given him the latest computerized statistical report on crime in America. Cloot studied it for a few minutes.

Cloot said, 'Nothing's changed.' And he began to rage. At first Christian thought him a nut. Cloot said many things . . .

'If only people knew the statistics on crime,' he said. 'If people only knew the crimes that never got into statistics. Burglars, with prior records, rarely go to prison. That home which the government shall not invade, that precious freedom, that sacred social contract, that sacred home, is invaded routinely by armed fellow citizens intent on theft, murder and rape.' Cloot recited that beloved bit of English law, 'The rain may enter, the wind may enter, but the king may not enter.'

'What a piece of bullshit that is,' Cloot said. He went on. 'California alone, by itself, had six times as many murders than the whole of England last year. In America murderers do less than five years in prison. Providing that by some miracle you could convict them.'

Cloot droned on in a grating voice that bored Christian . . .

The Supreme Court in its magestic innocence of everyday life, the lower courts in their venality, the army of greedy lawyers ready for battle as samurai, protected criminals so evil they came out of Grimms' fairy tales.

And the social scientists, the psychiatrists, the pundits of ethics wrapped up all these criminals in the mantle of environment and the general population who supplied jurors too cowardly to convict.

'The people of America are terrorized by a few million lunatics,' Cloot said. 'Afraid to walk the streets at night. Guarding their homes with private security that costs thirty billion dollars a year.'

Cloot rambled on that the whites feared the blacks, the blacks feared the whites, the rich feared the poor. Senior citizens carried guns in their shopping bags because they feared the young. Women in fear of rapists aspired to Black Belts and millions of them carried guns.

'Our fucking Bill of Rights,' Cloot said. 'We have the highest rates of crime in the civilized world.'

But Cloot especially hated one aspect. He said, 'Do you know that ninety-eight per cent of crimes go unpunished? Nietzsche said a long time ago, "A society when it becomes soft and tender takes side with those who harm it." The religious outfits with all their mercy shit forgive criminals. They have no right to forgive criminals, those bastards. The worst thing I ever saw was this mother on TV whose daughter was raped and killed in an awful way, saying "I forgive them". What fucking right did she have to forgive them?'

And then to Christian's slightly snobbish surprise, Cloot attacked literature. 'Orwell had it all wrong in *1984*,' he said. 'The individual is the beast, and Huxley in *Brave New World*, he made it out as a bad thing. But I wouldn't mind living in a Brave New World, it's better than this. It's the individual who is the tyrant, not the government.' And he went on.

Cloot hated lawyers in particular though he himself had a law degree. He thought the Supreme Court a joke. He thought that criminals had all the best of it in American society, and he was not above using all the evasions in his power to thwart any restrictions on his agency. He was careful not to do anything illegal, plant evidence or distort it too obviously but he was not above burying evidence he did not want used.

Christian was undecided about Cloot until their final interview. He had given Peter Cloot the huge statistical report to study and make notes on.

Cloot tapped the computer pages. 'Old stuff,' he said. 'Is this what you want to talk about?'

Christian said earnestly and a little ingenuously, 'I am really astonished by the figures. The population of this country is being terrorized. Maybe that's too strong a word. But was this never addressed by the former President during your term of office?'

Cloot puffed on his cigar. 'We tried. But Congress would never pass the legislation we needed. The newspapers and other media scream bloody murder about the Bill of Rights, the sacred Constitution. And the Civil Liberties outfits are always on our ass. To say nothing of the black lobbies to whom law and order are dirty words. And special groups and unorganized liberals. And those women, special types, who love criminals behind bars and petition to get them loose. So it was a no win situation for Congress.'

Christian pushed over a huge ashtray of red glass and

Cloot tapped his cigar ash into it. Christian picked up his copy of the report and asked, 'Was it this bad before?'

'Worse,' Cloot said. Smoke circled his head like a halo and he smiled sardonically through it. He was digesting the excellent lunch, enjoying his cigar, and so was in the proper state of physical relaxation to pontificate. 'Let me give you a little insight, buy it or not. The really amazing thing is that I've discussed this situation with the really powerful men in this country, the ones with all the money. I gave a speech to the Socrates Club. I thought that they would be concerned. But what a surprise. They had the clout to move Congress. they wouldn't do it. And you could never in a million years guess the reason. I couldn't.' He paused as if he expected Christian to guess.

His face grimaced in what could be a smile or an expression of contempt. 'The rich and powerful in this country can protect themselves. They don't rely on the police or government agencies. They surround themselves with expensive security systems. They have private bodyguards. They are sealed off from the criminal community. And the prudent ones don't get mixed up with the wild drug elements. They can sleep peacefully at night behind their electric walls.'

Cloot paused for a moment. Christian moved restlessly and took a sip of brandy as Cloot swallowed half his glass. Then Cloot went on.

'This is a private consultation so I can speak frankly. You are not allowed in politics to say that blacks commit far more crimes than is proportionate to their population. Sure we both know all the reasons, economic and cultural, and there's a long scandalous history in this country of repressing the black population. But there it is.'

Cloot picked up his cigar. 'By the way, whites are the more dangerous criminals. I never knew a black to be a serial killer, I never knew a black who stole as much money

111

as a Wall Street conniver. And never a black political assassin.'

Christian said, 'You're trying as hard as you can not to get to the point.'

Cloot laughed. 'OK,' he said. 'The point is this. Let's say we pass laws to crush crime, we are then punishing the black criminals more than anyone else. And where are those ungifted, uneducated, unpowered people going to go? What other resource do they have against our society? If they have no outlet in crime they will turn to political action. They will become active radicals. And they will shift the political balance of this country. We may not have a capitalist democracy.'

Christian said, 'Do you believe that crap?'

Cloot sighed. 'Jesus, who knows? But the people who run this country believe it. They figure, let the jackals feast on the helpless. What can they steal, a few billion dollars? A small price to pay. Thousands get raped, burglarized, murdered, mugged, it doesn't matter, it happens to unimportant people. Better that minor damage than a real political upheaval.'

Christian said, 'You're going too far.'

'That may be,' Cloot said.

'And when it goes too far,' Christian said, 'you'll have all kinds of vigilante groups, fascism in an American form.'

'But that's the kind of political action that can be controlled,' Cloot said. 'That will actually help the people who run our society.'

They were both silent, then Cloot went on.

'You show me that fucking computer report,' Peter Cloot said. 'Am I supposed to faint? When I was a young DA I saw those statistics in blood. We had a beeper twenty-four hours a day and in the middle of the night I'd get called on to the street. Husbands who took an axe to their wives and then served only five years in prison. Young doped-up punks murdering old ladies for their social security check, ninety bucks. And then the murderers get off because their civil rights were not observed. Burglars, stick-up artists, bank robbers, it was like winning a gold medal. What a fucking joke. And newspapers quoting *1984* and that fucking George Orwell. Listen I saw the parents of murdered girls weeping, their lives ruined for ever, and the killer getting a slap on the wrist because they had a high-powered lawyer, dumb jurors and some faggy church mogul going to bat for him. And what would they get, these killers, if you convicted them at all? Three years, five years. The criminal system in this country is a complete joke. The people who run this country, the rich, the church, the politicians, my fellow lawyers, they *like* things this way. No radical political movements, fat fees, very nice bribes. So what if a few hundred thousand ordinary people got murdered, who cares that millions get mugged, beaten and raped?' Cloot stopped himself and wiped his clammy face with the table napkin then said in a bewildered voice, 'It never made any sense.'

Then he smiled at Christian and picked up the computer report. 'I'd like to keep this,' he said. 'Not to wipe my ass with it as I should. Just to frame it and put up on the wall of my den where it will be safe. I know it will be safe because I have a fifty-thousand-dollar security system around my house.'

But Cloot had proved to be a superbly efficient Deputy in running the FBI, and tonight, grim-faced, he greeted Christian with a handful of memos and a three-page letter which he handed to him separately.

It was a letter composed with type cut from newspapers. Christian read. Another one of those crazy warnings that a home-made atom bomb would explode in New York City. Christian said, 'For this you pull me out of the President's office?'

Peter Cloot said, 'I waited until we went through all the checking procedures. It qualifies as a possible.'

'Oh Christ,' Christian said. 'Not now.' He read the letter

again but much more carefully. The different types of print disoriented him. The letter looked like a bizarre avant-garde painting. He sat down at his desk and read it slowly word for word. The letter was addressed to the *New York Times*. First he read the paragraphs that were isolated by heavy green marker to identify the hard information. The marked parts of the letter read:

'We have planted a nuclear weapon with minimum potential one half kiloton, and maximum of 2 kiloton, in the New York City area. This letter is written to your newspaper so that you may print it and warn the inhabitants of the city to vacate and escape harm.

'The device is set to trigger off seven days from the date above. So you know how necessary it is to publish this letter immediately.'

Klee looked at the date. The explosion would be Thursday. He read on:

'We have taken this action to prove to the people of the United States that the government must unite with the rest of the world on an equal partnership basis to control nuclear energy or our planet can be lost.

'There is no other way we can be bought off by money or by any other condition. By publishing this letter and forcing the evacuation of New York City you will save thousands of lives.

'To prove that this is not a crackpot letter, have the envelope and paper examined by government laboratories. They will find residues of plutonium oxide.

'Print this letter immediately.'

The rest of the letter was a lecture on political morality and an impassioned demand that the United States cease making nuclear weapons.

Christian said to Peter Cloot, 'Have you had it examined?'

'Yes,' Peter Cloot said, 'it does have residue. The individual letters are cut from newspapers and magazines to form the message but they give a clue. The writer or writers were smart enough to use papers from all over the country. But there is just a slight over normal edge for Boston newspapers. I sent an extra fifty men to help the bureau chief up there.'

Christian sighed. 'We have a long night ahead of us. Let's keep this very low key. And seal it off from the media. Command post will be my office and all papers to me. The President has enough headaches, let's just make this thing disappear. It's a piece of bullshit like all those other crank letters.'

'OK,' Peter Cloot said. 'But you know, someday one of them *will* be real.'

It was a long night. The reports kept flowing in. The Nuclear Energy and Research Agency chief was informed so that his Agency Search teams could be alerted. These teams were specially recruited personnel with sophisticated detecting equipment that could search out hidden nuclear bombs.

Christian had supper brought in for him and Cloot and read the reports. The *New York Times* of course had not published the letter, they had routinely turned it over to the FBI. Christian called the publisher of the *Times* and asked him to blackout the item until the investigation was completed. This was also a matter of routine. Newspapers had received thousands of similar letters over the years. But because of this very casualness the letter had gotten to them Monday instead of Saturday.

Sometime before midnight Peter Cloot returned to his own office to manage his staff which was receiving hundreds of calls from the agents in the field, most of them from Boston. Christian kept reading the reports as they were brought in. More than anything else he didn't want this to add to the President's burdens. For a few moments he thought about

115

the possibility that this might be another twist to the hijacker's plot, but even they would not dare to play for such high stakes. This had to be some aberration that the society had thrown up. There had been atomic scares before, crazies who had claimed they planted home-made atom bombs and demanded ransom of ten to a hundred million dollars. One letter had even asked for a portfolio of Wall Street stocks, shares of IBM, General Motors, Sears, Texaco and some of the gene technology companies. When the letter had been submitted to the Energy Department for a psycho profile the report had come back that the letter posed no bomb threat but that the terrorist was very savvy about the stock market. Which had led to the arrest of a minor Wall Street broker who had embezzled his clients' funds and was looking for a way out.

This had to be another of those crackpot things, Christian thought, but meanwhile it was causing trouble. Hundreds of millions of dollars would be spent. Luckily on this issue the media would suppress the letter. There were some things that those cold-hearted bastards didn't dare fuck around with. They knew that there were classified items in the atom bomb control laws that could be invoked, that could even make a hole in the sacred freedom of the Bill of Rights erected around them. He spent the next hours praying that this would all go away. That he would not have to go to the President in the morning and lay this load of crap on him.

6

In the Sultanate of Sherhaben, Yabril stood in the doorway of the hijacked aircraft preparing for the next act he would have to play. Then his absolute concentration lessened and he let himself check the surrounding desert. The Sultan had arranged for missiles to be in place, radar had been set up. An armored division of troops had established a perimeter so that the TV vans could come no nearer to the plane than one hundred yards, and beyond them there was a huge crowd. And Yabril thought that tomorrow he would have to give the order that the TV vans and the crowds would be allowed to come closer, much closer. There would be no danger of assault, the aircraft was lavishly booby-trapped, Yabril knew he could blow everything into fragments of metal and flesh so completely that the bones would have to be sifted out of the desert sands.

Finally he turned from the aircraft doorway and sat down next to Theresa Kennedy. They were alone in the First Class cabin. There were terrorist guards to keep the passenger hostages in the tourist section, there were guards in the cockpit with the crew.

Yabril did his best to put Theresa Kennedy at ease. He told her that the passengers, her fellow hostages, were being well looked after. Naturally, they were not all that comfortable, neither was she or himself. He said with a wry face, 'You know it is to my own best interests that no harm comes to you.'

Theresa Kennedy believed him. Despite everything, she

found that dark, intense face sympathetic, and though she knew he was dangerous she could not really dislike him. In her innocence she believed her high station made her invulnerable.

Yabril said almost pleadingly, 'You can help us, you can help your fellow hostages. Our cause is just, you once said so yourself a few years ago. But the American Jewish establishment was too strong. They shut you up.'

Theresa Kennedy shook her head. 'I'm sure you have your justifications, everybody always has. But the innocent people on this plane have never done you or your cause any harm. They are just people like you people. They should not suffer for the sins of your enemies.'

It gave Yabril a peculiar pleasure that she was courageous and intelligent. Her face so pleasant and pretty in the American fashion also pleased him, as if she were some kind of American doll.

Again he was struck by the fact that she was not afraid of him, was not fearful of what would happen to her. Again the blindness of the highborn to fate, the hubris of the rich and powerful. And of course it was in her family history.

'Miss Kennedy,' he said in a courteous voice that cajoled her to merely listen, 'it is well known to us that you are not the usual spoiled American woman, that your sympathies go out to the poor and oppressed of the world. You have doubts even about Israel's right to expel people from their own land to found a warring state of their own. Perhaps you would make a videotape saying this and be heard all over the world.'

Theresa Kennedy studied Yabril's face. His tan eyes were liquid and warm, the smile made his dark thin face almost boyish. She had been brought up to trust the world, to trust other human beings and to trust her intelligence and her own beliefs. She could see this man sincerely believed in what he was doing. In a curious way he inspired respect.

She was polite in her refusal. 'What you say may be true.

But I would never do anything to hurt my father.' She paused for a moment, then said, 'And I don't think your methods are intelligent. I don't think murder and terror change anything.'

With this remark Yabril felt a powerful surge of contempt. But he replied gently, 'Israel was established by terror and American money. Did they teach you that in your American college? We learned from Israel but without their hypocrisy. Our Arab oil sheiks were never as generous with money to us as your Jewish philanthropists were to Israel.'

Theresa Kennedy said, 'I believe in the state of Israel, I also believe the Palestinian people should have a homeland. I don't have any power with my father, we argue all the time. But nothing justifies what you're doing now.'

Yabril became impatient. 'You must realize that you are my treasure,' he said. 'I have made my demands. A hostage will be shot every hour after my deadline. And you will be the first.'

To Yabril's surprise, there was still no fear on her face. Was she stupid? Could such an obviously sheltered woman be so courageous? He was interested in finding out. So far she had been well treated. She had been isolated in the First Class cabin and treated with the utmost respect by her guards. She looked very angry, but calmed herself by sipping the tea he had served her.

Now she looked up at him. He noticed how severely her pale blonde hair framed the delicate features. Her eyes were bruised with fatigue, the lips without make-up, a pale pink.

Theresa Kennedy said in a flat even voice, 'Two of my great-uncles were killed by people like you. My family grew up with death. And my father worried about me when he became President. He warned me that the world had men like you, but I refused to believe him. Now I'm curious. Why do you act like such a villain? Do you think you can frighten the whole world by killing a young girl?'

Yabril thought, maybe not, but I killed a pope. She didn't

know that, not yet. For a moment he was tempted to tell her. The whole grand design. The undermining of authority which all men fear, the power of great nations and great churches. And how man's fear of power could be eroded by solitary acts of terror.

But he reached out a hand to touch her reassuringly. 'You will come to no harm from me,' he said. 'They will negotiate. Life is negotiation. You and I as we speak, we negotiate. Every terrible act, every word of insult, every word of praise is negotiation. Don't take what I've said too seriously.'

She laughed.

He was pleased she found him witty. She reminded him of Romeo, she had the same instinctive enthusiasm for the little pleasures of life, even just a play on words. Once Yabril had said to Romeo, 'God is the ultimate terrorist,' and Romeo had clapped his hands in delight.

And now Yabril's heart sickened, he felt a wave of dizziness. He was ashamed of his wanting to charm Theresa Kennedy. He had believed he had come to a time in his life when he was beyond such weakness. If only he could persuade her to make the videotape he would not have to kill her.

7

On the Tuesday morning after the Easter Sunday hijacking and the murder of the Pope, President Francis Kennedy entered the White House screening room to watch a CIA film smuggled from Sherhaben.

The White House screening room was a disgraceful affair, with ratty dingy green armchairs for the favored few and metal folding chairs for anyone under Cabinet level. The audience was CIA personnel, the Secretary of State, Secretary of Defense, their respective staffs, and the members of the White House Senior Staff.

All rose when the President entered. Kennedy took a green armchair, the CIA Director, Theodore Tappey, stood up alongside the screen to give comments.

The film started. It showed a supply truck pulling up to the back of the hijacked plane. The workers unloading wore brimmed hats against the sun, they were clad in brown twill trousers and short-sleeved brown cotton shirts. The film showed the workers leaving the plane and then froze on one of the workers. Under the floppy hat the features of Yabril could be seen, the dark angled face with brilliant eyes, the slight smile on his lips. Yabril got into the supply truck with the other workers.

The film stopped and Tappey spoke. 'That truck went to the compound of the Sultan of Sherhaben. Our information is that they had an elaborate banquet complete with dancing girls. Afterwards Yabril returned to the plane in the same fashion. Certainly the Sultan of Sherhaben is a fellow conspirator in these acts of terrorism.'

The voice of the Secretary of State boomed in the darkness. 'Certain only to us. Secret intelligence is always suspect. And even if we could prove it, we couldn't make it public. It would upset all political balances in the Persian Gulf. We would be forced to take retaliatory action, and that would be against our best interest.'

Otto Gray muttered, 'Jesus Christ.'

Christian Klee laughed outright.

All of the President's staff hated the Secretary of State whose agenda was primarily the placating of foreign governments.

Eugene Dazzy, who could write in the dark, a sure mark of administrative genius, he always told everyone, made notes on a pad.

Kennedy said dryly, '*We* know it. That's good enough. Thank you, Theodore. Please go on.'

The CIA Chief said, 'Our information boils down to this — you'll get the memos in detail later — This seems to be an operation cadre financed by the international terrorist group called the "First Hundred", or sometimes the "Christs of Violence". To repeat what I said in the previous meeting, it really is a liaison between revolutionary groups in different countries, supplying safe houses and material. And it is limited mostly to Germany, Italy, France and Japan, and very vaguely in Ireland and England. But according to our information even the First Hundred never really knew what was going on here. They thought the operation ended with the killing of the Pope. So what we come down to is that only this man Yabril, with the Sultan of Sherhaben, controls this conspiracy.'

The film started to roll again. It showed the airplane isolated on the tarmac, it showed the ring of soldiers and anti-aircraft guns that protected the approaches to the plane. It showed the crowds that were kept over a hundred yards away.

The CIA Director's voice sounded over the film. 'This film

122

and other sources indicate there can be no rescue mission. Unless we decide to just overpower the whole state of Sherhaben. And of course Russia will never allow that, nor perhaps will the other Arab states. Also, over fifty billion dollars of American money has gone to build up their city of Dak, which is another sort of hostage they hold. We are not going to blow away fifty billion dollars of our citizen investor money. Plus the fact that the missile sites are manned mostly by American mercenaries but at this point we come to something much more curious.'

On the screen appeared a wobbly shot of the hijacked plane's interior. The camera was obviously hand-held and moved down the aisle of the tourist section to show the mass of frightened passengers trapped into their seats. Then the camera moved back up into the First Class cabin and held on a passenger sitting there. Then Yabril moved into the picture. He wore cotton slacks of whitish brown and a tan short-sleeved shirt the color of the desert outside the plane. The film cut to Yabril sitting next to that lone passenger revealed now as Theresa Kennedy. Yabril and Theresa seemed to be talking in an animated and friendly way.

Theresa Kennedy had a small, amused smile on her face and this made her father, watching the screen, almost turn his head away. It was a smile he remembered from his own childhood, the smile of people entrenched in the central halls of power, who never dream they can be touched by the malicious evil of their fellow man. Francis Kennedy had seen that smile often on the faces of his dead uncles.

Kennedy asked the CIA director, 'How recent is that film and how did you get it?'

Theodore Tappey said, 'It is twelve hours old. We bought it at great cost, obviously from someone close to the terrorists. I can give you the details in private after this meeting, Mr President.'

Kennedy made a dismissive motion. He was not interested in details.

Theodore Tappey went on. 'Further information. None of the passengers have been mistreated. Also, curiously enough, the female members of the hijacking cadre have been replaced, certainly with the connivance of the Sultan. I regard this development as a little sinister.'

'In what way?' Kennedy asked sharply.

Tappey said, 'The terrorists on the plane are male. There are more of them, at least ten. They are heavily armed. It may be they are determined to slaughter their hostages if an attack is made. They may think that female guards would not be able to carry through such a slaughter. Our latest Intelligence evaluation forbids a rescue operation by force.'

Christian Klee said sharply, 'They may be using different personnel simply because this is a different phase of the operation. Or Yabril might just feel more comfortable with men, he's Arab, after all.'

Tappey smiled at him. He said, 'Chris, you know as well as I do that this replacement is an aberration. I think it's happened only once before. From your own experience in clandestine operations you know damn well this rules out a direct attack to rescue the hostages.'

Christian remained silent.

They watched the little bit of film remaining. Yabril and Theresa talking animatedly, seeming to grow more and more friendly. Then finally Yabril was actually patting her shoulder. It was obvious that he was reassuring her, giving her some good news, because Theresa laughed delightedly. Then Yabril made her an almost courtly bow, a gesture that she was under his protection and that she would come to no harm.

Francis Kennedy said, 'I'm afraid of that guy. Let's get Theresa out of there.'

Eugene Dazzy sat in his office going over all his options to help President Kennedy. First he called his mistress to tell her he would not be able to see her until the crisis was over.

124

Then he called his wife to check their social schedule and cancel everything. After much thought he called Bert Audick who over the last three years had been one of the most bitter enemies of the Kennedy administration.

'You've got to help us, Bert,' he said. 'I'll owe you a big one.'

Audick said, 'Listen, Eugene, in this we are all Americans together.'

Bert Audick had always been an oil man. Conceived in oil, raised in oil, matured in oil. Born wealthy, he increased that wealth a hundredfold. His privately held company was worth twenty billion dollars and he owned fifty-one per cent of it. Now at seventy he knew more about oil than any man in America. He knew every spot on the globe where it was buried beneath the earth.

In his Houston corporate headquarters, computer screens made a huge map of the world that showed the countless tankers at sea, their ports of origin and destinations. Who owned it, what price it had been bought for, how many tons it carried. He could slip any country a billion barrels of oil as easily as a man about town slips a fifty-dollar bill to a *maître d'*.

He had made part of his great fortune in the oil scare of the 1970s, when the OPEC cartel seemed to have the world by the throat. But it was Bert Audick who applied the squeeze. He had made billions of dollars out of a shortage he knew was just a sham.

But he had not done so out of pure greed. He loved oil and was outraged that this life-giving force could be bought so cheaply. He helped rig the price of oil with the romantic ardor of a youth rioting against the injustices of society. And then he had given a great part of his booty away to worthy charities.

He had built non-profit hospitals, free nursing homes for the elderly, art museums. He had established thousands of

125

college scholarships for the under-privileged without regard to race or creed. He had of course taken care of his relatives and friends, made distant cousins rich. He loved his country and his fellow Americans, and never contributed money for anything outside the United States. Except of course for the necessary bribes to foreign officials.

He did not love the political rulers of his country or its crushing machinery of government. They were too often his enemies with their regulatory laws, their anti-trust suits, their interference in his private affairs. Bert Audick was fiercely loyal to his country but it was his business, his democratic right, to squeeze his fellow citizens, make them pay for the oil he worshipped.

Audick believed in holding his oil in the ground as long as possible. He often thought lovingly of those billions and billions of dollars that lay in great puddles beneath the desert sands of Sherhaben and other places on earth, safe as they could be. He would keep that vast golden lake as long as possible. He would buy other people's oil, buy other oil companies. He would drill the oceans, buy into England's North Sea, get a piece of Venezuela. And then there was Alaska. Only he knew the size of the great fortune that lay beneath the ice.

Bert Audick had already swallowed two of the giant American oil companies, gulping them like a frog swallowing flies, so his enemies said. For he did look like a frog, the wide mouth in a great jowly face, eyes slightly popping. And yet he was an impressive man, tall with large bulk, massive head with a jaw as boxy as his oil rigs. But in his business dealings he was as lithe as a ballet dancer. He had a sophisticated intelligence apparatus that gave him a far more accurate estimate of the oil reserves of the Soviet Union than the CIA. Information he did not share with the United States government, as why should he, since he paid an enormous amount of cash to get it, and its value to him was its exclusivity.

And he truly believed, as did many Americans, indeed he proclaimed it as a lynchpin of a democratic society, that a free citizen in a free country has the right to put his personal interests ahead of the aims of elected government officials. For if every citizen promoted his own welfare how could the country not prosper?

On Dazzy's recommendation, Francis Kennedy agreed to see this man. Audick was one of the most influential men in the United States. Not with the public, to them he was a shadowy figure presented in the newspapers and *Fortune* magazine as a cartoonish Czar of Oil. But he had enormous influence with the elected representatives in the Congress and the House. He also had many friends and associates in the few thousand men who controlled the most important industries of the Unites States – the Socrates Club. The men in this club controlled the printed media, the TV media, ran companies that controlled the buying and shipping of grain, the Wall Street giants, the colossi of electronics and automobiles, the Templars of Money who ran the banks. And, most importantly, Audick was a personal friend of the Sultan of Sherhaben.

Bert Audick was escorted into the Cabinet Room where Francis Kennedy was meeting with his staff and the appropriate Cabinet members. Everybody understood that he had come not only to help the President but to caution him. It was Audick's oil company that had fifty billion dollars invested in the oilfields of Sherhaben and the principal city of Dak. He had a magical voice, friendly, persuasive and so sure of what he was saying that it seemed as if a cathedral bell tolled at the end of every sentence. He could have been a superb politician except that in all his life he had never been able to lie to the people of his country on political issues, and his beliefs were so far right that he could not be elected in the most conservative districts of the country.

He started off by expressing his deepest sympathy for

Kennedy with such sincerity that there could be no doubt that the rescuing of Theresa Kennedy was the main reason he had offered his service.

'Mr President,' he said to Kennedy, 'I have been in touch with all the people I know in the Arab countries. They disavow this terrible affair, and they will help us in any way they can. I am a personal friend of the Sultan of Sherhaben and I will bring all my influence to bear on him. I've been informed that there is certain evidence that the Sultan is part of the hijacking conspiracy and the murder of the Pope. I assure you that no matter what the evidence, the Sultan is on our side.'

This alerted Francis Kennedy. How did Audick know about the evidence against the Sultan? Only the Cabinet members and his own staff held this information and it had been given the highest security classification. Could it be that Audick was the Sultan's free ticket to absolution after this affair was over? That there would be a scenario where the Sultan and Audick would be the saviors of his daughter?

Then Audick went on. 'Mr President, I understand that you are prepared to meet the hijackers' demands. I think that is wise. True, it will be a blow to American prestige and authority. That can be repaired later. But let me give you my personal assurance on the matter that I know is closest to your heart. No harm will come to your daughter.' The cathedral bell in his voice tolled with assurance.

It was the certainty of this speech that made Kennedy doubt him. For Kennedy knew from his own experience in political warfare, that complete confidence is the most suspect quality in any kind of leader.

'Do you think we should give them the man who killed the Pope?' Kennedy asked. It didn't matter, he had given orders to grant Yabril everything, but he wanted to hear this man keep talking.

Audick misread the question. 'Mr President, I know you are a Catholic. But remember that this is mostly a Protestant country. Simply as a foreign policy matter we need not make the killing of a Catholic pope the most important of our concerns. It is necessary for the future of our country that we preserve our lifelines of oil. We need Sherhaben. We must act carefully, with intelligence, not passion. Again here is my personal assurance. Your daughter is safe.'

He was beyond a doubt sincere, and impressive. Kennedy thanked him and walked him to the door. When he was gone Kennedy turned to Dazzy and asked, 'What the hell did he really say?'

'He just wants to make points with you,' Dazzy said. 'And maybe he doesn't want you to get any ideas of using that fifty billion dollar oil city of Dak as a bargaining chip.' He paused for a moment and then said, 'I think he can help.'

Kennedy seemed lost in thought.

Christian took advantage of this and said, 'Francis, I have to see you alone.'

Kennedy excused himself from the meeting and took Christian to the Oval Office. Though Kennedy hated using the small room the other rooms of the White House were filled with advisors and staff planners awaiting final instructions.

Christian liked the Oval Office. The light coming from the three long bullet-proof windows, the two flags, one cheerful red white and blue flag of the country on the right of the small desk, on the left the Presidential flag more somber and dark blue. Kennedy waved to Christian to sit down. Christian wondered how the man could look so composed. Though they had been such close friends for so many years, he could detect no sign of emotion.

Kennedy said, 'A whole hour of useless discussion. I've already made clear we're going to give them everything they want. Still they go on.'

'We have more trouble,' Christian said. 'Right here at home. I hate to bother you but it's necessary.'

129

He briefed Kennedy on the atom bomb letter. 'It's probably all bullshit,' Christian said. 'There's one chance in a million there is such a bomb. But if there is it could destroy ten city blocks and kill thousands of people. Plus radioactive fallout would make the area uninhabitable for who knows how long. So we have to treat that one chance in a million seriously.'

Francis Kennedy sighed. 'I hope to hell you're not going to tell me this is tied up with the hijacker?'

'Who knows,' Christian said.

'Then keep this contained, clean it up without a fuss,' Kennedy said. 'Slap the Atomic Secrecy classification on it.' Kennedy flipped on the speaker to Eugene Dazzy's office. 'Euge,' he said, 'get me copies of the classified Atomic Secrecy Act. Also get me all the medical files on brain research. And set up a meeting with Dr Annaccone. Make the meeting after this hostage crisis is over.'

Kennedy switched off the intercom. He stood up and glanced through the windows of the Oval Office. He absently ran his hand over the furled cloth of the American flag. For a long time he stood there thinking.

Christian wondered at the man's ability to separate this from everything else that was happening. He said, 'I think this is a domestic problem, some kind of psychological fallout that has been predicted in think tank studies for years. We're closing in on some subjects.'

Again Kennedy stood by the window for a long time. Then he spoke softly. 'Chris, seal this off from every other compartment of government. This is just between you and me. Not even Dazzy or other members of my personal staff. It's just too much to add on to everything else.'

'I understand,' Christian said.

Eugene Dazzy walked into the office. 'Guess what,' he said. 'The Italian Security Chief, Sebbediccio, was delighted when he heard that we're going to turn that Pope-killer loose to that guy in Sherhaben. He says now he can track him down and kill the bastard.'

The city of Washington overflowed with the influx of media people and their equipment from all over the world. There was a hum in the air as in a crowded stadium and the streets were filled with people who gathered in vast crowds in front of the White House as if to share the suffering of the President. The skies were filled with transport aircraft, specially chartered overseas airliners. Government advisors and their staff were flying to foreign countries to confer about the crisis. Special envoys were flying in. An extra division of Army troops was brought into the area to patrol the city and guard the White House approaches. The huge crowds seemed to be prepared to maintain an all night vigil as if to reassure Francis Xavier Kennedy that he was not alone in his trouble. The noise of that crowd enveloped the White House and its grounds.

On television most of the regular programming had been preempted to report on the hostage crisis and to speculate on the fate of Theresa Kennedy. The word had leaked out that the President was willing to free the killer of the Pope to obtain the release of the hostages and his daughter. Political experts recruited by the TV networks were divided about the wisdom of such a move but they all agreed that President Kennedy had acted too hastily, that the opening demands were certainly open to negotiation as in the many other hostage crises over the past years. They more or less agreed that the President had panicked because of the danger to his daughter.

Some channels had religious groups praying for Theresa Kennedy's safety and pleading to their audiences to suppress any feelings of hatred for fellow human beings no matter how evil. There were a few channels, mercifully with small audiences, that had satirists portraying Francis Kennedy and the United States as a spineless wimp caving in to threats.

131

And then there was the eminent left-wing lawyer, Whitney Cheever III. He made his position clear, the terrorists were freedom fighters, that was understood and they had only done what any revolutionary would do in the fight against the worldwide tyranny of the United States. But Cheever's main point was that Kennedy was paying a huge ransom from the coffers of the United States government to ransom his daughter. Did anyone think, Cheever asked his audience, that if the hostages were no relation, or if they were black, the President would be so pliable? As for the killer of the Pope being released, Cheever did not condone assassination, but that killing was a problem for the Italian government, certainly not the United States with its separation of state and church. But then Cheever concluded by approving the deal Kennedy had made to release the hostages. It could lead to a new period of negotiation and understanding with the revolutionary forces in the world today. And it showed that the authority of the State could not so cavalierly trample the rights of individuals in the dust.

All these programs were recorded by the monitoring government agencies, the film of Cheever's speech was put in a special file for the attention of the Attorney General, Christian Klee.

And while all of this was going on the crowds outside the White House grew larger and larger through the night. The streets of Washington were clogged with vehicles and pedestrians all converging on the symbolic heart of their country. Many of them brought food and drink for the long vigil. They would wait through the night with their President, Francis Xavier Kennedy.

When Francis Kennedy went to bed Tuesday night, he was almost certain that the hostages would be released the next day. The stage set, Yabril would win. Romeo was being prepared for his trip to Sherhaben and freedom. On Kennedy's night table were stacked the papers prepared by the

CIA, the National Security Council, the Secretary of State, the Secretary of Defense and the covering memos from his own staff. When his butler, Jefferson brought him hot chocolate and biscuits, he settled down to read these reports.

They all said the same thing. His complete capitulation was an enormous loss of prestige for the United States. It would be obvious that the most powerful country on earth had been defeated and humiliated by a handful of determined men.

He barely noticed when Jefferson came into the room and wheeled out the table, asking him if he wanted more hot chocolate, saying, 'Good night, Mr President.'

He read on and read between the lines. He brought together the seemingly divergent viewpoints of the different agencies. He tried to put himself in the role of a rival world power reading these reports.

They would see that America was a country on its last decadent leg, an obese, arthritic giant getting its nose tweaked by malevolent urchins. Within the country itself there was an internal blood draining of the giant. The rich were getting much richer, the poor sank into the ground. The middle class fought desperately for their balance in the good life.

The world held the giant money-making America in contempt, waited for it to fall off its own fatty wealth. Perhaps not in a decade, not in two, perhaps not in three, but suddenly it would be a giant carcass eaten away by all these cancers.

Francis Kennedy recognized that this latest crisis, the killing of the Pope, the hijacking of the plane, the kidnapping of his daughter, the humiliating demands to which he had yielded, was a deliberate, planned blow at the moral authority of the United States.

But then there was also the internal attack, the planting of the atom bomb, if there was one. The cancer from within. The psychological profiles had predicted that such a thing

133

could happen and precautions had been taken. But not enough. And it had to be internal, it was too dangerous a ploy for terrorists, too rough a tickling of the obese giant. It was a wild card that the terrorists, no matter how bold, would never dare to play. It could open a Pandora's box of repression. And they knew that if governments, especially the United States, suspended the laws of civil liberties, any terrorist organization could easily be destroyed.

Francis Kennedy studied the reports that summarized known terrorist groups and the nations that lent them support. He was surprised to see that China gave the terrorist Arab groups more financial support than did Russia. But then that was understandable. The Russian-Arab axis was caught in a trap. The Russians had to support the Arabs against Israel because Israel was the American presence in the Far East. The Arab feudal regimes had to worry that Russia wanted to make their state apparatus disappear into communism. But there were specific organizations that at this moment did not seem to be linked with Yabril's operation; it was too bizarre and without a definite advantage for the cost involved, the negative aspect. The Russians had never advocated free enterprise in terrorism. But there were the splinter Arab groups, the Arab Front, the Saiqua, the PLFP-G and the host of others designated with just initials. Then there were the Red Brigades, the Japanese Red Brigade, the Italian Red Brigade, the German Red Brigade which had swallowed up all the German splinter groups in a murderous internecine warfare. And there was the famous 'First Hundred' that the CIA claimed did not exist but was simply a loose international linkage. Yabril and Romeo were classified as part of that group also known as the Christs of Violence. This infamous First Hundred was regarded with horror by even China and Russia.

But what was curious was that not even the First Hundred seemed to be controlling Yabril. Yabril had planned and executed this operation on his own. True he had drawn

134

cadre and material from the Red Brigades, but he had done this by using Romeo. Romeo had certainly been his right-hand man, but nothing else showed, except the final and surprising link with the Sultan of Sherhaben.

Finally it was all too much for Kennedy. In the morning, on the Wednesday, the negotiations would be completed, the hostages would be safe. Now there was nothing he could do but wait. All this took longer than the twenty-four-hour deadline, but it was all agreed. The terrorists would surely be patient.

Before he fell asleep he thought of his daughter Theresa and her bright confident smile as she spoke to Yabril, the reincarnated smile of his own dead uncles. The he fell into tortured dreams, and groaned aloud, called for help. When Jefferson came running to the bedroom, he stared at the agonized, sleep-masked face of the President, waited a moment, then woke him out of his nightmare. He brought in another cup of hot chocolate and gave Kennedy the sleeping pill the doctor had ordered.

As Francis Kennedy slept, Yabril rose. Yabril loved the early morning hours of the desert, the coolness fleeing the sun's eternal fire, the sky turning to incandescent red. He always thought in these moments of the Mohammedan Lucifer, called Azazel.

The angel Azazel, standing before God, refused to worship the creation of man, and God hurled Azazel from Paradise to ignite these desert sands into hellfire. Oh, to be Azazel, Yabril thought. When he had been young and romantic, he had used Azazel as his first operational name.

This morning the sun flaming with heat made him dizzy. Though he stood in the shaded door of the air-conditioned aircraft, a terrible surf of scalding air sent his body reeling backwards. He felt nausea and wondered if it was because of what he had to do. Now he would commit the final irrevocable act, the last move in his chess game of terror that

135

he had not told Romeo, the Sultan of Sherhaben, nor the supporting cadres of the Red Brigades. A final sacrilege.

Far away by the air terminal he saw the perimeter of the Sultan's troops that kept the thousands of newspaper, magazine and TV reporters at bay. He had the attention of the entire world, he held the daughter of the President of the United States. He had a bigger audience than any ruler, any Pope, any prophet. With his hands he could mask the globe. Yabril turned away from the open door to face the plane's interior.

Four men of his new cadre were eating breakfast in the First Class cabin. Twenty-four hours had passed since he gave the ultimatum. Time was up. He made them hurry, then sent them on their errands. One went with Yabril's handwritten order to the Chief of Security on the perimeter, ordering TV crews to be allowed close to the plane. Another of the cadre was given the stack of printed leaflets proclaiming that since Yabril's demands had not been met within the twenty-four hour deadline, one of the hostages would be executed.

Two men of the cadre were ordered to bring the President's daughter back from the isolated front row of the tourist cabin into the First Class cabin and Yabril's presence.

When Theresa Kennedy came into the First Class cabin and saw Yabril waiting her face relaxed into a relieved smile. Yabril wondered how she could look so lovely after spending these days on the plane. It was the skin, he thought, she had no oil in her skin to collect dirt. He smiled back at her and said in a kindly half-joking way, 'You look beautiful but a little untidy. Freshen yourself, put on some make-up, comb your hair. The TV cameras are waiting for us. The whole world will be watching and I don't want them to think I've been treating you badly.'

He let her into the aircraft toilet and waited. She took almost twenty minutes. He could hear flushing and he imagined her sitting there like a little girl and he felt a

136

needle-like pain lance his heart and he prayed, Azazel, Azazel be with me now. And then he heard the great thunderous roar of the crowd standing in the blazing desert sun; they had read the leaflets. He heard the vast threshing of the TV mobile units as they came closer.

Theresa Kennedy appeared. Yabril saw a look of sadness in her face. Also stubbornness. She had decided she would not speak, would not let him force her to make his videotape. She was well scrubbed, pretty, with faith in her strength. But she had lost some of her heart's innocence. Now she smiled at Yabril and said, 'I won't speak.'

Yabril took her by the hand. 'I just want them to see you,' he said. He led her to the open door of the aircraft, they stood on the ledge. The red air of the desert sun fired their bodies. Six mobile TV tractors seemed to guard the plane like prehistoric monsters, almost blocking the huge crowd beyond the perimeter. 'Just smile at them,' Yabril said, 'I want your father to see you are safe.'

At that moment he smoothed the back of her head, feeling the silky hair, pulling it to leave the nape of her neck clear, the white ivory skin so frighteningly pale, the only blemish a small black mole that stole down to her shoulder.

She flinched at his touch and turned to see what he was doing. His grip tightened and he forced her head to turn front so that the TV cameras could see the beauty of her face. The desert sun framed her in gold, his body was her shadow.

One hand raised and pressed against the roof door to give him balance, he pressed the front of his body into her back so that they teetered on the very edge, a tender touching. He drew the pistol with his right hand and held it to the exposed skin of her neck. And then before she could understand the touch of metal, he pulled the trigger and let her body fall from his.

She seemed to float upward into the air, into the sun, into the halo of her own blood. Then her body tumbled so that

137

her legs pointed to the sky and then turned again before she hit the cement runway, lying there, smashed beyond any mortality, with her ruined head cratered by the burning sun. At first the only sound was the whirring of TV cameras and mobile trucks, the grinding of sands, then rolling over the desert came the wail of thousands of people, an endless scream of terror.

The primal sound, without the expected jubilance, surprised Yabril. He stepped back from the door to the interior of the aircraft. He saw his cadre men looking at him with horror, with loathing, with almost animal terror. He said to them, 'Allah be praised,' but they did not answer him. He waited for a long moment then told them curtly, 'Now the world will know how serious we are. Now they will give us what we ask.' But his mind noted that the roar of the crowd had not had the ecstasy he expected. The reaction of his own men seemed ominous. The execution of the daughter of the President of the United States, that extinction of some exempt symbol of authority violated a taboo he had not taken into account. But so be it.

He thought for one moment of Theresa Kennedy, her sweet face, the violet smell of her white neck, he thought of her body caught in the red halo of dust. And he thought, let her be with Azazel, flung from the golden frame of heaven down into the desert sands for ever and for ever. His mind held one last picture of her body, her loose-fitting white slacks bunched around her calves, showing her sandalled painted feet. Fire from the sun rolled through the aircraft and he was drenched in sweat. And he thought, I am Azazel.

Before dawn on Wednesday morning, deep in nightmare, filled with the anguished roar of a huge crowd, President Kennedy found himself being shaken by Jefferson. And oddly, though he was now awake, he could still hear the massive roll of thunderous voices that penetrated the walls of the White House.

There was something different about Jefferson, he did not look like a maker of hot chocolate, a brusher of clothes, the deferential servant. He looked more like a man who had tensed his body and face to receive a dreadful blow. He was saying over and over, 'Mr President, wake up, wake up.'

But Kennedy was awake and he said, 'What the hell is that noise?'

The whole bedroom was awash with light from the overhead chandelier and an ensemble of men stood behind Jefferson. He recognized the naval officer who was the White House physician, the warrant officer entrusted with the nuclear football, and there was Eugene Dazzy, Arthur Wix and Christian Klee. He felt Jefferson almost lifting him out of the bed to stand him on his feet, then in a quick motion slipping him into a bathrobe. For some reason his knees sagged and Jefferson held him up.

All the men seemed stricken, the features of their faces disturbed, ghostly white, eyes unusually wide open, no lids. Kennedy stood facing them with astonishment and then with an overwhelming dread. For a moment he lost all sense of vision, all sense of hearing, the dread poisoned every sense in his being. The naval officer opened his black bag and took out a needle already prepared and Kennedy said, 'No.' He looked at the other men one by one but they did not speak. He said tentatively, 'It's OK, Chris, I knew he would do it. He killed Theresa, didn't he?' And then waited for Christian to say no, that it was something else, that it was some natural catastrophe, the blowing up of a nuclear installation, the death of a great head of state, the sinking of a battleship in the Persian Gulf, a devastating earthquake, flood, fire, pestilence. Anything else. But Christian, his face so pale, said, 'Yes.'

And it seemed to Kennedy that some long illness, some lurking fever crested over. He felt his body bow and then was aware that Christian was beside him, as if to shield him

139

from the rest of the people in the room because his face was streaming with tears and he was gasping to get his breath. Then all the people in the room seemed to come close, the doctor plunged the needle into his arm, Jefferson and Christian were lowering his body into the bed.

They waited for Francis Kennedy to recover from shock. Finally he gave them instructions. To commence all the necessary staff sections, to set up liaisons with congressional leaders and to clear the crowds from the streets of the city and from around the White House. And to bar all media. And that he would meet with them at seven a.m.

Just before daybreak, Francis Kennedy made everyone leave. Then Jefferson brought in a tray of hot chocolate and biscuits. 'I'll be right outside the door,' Jefferson said. 'I'll check with you every half-hour if that is OK, Mr President.' Kennedy nodded and Jefferson left.

Kennedy extinguished all the lights. The room was gray with approaching daybreak. He forced himself to think clearly. His grief was a calculated attack by an enemy and he tried to repulse that grief. He looked at the long oval windows, remembering as he always did that they were special glass, he could look out but nobody could see in, and they were bullet-proof. Also the vista he faced, the White House grounds, the buildings beyond, were occupied by Secret Service personnel, the park with special beams and dog patrols. He himself was always safe, Christian had kept his promise. But there had been no way to keep Theresa safe.

It was over, she was dead. And now after the initial wave of grief he wondered at his calmness. Was it because she had insisted on living her own life after her mother died? Refused to share his life in the White House because she was far to the left of both parties and so his political opponent? Was it a lack of love for his daughter?

He absolved himself. He loved Theresa and she was dead. It was just that he had been preparing himself for that death in the last days. His unconscious and cunning paranoia, rooted in the Kennedy history, had sent him warning signals.

There was the co-ordination of the killing of the Pope and the hijacking of the plane that held the daughter of the leader of the most powerful nation on earth. There was the delay in the demands until the assassin had been in place and captured in the United States. Then the deliberate arrogance of the demand for the release of the assassin of the Pope.

By a supreme effort of will Francis Kennedy banished all personal feeling from his mind. He tried to follow a logical line. It was really all so simple.

On the surface a pope and a young girl had lost their lives. Essentially not terribly important in the world scale. Religious leaders can be canonized, young girls mourned with sweet regret. But there was something else. The people the world over would have a contempt for the United States and its leaders. Other attacks would be launched in ways not foreseen. Authority spat upon cannot keep order. Authority taunted and defeated cannot presume to hold together the fabric of its particular civilization. How could he defend?

The door of the bedroom opened and light flooded in from the hall. But the bedroom now aglow with the rising sun blotted it out. Jefferson, in fresh shirt and jacket, wheeled the breakfast table through and prepared it for Kennedy. He gave Kennedy a searching look, as if enquiring whether to stay, then finally went out.

Kennedy felt tears on his face and knew suddenly that they were the tears of impotence. Again he realized that his grief was gone and wondered. Then he felt consciously overwhelming his brain the waves of blood carrying terrible rage, a rage he had never known and which all his life he had disdained in others. He tried to resist it.

He thought now of how his staff had tried to comfort him.

Christian had shown his personal affection shared over

141

long years, Christian had embraced him, helped him to his bed. Oddblood Gray, usually so cool and impersonal, had gripped him by the shoulders and just whispered, 'I'm sorry, I'm goddamn sorry.'

Arthur Wix and Eugene Dazzy had been more reserved. They had touched him briefly and murmured something he could not hear. And Kennedy had noted the fact that Eugene Dazzy as his Chief of Staff had been one of the first to leave the bedroom to get things organized in the rest of the White House. Wix had left with Dazzy. As head of the National Security Council he had urgent work and perhaps he was afraid of hearing some wild order of retaliation from a man overwrought by a father's grief.

In the short time before Jefferson came back with the breakfast, Francis Kennedy knew his life would be completely different, perhaps out of his control. He tried to exclude anger from his reasoning process.

He remembered strategy sessions in which such events were discussed. Arthur Wix had been the most emphatic on strong action. He brought up the former President, Jimmy Carter.

'When Iran held those hostages, Carter should have taken strong action, no matter what the cost,' Wix said. 'When he ran for re-election the public spurned him because they could not forgive him the months of humiliation they had to bear, that they, the strongest nation on earth, had to eat shit a small country shoveled over them.'

Otto Gray said, 'Carter knew that, he was a very decent man. He put getting the hostages back alive ahead of his re-election.'

Wix said scornfully, 'Sure Carter was decent, but so what? That wasn't his job. The American public didn't care if the hostages got out alive. Not at the price we paid.'

Dazzy said, 'It came out OK. Not one of those hostages was killed. They all got back to their families.'

'You're missing the point,' Wix said. 'Carter lost the

election. When all he had to do was make a military attack and kill a bunch of Iranians even if the hostages got killed in the process. Then he would have been re-elected in a landslide.'

Eugene Dazzy said thoughtfully, 'You know, it could have gone the other way. Carter holding off and the hostages still getting killed. Then Carter, despite his good conscience would have been driven out of office.'

'Tarred and feathered,' Wix said, in his voice his habitual disdain for anyone ineffectual. 'His balls cut off.'

Francis Kennedy did not remember what he had said in that discussion. But now his mind went back almost forty years. He was a seven-year-old boy playing on the lawn and around the porticoes of the White House, running in flowers and grass and then on rich marble, playing with the children of his Uncle John and Uncle Bobby. And the two uncles so tall and slim and fair had played with them a few minutes before ascending into their waiting helicopter like gods. As a child he had always liked his Uncle John best because he had known all his secrets. He had once seen his Uncle John kiss a woman, then lead her into his bedroom. And he had seen them come out an hour later. He had never forgotten the look on Uncle John's face, such a happy look as if he had received some unforgettable gift. They had never noticed the little boy hidden behind one of the tables in the hallway. At that time of innocence the Secret Service were not so close to the President.

And there were other scenes out of his childhood, vivid tableaux of power. His two uncles being treated like royalty by men and women much older than themselves. The music starting when his Uncle John stepped out on the lawn, all faces turning toward him, the cessation of speech until he spoke. His two uncles sharing their power and their grace in wearing it. How confidently they waited for the helicopters to drop out of the sky, how safe they seemed surrounded by strong men who shielded them from hurt, how they were whisked up to the heavens, how grandly they descended from aloft . . .

Their smiles gave light, their godhead flashed knowledge and command from their eyes, the magnetism radiated from their bodies. And with all this they took the time to play with the little boys and girls who were their sons and daughters, their nieces and nephews, playing with the utmost seriousness, gods who visited tiny mortals in their keeping. And then. And then . . .

President John Fitzgerald Kennedy, born rich, married to a woman who was beautiful, leader of the most powerful nation on earth, had been destroyed by such an insignificant little man with only a cheap thin tube of iron. A little man without any resources, with barely the money to buy a rifle. And so, a little boy, Francis Xavier Kennedy, had been banished from the fairyland of power and happiness that he thought would last for ever.

Francis Kennedy, forty years later, remembered that terrible day. He had been playing with the other children and then had gone apart to sit absorbed in the Rose Garden tearing pink silky flowers into ribbons. And then suddenly a swarm of women weeping hysterically swept them into the White House. Into the Red Room, he remembered, filled with people weeping, until his mother had appeared and taken him away. And he had never seen his little friends again, had never played on that lawn again, or dodged around the portico pillars or the brown-gold marble floors.

But he had watched on television, with his weeping mother, the funeral of Uncle John, the gun carriage, the riderless horse, the millions of grief-stricken people and had seen his little playmate as one of the actors on the worldwide stage. And his Uncle Bobby and his Aunt Jackie. His mother at some point took him into her arms and said, 'Don't look, don't look,' and he was blinded by her long hair and sticky tears.

And then his Uncle Bobby was killed a few years later,

and his mother had taken him to a hunting lodge in the Sierra mountains that had no television. It was not until he was an adult that he saw the tapes of that murder. And again it was an insignificant man with a cheap tube of iron who destroyed what was left of his mother's world.

Now, the shaft of yellow light from the open door cut through his memories and he saw that Jefferson had wheeled in a fresh table. Francis Kennedy said quietly, 'Take that away and give me an hour. Don't interrupt me before then.' He had rarely spoken so abruptly or sternly and Jefferson gave him an appraising look. Then he said, 'Yes, Mr President,' and wheeled the table back out and closed the door.

The sun was strong enough to light the bedroom, yet not to give it heat. But the throb of Washington entered the room. The television trucks were filling streets outside the gates and countless car motors hummed like a giant swarm of insects. Planes flew constantly overhead, all military – air space had been closed to civilian traffic.

President Francis Kennedy tried to fight the overwhelming rage, the bitter nauseating bile in his mouth. What was supposed to be the greatest triumph of his life had proved to be his greatest misfortune. He had been elected to the Presidency and his wife had died before he assumed the office. His great programs for a utopian America had been smashed to bits by Congress and he had not been strong enough to muster his will, his strength, his intelligence to overcome that defeat. And now his daughter had paid the price for his ambition and his dreams. Nauseating saliva made him gag as it ran over his tongue and lips. His body seemed to fill with a poison that weakened him in every limb and only rage could make him well, and at that moment something happened in his brain, an electric charge fighting the sickness of his body cells. So much energy flowed through his body that he flung his arms outward, fists clenched to the now sun-filled windows.

He had power, he would use that power. He could make his enemies tremble, he could make their saliva bitter in their mouths. He could sweep away all the small insignificant men with their cheap tubes of iron, all those who had brought such tragedy into his life and to his family.

He felt now like a man who, long sick and feeble, is finally cured of a serious illness, wakes one morning and has regained his strength. He felt an exhilaration, almost a peace he had not felt since before his wife died. He sat on the bed and tried to control his feelings, to restore caution and a rational train of thought. More calmly he reviewed all his options and all their dangers and then finally he knew what he must do and what dangers he must forestall. He felt one last thrust of pain that his daughter no longer existed. Then he opened the door and called out for Jefferson.

BOOK III

8

Just four hours after the killing of his daughter, Francis Kennedy met with his staff. They breakfasted in the family dining room of the White House with its small fireplace and yellow-white walls and rugs. This was a preliminary to the larger meeting which would include the Vice President, the Cabinet and the representatives of the Senate and Congress.

Eugene Dazzy as Chief of the President's staff had prepared a memo of staff recommendations made in the hours since the killing of Theresa Kennedy. Otto Gray had briefed by phone the leaders of Congress, Wix had briefed members of the National Security Council and the Chief of the Central Intelligence Agency and the Chief of the Joint Chiefs of Staff. Christian Klee had consulted with no one. The situation was beyond any legal theory.

While Kennedy read Dazzy's memo, the other men ate breakfast. Wix had milk and toast. Oddblood Gray tried to eat some eggs and bacon and a small steak but gave up after a mouthful of each. Dazzy and Klee made no pretense of eating, they watched Kennedy reading the memo.

Kennedy put the six pages on top of Dazzy's briefcase. None of the recommendations even approached what he planned to do. But he had to be careful.

'Thank you,' he said. 'It covers all options you could have foreseen. But I have something else in mind.' He smiled at them to show he was in command of his feelings, not knowing how ghastly the smile appeared on his bloodless face.

Eugene Dazzy said, 'Mr President, could you please initial the memo to show it's been read.' Kennedy noted the formality of the language and knew it came from the awkwardness of the terrible event of the morning. Kennedy wrote 'NO' in large letters on the memo and signed it in full.

Then he surveyed each one of them in turn before he spoke. He wanted to show them how calm he was, that he was not acting in angry grief, that he was rational, that what he was going to say was logic unmarred by personal emotions. He spoke very slowly.

'I wanted to tell you what I'm going to tell everyone else at the meeting later. This is not a consultation. This is a plea for your support. I want us all to be together on this. Anybody who feels strongly that they can't go along, I want them to resign right now before we go into that meeting.'

Very quickly Kennedy gave his analysis of the situation and what he was going to do. He could see that they were stunned, even Christian. Not by the analysis but the solution he proposed. And they were stunned too by the curtness he showed. He was rarely ceremonious in their staff meetings. His invitation of their resignations was completely out of character. He made it very clear to them. They would go along without any discussion or resign.

This demand by President Francis Kennedy to the four men of his Senior Staff was in the nature of an insult to a close family. The President's Senior Staff was personally picked by the President. They were responsible solely to him. He could appoint them, he could fire them. The President was like a Cyclops with one brain and four arms. The Senior Staff were his four arms. It went without saying that they would approve Francis Kennedy's decision. But it was an insult that they were forbidden to analyze and discuss it. After all, they were not the Cabinet members who were approved by Congress. The Presdent's staff must sink with the President.

Official distinctions aside, the Senior Staff was always

much closer to the President than anyone in the Cabinet or Congress. In fact the staff had evolved to weaken the different Secretaries in the Cabinet. And in Kennedy's case, all four of these men were his closest personal friends. And since the death of his wife, his only personal family. Francis Kennedy knew that he had insulted them and he watched their reactions closely.

Christian Klee, he saw, didn't give a damn. Christian was his dearest and closest friend of the four. The one who had always held him in some sort of reverence. Which always surprised Kennedy because he knew that Christian valued physical bravery and knew that Kennedy had a fear of assassination. It was Christian who had begged Francis to run for the Presidency and guaranteed his personal safety if he was appointed Attorney General and head of the FBI and Secret Service. And Christian believed in Kennedy's political theories more as a patriot than as a left-wing idealist. Kennedy knew that Christian was with him.

Arthur Wix was the man whose reaction he feared most. Wix believed in analyzing every situation in depth. Francis Kennedy had met Wix ten years before when he had first run for the Senate. Wix was an Eastern Seaboard liberal, a professor of ethics and political science at Columbia University. He was also a very rich man who had contempt for money. Their relationship had grown into a friendship based on their intellectual gifts. Kennedy thought Arthur Wix the most intelligent man he had ever met. Wix thought Kennedy the most moral man in politics. This was not, could not be, the basis of a warm friendship, but did form the basis for a trusting relationship. Kennedy could see that Wix had to make an effort to restrain a protest against his ultimatum. But restrain he did, he would agree out of trust.

The third man, his Chief of Staff, Eugene Dazzy, Kennedy was sure of because of the political realities involved. Eugene Dazzy had been the head of a huge computer firm ten years before when Francis Kennedy first entered politics. He had

151

been a cruncher, a man who could eat up rival companies, but he had come originally from a poor family, and he retained his sense of justice more out of a practical sense than a romantic idealism. He had come to a belief that concentrated money held too much power in America and that in the long run this would destroy the true democracy. And so when Francis Kennedy entered politics under the banner of a true social democracy, Eugene Dazzy organized the financial support that helped Kennedy ascend to the Presidency.

During that time a curious friendship had evolved. Dazzy was an eccentric. A big wheel businessman who cared nothing for outward appearances. A huge rumpled man who dressed in cheap suits and ties, he also always wore a Walkman on his head to listen to music while in his office. He loved music and he loved young women but his marriage had lasted thirty years. His wife often claimed he wore the Walkman radio cassette player to discourage conversation, not to listen to music. She never mentioned his women.

But what had astonished and fascinated Francis Kennedy most was that Eugene Dazzy was such a paradox. A rare combination of hard-headed businessman and a devoted student of literature with a passionate love of poetry, especially Yeats. Dazzy had been chosen as staff because he was a master of the 'half yes' and still had the sensitivity to give a flat 'no' without making an implacable enemy. But he was the President's shield against the Cabinet and the Congress. The Secretary of State and the Speaker of the House had to satisfy Dazzy before they could get to see the President.

But what brought Kennedy and Dazzy close in a more personal way was the exercise to pardon criminals. Dazzy would screen the Presidential Pardoning Committee for outlandish cases where a citizen had been mangled by the judicial system or the bureaucracy and would persuade the President to use his power to pardon. 'Look at it this way,'

152

Eugene Dazzy told Francis Kennedy, 'the President of the United States has the power to pardon anyone. The Congress and the Courts can't interfere. Think how that burns their ass. You have to use that power as much as you can, just for that reason.'

Francis Kennedy had not studied and practised the law without being subjected to the best of cons. So in the beginning he had watched Dazzy closely on the pardoning business. But each case Dazzy brought to his attention had its own particular poetic merit. And they rarely disagreed. And these special regal mercies to their fellow man created a special bond between them.

And so Kennedy could see that Dazzy would agree, would not insist on a discussion. Which left only Oddblood Gray.

Oddblood Gray's association with Francis Kennedy was longer than that of Wix and Dazzy. Gray had been a firebrand on the left of the black political movement when they first met. A tall imposing man, he had been a brilliant scholar and a first-rate orator in his college days. Kennedy had spotted under the firebrand, a man with a natural courtesy and diplomacy, a man who could persuade without threats. And then, in a potentially violent situation in New York, Kennedy had won Oddblood's admiration and trust. Kennedy had used his extraordinary legal skills, his intelligence and charm, his complete lack of racial bias to defuse the situation, to serve the agreement and win the admiration of both sides.

Afterwards Oddblood Gray had asked him, 'How the hell did you do that?'

Kennedy had grinned and said, 'Easy. I convinced them there was nothing in it for me.'

After that, Oddblood Gray had drifted from the left of the movement to the right. Which lessened his power in the movement but brought him to the center of national power. He had supported Kennedy in his political career, urged him to run for the Presidency. Kennedy appointed Oddblood

Gray to his staff as liaison to the Congress, head man to get the President's bills pushed through.

Now Oddblood Gray yielded his judgment to his trust.

But superseding all this, even the admiration all four of these men held for Kennedy, for his moral character, his intelligence, his charm, his unending string of achievements, was their respect for his gallantry when he met with his first defeat, the death of his wife, Catherine. That he persevered in his campaign for the Presidency, that he still pursued his aims for political and social reform. And their affection for him deepened when he searched for some personal stability by designating the four of them as his personal family.

Each night at least one of them ate dinner with Kennedy in the White House. There were many times when they all dined together as friends. Enthusiastically making plans for the betterment of their country, discussing the details of particular bills to Congress, and outlining strategies to deal with foreign countries. They were often as excited as when they were young college students as they plotted against the oligarchy of the rich, and still they suffered over the anarchy of the poor. After dinner they all went home to dream of a new and better America that they would create together.

But they had been defeated by the Congress and the Socrates Club. Not only President Francis Xavier Kennedy, but all of them.

And so now when Kennedy looked around the breakfast table, they all nodded their assent and then prepared to go to the general meeting in the Cabinet Room. It was eleven a.m. Wednesday morning in Washington.

In the Cabinet Room the most politically significant people in the government had gathered to decide what the country should do. There was the Vice President Helen DuPray, there were the members of the Cabinet, the head of the CIA, the Chief of the Joint Chiefs of Staff, not usually present at such meetings but instructed to be so by Eugene Dazzy following the President's request. When Kennedy entered the room they all rose.

Kennedy motioned to them to sit down.

Only the Secretary of State remained standing. He said, 'Mr President, all of us here wish to express our heartbreak at your loss. We offer our personal condolences, our love. We assure you of our utmost loyalty and devotion in your personal crisis and this crisis in our nation. We are here to give you more than our professional counsel. We are here to give you our indiviaul devotion.' There were tears in the eyes of the Secretary of State. And he was a man noted for his coolness and reserve.

Kennedy bowed his head for a moment. He was the only man in the room who seemed to show no emotion except for the paleness of his face. He looked at them all for a long moment, as if acknowledging every person in the room, their feelings of affection and his gratefulness. Knowing that he was about to shatter this good feeling. He said, 'I want to thank all of you, I am grateful and I am counting on you. But now I beg all of you to put my personal misfortune out of the context of this meeting. We are here to decide what is best for our country. This is our duty and sacred obligation. The decisions I have made are strictly non-personal.' He paused for a moment to let the shock and recognition sink in that he alone would control.

Helen DuPray thought, 'Oh Christ, he's going to do it.'

Kennedy went on. 'This meeting will deal with our options. I doubt that any of your options will be taken but I must give you your opportunity to argue them. But first let me present my scenario. Let me say that I have the support of my personal staff.' He paused again to project all his personal magnetism. He stood up and said, 'One: The analysis. All the recent tragic events have been the dynamic of one boldly conceived and ruthlessly executed masterplan. The murder of the Pope on Easter Sunday, the hijacking of

155

the plane on the same day, the deliberate logistical impossibility of the demands for the release of the hostages, and though I agreed to meet all those demands, finally the unnecessary murder of my daughter early this morning. And even the capture of the assassin of the Pope here in our country, an event far beyond the realm of any chance of destiny, that too was part of the overall plan so that they could demand the release of the assassin. The evidence supporting this analysis is overwhelming.'

He could see the looks of disbelief on their faces. He paused and then went on.

'But what could be the purpose of such a terrifying and complicated scenario? There is in the world today a contempt for authority, the authority of the state, but specifically a contempt for the moral authority of the United States. It goes far beyond the usual historical contempt for authority exhibited by the young, which is often a good thing. The purpose of this terrorist plan is to discredit the United States as an authority figure. Not only in the lives of billions of common people but in the eyes of the governments of the world. We must at some time answer these challenges and that time is now.

'For the record. Russia has no part in this plot. The Arab states have no part. Except for Sherhaben. Certainly the terrorist worldwide underground know as the "First Hundred" gave logistical and personnel support. But the evidence points to only one man in control. And it seems that he does not accept being controlled except perhaps by the Sultan of Sherhaben.'

Again he paused. He was surprised at his own calm. He went on.

'We now know for certain that the Sultan is an accomplice. His troops are stationed to guard the aircraft from outside attacks, not to help us with the hostages. The Sultan claims to act in our interest, but in reality is involved in these acts. However, to give him his due, there is evidence that he did not know that Yabril would murder my daughter.'

Kennedy paused but it was not a pause that inviteed interruption. He glanced around the table to again impress them with his calmness. Then he said, 'Second: The prognosis. This is not the usual hostage situation. This is a clever plot to humiliate the United States to the utmost. To make the United States beg for the return of the hostages after suffering a series of humiliations that make us seem impotent. It is a situation that will be wrung dry for weeks with media coverage all over the world. And with no guarantee that all the remaining hostages will be returned safely. Under those circumstances I cannot imagine anything but chaos afterwards. Our own people will lose faith in us and our country.'

Again Kennedy paused, he saw that he was making an impression now. That the men in this room understood that he had a point. He went on.

'Remedies: I've studied the memo on options we have. I think they are the usual lame recourses of the past. Economic sanctions, armed rescue missions, political arm-twisting, concessions given in secret while maintaining that we never negotiate with terrorists. The concern that the Soviet Union will refuse to permit us to make a large-scale military assault in the Persian Gulf. All these imply that we must submit and accept our profound humiliation in the eyes of the world. And in my opinion more of the hostages may well be lost.'

The Secretary of State interrupted. 'My department has just received a definite promise from the Sultan of Sherhaben to release all the hostages when the terrorists' demands have been met. He is outraged by Yabril's action and claims he is ready to launch an assault on the plane. He has secured Yabril's promise to release fifty of the hostages now to show good faith.'

Kennedy stared at him for a moment. The cerulean eyes seemed veined with tiny black dots. Then his voice, cold with taut courtesy, and so controlled that the words rang metallically, said, 'Mr Secretary, when I am done, everyone here will be given time to speak. Until that time please do not interrupt. Their offer will be suppressed, it will not be made known to the media.'

The Secretary of State was obviously surprised. The President had never spoken so coolly to him before, had never so blatantly shown his power. The Secretary of State bowed his head to study his copy of the memo, only his cheeks reddened slightly. Kennedy went on.

'Solution: I hereby instruct the Chief of Staff to direct and plan an air strike on the oilfields of Sherhaben and their industrial oil city of Dak. The mission of the airstrike will be the destruction of all oil equipment, drilling rigs, pipelines, etc. The city will be destroyed. Four hours before the bombing leaflets will be dropped on the city warning the inhabitants to evacuate. The air strike will take place exactly thirty-six hours from now. That is on Thursday, eleven p.m. Washington time.'

There was dead silence in the room that held more than thirty people who wielded all the arms of power in America. Kennedy went on.

'The Secretary of State will contact the necessary countries for overflight approval. He will make it plain to them that any refusal will be a cessation of all economic and military accommodations with this country. That the results of a refusal will be dire.'

The Secretary of State seemed to levitate from his seat to protest, then restrained himself. There was a murmur through the room of suprise or shock.

Kennedy held up his hands, the gesture almost angry, but he was smiling at them, a smile that seemed to be one of reassurance. He seemed to become less commanding, almost casual, smiling at the Secretary of State and speaking directly to him. 'The Secretary of State will send to me, at once, the Ambassador from the Sultan of Sherhaben. I will tell the

Ambassador this: the Sultan must deliver up the hostages by tomorrow afternoon. He will deliver up the terrorist, Yabril, in a way that he will not be able to take his own life. If the Sultan refuses, the entire country of Sherhaben itself will cease to exist.' Kennedy paused for a moment, the room was absolutely still. 'This meeting has the highest security classification. There will be no leaks. If there are, the most extreme action under the law will be taken. Now you all can speak.'

He could see the audience was stunned by his words, that his staff had looked down refusing to meet the eyes of the others in the room.

Kennedy sat down, sprawling in his black leather chair, his legs out from under the table and visible to the side. He stared out into the Rose Garden as the meeting continued.

He heard the Secretary of State say, 'Mr President, again I must argue your decision. This will be a disaster for the United States. We will become a pariah among nations by using our force to crush a small nation.' And the voice went on and on but he could not hear the words.

Then he heard the voice of the Secretary of the Interior, a voice almost flat and yet commanding attention. 'Mr President, when we destroy Dak, we destroy fifty billion American dollars, that's American oil company money, money the middle class of American spent to buy stock in the oil companies. Also, we curtail our import of oil. The price of gasoline will double for the consumers of this country.'

There was the confused babble of other arguments. Why did the city of Dak have to be destroyed before any satisfaction was given? There were many avenues still be be explored. The great danger was in acting too hastily. Kennedy looked at his watch. This had been going on for over an hour. He stood up.

'I thank each of you for your advice,' he said. 'Certainly the Sultan of Sherhaben could save the city of Dak by meeting my demands immediately. But he won't. The city of Dak must be destroyed or our threats will be ignored. The alternative is for us to govern a country that any man with courage and small weapons can humiliate. Then we might as well scrap our Navy and Army and save the money. I see our course very clearly and I will follow it.

'Now as to the fifty billion dollar loss to American stockholders. Bert Audick heads the consortium that owns that property. He has already made his fifty billion dollars and more. We will do our best to help him, of course. I will permit Mr Audick an opportunity to save his investment in another way. I am sending a plane to Sherhaben to pick up the hostages and a military plane to transport the terrorists to this country to stand trial. The Secretary of State will invite Mr Audick to go to Sherhaben on one of those planes. His job will be to help persuade the Sultan to accept my terms. To persuade him that the only way to save the city of Dak, the country of Sherhaben and the American oil in that country is to accede to my demands. That's the deal.'

The Secretary of Defense said, 'If the Sultan does not agree that means we lose two more planes, Audick, and the hostages.'

Kennedy said, 'Most likely. Let's see if Audick has the balls. But he's smart. He will know as I do, that the Sultan must agree. I'm so sure that I am also sending the National Security Advisor, Mr Wix.'

The CIA Chief said, 'Mr President, you must know that the anti-aircraft guns around Dak are manned by Americans on civilian contract to the Sherhaben government and the American oil companies. Specially trained Americans who man missile sites. They may put up a fight.'

Kennedy smiled. 'Audick will order them to evacuate. Of course, as Americans, if they fight us they will be traitors, and the Americans who pay them will also be prosecuted as traitors.'

He paused to let that sink in. Audick would be prosecuted. He turned to Christian. 'Chris, you can start working on the legal end.'

Among those present were two members of the legislative branch. The Senate Majority Leader, Thomas Lambertino, and the Speaker of the House, Alfred Jintz. It was the Senator who spoke first. He said, 'I think this too drastic a course of action to be taken without a full discussion in both houses of the Congress.'

Kennedy said to him courteously, 'With all due respect, there is no time. And it is within my power as the Chief Executive to take this action. Without question the legislative branch can review it later and take action as they see fit. But I sincerely hope that Congress will support me and this nation in its extremity.'

Senator Lambertino said almost sorrowfully, 'This is dire, the consequences severe. I implore you, Mr President not to act so quickly.'

For the first time Francis Kennedy became less than courteous. 'I haven't won a battle in the Congress in all the three years of my administration,' he said. 'We can argue all the complicated options until the hostages are dead and the United States is ridiculed in every nation and every little village in the world. I hold by my analysis and my solution, my decision is within my power as Chief Executive. When the crisis is over I will go before the people and give them a full report. Until then, I remind you all again, this discussion is of the highest classification. Now I know you all have work to do. Report your progress to my Chief of Staff.'

It was Alfred Jintz, the Speaker of the House, who answered. 'Mr President,' he said, 'I had hoped not to say this. But Congress now insists that you remove yourself from these negotiations. Therefore, I must give notice that this very day the Congress and the Senate will do everything to prevent your course of action on the grounds that your personal tragedy makes you incompetent.'

Kennedy stood over them. His face with its beautifully planed lines was frozen into a mask. His satiny blue eyes were as blind as a statue. 'You do so at your peril,' he said, 'and America's.' He left the room.

All the others rose and remained standing until the door closed behind him and his two Secret Service bodyguards.

In the Cabinet room, there was a flurry of movement, a babble of voices. Oddblood Gray huddled with Senator Lambertino and Congressman Jintz. But their faces were grim, their voices cold. The Congressmen said, 'We can't allow this to happen. I think the President's staff has been delinquent in not dissuading him from this course of action.'

Oddblood Gray said, 'He convinced me he was not acting out of personal anger. That it was the most effective solution to the problem. It is dire of course, but so are the times. We can't let the situation be drawn out. That can be catastrophic.'

Senator Lambertino said, 'This is the first time that I have ever known Francis Kennedy to act in so high-handed a fashion. He was always a courteous President to the legislative branch. He could at least have pretended that we were party to the decision process.'

Oddblood Gray said, 'He's under a great deal of stress. It would be helpful if the Congress did not add to that stress.' Fat chance, he thought as he said it.

Congressman Jintz said worriedly, 'Stress may be the issue here.' Oddblood Gray thought, Oh shit, hastily said a cordial farewell and ran back to his office to make the hundreds of calls to members of the Congress.

The National Security Advisor, Arthur Wix, was trying to sound out the Secretary of Defense. And making sure that there would be an immediate meeting with the Joint Chiefs of Staff. But the Secretary of Defense seemed to be stunned by events and mumbled his answers, agreeing but not volunteering anything.

Eugene Dazzy had noted Oddblood Gray's difficulties with the legislators. There was going to be big trouble. He looked around for Christian Klee. But Klee had vanished, which surprised Dazzy, it was not like him to disappear at a crucial moment like this.

Dazzy turned to Helen DuPray. 'What do you think?' he asked her.

She looked at him coolly. She was a very beautiful woman, Dazzy thought. He must invite her to dinner. Then she said, 'I think you and the rest of the President's staff have let him down. His response to this crisis is far too drastic.'

Dazzy was angry. 'His position has logic and even if we disagreed we have to support him.' He did not tell her of Kennedy's ultimatum to the staff.

Helen DuPray said, 'It's how Francis presented it. Obviously, Congress will try to take the negotiations out of his hands. They will try to suspend him from office.'

'Over the graves of his staff,' Dazzy said.

Helen DuPray said to him quietly, 'Please be careful. Our country is in great danger.'

In his office Dazzy got his personal secretaries working, his aides briefed other staff on what was to be done. It would be his job to co-ordinate everything for the President. When the direct telephone line from the President's office rang, he answered it so quickly that papers flew out of his hand and on to the floor. He said, 'Yes, Mr President.' And he heard the calm voice of Francis Kennedy say the words he knew he would say, that he had been dreading to hear.

Kennedy said, 'Euge?' in that questioning, friendly way, 'I'd like to have my personal staff meet me in the Yellow Oval Room. Arrange to show the film of the television news coverage of my daughter's death.'

Eugene Dazzy said, 'Sir, maybe it would be better if you witnessed that by yourself, without anyone present.'

'No,' the President said. 'I want all of us to see it together.'

'Yes, sir,' Eugene Dazzy said. He did not mention that the personal staff had already viewed the film of Theresa Kennedy's murder.

9

On this Wednesday afternoon Peter Cloot was certainly the only official in Washington who paid almost no attention to the news that the President's daughter had been murdered. His energies were focused on the nuclear bomb threat.

As Deputy Chief of the FBI he had almost full responsibility for that agency. Christian Klee was the titular head but only to hold the reins of power, to bring it more firmly under the direction of the Attorney General's office which Christian Klee also held. That combination of offices had always bothered Peter Cloot. It also bothered him that the Secret Service had also been placed under Klee. That was too much concentration of power for Cloot's taste. He also knew that there was a separate elite branch ostensibly in the FBI Table of Organization that Klee administered directly and that this Special Security branch was composed of Christian Klee's former colleagues in the CIA. That affronted him.

But this nuclear threat was Peter Cloot's baby. He would run this show. And luckily there were specific directives to guide him and he had attended the think-tank seminars that directly addressed the problem of internal nuclear threats. If anyone was an expert on this particular situation it was Cloot. And there was no shortage of manpower. During Klee's tenure the number of FBI personnel had increased threefold.

When he had first seen the threatening letter with its accompanying diagrams Cloot had taken the immediate action as outlined in the standing directives. He had also felt a thrill of fear. Up to this time there had been hundreds of such threats, only a few of them plausible, but none so convincing as this. All these threats had been kept secret again according to directives.

Immediately, Cloot forwarded the letter to the Department of Energy Command Post in Maryland, using the special communications facilities for this purpose only. He also alerted the Department of Energy Search Teams based in Las Vegas called NEST. NEST was already flying their pod containing tools and detection equipment to New York. Other planes would be flying specially trained personnel into the city, where they would use disguised vans loaded with sophisticated equipment to explore the streets of New York. Helicopters would be used, men on foot carrying Geiger counter briefcases would cover the city. But all this was not Cloot's headache. All he would have to do was supply armed FBI guards to protect the NEST searchers. Cloot's job was to find the villains.

The Maryland Department of Energy people had studied the letter and sent him a psychological profile of the writer. Those guys were really amazing, Cloot thought, he didn't know how they did it. Of course one of the obvious clues was that the letter did not ask for money. Also it did define a definite political position. As soon as he got the profile Cloot sent a thousand men checking.

The profile had said that the letter writer was probably very young and highly educated. That he was probably a student of physics in a highly rated university. And on this information alone Cloot in a matter of hours had two very good suspects and after that it was amazingly easy. He had worked all through the night, directing his field office teams. When he was informed of the murder of Theresa Kennedy he had resolutely put it out of his mind except for the flash that all this stuff might be linked together in some way. But his job tonight was to find the author of the nuclear bomb threat. Thank God the bastard was an idealist. It made him easier to track down. There were a million greedy son-of-a-bitches who would do something like this for money and it would have been tough to find them.

While he waited for the information to come in he put the files of all previous nuclear threats though his computer. There had never been a nuclear weapon found, and those blackmailers who had been caught while trying to collect their bribe money had confessed that there had never been one. They had, some of them, been men with a smattering of science. Others had picked up convincing information from a left-wing magazine that had printed an article describing how to make a nuclear weapon. The magazine had been leaned on not to publish that article but it had gone to the Supreme Court which had ruled that suppression would be a violation of free speech. Even thinking of that now made Peter Cloot tremble with rage. The fucking country was going to destroy itself. One thing he noted with interest. None of the over two hundred cases had involved a woman or black or even a foreign terrorist. They were all fucking true blue greedy American men.

When he had finished with the computer files he thought a minute about his boss, Christian Klee. He really didn't like the way Klee was running things. Klee thought the whole job of the FBI was to guard the President of the United States. Klee didn't use only the Secret Service Division but had special squads in every FBI office in the country whose main job was to sniff out possible dangers to the office of the President. Klee diverted a great deal of manpower from other operations of the FBI to do this.

Cloot was leery of Christian Klee's power, his Special Division of ex-CIA men. What the hell did they do? Peter Cloot didn't know and he had every right to know. That division reported directly to Klee and that was a very bad thing in a government agency so sensitive to public opinion as the FBI. So far nothing had happened. Peter Cloot spent

166

a great deal of time covering his ass, making sure that he could not be caught in the fireworks when that Special Division pulled some shit that would bring the Congress down on their heads with their special investigation committees.

At one in the morning Cloot's assistant deputy came in to report that two suspects were under surveillance, proof was in hand that confirmed the psychological profile, there was other circumstantial evidence. Only the order to make the arrest was needed.

Cloot said to his deputy, 'I have to brief Klee first. Stay here while I call him.'

Cloot knew that Klee would be in the President's Chief of Staff office or that the omnipotent White House telephone operators would track him down if he was not. He got Klee on his first try.

'We have that special case all wrapped up,' Cloot told him. 'But I think I should brief you before we bring them in, can you come over?'

Klee's voice was strained. 'No, I cannot. I have to be with the President now, surely you understand that.'

'Shall I just go ahead and fill you in later?' Cloot asked.

There was a long pause at the other end. Then Klee said, 'I think we have time for you to come over here. If I'm not available, just wait. But you have to rush.'

'I'm on my way,' Peter Cloot said.

It had not been necessary to either of them to suggest doing the briefing over the phone. That was out of the question. Anybody could pick messages out of the infinite trailways of airspace.

Peter Cloot got to the White House and was escorted into a small briefing room. Christian Klee was waiting for him, his prosthesis was off and he was massaging his stump through his stocking.

'I only have a few minutes,' Klee said. 'Big meeting with the President.'

'Jesus, I'm sorry about that,' Cloot said. 'How is he taking it?'

Klee shook his head, 'You can't ever tell with Francis. He seems OK.' He shook his head in a sort of bewilderment then said briskly, 'OK, let's have it.' He looked at Cloot with a sort of distaste. The man's physical appearance always irritated him.

Cloot never looked tired and he was one of those men whose shirt and suit never got wrinkled. He always wore ties of knitted wool with square knots, usually of a light gray color and sometimes a sort of bloody black.

'We spotted them,' Cloot said. 'Two young kids, twenty years old in MIT nuclear labs. Geniuses, IQs in the 160s, come from wealthy families, left wing, marched with the nuclear protesters. They have access to classified memoranda. They fit the think-tank profile. They are sitting in their lab up in Boston, working on some government and university project. A couple of months ago they came to New York and a buddy got them laid and they loved it. He was sure it was their first time. A deadly combination, idealism and the raging hormones of youth. Right now I have them sealed off.'

'Do you have any firm evidence?' Christian asked. 'Anything concrete?'

'We're not trying them or even indicting them,' Cloot said. 'This is preventive arrest as authorized under the atom bomb laws. Once we have them, they'll confess and tell us where the damn thing is if there is one. I don't think there is. I think that part is bullshit. But they certainly wrote the letter. They fit the profile. Also the date of the letter, the day they registered at the Hilton in New York. That's the clincher.'

Christian had often marveled at the resources of all the government agencies with their computers and high-grade electronic gear. It was amazing that they could eavesdrop on anyone anywhere no matter what precautions were taken. That computers could scan hotel registers all over the city in

168

less than an hour. And other complicated serious things. At ghastly expense, of course.

'OK, we'll grab them,' Christian said. 'But I'm not sure you can make them confess. They're smart kids.'

Cloot stared into Christian's eyes. 'OK, Chris, they don't confess, we're a civilized country. We just let the bomb explode and kill thousands of people.' He smiled for a moment almost maliciously. 'Or you go to the President and make him sign a Medical Interrogation order. Section IX of the Atomic Weapons Control Act.'

Which was what Cloot had been coming to all the time.

Christian had been avoiding the same thought all night. He had always been shocked that the country like the United States could have such a secret law. The press could easily have uncovered it but again there was that covenant between the owners of the media and the governors of the country. So the law was not really known to the public, as was true of many laws governing nuclear science.

Christian knew Section IX very well. As a lawyer he had marveled at it. It was that savagery in the law that had always repelled him.

Section IX essentially gave the President the right to order a chemical brain scan that had been developed to make anyone tell the truth, a lie detector right in the brain. The law had been especially designed to extract information about the planting of a nuclear device, it fitted this case perfectly. There would be no torture, the victim would suffer no physical pain. Simply the neurons of the brain would be measured so that he would invariably tell the truth when asked questions. It would be humane, the only catch being that nobody really knew what happened to the brain after the operation. Experiments indicated that in rare cases there would be some loss of memory, some slight loss of functioning. He would not be retarded, that would be unconscionable, but as the old joke had it, there went the music lessons. The only catch was that there was a ten per cent chance that

169

there would be complete memory loss. Complete long-term amnesia. The subject's entire past would be erased.

Christian said, 'Just a long shot, but could this be linking up with the hijacking and the Pope? Even that guy being captured on Long Island looks like a trick. Could this all be a part of it, a smoke screen, a booby trap?'

Cloot studied him for a long time as if debating his answer. But when the answer came it showed no doubt. 'Not a chance,' Cloot said. 'This is one of those famous coincidences of history.'

'That always lead to tragedy,' Christian said wryly.

Cloot went on. 'These two kids are just crazy in their own genius style. They are political. They are obsessed by nuclear danger to the whole world. They are not interested in current political quarrels. They don't give a shit about the Arabs and Israel or the poor and rich in America. Or the Democrats and Republicans. They just want the globe to rotate faster on its axis. You know.' He smiled contemptuously. 'They all think they're God. Nothing can touch them.'

But Christian's mind was at rest on one thing. If Cloot did not suspect a link between this crazy atom bomb stuff and the hijackers, there could be none. Cloot suspected everyone of everything. But then another thought occurred. There was political shrapnel flying all around with these two problems. Don't move too fast, he thought. Francis was in terrible danger now. Kennedy would have to be protected. Maybe they could play one off against the other.

He said to Cloot, 'Listen, Peter, I want this to be the most secret of operations. Seal it off from everybody else. I want those two kids grabbed and put into the hospital detention facility we have here in Washington. Just you and me and the agents we use from Special Division. Shove the agents' noses into the Atomic Security Act, absolute secrecy. Nobody sees them, nobody talks to them except me. I'll do the interrogation personally.'

Cloot gave him a funny look. He didn't like the operation

being turned over to Klee's Special Division. 'The medical team will want to see a Presidential order before they shoot chemicals into those kids' brains.'

Christian said, 'I'll ask the President.'

Peter Cloot said casually, 'Time is crucial on this thing, and you said nobody interrogates except you. Does that include me? What if you're tied up with the President?'

Christian Klee smiled and said, 'Don't worry, I'll be there. Nobody but me, Peter. Now give me the details.' He had other things on his mind. Shortly he would meet with the chiefs of his FBI Special Division and order them to mount an electronic and computer surveillance on the most important members of the Congress and the Socrates Club.

The Department of Energy's command post in Maryland, officially known as the Emergency Action Co-ordination Team, sat on think-tank profiles of possible nuclear bomb terrorists. It had profiles of psychotics and how they might pick up enough knowledge to present a plausible threat. It had profiles on idealists who might try to explode a nuclear weapon. It had profiles on fortune hunters who would demand money, agents of foreign terrorist organizations who might bring themselves to commit such a terrible act. They had profiles that fitted almost exactly the case of Adam Gresse and Henry Tibbot. This made it an easy task for Peter Cloot and his three thousand agents.

Adam Gresse and Henry Tibbot were certified as scientific whiz-kids at the age of twelve, and were furnished with the finest education that a wealthy and a supportive federal government can provide. They were instructed in the humanities, in art, in law, and the immortal struggle of the upstarts in history, Antigone, Baudelaire, Sacco and Vanzetti, Martin Luther King. They were as perfectly educated as civilization could make them.

But they were young and their raging hormones warred with their sensibilities. The vulgarities of life, political and

171

intellectual, produced in them what could only be called a contempt for an existing world that must be made better.

They admitted even to themselves that the excitement of stealing their materials from the official programs, the gratification of solving the technical problems, the excitement of finally constructing a viable and explodable two-kiloton nuclear bomb, gave them such a feeling of power that it cemented their final decision to use it. But they never intended it to explode.

They would plant the bomb. They would send a letter to the *New York Times* that declared their intent. That this was a warning that if nations continued to manufacture nuclear weapons to further their own narrow interests, then every individual had the right to also develop nuclear weapons to stop the dictators of the world from burning the entire universe into cinders. They had no knowledge of the elaborate and secret measures that had been taken by government agencies to thwart just such threats. They also had no knowledge of how the real world worked. They could not conceive of that underworld of everyday life where seemingly inconsequential carelessness has dire consequences. It was beyond their comprehension that a mail clerk in the *New York Times* would get the sack of incoming letters two days late and so hold up their warning letter. Nor did they realize that that letter would immediately be handed over to the FBI.

And so they had planted their tiny atomic bomb, a bomb they had constructed with much labor and ingenuity. They were perhaps so proud of their labors they could not resist using it for such a high cause.

Adam Gresse and Henry Tibbot kept watching the newspapers, but their letter did not appear on the front page of the *New York Times*. There were no news items. They had not been given the opportunity to lead the authorities to the bomb after their demand was met. They were being ignored. This frightened them and yet angered them too. Now the

172

bomb would explode and cause thousands of deaths. But possibly that would be for the best. How else could the world be alerted to the dangers of the use of atomic power? How else could the necessary action be taken for the men in authority to install the proper safeguards? They had calculated that the bomb would destroy at least four to six square blocks of New York City. They regretted that, it would cost a certain amount of human lives. But it would be a small price for mankind to pay to see the error of its ways. Impregnable safeguards must be established, the making of nuclear bombs must be banned by all the nations of the world.

On Wednesday Gresse and Tibbot worked in the laboratory until after everyone in the Institute had gone home and then they argued whether they should make a phone call to alert the authorities. At the beginning it had never been their intention to actually let the bomb go off. They had wanted to see their letter of warning published in the *New York Times* and then they would go back to New York to disarm the bomb. But now it seemed a war of wills. Were they to be treated as children, sneered at, when they could accomplish so much for humanity? Or would they be listened to? In all conscience they could not go on with their scientific work if it was to be misused by the political establishment.

They had chosen New York City to be punished because on their visits there they had been so horrified by the feeling of evil that seemed to them to pervade the streets. The threatening beggars, the insolent drivers of wheeled vehicles, the rudeness of clerks in stores, the countless burglaries, street muggings and murders. They had been particularly revolted by Times Square, that area so crowded with people that it seemed to them like a huge sink of cockroaches. In Times Square, the pimps, the dope pushers, the whores seemed so menacing that Gresse and Tibbot had retreated with fright to their hotel room uptown. And so with fully justifiable anger they had decided to plant the bomb in Times

173

Square itself. They would have been horrified and hurt if it was pointed out to them that most of the faces they had seen in Times Square were black.

Adam Gresse and Henry Tibbot were as shocked as the rest of the nation when the television screen showed the murder of Theresa Kennedy. But they were also a little annoyed that this diverted attention from their own operation, more important to the fate of humanity.

But they had become nervous. Adam had heard peculiar clickings on his telephone, he had noticed that his car seemed to be followed, he had felt an electric disturbance when certain men passed him in the street. He told Tibbot about these things.

Henry Tibbot was very tall and very lean. He seemed to be made of wires joined together with scraps of flesh and transparent skin. He had a better scientific mind than Adam and stronger nerves. 'You're reacting like all criminals act,' he told Adam. 'It's normal. Every time there's a knock on the door I think it's the Feds.'

'And if it is one time?' Adam Gresse asked.

'Keep your mouth shut until the lawyer comes,' Henry Tibbot said. 'That is the most important thing. We would get twenty-five years just for writing the letter. So if the bomb explodes it will just be a few more years.'

'Do you think they can trace us?' Adam asked.

'Not a chance,' Henry Tibbot said. 'We've gotten rid of anything that could be evidence. Christ, are we smarter than them or not?'

This reassured Adam but he wavered a bit. 'Maybe we should make a call and tell them where it is,' he said.

'No,' Henry Tibbot said. 'They are on the alert now. They will be ready to zero in on our call. That will be the only way to catch us. Just remember, if things go wrong, just keep your mouth shut. Now let's go to work.'

Adam Gresse and Henry Tibbot were working late in the lab this night really because they wanted to be together.

They wanted to talk about what they had done, what recourse they had. They were young men of intense will, they had been brought up to have the courage of their convictions, to detest an authority that refused to be swayed with a reasonable argument. Though they conjured up mathematical formulae that might change the destiny of mankind they had no idea of the complicated relationships of civilization. Glorious achievers, they had not yet grown into humanity.

As they were preparing to leave, the phone rang. It was Henry Tibbot's father. He said to Henry. 'Son, listen carefully. You are about to be arrested by the FBI. Say nothing to them until they let you see your lawyer. Say nothing. I know . . .'

At that moment the door of the room opened and men swarmed in.

10

The rich in America, without a doubt are more socially conscious than the rich in any other country of the world. This is true, of course, especially of the extremely rich, those who own and run huge corporations, exercise their economic strength in politics, propagandize all the forms of culture. And this was especially true of members of the Socrates Club.

The Socratic Country Golf and Tennis Club of Southern California had been formed and founded nearly seventy years before by real estate, media, cinematic and agricultural tycoons, as a politically liberal organization devoted to recreation. It was an exclusive resort, you had to be very rich to join. Technically, you could be black or white, Jewish or Catholic, man or woman, artist or magnate. In reality there were very few blacks and no women.

The Socrates Country Club finally evolved into a club for the very enlightened, very responsible rich. Prudently, it had an ex-Deputy Director of CIA Operations as head of Security Systems, and its electronic fences were the highest in America.

Four times a year, the club was used as a retreat for fifty to a hundred men who in effect owned nearly everything in America. They came for a week and in that week, service was reduced to a minimum. They made their own beds, served their own drinks and sometimes even cooked their own food in the evening on outside barbecues. There were of course some waiters, cooks and some maids, and there were the inevitable aides to those important men; after all, the world of American business and politics could not come to a stop while they recharged their spiritual batteries.

During this week-long stay these men would gather into small groups and spend their time in private discussions. They would have seminars headed by distinguished professors from the most famous universities on questions of ethics, philosophy, the responsibility of the fortunate elite to the less fortunate in society. They would be given lectures by famous scientists on the benefits and dangers of nuclear weapons, brain research, the exploration of space, on economics.

They also played tennis, swam in the pool, had backgammon and bridge tournaments and discussed far into the night on virtue and villainy, on women and love, on marriage and adventure. And these were responsible men, the most responsible men in American society. But they were trying to do two things, they were trying to become better human beings while recovering their adolescence, and they were trying to unite in bringing about a better society as they perceived a better society to be.

After a week together they returned to their normal lives, refreshed with new hope, a desire to help mankind, and a sharper perception of how all their activities could be meshed to preserve the structure of their society, and perhaps with closer personal relationships that could help them do business.

This present week had started on the Monday after Easter Sunday. Because of the crisis in national affairs with the killing of the Pope and the hijacking of the plane carrying the President's daughter and her murderer, the attendance had dropped to less than twenty.

George Greenwell was the oldest of these men. At eighty, he could still play tennis doubles, but out of a carefully bred courtesy did not inflict himself on the younger men who would be forced to play a forgiving style. Yet, he was still a tiger in long sessions of backgammon.

Greenwell considered the national crisis none of his business unless it involved grain in some way. For his company was privately owned and controlled most of the wheat in America. His shining hour had been thirty years ago when the United States had embargoed grain to Russia as a political ploy, to muscle Russia in the Cold War.

George Greenwell was a patriot but not a fool. He knew that Russia could not yield to such pressure. He also knew that the Washington-imposed embargo would ruin American farmers. So he had defied the President of the United States and shipped the forbidden grain by diverting it to other foreign companies who relayed it to Russia. He had brought down the wrath of the American executive branch on his head. Laws had been presented to Congress to curtail the power of his family-held company, to make it public, to put it under some sort of regulatory control. But the Greenwell money contributed to Congressmen and Senators soon put a stop to that nonsense.

Greenwell loved the Socrates Country Club because it was luxurious but not so luxurious as to invite the envy of the less fortunate. Also, because it was not known to the media, for its members owned most of the TV stations, newspapers and magazines. And also it made him feel young, enabled him to participate socially in the lives of younger men who were equal in power.

He had made a good deal of extra money during that grain embargo, buying wheat and corn from embattled American farmers and selling it dear to a desperate Russia. But he had made sure that the extra money benefited the people of the United States. What he had done had been a matter of principle. The principle being that his intelligence was greater than that of government functionaries. The extra money, hundreds of millions of dollars, had been funneled into museums, educational foundations, cultural programs on TV, especially music, which was Greenwell's passion.

Greenwell prided himself on being civilized, based on his being sent to the best schools, where he was taught the social behavior of the responsible rich and a civilized feeling of affection for his fellow man. That he was strict in the dealings of his business was his form of art, the mathematics of millions of tons of grain sounded in his brain as clearly and sweetly as chamber music.

One of his few moments of ignoble rage had occurred when a very young professor of music in a university chair established by one of his foundations, published an essay that elevated jazz and rock and roll music above Brahms and Schubert and dared to call classical music 'Funeral'. George Greenwell had vowed to have the professor removed from his chair but his inbred courtesy prevailed. Then, the young professor had published another essay in which the unfortunate phrase was 'Who gives a shit for Beethoven?' And that was the end of that. The young professor never really knew what happened but a year later he was giving piano lessons in San Francisco.

The Socrates Country Club had one extravagance, an elaborate communications system. On the morning that President Francis Xavier Kennedy announced to the secret meeting of advisors the ultimatum he would give the Sultan of Sherhaben, all twenty men in the Socrates Country Club had the information within the hour. Only Greenwell knew that this information had been supplied by Oliver Ollifant, the Oracle.

It was a matter of doctrine that these yearly retreats of great men were in no way used to plan or conspire, they were merely a way to communicate general aims, to inform a general interest, to clear away confusion as to the general operation of a complicated society. In that spirit George Greenwell on Tuesday invited three other great men to one

179

of the cheerful pavilions just outside the tennis courts to have lunch.

The youngest of these men, Lawrence Salentine, owned a major TV network and some cable companies, newspapers in three major cities, five magazines and one of the biggest movie studios. He owned, through subsidiaries, a major book publishing house. He also owned twelve local TV stations in major cities. That was in the United States alone. He was also a powerful presence in the media of foreign countries. Salentine was a lean and handsome man with a full head of silvery hair, a crown of curls in the style of Roman emperors, but now much in fashion with intellectuals and people in the arts and in Hollywood. He was impressive in appearance and in intelligence and one of the men most powerful in the politics of America. There was not a Congressman or Senator or a member of the Cabinet who did not return his calls. He had not however been able to become friendly with President Kennedy who seemed to take personally the hostile attitude the media had shown the new social programs prepared by the Kennedy administration.

The second man was Louis Inch who owned more important real estate in the great cities of America then any other company or individual. As a very young man – he was now only forty – he had grasped the true importance of building straight up into the air to an impossible degree. He had bought rights over many existing buildings and then built the enormous skyscrapers that increased the value of buildings tenfold. He more than anyone else had changed the very light of the cities, had made endless dark canyons between commercial buildings that proved to be more needed than anyone supposed. He had made rents so impossibly high in New York, Chicago and Los Angeles for ordinary families that only the rich or very well off could live comfortable in these cities. He had cajoled and bribed municipal officials to give him tax abatements; to do away with rent controls to such a degree that he boasted that his rental charge per square foot would someday equal Tokyo.

His political influence, despite his ambitions, was less than anyone in the pavilion. He had a personal wealth of over five billion dollars but his wealth had the inertness of land. His real strength was more sinister. His aims were the amassing of wealth and power without real responsibility to the civilization he lived in. He had extensively bribed public officials and construction unions. He owned casino hotels in Atlantic City and Las Vegas, shutting out the mobster overlords in these cities. But in doing so he had, in the curious way of the democratic process, acquired the support of the secondary figures in criminal empires. All the service departments of his numerous hotels had contracts with firms that supplied tableware, laundry services, service help, liquor and food. He was a link through subordinates to this criminal underworld. He was of course not so foolish as to make that link more than a microscopic thread. The name of Louis Inch had never been touched by any hint of scandal. This was due not only to his sense of prudence, but the absence of any personal charisma.

For all these reasons he was actually despised on a personal level by nearly all the members of the Socrates Country Club. But he was tolerated because by his particular brand of magic, one of his own companies owned land surrounding the Club and there was always the underlying fear that he might put up cheap housing for fifty thousand families and drown the Club area with Hispanics and blacks.

The third man, Martin Mutford, was dressed in slacks, pure white shirt open at the collar, and a blue blazer. He was a man of sixty and he was perhaps the most powerful of the four because he had control of money in so many different areas. As a young man he had been one of the Oracle's protégés and had learned his lessons well. In fact he would tell admiring stories about the Oracle to the delight of the audiences in the Socrates Country Club.

Martin Mutford had based his career on investment banking and because of the influence of the Oracle, or so he claimed, he had gotten off to a shaky start. As a young man he had been sexually vigorous, as he put it. Much to his surprise the husbands of some of the young wives he seduced came looking for him not for revenge but for a bank loan. They had little smiles on their faces and were very good-humored. By instinct he granted the personal loans which he knew they would never pay back. At the time he did not know that loan officials at banks took gifts and bribes to give unsafe loans to small businesses. The paperwork was easy to get around, the people who ran banks wanted to loan money, that was their business, that was their profit and so their regulations were purposely written to make it easy for loan officers. Of course there had to be a parade of paperwork, memo of interviews, etc. But Martin Mutford cost the bank a few hundred thousand dollars before he was transferred to another branch and another city by what he thought was fortunate circumstance but what he later realized was simply a tolerant shrug of his superiors.

The errors of youth behind him, forgiven, forgotten, valuable lessons learned, Mutford rose in his world.

Thirty years later he sat in the pavilion of the Socrates Country Club and was the most powerful financial figure in the United States. He was chairman of a great bank, he owned substantial stock in the TV networks, he and his friends had control of the giant automobile industry, and had linked up with the air travel industry. He had used money as a spider web to snare a large share of electronics. Even in those areas he did not control were the thin filaments hanging that showed he had at least tried. He also sat above Wall Street investment firms who put together deals to buy out conglomerates to add to another huge conglomerate. When these battles were at their most fierce Martin Mutford could send out a wave of money as drenching as the sea to

182

settle the issue. Like the other three he 'owned' certain members of the Congress and the Senate.

The four men sat at the round table in the pavilion outside the tennis courts. California flowers and New England-like greenery surrounded them. George Greenwell said, 'What do you fellows think of the President's decision?'

Martin Mutford said, 'It's a damn shame what they did to his daughter. But destroying fifty billion dollars of property is way out of proportion.'

A waiter, a Hispanic wearing white slacks and a white silky-looking short-sleeved shirt with the club logo, took their drink orders.

Lawrence Salentine said thoughtfully, 'The American people will think of Kennedy as a real hero if he pulls it off. He will be re-elected in a landslide.'

George Greenwell said, 'But it is far too drastic a response, we all know that. Foreign relations will be injured for years to come.'

Martin Mutford said, 'The country is running wonderfully well. The legislative branch finally has the executive branch under some sort of control. Will the country benefit in a swing of power the opposite way?'

Louis Inch said, 'What the hell can Kennedy do even if he gets re-elected? The Congress controls and we have a big say with them. There are not more than fifty members of the House who are elected without our money. And in the Senate, there's not a man among them that is not a millionaire. We don't have to worry about the President.'

George Greenwell had been looking beyond the tennis courts to the marvelous Pacific Ocean so quiet yet majestic. The ocean which at this moment was cradling billions of dollars worth of ships carrying his grain all over the world. It gave him a slightly guilty feeling that he could starve or feed the world.

He started to speak but then the waiter came with their drinks. Greenwell was prudent at his age and had asked for

183

mineral water. He sipped at his glass and after the waiter left he spoke in careful modulated tones. He was always exquisitely courteous, the courtesy that comes to a man who has regretfully made brutal decisions in his life. 'We must never forget,' he said, 'that the office of the President of the United States can be a very great danger to the democratic process.'

Salentine said, 'That's nonsense. The other officials in the government prevent him from making a personal decision. The military, benighted as they are, would not permit it unless it was reasonable, you know that George.'

George Greenwell said, 'That's true, of course. In normal times. But look at Lincoln, he actually suspended habeas corpus and civil liberties during the Civil War, look at Franklin Roosevelt, he got us into World War II. Look at the personal powers of the President. He has the power to absolutely pardon any crime. That is the power of a king. Do you know what can be done with such a power? What allegiance that can create? He has almost infinite powers if there is not a strong Congress to check him. Luckily we have such a Congress. But we must look ahead, we must make sure that the executive arm remains subordinate to the duly elected representatives of the people.'

Salentine said, 'With TV and other media Kennedy wouldn't last a day if he tried anything dictatorial. He simply hadn't got that option. The strongest belief in America today is the creed of individual freedom.' He paused for a moment and said, 'As you know well, George. You defied that infamous embargo.'

Greenwell said, 'You're missing the point. A bold president can surmout those obstacles. And Kennedy is being very bold in this crisis.

Louis Inch said impatiently, 'Are you arguing we should present a united front against Kennedy's ultimatum to Sherhaben? Personally, I think it's great that he's being

184

tough. Force works, pressure works, on governments as well as people.'

Early in his career Louis Inch had used pressure tactics on tenants in housing developments under rent control when he wanted to empty the buildings. He had withheld heat, water and prohibited maintenance, he had made the lives of thousands of people uncomfortable. He had 'tipped' certain sections of suburbia, flooding them with blacks to drive out white residents, he had bribed city and state governments, he made rich the Federal regulators. He knew what he was talking about. Success was built on applying pressure.

George Greenwell said, 'Again, you're missing the point. In an hour we have a screen conference call with Bert Audick. Please forgive me that I promised this without consulting you, I thought it too urgent to wait, events are moving so quickly. But it's Bert Audick whose fifty billion dollars will be destroyed, he is terribly concerned. And it is important to look into the future. If the President can do this to Audick, he can do it to us.'

'Kennedy is unsound,' Martin Mutford said thoughtfully.

Salentine said, 'I think we should have some sort of consensus before the conference call with Audick.'

'He's really perverted with his oil preservation,' Inch said. Inch had always felt oil in some way conflicted with the interests of real estate.

'We owe it to Bert to give him our fullest consideration,' Greenwell said.

The four men were gathered in the communications center of the Socrates Country Club when the image of Bert Audick flashed on the TV screen. He greeted them with a smile, but the face on the screen was an unnatural red which could be the color tuning or some sort of rage. Audick's voice was calm.

'I'm going to Sherhaben,' he said. 'It may be a last look at my fifty billion bucks.'

The men in the room could speak to the image as if he

were present at the club. They could see their own images on their monitor, the image that Audick could see in his office. They had to guard their faces as well as their voices.

'You're actually going?' Louis Inch said.

'Yes,' Audick said. 'The Sultan is a friend of mine and this is a very touchy situation. I can do a lot of good for our country if I'm there personally.'

Lawrence Salentine said, 'According to the correspondents on my media payroll, Congress and the Senate are trying to veto the President's decision. Is that possible?'

The image of Audick smiled at them. 'Not only possible but almost certain. I've talked to Cabinet members. They are proposing that the President be removed temporarily from office by reason of his personal vendetta which shows a temporary imbalance of the mind. Under an Amendment of the Constitution that is legal. We need only get the signatures of the Cabinet and the Vice President on a petition that Congress will ratify. Even if the impeachment is for only thirty days, we can halt the destruction of Dak. And I guarantee that the hostages will be released while I am in Sherhaben. But I think all of you should offer support to Congress to remove the President. You owe that to American democracy, as I owe it to my stockholders. We all know damn well that if anybody but his daughter had been killed, he would never have chosen this course of action.'

George Greenwell said, 'Bert, the four of us have talked this over and we have agreed to support you and the Congress, that's our duty. We will make the necessary phone calls, our efforts will be co-ordinated. But Lawrence Salentine has a few pertinent observations he'd like to present.'

Audick's face on the screen showed anger and disgust. He said, 'Larry, this is no time for your media to sit on the fence, believe me. If Kennedy can cost me fifty billion dollars there may come a time when all your TV stations could be without a Federal licence and then you can go fuck yourself. I won't lift a finger to help you.'

George Greenwell winced at the vulgarity and directness of the response. Louis Inch and Martin Mutford smiled. Lawrence Salentine showed no emotion. He answered in a calm soothing voice.

'Bert,' he said. 'I'm with you all the way, never doubt that. I think a man who arbitrarily decides to destroy fifty billion dollars to reinforce a threat, is undoubtedly unbalanced and not fit to head the government of the United States. I'm with you, I assure you. The television media will be breaking into their scheduled programs with bulletins that President Kennedy is being psychiatrically evaluated, that the trauma of his daughter's death may have temporarily disordered his reason. That should prepare the groundwork for Congress. But this touches an area where I have a little more expertise than most. The President's decision will be embraced by the American people, the natural mob reaction to all acts of national power plays. If the President succeeds in his action and he gets the hostages back, he will command untold allegiance and votes. Kennedy has intelligence and energy, if he gets one foot in the door he can sweep Congress away.' Salentine paused for a moment, trying to choose his words very carefully. 'But if his threats fail, hostages killed, problem not solved, then Kennedy is finished as a political power.'

On the console the image of Bert Audick flinched. He said in a very quiet serious tone, 'That is not an alternative. If it goes that far, then the hostages must be saved, our country must win. Besides the fifty billion dollars will already be lost. No true American wants the Kennedy mission to fail. They may not want a mission with such drastic action, but once started we must see that it succeeds.'

'I agree,' Salentine said, though he did not. 'I absolutely agree. I have another point. Once the President sees the danger of Congress, the first thing he will want to do is address the nation on television. Whatever Kennedy's faults, he is a magician on the tube. Once he presents his case on that TV screen the Congress will be in a great deal of trouble

187

in this country. What if Congress does depose Kennedy for thirty days? Then there is the possibility that the President is right in his diagnosis, that the kidnappers make this a long drawn out affair with Kennedy on the sidelines, out of all the heat.' Again Salentine paused trying to be careful. He said, 'Then Kennedy becomes an even greater hero. Our best scenario is to just let him alone, win or lose. That way there is no long-term danger to the political structure of this country. That may be best.'

'I lose fifty billion dollars that way, right?' Bert Audick said. The face on the huge TV screen was reddening with anger. There had never been anything wrong with the color control.

Mutford said, 'It is a considerable sum of money, but it's not the end of the world.'

Bert Audick's face on the screen was an astonishing bloody red. Salentine thought again that it might be the controls, no man could stay alive and turn such vivid hues, the fucking oil maniac wasn't an autumn forest. But then Audick's voice reverberated through the room.

'Fuck you, Martin, fuck you. And it's more than fifty billion. What about the loss of revenue while we rebuild Dak? Will your banks loan me the money then without interest? You've got more cash up your asshole than the US Treasury, but would you give me the fifty billion? Like shit you would.'

George Greenwell said hastily, 'Bert, Bert, we are with you. Salentine was just pointing out a few options you may not have thought of under the pressure of events. In any event we could not stop Congress's action even if we tried. Congress will not permit the Executive to dominate on such an issue. Now we all have work to do, so I suggest this conference come to an end.'

Salentine smiled and said, 'Bert, those bulletins about the President's mental condition will be on television in three hours. The other networks will follow our lead. Call me and

188

tell me what you think, you may have some ideas. And one other thing, if Congress votes to depose the President before he requests time on TV, the networks can refuse him the time on the basis that he has been certified as mentally incompetent and no longer President.

'You do that,' Audick said, his face now a natural color. And the conference call ended with courteous goodbyes.

Lawrence Salentine said, 'Gentlemen, I suggest we all fly to Washington in my plane. I think we should all pay a visit to our old friend Oliver Ollifant.'

Martin Mutford smiled. 'The Oracle, my old mentor. He'll give us some answers.'

Within the hour they were all on their way to Washington.

Summoned to meet with President Kennedy, the Ambassador of Sherhaben, Sharif Waleeb, was shown secret CIA video tapes of Yabril having dinner with the Sultan in the Sultan's palace. The Sherhaben Ambassador was genuinely shocked. How could his Sultan be involved in such a dangerous endeavour? Sherhaben was a tiny country, a gentle country, peace loving, as was wise for a militarily weak power.

The meeting was in the Oval office with Bert Audick present. The President was accompanied by two staff members, Arnold Wix, the National Security Advisor, and Eugene Dazzy, the Chief of Staff.

After he was formally presented, the Sherhaben Ambassador said to Kennedy, 'My dear Mr President, you must believe I had no knowledge of this. You have my personal, my most abject, my most heartfelt apologies.' He was close to tears. 'But I must say one thing I truly believe. The Sultan could never have agreed to harm your poor daughter.'

Francis Kennedy said gravely, 'I hope that is true because then he will agree to my proposal.'

The Ambassador listened with an apprehension that was more personal than political. He had been educated at an American university, and he was an admirer of the American

189

way of life. He loved American food, American alcoholic drinks, American women and their rebelliousness to the male yoke. He loved American music and films. He had donated money to all the necessary politicos and made bureaucrats in the American State Department rich. He was an expert on oil and a friend of Bert Audick.

Now he despaired for his personal misfortune, but he was not really worried about Sherhaben and its Sultan. The worst that could happen would be economic sanctions. The American CIA would mount covert operations to displace the Sultan, but this might be to his advantage.

So he was profoundly shocked by Kennedy's carefully articulated speech to him. 'You must listen closely,' Francis Kennedy said. 'In three hours you will be on a plane to Sherhaben to bring my message to your Sultan personally. Mr Bert Audick, whom you know, and my National Security Advisor, Arnold Wix, will accompany you. And the message is this. In twenty-four hours your city of Dak will be destroyed.'

The Ambassador, horrified, his throat constricted, could not speak.

Kennedy continued, 'The hostages must be released and the terrorist Yabril must be turned over to us. Alive. If the Sultan does not do this, the state of Sherhaben itself will cease to exist.'

The Ambassador looked so stricken that Kennedy thought he might have trouble comprehending. Kennedy paused for a moment and then he went on reassuringly. 'All this will be in the documents I will send with you to present to your Sultan.'

Ambassador Waleeb said dazedly, 'Mr President, forgive me, you said something about destroying Dak?'

Kennedy said, 'That is correct. Your Sultan will not believe my threats until he sees the city of Dak in ruins. Let me repeat: the hostages must be released, Yabril must be surrendered and secured so that he cannot take his own life. There will be no more negotiations.'

The Ambassador said incredulously, 'You cannot threaten to destroy a free country, tiny as it is. And if you destroy Dak you destroy fifty billions of dollars of American investment.'

'That may be true,' Kennedy said. 'We will see. Make sure your Sultan understands that I am immovable in this matter, that is your function. You, Mr Audick and Mr Wix will go in one of my personal planes. Two other aircraft will accompany you. One to bring back the hostages and the body of my daughter. The other to bring back Yabril.'

The Ambassador could not speak, he could scarcely think. This was surely a nightmare. The President had gone mad.

When he was alone with Bert Audick, Audick said to him grimly, 'That bastard meant what he said but we have a card to play. I'll talk to you on the plane.'

In the Oval Office Eugene Dazzy took notes.

Francis Kennedy said, 'Have you arranged for all the documents to be delivered to the Ambassador's office and to the plane?'

Dazzy said, 'We dressed it up a little. Wiping out Dak is bad enough but we can't say in print we will destroy the whole country of Sherhaben. But your message is clear. Why send Wix?'

Kennedy smiled and said, 'The Sultan will know that when I send him my National Security Advisor I'm very serious. And Arthur will repeat my verbal message.'

'Do you think it will work?' Dazzy said.

'He'll wait for Dak to go down,' Kennedy said. 'Then it sure as hell will work unless he's crazy.' He paused for a moment and then said, 'Tell Christian I want to have dinner with him before we see that film tonight.'

11

To impeach the President of the United States in twenty-four hours seemed almost impossible. But four hours after Kennedy's ultimatum to Sherhaben, Congress and the Socrates Club had this victory well within their grasp.

After Christian Klee had left the meeting, the computer surveillance section of his FBI Special Division gave him a complete report on the activities of the leaders of Congress and the members of the Socrates Club. Three thousand calls were listed. Charts and records of all the meetings held were also part of the report. The evidence was clear and overwhelming. Within the next twenty-four hours, the House and Senate of the United States would try to impeach the President.

Christian, trembling with rage, put the reports in his briefcase and rushed over to the White House. But before he left, he told Peter Cloot to move ten thousand agents from their normal duty posts and send them to Washington.

At this same time late Wednesday Senator Thomas Lambertino, the strong man of the Senate, with his aide Elizabeth Stone and Congressman Alfred Jintz, the Democratic Speaker of the House, were meeting in Lambertino's office. Patsy Troyca, chief aide to Congressman Jintz, was there to cover up, as he often said, the asshole of his boss who was an idiot *manqué*. About Patsy Troyca's cunning there was no doubt, not only in his own mind, but on Capitol Hill.

In that warren of rabbity legislators, Patsy Troyca was also a champion womanizer and genteel promoter of avuncular relationships between the sexes. Troyca had already noted that the Senator's chief aide, Elizabeth Stone, was a beauty but he had to find out how devoted she was. And right now he had to concentrate on the business at hand.

Troyca read aloud the pertinent sentences of the Twenty-fifth Amendment to the United States Constitution, editing out odd sentences and words. He read slowly and carefully in a beautifully controlled tenor voice.

'Whenever the Vice President and majority of either of the principal officers of the executive departments,' Troyca said – then in an aside to Jintz, he whispered, 'that's the Cabinet.' Then his voice grew more emphatic – 'or of *such other body as Congress may by law provide*, transmit to the Senate and House of Representatives their written declaration that the President is unable to discharge the powers and duties of his office, the Vice President shall immediately assume the powers and dutes of the office as Acting President.'

'Bullshit,' Congressman Jintz yelled. 'It can't be that easy to impeach a President.'

'It's not,' said Senator Lambertino in a soothing voice. 'Read on, Patsy.'

Patsy Troyca thought bitterly that it was typical that his boss did not know the Constitution, holy as it was. He gave up. Fuck the Constitution, Jintz would never understand. He would have to put it in plain language. He said, 'Essentially, the Vice President and the Cabinet must sign a declaration of incompetence to impeach Kennedy. Then the Vice President becomes President. One second later Kennedy enters his counter-declaration and says he's OK. He's President again. Then Congress decides. During that delay Kennedy can do what he wants.'

Congressman Jintz said, 'And there goes Dak.'

Senator Lambertino said, 'Most of the Cabinet members will sign the declaration. We'll have to wait for the Vice President, we can't proceed without her signature. Congress will have to meet no later than ten p.m. Thursday to decide the issue in time to prevent the destruction of Dak. And to

193

win we must have a two-thirds vote of each the House and Senate. Now can the House do the job? I guarantee the Senate.'

'Sure,' Congressman Jintz said. 'I got a call from the Socrates Country Club, they are going to lean on every member of the house,'

Patsy Troyca said respectfully, 'The Constitution says, "Any other body the Congress may by law provide." Why not bypass all that Cabinet and Vice Presidential signing and make Congress that body? Then they can decide forthwith.'

Congressman Jintz said patiently, 'Patsy, it won't work. It can't look like a vendetta. The voting public would be on his side and we'd have to pay for it later. Remember Kennedy is popular with the people, a demagogue has that advantage over responsible legislators.'

Senator Lambertino said, 'We should have no trouble following procedure. The President's ultimatum to Sherhaben is far too extreme and shows a mind temporarily unbalanced by his personal tragedy. For which I have the utmost sympathy and sorrow. As indeed do we all.'

Congressman Jintz said, 'My people in the House come up for re-election every two years. Kennedy could knock a bunch of them out if he's declared competent after the thirty-day period. We have to *keep* him out.'

Senator Lambertino nodded. He knew that the Senatorial six-year term always grated on House members. 'That's true,' he said, 'but remember it will be established that he has serious psychological problems and that can be used to keep him out of office simply by the Democratic party refusing him the nomination.'

Patsy Troyca had noted one thing. Elizabeth Stone, the chief aide to the Senator, had not uttered a word during the meeting. But she had a brain for a boss, she didn't have to protect Lambertino from his own stupidity.

So Troyca said, 'If I may summarize, if the Vice President

194

and the majority of the Cabinet vote to impeach the President, they will sign the declaration this afternoon. The President's personal staff will still refuse to sign. It would be a great help if they did, but they won't. According to the Constitutional procedure the one essential signature is that of the Vice President. A Vice President, by tradition, endorses all of the President's policies. Are we absolutely positive she will sign? Or that she won't delay? Time is of the essence.'

Jintz laughed and said, 'What Vice President doesn't want to be President? She's been hoping for the last three years that he has a heart attack.'

For the first time Elizabeth Stone spoke. 'The Vice President does not think in that fashion. She is absolutely loyal to the President,' she said coolly. 'It is true that she is almost certain to sign the declaration. But for all the right reasons.'

Congressman Jintz looked at her with patient resignation and made a pacifying gesture. Lambertino frowned. Troyca kept his face impassive, but inwardly he was delighted.

Patsy Troyca said, 'I still say bypass everybody. Let Congress go right to the bottom line.'

Congressman Jintz rose from his comfortable armchair. 'Don't wory, Patsy, the Vice President can't seem to be too much in a hurry to push Kennedy out. She will sign. She just doesn't want to look like a usurper.' Usurper was a word often used in the House of Representatives in reference to President Kennedy.

Senator Lambertino regarded Troyca with distaste. He disliked a certain familiarity in the man's manner, the questioning of the plans of his betters. 'This action to impeach the President is certainly legal if unprecedented,' he said. 'The Twenty-fifth Amendment to the Constitution doesn't specify medical evidence. But his decision to destroy Dak is evidence.'

Patsy Troyca couldn't resist. 'Once you do this there will certainly be a precedent. A two-thirds vote of Congress can impeach any President. In theory anyway.' He noted with satisfaction that he had won Elizabeth Stone's attention at least. So he went on. 'We'd be another banana republic only in reverse, the legislature being the dictator.'

Senator Lambertino said curtly, 'By definition that cannot be true. The legislature is elected by the people directly, it cannot dictate as one man can.'

Patsy Troyca thought with contempt, not unless the Socrates Country Club gets on your ass. Then he realized what had made the Senator angry. The Senator thought of himself as Presidential timber and didn't like someone saying that the Congress could get rid of the President whenever it liked.

Jintz said, 'Let's wind this up, we all have a hell of a lot of work to do. This is really a move to a more genuine democracy.'

Patsy Troyca was still not used to the direct simplicity of great men like the Senator and the Speaker, how with such sincerity they struck to the very heart of their own self-interest. He saw a certain look on the face of Elizabeth Stone and realized she was thinking exactly what he was thinking. Oh, he was going to take his shot at her no matter what the cost. But he said with his patented sincerity, humbly, 'Is it at all possible that the President may declare that Congress is overruling an executive order that they disagree with and then defy the vote of the Congress? May he not go to the nation on television tonight before the Congress meets? And won't it seem plausible to the public that since Kennedy's staff refuses to sign the declaration, Kennedy is OK? There could be a great deal of trouble. Especially if the hostages are killed after Kennedy has been impeached. There could be tremendous repercussions on the Congress.'

Neither the Senator nor the Congressman seemed impressed by this analysis. Jintz patted him on the shoulder and said, 'Patsy, we've got it all covered, you just make sure the paperwork gets done.'

At that moment the phone rang and Elizabeth Stone

picked it up. She listened for a moment and then said, 'Senator, it's the Vice President.'

Before making her decision, Vice President Helen DuPray decided to take her daily run.

The first woman Vice President of the United States, she was fifty-five years of age and by any standard an extraordinarily intelligent woman. She was still beautiful, possibly because when in her twenties, then a pregnant wife and Assistant District Attorney, she became a health food nut. She had also become a runner in her teens before she was married. An early lover had taken her on his runs, five miles a day and not jogging. He had quoted Latin, 'In corpore sanus mente sanus,' and translated for her, 'If one is healthy in body, one is healthy in mind.' For his condescension in translating and his taking literally the truth of the quotation (how many healthy minds have been brought to dust by a too healthy body?) she had 'discharged' him as a lover.

But just as important were her dietary disciplines, which dissolved the poisons in her system and generated a high energy level with the extra bonus of a magnificent figure. Her political opponents would joke that she had no taste buds but this was not true. She could enjoy a rosy peach, a mellow pear, the tangy taste of fresh vegetables, and in her dark days of the soul which no one escapes she could eat a gallon jar of chocolate cookies.

She had become a health food nut by chance. In her early days as a District Attorney she had prosecuted a diet book author for making fraudulent and injurious claims. To prepare for the case she had researched the subject, read everything in the field of nutrition, on the premise that to detect the false you must know what is true. She had convicted the author, made him pay an enormous fine but always felt she owed him a debt.

And even as Vice President of the United States Helen DuPray ate sparingly and always ran at least five miles a day. On weekends, she did ten miles. Now, on what could be the most important day of her life, the declaration to impeach the President waiting for her signature, she decided to take a mind-clearing run.

Her Secret Service guard had to pay the price. Originally the chief of her security detail thought her morning run would be no problem. After all, his men were good physical specimens. But Vice President DuPray not only took her runs early in the morning through woods where guards could not follow, but her once-a-week ten-mile run left her security men straggling far to her rear. The Chief was amazed that this woman, in her fifties, could run so fast. And so long.

The Vice President did not want her run disturbed, it was after all a sacred thing in her life. It had replaced 'fun', meaning it had replaced the enjoyment of food, liquor and sex, the warmth and tenderness that had gone out of her life when her husband had died six years before.

She had lengthened her runs and put aside all thoughts of remarrying; she was too far up the political ladder to risk allying herself to a man who might be a booby trap, with secret skeletons in his closet to drag her down. Her two daughters and an active social life were enough and she had many friends, male and female.

She had won the support of the feminist groups of the country not with the usual empty political blandishments but with a cold intelligence and a steadfast integrity. She had mounted an unrelenting attack on the anti-abortionists and had crucified in debate those male chauvinists who without personal risk tried to legislate what women might do with their bodies. She had won that fight and in the process climbed high up the political ladder. From a lifetime of living she disdained the theories that men and women should be more alike, she celebrated their differences. The difference was valuable in a moral sense, as a variation in music is valuable, as a variation in gods is valuable. Oh, yes there was a difference. She had learned from her political life, from her years as a district attorney, that women were better than men in the most important things in life. And she had the statistics to prove it. Men committed far more murders, robbed more banks, perjured themselves more, betrayed their friends and loved ones more. As public officials they were far more corrupt, as believers in God they were far more cruel, as lovers they were far more selfish, in all fields they exercised power far more ruthlessly. Men were far more likely to destroy the world with war because they feared death so much more than women. But all this aside, she had no quarrel with men.

Helen DuPray started running from her chauffeured car parked in the woods of the Washington suburb. Running from the fateful document waiting on her desk. The Secret Service men spread out, one ahead, another behind, two on the flanks all at least twenty paces from her. There had been a time when she had delighted in making them sweat to keep up. After all they were fully clothed while she was in running gear, and they were loaded with guns, ammo, communications equipment. They had a rough time until the chief of security detail, losing patience, recruited champion runners from small colleges, and that had chastened Helen DuPray a bit.

The higher Helen DuPray rose on the political ladder, the earlier in the morning she got up to run. Her greatest pleasure was when one of her daughters ran with her. It also made for great photos in the media. Everything counted.

Vice President Helen DuPray had overcome many handicaps to achieve such high office. Obviously, the first was being a woman, and then, not so obviously, being beautiful. Beauty because of its external power often aroused hostility in both sexes. She overcame this hostility with her intelligence, her modesty and an ingrained sense of morality. She also had her fair share of cunning. It was commonplace in American politics that the electorate preferred handsome males and ugly females as candidates for office. So Helen

DuPray had transformed a seductive beauty into the stern handsomeness of a Joan of Arc. She wore her silver blond hair close cropped, she kept her body lean and boyish, she suppressed her breasts with tailored suits. For armor she wore a necklace of pearls and on her fingers only her gold wedding ring. A scarf, a frilly blouse, sometimes gloves, were her badges of womanhood. She projected an image of stern femininity until she smiled or laughed and then her sexuality flashed out brilliant as lightning. She was feminine without being flirtatious, she was strong without a hint of masculinity. She was in short the very model for the first woman President of the United States. Which she must become if she signed the declaration on her desk.

Now she was in the final stage of her run, emerging from the woods and on to a road where another car was waiting. Her detail of Secret Service men closed in like a collapsing diamond and she was on her way to the Vice President's mansion. After showering she dressed in her 'working' clothes, a severely cut skirt and jacket, and left for her office. The declaration was waiting for her.

It was strange, she thought. She had fought all her life to escape the trap of a single funneled life. She had been a brilliant lawyer while having two children, she had pursued a political career while happily and faithfully married. She had been a partner in a powerful law firm, then a Congresswoman, then a Senator and all the time a devoted and caring mother. She had managed her life impeccably only to wind up another kind of housewife, namely the Vice President of the United States.

As Vice President she had to tidy up after her political husband, the President, and perform his menial tasks. She received leaders of small nations, served on powerless committees with high-sounding titles, accepted condescending briefings, gave advice that was accepted with courtesy but not given truly respectful consideration. She had to parrot

200

the opinions and support the policies of her political husband.

She admired President Francis Xavier Kennedy and was grateful that he had selected her to be on the ticket with him as Vice President, but she differed with him on many things. She was sometimes amused that as a married woman she had escaped being trapped as an unequal partner, yet now in the highest political office ever achieved by an American woman, political laws made her subservient to a political husband.

But today she could become a political widow and she certainly could not complain about her insurance policy, the Presidency of the United States of America. After all, this had become an unhappy 'marriage'. Francis Kennedy had moved too quickly, too aggressively. Helen DuPray had begun fantasizing about his death, as many unhappy wives do.

But by signing this declaration she could become a political divorcée and get all the loot. She could take his place. For a lesser woman this would have been a miraculous delight.

She knew it was impossible to control the pragmatic exercises of the brain, so she did not really feel guilty about her fantasies, but she might feel guilty about a reality she had helped become true. When rumors floated that Kennedy would not run for a second term, she had alerted her political network. Kennedy had then given his blessing. This was all changed.

Now she had to clear her mind. The declaration, the petition, had already been signed by most of the Cabinet, the Secretary of State, the Secretary of Defense, Treasury and others. CIA was missing, that clever, unscrupulous bastard, Tappey. And of course, Christian Klee, a man she detested. But she had to make up her mind according to her judgment and her conscience. She had to act for the public good, not out of her own ambition.

201

Could she sign, commit an act of personal betrayal and keep her self-respect? But what was personal was extraneous. Consider only the facts.

Like Christian Klee and many others she had noted the change in Kennedy after his wife died just before his election to the Presidency. The loss of energy, the loss of political skills. Helen DuPray knew, as everyone knew, that to make the Presidency work you could only lead by building a consensus with the legislative branch. You had to court and cajole and maybe give a few kicks. You had to outflank, infiltrate and seduce the bureaucracy. You had to have the Cabinet under your thumb and your personal senior staff had to be a band of Attila the Huns and a gaggle of Solomons. You had to haggle, you had to reward and you had to throw a few thunderbolts. In some way you had to make everyone say, 'Yes, for the good of the country and the good of me.'

Not doing these things had been Kennedy's faults as President, also that he was too far ahead of his time. His staff should have known better. A man as intelligent as Kennedy should have known better. And yet she sensed in Kennedy's ill-fated moves a kind of moral desperation, an all-out gamble on good against evil.

But after his defeats he had retreated into his office like a sullen child and like a child put out the word that he would not run for re-election. And she believed, and hoped she was not regressing into an outmoded female sentimentality, that the death of Kennedy's wife was the root for the failure of his administration. But then did extraordinary men like Kennedy fall apart because of some personal tragedy? The answer to that was yes. Or maybe the power load of the Presidency had been too much for him. She herself had been born to politics but she had always thought that Kennedy himself had not the temperament. He was more scholar, scientist, teacher. He had too much idealism, he was in the best sense of the word, naive. That is, he was trusting.

202

But a central fact. The Congress, both houses, had waged brutal war against the executive branch, and won the war. Well it would not happen to her.

Now, she picked up the declaration from her desk, and analyzed it. The case presented was that Francis Xavier Kennedy was no longer capable of exercising the duties of President because of a temporary mental breakdown. Caused by the murder of his daughter. Which now affected his judgement, so that his decision to destroy the city of Dak and threaten to destroy a sovereign nation, became an irrational act, far out of proportion to the case, a dangerous precedent that must turn world opinion against the United States.

But then there was Kennedy's argument which he had presented at the staff and Cabinet conference.

This was an international conspiracy in which the Pope of the Catholic Church had been assassinated and the daughter of the President of the United States murdered. A number of hostages were still being held and the conspiracy could spin out the situation for weeks or even months. And the United States would have to set the killer of the Pope free. What an enormous loss of authority to the most powerful nation on earth, the leader of democracy and, of course, democratic capitalism.

So who was to say that the Draconian answer proposed by the President was not the correct answer? Certainly, if Kennedy was not bluffing, his measures would succeed. The Sultan of Sherhaben must go to his knees. What were the real values here?

Point: Damage – Kennedy had made his decision without proper discussion with his Cabinet, his staff, the leaders of Congress. That was very grave. That indicated danger. A gang leader ordering a vendetta.

But: He had known they would all be against him. He was convinced he was right. Time was short. This was the decisiveness of Francis Kennedy in the years before he became President.

Point: He had acted within the powers of the Chief Executive. His decision was legal. The declaration to impeach Kennedy had not been signed by any member of his personal staff, those people close to him. Therefore the charge of unfitness and mental instability was a matter of opinion which rested on the decision he had made. Therefore, this declaration to impeach was an illegal attempt to circumvent the power resting in the Executive branch of the government. The Congress disagreed with the Presidential decision and so, therefore, was attempting to reverse his decision by removing him. Clearly in violation of the Constitution.

Those were the moral and legal issues. Now she had to decide what was in her own best interests. That was not unreasonable in a politician.

She knew the mechanics. The Cabinet had signed, so now if she signed this declaration she would be the President of the United States. Then Kennedy would sign his declaration and she would be Vice President again. Then Congress would meet and in a two-thirds vote impeach Kennedy and she would be the President for at least thirty days, until the crisis was over.

The plus factor: She would be the first woman President of the United States for a few moments at the very least. Maybe for the rest of Kennedy's term which would end the following January. But no illusions. She would never get the nomination after the term ran out.

She would achieve the Presidency by what some would see as an act of betrayal. And she a woman. It was enough that the literature of civilization had always portrayed women as causing the downfall of great men, that there was the ever-present myth that men could never trust women. It would be regarded as 'unfaithful': that great sin of womankind which men never forgave. And she would be betraying the great national myth of the Kennedys. She would be another Mordred.

And it struck her. She smiled as she realized that she was in a 'no lose' situation. Just by refusing to sign the declaration.

Congress would not be denied.

Congress, possibly acting illegally without her signature, would impeach Kennedy and the Constitution decreed that she would succeed to the Presidency. But she would have proved her 'faithfulness' and if and when Francis Kennedy was restored after thirty days, she would still have his support. She would still have the Kennedy power group behind her nomination. As for the Congress, they were her enemies no matter what she did. So why be their political Jezebel? Their Delilah?

It became clearer and clearer to her. If she signed the declaration the voting public would never forgive her and the politicians would hold her in contempt. And then when and if she became President, they would most likely try to perform the same castrative act on her. They would, she thought, probably blame it on her menstrual flow, the cruel male expression would be the inspiration for comics all over the country.

She made her decision. She would *not* sign the declaration. That would show she was not greedily ambitious, that she was loyal.

She started writing the statement she would give to her administrative aide to prepare. In it she simply wrote that she could not sign, with a clear conscience, a document that would elevate her to such high power. That she would remain neutral in this struggle. But even this could be dangerous. She crumpled up the paper. She would just refuse to sign, Congress would carry it forward from there. She placed a call to Senator Lambertino. After that she would call other legislators and explain her position. But nothing in writing.

*

Vice President Helen DuPray's refusal to sign was a shocking blow to Congressman Jintz and Senator Lambertino. Only a female could be so contrary, blind to political necessity, so dull of wit not to grab this chance to be President of the United States. But they would have to do without her. They went over their options, the deed must be done. Patsy Troyca had been on the right track, all the preliminary steps must be eliminated. The Congress must designate itself the body to decide from the very beginning. But Lambertino and Jintz were still trying for some way to make Congress seem impartial. They never noticed that in that moment Patsy Troyca fell in love with Elizabeth Stone.

'Never fuck a woman over thirty,' had always been Patsy Troyca's creed. But for the first time he was thinking the exception might be the aide to Senator Lambertino. She was tall and willowy with wide gray eyes and a face that was sweet in repose. She was obviously intelligent yet knew how to keep her mouth shut. But what made him fall in love was that when they learned Vice President Helen DuPray was refusing to sign the declaration, she gave Patsy a smile that acknowledged him as a prophet, only he had proposed the correct solution.

For Troyca there were many good reasons for his stance. One, women didn't really like to fuck as much as men, they were more at risk in many different ways. But before thirty, they had more juice and less brains. Over thirty their eyes got squinty, they got too crafty, they started to think that men had it too good, were getting the better of nature and society's bargain. You never knew whether you were getting a casual piece of ass or signing some sort of promissory note. But Elizabeth Stone looked demurely horny in that slender virginal way some women have, and besides she had more power than him. He would not have to worry that she was hustling. It didn't matter that she must be close to forty.

Planning strategy with Congressman Jintz, Senator Lambertino noted that Troyca had an interest in his female aide.

That didn't bother him. Lambertino was one of the personally virtuous men in the Congress. He was sexually clean, with a wife of thirty years and four grown children. He was financially clean, wealthy in his own right. He was as politically clean as any political man in America can be but in addition he genuinely had the interest of the people and country at heart. True he was ambitious, but that was the very essence of political life. His virtue did not make him innocent of the machinations of the world. The refusal of the Vice President to sign the declaration had astonished Congressman Jintz but the Senator was not so easily surprised. He had always thought the Vice President a very clever woman. Lambertino wished her well, especially since he believed that no woman had the enduring political connections, or money patrons, to win the Presidency. She would be a very vulnerable opponent in a fight for the coming nomination.

'We have to move fast,' Senator Lambertino said. 'The Congress must designate a body or itself to declare the President unfit.'

'How about ten Senators on a blue ribbon panel?' Congressman Jintz said with a sly grin.

Senator Lambertino said, with a burst of irritation, 'How about a fifty House of Representatives committee with their heads up their asses.'

Jintz said placatingly, 'I have a helpful surprise for you, Senator. I think I can get one of the President's staff to sign the declaration to impeach him.'

That would do the trick, Troyca thought. But which one could it be? Never Klee, not Dazzy. It had to be either Oddblood Gray or the NSA guy, Wix. He thought, no, Wix was in Sherhaben.

Lambertino said briskly, 'We have a very painful duty today. A historical duty. We better get started.'

Troyca was surprised that Lambertino did not ask for the

name of the Staff member. Then he realized that the Senator did not want to know.

'You have my hand on that,' Jintz said and extended his arm to give that handshake that was famous as an unbreakable pledge.

Albert Jintz had achieved his eminence as a great Speaker of the House by being a man of his word. The newspapers often carried articles to this effect. A Jintz handshake was better than any handcuffing legal document. Though he looked like an alcoholic bank embezzler cartoon, short and round, cherry-red nose, head dripping with white hair like a Christmas tree in a snowstorm, he was considered the most honorable man in Congress, politically. When he promised a chunk of pork from the bottomless barrel of the budget, that pork was delivered. When a fellow Congressman wanted a bill blocked, and Jintz owed him a political debt, that bill was blocked. When a Congressman who wanted a personal bill paid his quid pro quo, it was a done deal. True he often leaked secret matters to the press but that was why so many articles on his impeccable handshake were printed.

And now this afternoon Jintz had to do the scut work of making sure the House would vote for the impeachment of President Kennedy. Make hundreds of phone calls, thousands of promises, to insure that two-thirds vote. It was not that Congress wouldn't do it, but a price had to be paid. And it all had to be done in less than twenty-four hours.

Patsy Troyca moved through his Congressman's suite of offices, his brain marshaling all the phone calls he had to make, all the documents he had to prepare. He knew he was involved in a great moment of history and he also knew that his career could be washed away if there was some terrible reversal. He was amazed that men like Jintz and Lambertino, whom he held in a certain kind of contempt, could be so courageous as to put themselves in the front line of battle.

This was a very dangerous step they were taking. Under a very shady interpretation of the Constitution they were prepared to make the Congress a body that could impeach the President of the United States.

He moved through the spooky green light of a dozen computers being worked by office staff. Thank God for computers. How the hell did things ever get done before? Passing one computer operator he touched her shoulder in a comradely gesture that could not be taken for sexual harassment and said, 'Don't make any dates – we'll be here until morning.'

The *New York Times* magazine section had recently published an article on the sexual mores of Capitol Hill, the building that housed both the Senate and the House and their staffs. The article noted that of the elected hundred Senators and 435 Congressmen and their huge staffs, the population was in the many thousands, of which more than half were females.

The article had suggested that there was a great deal of sexual activity among these free citizens. The article had said that due to long hours and the tension of working under political deadlines the staff had little social life and had to perforce seek a little recreation on the job. It was noted that Congressional offices and Senator suites were furnished with couches. The article explained that in government bureaus there were special medical clinics and doctors whose duties were the discreet treatment of venereal infection. The records were of course confidential, but the writer claimed he had been given a peek and the percentage of infection was higher than the national average. The writer attributed this not so much to promiscuity as to the incestuous social environment. The writer then wondered if all this fornication was affecting the quality of law-making on Capitol Hill which he referred to as the 'Rabbit Warren'.

Patsy Troyca had taken the article personally. He averaged a sixteen-hour working day six days a week and was on call

Sundays. Was he not entitled to a normal sex life like any other citizen? Damn it, he didn't have time to go to parties, to romance women, to commit himself to a relationship. It all had to happen here, in the countless suites and corridors, in the smoky green light of computers and military ringing of telephones. You had to fit it into a few minutes of banter, a meaningful smile, the involved strategies of work. That fucking *Times* writer went to all the publisher parties, took out people for long lunches, chatted leisurely with journalist colleagues, could go to hookers without a newspaper reporting the seamy details.

Troyca went into his private office, then into the bathroom, and gave a sigh of relief as he sat on the toilet, pen in hand. He scribbled notes on all the things he had to do. He washed his hands, juggling pad and pen, Congressional logo etched in gold computer lines; and feeling much better (the tension of impeaching a President had knotted his stomach) went to the small mobile liquor cart, took ice from the tiny refrigerator to fix himself a gin and tonic. He thought about Elizabeth Stone. He was sure there was nothing between her and her Senator boss. And she was smart, smarter then him, she had kept her mouth shut.

The door of his office opened and the girl he had patted on the shoulder came into the office. She had an armful of computer printout sheets and Patsy Troyca sat at his desk to go over them. She stood beside him. He could feel the heat of her body, a heat generated by the long hours she had put in on the computer that day.

Patsy Troyca had interviewed this girl when she had applied for the job. He often said that if only the girls who worked in the office kept looking as good as on their interview day, he could put them all in *Playboy*. And if they remained as demure and sweet he would marry them. The girl's name was Janet Wyngale and she was really beautiful. The first day he saw her, a line from Dante had flashed through Patsy Troyca's mind, 'Here is the goddess that will subjugate me.' Of course he would not allow such a misfortune to happen. But she was that beautiful, that first day. She was never as beautiful again. Her hair was still blonde, but not gold, her eyes were still that amazing blue but she wore glasses and was a little ugly without the first perfect make-up. Nor were her lips as cherry-red. Her body was not as voluptuous as the first day, which was natural since she was a hard worker and dressed comfortably now to increase her efficiency. He had, all in all, made a good decision, she was not yet squinty-eyed.

Janet Wyngale, what a great name. She was leaning over his shoulder to point out things on the computer sheets. He was conscious she switched her feet so that she was standing more beside him than behind him. Her golden hair brushed his cheek, silky warm and smelling of minced flowers.

'Your perfume is great,' Patsy Troyca said, and he was almost shivering when the heat of her body gusted over him. She didn't move or say anything. But her hair was like a Geiger counter over his cheek picking up the radiating lust in his body. It was a friendly lust, two buddies in a jam together. They would be going over computer sheets all through the night, answering a witch's brew of telephone calls, calling emergency meetings. They would fight side by side.

Holding the computer sheets in his left hand, Patsy Troyca let his right hand touch the back side of her thigh under her skirt. She didn't move. They were both staring intently at the computer sheets. He let his hand stay perfectly still, let it burn on satiny skin that electrified his scrotum. He was not conscious that the computer sheets had fallen to the desk. Her flowered hair drowned his face and he swiveled and both his hands were under her skirt, both his hands like little feet running over that field so satiny under the synthesized nylon of her panties. Underneath to the pubic hair and the wet agonizing sweetness of the flesh beneath. Patsy Troyca levitated from his seat, it seemed to him he was motionless in the air, his body forming a supernatural eagle's nest into which Janet Wyngale, with a fluttering of wings, came to rest on his lap. Miraculously she was sitting right on his cock which had mysteriously emerged and they were face to face kissing; he drowning in blonde minced flowers, groaning with passion and Janet Wyngale kept repeating a passionate endearment which he finally understood. 'Lock the door,' she was saying and Patsy Troyca freed his wet left hand and flipped the electronic button which enclosed them in that perfect brief moment of ecstasy. Both tumbled to the floor in a graceful wing-like dive and she had her long legs wrapped around his neck, and he could see the long milk-white thighs and they climaxed together in perfect unison, Patsy Troyca whispered ecstatically, 'Ah, heaven, heaven.'

Then miraculously they were both standing, rosy-cheeked, their eyes flashing with delight, renewed, jubilant, ready to face the grueling long hours of work together. Gallantly Patsy Troyca passed her the gin and tonic with its joyful tinkling of ice cubes. Graciously and thankfully she wet her parched mouth. Sincerely and gratefully Patsy Troyca said, 'That was wonderful.' Lovingly she patted his neck and kissed him. 'It was great.'

Moments later they were back at the desk studying the computer sheets in earnest, concentrating on the language and the figures. Janet was a wonderful editor. Patsy Troyca felt an enormous gratitude. He murmured with genuine courtesy, 'Janet, I'm really crazy about you. As soon as this crisis is over we got to have a date, OK?'

'Umm,' Janet said. She gave him a warm smile. A friendly smile. 'I love working with you,' she said.

12

Television never had such a glorious week. On Sunday the assassination of the Pope had been repeated scores of times on the networks, on the cable channels, on PBS special reports. On Tuesday the murder of Theresa Kennedy had been even more continuously repeated, her murder floated through the airways of the universe endlessly and endlessly. Messages of sympathy by the millions poured into the White House. In all of the great cities the citizens of America appeared on the streets wearing black armbands. And so when the television stations climaxed late Wednesday with the leaked news of President Francis Kennedy's ultimatum to the Sultan of Sherhaben, great mobs congregated all through the United States in a wild frenzy of jubilation. There was no question they supported the President's decision. Indeed the TV correspondents who interviewed citizens on the street were appalled at the ferocity of the comments. The common cry was 'Nuke the bastards'. Finally orders came from the top TV network news chiefs to stop covering the street scenes and to halt the interviews. The orders originated from Lawrence Salentine who had formed a council with the other owners of the media.

In the White House President Francis Kennedy didn't have time to grieve for his daughter. He was on the hotline to Russia to reassure them there was to be no territorial grabbing in the Far East. He was on the phone to heads of other states to plead for co-operation and to make them understand his own stance was irrevocable. That the President of the United States was not bluffing, the city of Dak would be destroyed, and that if the ultimatum was not obeyed the Sultanate of Sherhaben too would be destroyed.

Arthur Wix and Bert Audick were already on their way to Sherhaben in a fast jet passenger plane not yet available to the civilian aircraft industry. Oddblood Gray was frantically trying to rally Congress behind the President and by the end of the day knew he had failed. Eugene Dazzy calmly dealt with all the memoranda from Cabinet members and the Defense establishment, his Walkman firmly set over his ears to discourage unnecessary conversation from his staff. Christian Klee was appearing and disappearing on mysterious errands.

Senator Thomas Lambertino and Congressman Alfred Jintz held constant meetings through Wednesday with colleagues in the House and Senate on the action to impeach Kennedy. The Socrates Club called in all their markers. True the interpretation of the Constitution was a little murky, that Congress could designate itself as the deciding body, but the situation warranted such a drastic action. Kennedy's ultimatum to Sherhaben was so obviously based on personal emotions and not on reasons of State.

By late Wednesday the coalition was set. Both Houses, with barely two-thirds of the vote assured, would convene on Thursday night, just hours before Kennedy's deadline to destroy the city of Dak.

Lambertino and Jintz kept Oddblood Gray fully informed, hoping he could persuade Francis Kennedy to rescind his ultimatum to Sherhaben. Oddblood Gray told them that the President would not do so. He then briefed Francis Kennedy.

Francis Kennedy said, 'Otto, I think you and Chris and Dazzy should have late dinner with me tonight. Make it about eleven. And don't plan to get home right away.'

The President and his staff ate in the Yellow Room which was Kennedy's favorite though this was a lot of extra work for the kitchen and waiters. As usual the meal was very simple for Kennedy, a small grilled steak, a dish of thinly

214

sliced tomatoes and then coffee with a variety of cream and fruit tarts. Christian and the others were offered the option of fish. None of them ate more than a few bites.

Kennedy seemed to be perfectly at ease, the others were awkward. They all wore black armbands on their jacket sleeves, as did Kennedy. Everyone in the White House including the servants wore the identical black band and it seemed archaic to Christian. He knew that Eugene Dazzy had sent out the memorandum for this to be done.

'Christian,' he said. 'I think it's time we share our problem. But it goes no further. No memorandum.'

'It's serious,' Christian said. And he outlined what had happened in the atomic bomb scare. He informed them that the two young men had refused to talk on the advice of their lawyer.

Oddblood Gray said incredulously, 'There's a nuclear device planted in New York City? I don't believe it. All this shit can't be happening at once.'

Eugene Dazzy said, 'Are you sure they really did plant a nuclear device?'

Christian said, 'I think there is only a ten per cent chance.' He believed that there was more than a ninety per cent chance but he was not willing to tell them that.

'What are you doing about it?' Dazzy said.

'We've got the nuclear search teams out,' Christian said. 'But there's a time element.' He spoke directly to Kennedy. 'I still need your signature to activate the Medical Interrogation Team for the PET test.' He explained the secret law in the Atomic Security Bill.

'No,' Francis Kennedy said.

They were all astonished by the President's refusal.

'We can't take a chance,' Dazzy said. 'Sign the order.'

Kennedy smiled and said, 'The invading of an individual's brain by government officials is a dangerous action.' He paused for a moment and said, 'We can't sacrifice a citizen's

215

individual rights just on suspicion. Especially such potentially valuable citizens as those two young men. Chris when you have more confirmation, ask again.' Then Kennedy said to Oddblood Gray, 'Otto, brief Christian and Dazzy on the Congress.'

Gray said, 'Here is their game plan. They know now that the Vice President will not sign the declaration to impeach you under the Twenty-fifth Amendment. But enough of the Cabinet members have signed so that they can still take action. They will designate Congress as the other body to determine your fitness. They will convene late Thursday and then vote to impeach. Just to cancel you from the negotiations for the release of the hostages. Their argument is that you are under too much stress because of the death of your daughter.

'When you're removed, the Secretary of Defense will countermand your orders to bomb Dak. They are counting on Bert Audick to convince the Sultan to release the hostages during that thirty-day period. The Sultan will almost certainly comply.'

Kennedy turned to Dazzy. 'Put out a directive. No member of this government will contact Sherhaben. That will be regarded as treason.'

Eugene Dazzy said softly, 'With most of your Cabinet against you, there is no possibility your orders will be carried out. At this moment you have no power.'

Kennedy turned to Christian Klee. 'Chris,' he said, 'they need a two-thirds vote to remove me from office, right?'

'Yes,' Christian said. 'But without the Vice President's signature, it's basically illegal.'

Kennedy looked into his eyes. 'Isn't there anything you can do?'

In that moment Christian Klee's mind made another leap. Francis thought he could do something, but what was it? Christian said tentatively, 'We can call on the Supreme

Court and say the Congress is acting against the Constitution. The language is vague in the Twenty-fifth Amendment. Or we can argue that Congress is acting contrary to the spirit of the Amendment by substituting themselves as the instigating party after the Vice President refuses to sign. I can contact the Court so they'll rule right after Congress votes.'

He saw the look of disappointment in Kennedy's eyes and he racked his brain furiously. He was missing something.

Oddblood Gray said worriedly, 'The Congress is going to attack your mental capacity. They keep bringing up the week you disappeared. Just before your inauguration.'

Kennedy said, 'That's nobody's business.'

Christian became aware that the others were waiting for him to speak. They knew he had been with the President that mysterious week. He said, 'What happened in that week won't damage us.'

Francis Kennedy said, 'Euge, prepare the papers for firing the whole Cabinet except for Theodore Tappey. Prepare them as soon as possible and I'll sign right away. Have the Press Secretary give it to the media before Congress meets.'

Eugene Dazzy made notes then asked, 'What about the Chairman of the Joint Chiefs of Staff? Fire him too?'

'No,' Francis Kennedy said. 'Basically he's with us, the others ruled against him. Congress couldn't do this if it weren't for those bastards in the Socrates Club.'

Christian said, 'I've been handling the interrogation of the two young kids. They choose to remain silent. And if their lawyer has it his way, they will be released on bail tomorrow.'

Dazzy said sharply, 'There's a section in the Atomic Security Act that enables you to hold them. It suspends the right of habeas corpus, civil liberties. You must know that, Christian.'

'Number one,' Christian said, 'what's the point of holding them if Francis refuses to sign the medical interrogation order? Their lawyer applies for bail and if we refuse them we still must have the President's signature to suspend

217

habeas corpus in this case. Francis, are you willing to sign an order for a suspension of habeas corpus?'

Kennedy smiled at him. 'No, Congress will use that against me.'

Christian was confident now. Still, for a moment, he felt a little sick and bile rose in his mouth. Then it passed and he knew what Kennedy wanted, he knew what he had to do.

Kennedy sipped his coffee, they had finished their meal, but none of them had taken more than a few bites. Kennedy said, 'Let's discuss the real crisis. Am I still going to be President in forty-eight hours?'

Oddblood Gray said, 'Rescind the order to bomb Dak, turn over the negotiations to a special team, and no action to remove you will be taken by Congress.'

'Who gave you that deal?' Kennedy asked.

'Senator Lambertino and Congressman Jintz,' Otto Gray said. 'Lambertino is a genuine good guy and Jintz is responsible, in a political affair like this. They wouldn't double-cross us.'

'OK, that's another option,' Kennedy said. 'That and going to the Supreme Court. What else?'

Eugene Dazzy said, 'Go on TV tomorrow before Congress convenes and appeal to the nation. The people will be for you and that may give Congress pause.'

'OK,' Kennedy said. 'Euge, clear it with the TV people for me to go on over all the networks. Just fifteen minutes is what we need.'

Eugene Dazzy said softly, 'Francis, it's an awful big step we're taking. The President and the Congress in such a direct confrontation and then calling upon the masses to take action? It could get very messy.'

Oddblood Gray said, 'I think the President is making the right decision. That guy Yabril will string us out for weeks and make this country look like a big lump of shit.'

Christian said, 'There's a rumor that one of the staff in

218

this room or Arthur Wix is going to sign that declaration to remove the President. Whoever it is should speak now.'

Kennedy said impatiently, 'That rumor is nonsense. If one of you were going to do that you would have resigned beforehand. I know all of you too well, none of you could betray me.'

After dinner they went from the Yellow Room to the little movie theater on the other side of the White House. Francis Kennedy had told Dazzy that he wanted to see all the TV footage of the murder of his daughter.

In the darkness, the nervous voice of Eugene Dazzy said, 'The TV coverage starts now.' For a few seconds the movie screen was streaked with black lines that seemed to scramble from top to bottom.

The screen lit up with brilliant colors, the TV cameras covering the hugh aircraft squatting on the desert sand like some horror bug. Then the cameras zoomed to the figure of Yabril presenting Theresa Kennedy in the doorway. Kennedy saw that his daughter was smiling slightly and then she waved to the camera. It was an odd wave, a wave of reassurance, yet of subjugation. Yabril was beside her, then slightly behind her. And then there was the movement of the right arm, the gun not visible, and the flat report of the shot and then the billowing ghostly pink mist and the body of Theresa Kennedy falling. Kennedy heard the wail of the crowd and recognized it as grief and not triumph. Then the figure of Yabril appeared in the doorway. He held his gun aloft, an oily gleaming tube of black metal. He held it as a gladiator holds a sword but there were no cheers. The film came to an end. Eugene Dazzy had edited it severely.

The lights came on but Francis Kennedy remained still. He was surprised that he felt a weakening of his body. He couldn't move his legs or his torso. But his mind was clear, there was no shock or disorder in his brain. He did not feel the helplessness of tragedy's victim. He would not have to

219

struggle against fate or God. He only had to struggle against his enemies in this world and he would conquer them.

He would not let mortal man defeat him. When his wife had died he had no recourse against the hand of God, the faults of nature. He had bowed his entire being in acceptance. But his daughter's malicious man-made death, oh, that he could punish, and redress. That was within his material world. This time he would not bow his head. Woe to that world, to his enemies, woe to the wicked in this world.

When he was finally able to lift his body from the chair he smiled reassuringly to the men around him. He had accomplished his purpose. He had made his closest and most powerful friends suffer with him. They would not now so easily oppose the actions he must take.

Christian thought about that day in early December, over three years ago, when Francis Kennedy, the President elect of the United States, who would be sworn into office the following January, had waited for him outside the monastery in Vermont. For that was the secret that newspapers and his political opponents often referred to. That Kennedy had disappeared for a week. There had been speculations that he had been under psychiatric care, that he had broken down, that he had a secret love affair. But only two people knew the truth, the Abbot of the monstery and Christian Klee.

It was a week after his election that Christian had driven Francis Kennedy to the Catholic monstery just outside of White River Junction in Vermont. They were greeted by the Abbot who was the only one who knew Kennedy's identity.

The resident monks lived apart from the world, cut off from all media and even the town itself. These monks communicated only with God and the earth on which they grew their livelihood. They had all taken a vow of silence and did not speak except in prayer or yelps of pain when they were ill or injured themselves in some domestic accident.

Only the Abbot had a television set and access to news-papers. The TV news programs were a constant source of amusement to him. He particularly fancied the concept of the 'anchor man' on the night broadcasts and often ironically thought of himself for humility.

When the car drove up, the Abbot was waiting for them at the monastery gate, flanked by two monks in ragged brown robes and sandaled feet. Christian took Kennedy's bag from the trunk and watched the Abbot shake hands with the President elect. The Abbot seemed more like an inn keeper than a holy man. He had a jolly grin to welcome them and when he was introduced to Christian he said jocularly, 'Why don't you stay? A week of silence wouldn't do you any harm. I've seen you on television and you must be tired of talking.'

Christian smiled his thanks but did not reply. He was looking at Francis Kennedy as they shook hands. The handsome face was very composed, the handshake was not emotional, Kennedy was not a demonstrative man. He seemed not to be grieving the death of his wife. He had more the preoccupied look of a man forced to go into hospital for a minor operation.

'Let's hope we can keep this secret,' Christian had said. People don't like these religious retreats. They might think you've gone nuts.'

Francis Kennedy's face twisted into a little smile. A controlled but natural courtesy. 'They won't find out,' he said. 'And I know you'll cover. Pick me up in a week. That should be enough time.'

Christian thought, what would happen to Francis in those days? He felt close to tears. He took hold of Francis by the shoulders and said, 'Do you want me to stay with you?' Kennedy had shaken his head and walked through the gates of the monastery. On that day Christian thought he had seemed OK.

The day after Christmas was so clear and bright, so

221

cleansed by cold that it seemed as if the whole world was enclosed in glass, the sky a mirror, the earth brown steel. And when Christian drove up to the monastery gate, Francis Kennedy was alone, waiting for him without any luggage, his hands stretched over his head, his body taut and straining upward. He seemed to be exulting in his freedom.

When Christian got out of the car to greet him, Francis Kennedy gave him a quick embrace and a shout of joyous welcome. He seemed to have been rejuvenated by his stay in the monastery. He smiled at Christian and it was one of his rare brilliant smiles that had enchanted multitudes. The smile that reassured the world that happiness could be won, that man was good, that the world would go on forever to better and better things. It was a smile that made you love him because of its delight in his seeing you. Christian had felt such relief at seeing that smile. Francis would be OK. He would be as strong as he had always been. He would be the hope of the world, the strong guardian of his country and fellow man. Now they would do great deeds together.

And then with that same brilliant smile Kennedy took Christian by the arm, looked into his eyes, and said, simply and yet with amusement, as if it didn't really mean anything, as if he were reporting some minor detail of information, 'God didn't help.'

And in the cold scrubbed world of a winter morning. Christian saw that finally something had been broken in Kennedy. That he would never be the same man again. That part of his mind had been chopped away. He would be almost the same but now there was a timy lump of falseness that had never before existed. He saw that Kennedy himself did not know this and that nobody else would know. And that he, Christian, only knew because he was the one who was here at his point of time, to see the brilliant smile and hear the joking words, 'God didn't help.'

Christian said, 'What the hell, you only gave him seven days.'

Kennedy laughed. 'And he's a busy man,' he said.

So they had gotten into the car. They had a wonderful day. Kennedy had never been more witty, had never been in such high spirits. He was full of plans, anxious to get his administration together and make wonderful things happen in the four years to come. He seemed to be a man who had reconciled himself to his misfortune, renewed his energies. And it almost convinced Christian.

Late Tuesday afternoon Christian Klee slipped away from the frenetic White House for a few hours to get all the ducks in a row. He had to see first of all Eugene Dazzy, then a certain Jeralyn Albanese, then the Oracle, and also the great Dr Zed Annaccone.

Dazzy he cornered for a few moments in the Chief of Staff's office and that was easy. His next stop was Dr Annaccone in the building of the National Science Institute and he wanted to make that fast. He had to be in the White House when Kennedy called for a final strategy meeting before Congress voted. He thought grimly he would solve a few of the problems this afternoon, give Francis Kennedy a fighting chance. And then his mind did a curious trick. Somewhere this afternoon he would have to secretly interrogate Adam Gresse and Henry Tibbot but his mind refused to include the two young scientists in his agenda. He would have to do it but he would not think about it, it would not be part of his agenda until he did it.

Dr Zed Annaccone was one of those short thin men with a big chest. His face was extraordinarily alert and the expression on it was not really supercilious, just the confidence of a man who believed he knew more about the important things on this earth than anyone else. Which was quite true.

Dr Annaccone was the Medical Science Advisor to the President of the United States. He was also the Director of

223

the National Brain Research Institute and the administrative head of the Medical Advisory Board of the Atomic Security Commission. Once at a White House dinner party, Klee had heard him say that the brain was such a sophisticated organ that it could produce whatever chemicals the body needed. And Klee simply thought, 'So what?'

The Doctor, reading his mind, patted him on the shoulder and said, 'That fact is more important to civilisation than anything you guys can do here in the White House. And all we need is a billion dollars to prove it. What the hell is that, one aircraft carrier?' Then he had smiled at Klee to show that he meant no offense.

And now he was smiling when Klee walked into his office.

'So,' Dr Annaccone said, 'finally even the lawyers come to me. You realize our philosophies are directly opposed?'

Klee knew that Dr Annaccone was about to make a joke about the legal profession and was slightly irritated. Why did people always have wise-ass remarks about lawyers?

'Truth,' Dr Annaccone said. 'Lawyers always seek to obscure it, we scientists try to reveal it.' He smiled again.

'No, no,' Klee said and smiled to show he had a sense of humor. 'I'm here for information. We have a situation that calls for that special PET study under the Atomic Security Act.'

'You know you have to get the President's signature on that?' Dr Annaccone said. 'Personally I'd do the procedure for many other situations but the civil libertarians would kick my ass.'

'I know,' Christian said. Then he explained the situation of the atom bomb and capture of Gresse and Tibbot. 'Nobody thinks there is really a bomb, but if there is, then the time factor is crucially important. And the President refused to sign the order.'

'Why?' Dr Annaccone asked.

'Because of the possible brain damage that could occur during the procedure,' Klee said.

This seemed to surprise Annaccone. He thought for a moment. 'The possibility of significant brain damage is very small,' he said. 'Maybe ten per cent. The greater danger is the rare incidence of cardiac arrest and the even rarer side effect post procedure of complete and total memory loss. Complete amnesia. But even that shouldn't dissuade him in this case. I've sent the President papers on it, I hope he reads them.'

'He reads everything,' Christian said. 'But I'm afraid it won't change his mind.'

'Too bad we don't have more time,' Dr Annaccone said. 'We are just completing tests that will result in an infallible lie detector based on computer measurement of the chemical changes in the brain. The new test is much like the PET but without the ten per cent damage risk. It will be completely safe. But we can't use that now, there would be too many elements of doubt until further data are compiled to satisfy the legal requirements.'

Christian felt a tinge of excitement. 'A safe, infallible lie detector that would be admitted into court?' he said.

'As to being admitted into a court of law, I don't know,' Dr Annaccone said. 'Scientifically, when our tests have been thoroughly analyzed and compiled by the computers, the new brain lie detector test will be as infallible as DNA and fingerprinting. That's one thing. But to get it enacted into law is another. The Civil Liberties groups will fight it to the death. They're convinced that a man should not be used to testify against himself. And how would people in Congress like the idea that they could be made to take such a test under criminal law?'

Klee said, 'I wouldn't like to take it.'

Annaccone laughed. 'Congress would be signing their own political death warrant. And yet where's the true logic? Our laws were made to prevent confessions obtained by foul means. However, this is science.' He paused for a moment.

225

'How about business leaders or even errant husbands and wives?'

'That's a little creepy,' Klee admitted.

Dr Annaccone said, 'But what about all those old sayings. Like "The truth shall make you free?" Like, "Truth is the greatest of virtues." Like, "Truth is the very essence of life." That man's struggle to discover truth is his greatest ideal?' Dr Annaccone laughed. 'When our tests are verified, I'll bet my Institute budget will get chopped.'

Christian said, 'That's my area of competence. We dress up the law. We specify that your test can only be used in important criminal cases. We restrict its use to the government. Make it like a strictly controlled narcotic substance or arms manufacturing. So if you can get the test proven scientifically, I can get the legislation.' Then he asked, 'Exactly how the hell does that work anyway?'

'The new PET?' Dr Annaccone said. 'It's very simple. Physically not invasive. No surgeon with a blade in his hand. No obvious scars. Just a small injection of a chemical substance into the brain through the blood vessels. Chemical self-sabotage with psychopharmaceuticals.'

'It's voodoo to me,' Christian said. 'You should be in jail with those two physics guys.'

Dr Annaccone laughed. 'No connection,' he said. 'Those guys work to blow up the world. I work to get at the inner truths. How man really thinks, what he really feels.'

Dr Zed Annaccone had caused President Kennedy more political trouble than any other member of the administration. And he had done it by doing his job too well. His National Science Institute had provided a hailstorm of political fire by harvesting vital organs from dead babies to use as transplants. Dr Annaccone had used funds for genetic engineering experiments on human volunteers. Genetic transplants for people prone to cancer, to Alzheimer's, to all the still mysterious maladies that struck kidneys, livers, eyes. He had proposed a program of genetic experiments that outraged most of the different church establishments, the general public and the political powers. And Dr Annaccone didn't really know why there was such a fuss. He had contempt for his opponents and he showed it.

But even he knew that a brain lie detector test meant legal trouble. 'This will be perhaps the most important discovery in the medical history of our time,' Dr Annaccone said. 'Imagine if we can read the brain. All your lawyers will be out of a job.'

Christian said. 'Do you think it's possible to figure out how the brain works, really?

Dr Annaccone shrugged. 'No,' he said. 'If the brain were that simple, we would be too simple to figure it out.' He gave Christian another grin. 'Catch 22. Our brain will never catch up with the brain. Because of that, no matter what happens, mankind can never be more than a higher form of animal.' He was overjoyed by this fact.

He became abstracted for a moment. 'You know there's a "ghost in the machine," Koestler's phrase. Man has two brains really, the primitive brain and the overlying civilized brain. Have you noticed there is a certain unexplainable malice in human beings. A useless malice?'

Christian said, 'Call the President about the PET. Try to persuade him.'

Dr Annaccone said, 'I will. He is really being too chicken. The procedure won't damage those kids a bit.'

Christian Klee next went to pay a call on Jeralyn Albanese who owned the famous restaurant in Washington DC, naturally named 'Jera'. It had three huge dining rooms separated from each other by a very lush lounge bar. The Republicans gravitated to one dining room, the Democrats to another, and members of the Executive Branch and the White House ate in the third room. The one thing on which all parties agreed was that the food was delicious, the service

227

superb, and the hostess one of the most charming women in the world.

Twenty years ago, Jeralyn, then a woman of thirty, had been employed by a lobbyist for the banking industry. He had introduced her to Martin Mutford, who had not yet earned the nickname 'Private' but was already on the rise. Martin Mutford had been charmed by her wit, her brashness, and her sense of adventure. For five years, they had an affair which did not interfere with their private lives. Jeralyn Albanese continued her career as a lobbyist, a career much more complicated and refined than generally supposed, requiring a great deal of research skill and administrative genius. Oddly enough, one of her most valuable assets was having been a champion college tennis player.

As an assistant to the chief lobbyist or the banking industry, a good part of her week was amassing financial data to convince experts on the Congressional Finance Committees to pass legislation favorable to banking. Then she included hostess conference dinners with Congressmen and Senators. She was astonished by the horniness of these calm, judicial legislators. In private, they were rioting gold-dust miners, they drank to excess, they sang lustily, they grabbed her ass in a spirit of old time American folksiness. She was amazed and delighted by their lust. It developed naturally that she went to the Bahamas and to Las Vegas with the younger and more personable Congressmen, always under the disguise of conferences, and even once to London to a convention of economic advisors from all over the world. Not to influence the vote on a bill, not to perpetrate a swindle, but if the vote on a bill was borderline, when a girl as pretty as Jeralyn Albanese presented the customary foot-high stack of opinion papers written by eminent economists, you had a very good chance of getting that teetering vote. As Martin Mutford said, 'On the close ones it's very hard for a man to vote against a girl who sucked his cock the night before.'

It was Mutford who had taught her to appreciate the finer things in life. He had taken her to the museums in New York, he had taken her to the Hamptons to mingle with the rich and the artists, the old money and the new money, the famous journalists and the TV anchors, the writers who did serious novels and the important screenplays of big movies. Another pretty face didn't make much of a splash there, but being a good tennis player gave her an edge.

Jeralyn had more men fall in love with her because of her tennis playing than her beauty, the intrinsic grace of her female form more revealed by tennis. And it was a sport that men who were mere 'hackers', as politicians and artists usually were, loved to play with good looking women. In mixed doubles, Jeralyn could establish a sporting rapport with partners, her golden skin and lovely limbs linked to her partner in their struggle for conquest.

But there came a time when Jeralyn had to think of her future. She was not married, and at forty years of age the Congressmen she would have to lobby were in their unappealing sixties and seventies.

Martin Mutford was eager to promote her in the high realms of banking, but after the excitement of Washington, banking seemed dull. American lawmakers were so fascinating with their outrageous mendacity in public affairs, their charming innocence in sexual relationships. It was Martin Mutford who came up with the solution. He, too, did not want to lose Jeralyn in a maze of computer reports. In Washington her beautifully furnished apartment was a refuge from his heavy responsibilities. It was Martin Mutford who came up with the idea that she could own and run a restaurant that would be a political hub.

The funds were supplied by American Sterling Trustees, a lobbyist group that represented banking interests, in the form of a five million dollar loan. Jeralyn had the restaurant built to her specification. It would be an exclusive club, an auxiliary home for the politicos of Washington. Many

229

Congressmen were separated from their families while Congress was in session and the Jera restaurant was a place where they could spend lonely nights. In addition to the three dining rooms and waiting lounge and bar, there was a room with TV and a reading room that had a copy of all the major magazines published in the United States and England. There was another room for chess or checkers or cards. But the ultimate attraction was the residential building built on top of the restaurant.

It was three storeys high and held twenty apartments. These apartments were rented by the lobbyists who loaned them out to Congressmen and important bureaucrats for secretive liaisons. 'Jera' was known to be the very soul of discretion in these matters. Jeralyn kept the keys.

It amazed Jeralyn that these hardworking men had the time for so much dalliance. They were indefatigable. And it was the older ones with established families, some with grandchildren, who were the most active. Jeralyn loved to see these same Congressmen and Senators on television, so sedate and distinguished looking, lecturing on morals, decrying drugs and loose living and the importance of old-fashioned values. She never felt they were hypocrites really. After all, men who had spent so much of their lives and time and energy for their country deserved extra consideration.

She really didn't like the arrogance, the smarmy self-assured smugness of the younger Congressmen, but she loved the old guys, like the stern-faced wrathful Senator who never smiled in public but cavorted at least twice a week bare-assed with young 'models'. And old Congressman Jintz with his body like a scarred zeppelin and a face so ugly that the whole country believed he was honest. All of them looked absolutely awful in private, shedding their clothes. But they charmed her. Why did men keep wanting to do that?

Rarely did the women members of Congress come to the restaurant and never did they make use of the apartments.

Feminism had not yet advanced so far. To make up for this Jeralyn gave little lunches in the restaurant for some of her girlfriends in the arts, pretty actresses, singers and dancers.

It was none of her business if these young pretty women struck up friendships with the highly placed servants of the people of the United States. But she was surprised when Eugene Dazzy, the huge slobby Chief of Staff to the President of the United States, took up with a promising young dancer and arranged for Jeralyn to slip him a key to one of the apartments above the restaurant. She was even more astonished when the liaison grew to the status of a 'relationship'. Not that Dazzy had that much time at his disposal, the most he spent in the apartment was a few hours after lunch. And Jeralyn was under no illusion as to what the rent-paying lobbyist could get out of it. Dazzy's decisions would not be influenced, but at least he would, on rare occasions, take the lobbyists' calls to the White House so that the lobbyists' clients would be impressed by such access.

Jeralyn gave all this information to Martin Mutford when they gossiped together. It was understood that the information between the two of them was not to be used in any way and certainly not in any form of blackmail. That could be disastrous and destroy the main purpose of the restaurant, which was to further the atmosphere of good fellowship and earned a sympathetic ear for the lobbyists who were footing the bill. Plus the fact that the restaurant was Jeralyn's main source of livelihood and she would not allow it to be jeopardized.

So Jeralyn was very much surprised when Christian Klee dropped in on her when the restaurant was almost empty between lunch and dinner. She received him in her office. She liked Klee though he ate at 'Jera' infrequently and had never tried to make use of the apartments above. But she had no feeling of apprehension, she knew that there was nothing he could reproach her for. If some scandal was brewing, no matter what newspaper reporters were up to, or what one of the young girls would say, she was in the clear.

She murmured some words of commiseration about the terrible times he must be going through, what with the murders and the hijacking, but careful not to sound as if she were fishing for inside information. Klee thanked her.

Then he said, 'Jeralyn, we've known each other a long time and I want to alert you, for your protection. I know what I'm about to say will shock you as much as it does me.'

Oh, shit, Jeralyn thought. Somebody is making trouble for me.

Christian Klee went on. 'A lobbyist for financial interests is a good friend of Eugene Dazzy and he tried to lay some bullshit on him. He urged Dazzy to sign a paper that would do President Kennedy a great deal of harm. He warned Dazzy that his using your apartments could be made public and ruin his career and his marriage.' Klee laughed. 'Jesus, who would ever have thought Eugene was capable of a thing like that. What the hell, I guess we're all human.'

Jeralyn was not fooled by Christian's good humor. She knew she had to be very careful or her whole life might go down the drain. Klee was Attorney General of the United States. And had acquired the reputation of being a very dangerous man. He could give her more trouble than she could handle, even though her ace in the hole was Martin Mutford. She said, 'I didn't have anything to do with all that. Sure, I gave Dazzy the key to one of the apartments upstairs. But hell, that was just a courtesy of the house. There are no records of any kind. Nobody could pin anything on me or Dazzy.'

'Sure, I know that,' Christian said. 'But don't you see, that lobbyist would never dare pull that shit on his own? Somebody higher up told him what to do.'

Jeralyn said uneasily, 'Christian, I swear I never blabbed to anyone. I would never put my restaurant in jeopardy. I'm not that dumb.'

'I know, I know,' Christian said reassuringly. 'But you and Martin have been very good friends for a very long time. You may have told him, just as a piece of gossip.'

Now Jeralyn was really horrified. Suddenly she was between two powerful men who were about to do battle. More than anything else in the world she wanted to step outside the arena. She also knew that the worst thing to do was lie.

'Martin would never try such a dumb thing,' she said. 'Not that kind of stupid blackmail.' By saying this, she admitted she had told Martin and yet she could deny that she had explicitly confessed.

Christian was still reassuring. He saw that she had not guessed the real purpose of his visit. He said, 'Eugene Dazzy told the lobbyist to go fuck himself. Then he told me the story and I said I would take care of it. Now, of course, I know they can't expose Dazzy. For one thing, I'd come down on you and this place so you'd think a tank hit you. I'd make you identify all the people in Congress who used those apartments. There would be one hell of a scandal. Your friend was just hoping Dazzy would lose his nerve. But Eugene figured that one out.'

Jeralyn was still unbelieving. 'Martin would never instigate something so dangerous. He's a banker.' She smiled at Christian who sighed and decided it was time to get tough.

'Listen, Jeralyn,' he said. 'Old "Take Me Private" Martin is not your usual nice stolid conservative banker. He's had a few trouble spots in his life. And he didn't make his billions by playing it safe. He's cut things a bit close before.' He paused for a moment. 'Now he's meddling in something very dangerous for you and for him.'

Jeralyn gave a contemptuous wave of her hand. 'You said yourself you knew I had nothing to do with what the hell ever he is doing.'

'True,' Christian said. 'I know that. But now Martin is a

233

man I have to watch. And I want you to help me watch him.'

Jeralyn was adamant. 'Like hell,' she said. 'Martin has always treated me decently. He's a real friend.'

Christian said, 'I don't want you to be a spy. I don't want any information about his business dealing or about his personal life. All I'm asking is that if you know anything or find out any moves he's going to make against the President, you give me fair warning.'

'Oh, fuck you,' Jeralyn said. 'Get the hell out of here, I have to get ready for the supper crowd.'

'Sure,' Christian said amiably. 'I'm leaving. But remember this, I *am* the Attorney General of the United States. We're in tough times and it doesn't hurt to have me as a friend. So use your own judgment when the time comes. If you slip me just a little warning, no one will ever know. Use your own good sense.'

He left. He had accomplished his purpose. Jeralyn might tell Martin Mutford about their interview, which was fine, for that would make Mutford more cautious. Or she would not tell Martin and when the time came, she'd snitch. Either way he couldn't lose.

Christian Klee had spent no more than thirty minutes with Jeralyn Albanese. Back in his official car he had the driver put on the siren. He had to get back to the White House as soon as possible, Kennedy would be looking for him. But first he had another stop to make. He had received a message from the Oracle. It was a request that he come to see him at his mansion and the message had been urgently phrased.

As his car snaked through traffic, siren screaming, he stared at the monuments, the buildings of marble with fluted columns, the stately domed buildings of embassies with flags flying, the eternal architecture with which established authority proclaimed its existence and supreme power. How worthless they seemed now, just waiting to be razed by

234

outside barbaric hordes, if not physically, then psychologically.

He reviewed the meeting he'd had with Dazzy. The rumor that one of the White House personal staff would sign the petition to remove Kennedy from the Presidency had set off warning signals. After the meeting, he had followed Eugene Dazzy back to the Office of the Chief of Staff.

Eugene Dazzy was at his desk surrounded by three secretaries taking notes for actions to be taken by his own personal staff. He wore his Walkman over his ears but the sound was turned off. And his usual good-humored face was grim. He looked up and said, 'Chris, this is the worst possible time for you to come snooping around.'

Christian said, 'Eugene, don't bullshit me. Nobody seems curious to know who the rumored traitor on the staff is. That means everybody knows, except me. And I'm the guy who should know.'

Dazzy dismissed his secretaries. They were alone in the office. Dazzy smiled at Christian. 'It never occurred to me you didn't know. You keep track of everything with your FBI and Secret Service, your stealth intelligence and listening devices. Those thousands of agents the Congress doesn't know you have on the payroll. How come you're so ignorant?'

Christian said coldly, 'I know you're fucking some dancer twice a week in those apartments that belong to Jeralyn's restaurant.'

Dazzy sighed. 'That's it. This lobbyist who loans me the apartment came to see me. He asked me to sign the removal of the President document. He wasn't crude about it, there were no direct threats but the implication was clear. Sign it or my little sins would be all over the papers and television.' Dazzy laughed. 'I couldn't believe it. How could they be so dumb?'

Christian said, 'So what answer did you give?'

Dazzy smiled. 'I crossed his name off my "friends" list. I

barred him access. And I told him I would give my old buddy Christian Klee his name as a potential threat to the security of the President. Then I told Francis. He told me to forget the whole thing.'

Christian said, 'Who sent the guy?'

Dazzy said 'The only guy who would dare is a member of the Socrates Club. And that would be our old friend, Martin "Take Me Private" Mutford.'

Christian said, 'He's smarter than that.'

'Sure he is,' Dazzy said grimly. 'Everybody is smarter than that until they get desperate. When the VP refused to sign the impeachment memorandum, they became desperate. Besides, you never know when somebody will cave in.'

Christian still didn't like it. 'But they know you. They know that under all that flab you're a tough guy. I've seen you in action. You ran one of the biggest companies in the United States, you cut IBM a new asshole just five years ago. How could they think you'd cave in?'

Dazzy shrugged. 'Everybody always thinks they're tougher than anybody else.' He paused. 'You do it yourself, though you don't advertise it. I do it. So does Wix and so does Gray. Francis doesn't think it. He just can be. And we have to be careful for Francis. We have to be careful he doesn't get too tough.'

The driver cut off the siren and they were gliding through the gates of the Oracle's estate. Christian noted that there were three limousines waiting in the circular driveway. And it was curious that the drivers were in their seats behind the wheel and not outside smoking cigarettes. Beside each car lounged a tall well-dressed man. Christian nailed them at once. Bodyguards. So the Oracle had important visitors.

Christian was greeted by the butler who led him to a living room furnished for a conference. The Oracle was in his wheelchair waiting. Around the table were five members of

236

the Socrates Club. Christian was surprised to see them. His latest report was that all five had been in California.

The Oracle motored his wheelchair to the head of the table. 'You must forgive me, Christian, for this slight deception,' he said, 'I felt it was important that you meet with my friends at this critical time. They are anxious to talk to you.'

Servants had set the conference table with coffee and sandwiches. There were also drinks being served, the servers summoned by a buzzer the Oracle could reach beneath the table. The five members of the Socrates Club had already refreshed themselves. Martin Mutford had lit up a huge cigar and unbuttoned his collar, loosened his tie. He looked a little grim, but Christian knew that his grimness of face was often a tightening of the muscles to conceal fear.

He said, 'Martin, Eugene Dazzy told me one of your lobbyists gave him some bad advice today. I hope you had nothing to do with that.'

'Dazzy can weed out good from bad,' Mutford said. 'Otherwise he wouldn't be the President's Chief of Staff.'

'Sure he can,' Christian said. 'And he doesn't need advice from me on how to break balls. But I can give him a hand.'

Christian could see that the Oracle and George Greenwell did not know what he was talking about. But Lawrence Salentine and Louis Inch were smiling slightly.

Louis Inch said impatiently, 'That's unimportant, not relevant to our meeting here tonight.'

'What the hell is the purpose?' Christian said.

It was Lawrence Salentine who answered him in a smooth calming voice, he was used to handling confrontations. 'This is a very difficult time,' he said. 'I think even a dangerous time. All the people here favor the deposing of President Kennedy for a period of thirty days. Congress will vote tomorrow night in special session. Vice President DuPray's refusal to sign makes things difficult, but not impossible. It would be very helpful if you as a member of the President's personal staff would sign. That is what we are asking you to do.'

Christian was so astonished he could not answer. The Oracle broke in. 'I agree. It will be better for Kennedy not to handle this particular issue. His action today was completely irrational and springs from a desire for vengeance. It could lead to terrible events. Christian, I implore you to listen to these men.'

Christian Klee said very deliberately, 'There is not one chance in hell.' He spoke directly to the Oracle. 'How could you be party to this? How can you, of all people, be against me?'

The Oracle shook his head. 'I'm not against you,' he said.

Lawrence Salentine said, 'He can't just destroy fifty billion dollars because he suffered a personal tragedy. That's not what democracy is about.'

Christian had regained his composure. He said in a reasonable tone of voice, 'That is not the truth. Francis Kennedy has reasoned this out. He doesn't want the hijackers to string us along for weeks milking TV time on your networks, Mr Salentine, with the United States being held up to ridicule. For Christ's sake, they killed the Pope of the Catholic Church, they murdered the daughter of the President of the United States. You want to negotiate with them now? You want to set the killer of the Pope free? You call yourself patriots? You say you worry about this country? You are a bunch of hypocrites.'

For the first time, George Greenwell spoke. 'What about the other hostages? Are you willing to sacrifice them?'

And Christian shot back without thinking. 'Yes.' He paused and then said, 'I think the President's way is the best possible chance to get them out alive.'

George Greenwell said, 'Bert Audick is in Sherhaben now, as you know. He has assured us that he can persuade the hijackers and the Sultan to release the remaining hostages.'

Christian said contemptuously, 'I heard him assure the

238

President of the United States that no harm would come to Theresa Kennedy. And now she's dead.'

Lawrence Salentine said, 'Mr Klee, we can argue all these minor points till Domesday. We haven't got the time. We were hoping you would join us and make it easier. What must be done will be done whether you agree to it or not. I assure you of that. But why make this struggle more divisive? Why not serve the President by working with us?'

Christian Klee looked at him coldly. 'Don't bullshit me. Let me tell you this, I know you men carry a lot of weight in this country, weight that is unconstitutional. My office will investigate all of you as soon as this crisis is over.'

George Greenwell gave a sigh. The violent and senseless ire of young men was boring to a man of his experience and age. He said to Christian, 'Mr Klee, we all thank you for coming. And I hope there will be no personal animosity. We are acting to help our country.'

Christian said, 'You are acting to save Audick his fifty billion dollars.' He had a flash of insight. These men did not have a real hope of recruiting him. This was simply intimidation. That he would possibly remain neutral. Then he got their sense of fear. They feared him. That he had the power and more importantly he had the will. And the only one who could have warned them about him was the Oracle.

They were all silent. Then the Oracle said, 'You can go, I know you have to get back. Call me and let me know what's happening. Keep me abreast.'

Christian, hurt by the Oracle's betrayal, said, 'You could have warned me.'

The Oracle shook his head. 'You wouldn't have come. And I couldn't convince my friends that you wouldn't sign. I had to give them their shot.' He paused for a moment. 'I'll see you out,' he said to Christian. And he rolled his wheelchair out of the room. Christian followed him.

Before Christian left the room he turned to the members of the Socrates Club and said, 'Gentlemen, I beg of you, don't let the Congress do this.' He gave off such a grave menace that nobody spoke.

When the Oracle and Klee were alone on the top of the ramp leading to the entrance foyer, the Oracle braced his wheelchair. He lifted his head, so freckled with the brown of aging skin, and said to Christian, 'You are my godson, and you are my heir. All this doesn't change my affection for you. But be warned. I love my country and I perceive your Francis Kennedy as a great danger.'

For the first time Christian Klee felt a bitterness against this old man he had always loved. 'You and your Socrates Club have Francis by the balls,' he said. 'You people are the danger.'

The Oracle was studying him. 'But you don't seem too worried. Christian, I beg of you don't be rash. Don't do something irrevocable. I know you have a great deal of power and more importantly a great deal of cunning. You are gifted, I know. But don't try to overpower history.'

'I don't know what you are talking about,' Christian said. He was in a hurry now. He had his last stop to make before going back to the White House. He had to interrogate Gresse and Tibbot.

The Oracle sighed, 'Remember, no matter what happens I still have my affection. You are the only living person I love. And if it is within my power I will never let anything happen to you. Call me, keep me abreast.'

Christian felt again his old affection for the Oracle. He squeezed his shoulder and said, 'What the hell, it's only a political difference, we've had them before. Don't worry, I'll call you.'

The Oracle gave him a crooked smile. 'And don't forget my birthday party. When this is all over if we are both alive.'

And Christian to his astonishment saw the tears dropping on to that withered, aged, seamed face. He leaned only to kiss that cheek, so parched that it was cool as glass.

*

240

When Christian Klee got back to the White House, he went directly to Oddblood Gray's office but the secretary told him that Gray was having a conference with Congressman Jintz and Senator Lambertino. The secretary looked frightened. She had heard rumors that Congress was trying to remove President Kennedy from office.

Christian said, 'Buzz him, tell him it's important and let me use your desk and phone. You go to the ladies' room.'

Gray answered the phone, thinking he was talking to his secretary. 'It better be important,' he said.

Christian said, 'Otto, it's Chris. Listen I've just been asked by some guys in the Socrates Club to sign the removal memo. Dazzy was asked to sign, they tried to blackmail him over that affair with the dancer. I know Wix is on his way to Sherhaben so he's not signing the petition. Are you signing?'

Oddblood Gray's voice was very silky. 'It's funny, I've just been asked to sign by the two gentlemen in my office. I already told them I would not. And I told them nobody else on the personal staff would sign. I didn't have to ask you.' There was sarcasm in his voice.

Christian said impatiently, 'I knew you wouldn't sign, Otto. But I had to ask. But look, put out some lightning bolts. Tell those guys that as the Attorney General, I'm launching an investigation into the blackmail threat on Dazzy. Also, that I have a lot of stuff on some of those Congressmen and Senators that won't look too good in the papers and I'll leak it. Especially their business with members of the Socrates Club. This is no time for your English Oxford bullshit.'

Oddblood Gray said smoothly, 'Thanks for the advice, old buddy. But why don't you take care of your stuff and I'll take care of mine. And don't ask other people to wave your sword around, wave it yourself.'

There had always been a subtle antagonism between Oddblood Gray and Christian Klee. Personally they liked and respected each other. Both were physically impressive, Gray had a social bravery. But he had achieved everything on his own. Christian Klee had been born to wealth but had refused to live the life of a rich man. He had been a physically brave officer and then a CIA Field Director directly involved in clandestine operations. They were both respected men in the world. They were both devoted to Francis Kennedy. They were both skilled lawyers.

And yet they were both wary of each other. Oddblood Gray had the utmost faith in the progress of society through law, which was why he was so valuable as the President's liaison man with Congress. And he had always distrusted the consolidation of power Klee had put together. It was too much that in a country like the United States any man should be Director of the FBI, Chief of the Secret Service and also Attorney General. True, Francis Kennedy had explained his reasons for this concentration of power. That it was to help protect the President himself against the threat of assassination. But Gray still didn't like it.

Christian Klee had always been a little impatient with Gray's scrupulous attention to every legality. Gray could afford to be the punctilious statesman. He dealt with politicians and political problems. But Christian Klee felt he had to shovel away the murderous shit of everyday life. The election of Francis Kennedy had brought all the cockroaches from the fabric of America. Only Klee knew the thousands of murder threats the President had received. Only Klee could stamp those cockroaches dead. And he couldn't always observe the finer points of the law to do his job. Or so Klee believed.

Now was a case in point. Klee wanted to use power, Gray the velvet glove.

'OK,' said Christian said. 'I'll do what I have to do.'

'Fine,' Oddblood Gray said. 'Now me and you can go together to see the President. He wants us in the Cabinet Room as soon as I'm through here.'

Oddblood Gray had been deliberately indiscreet while on the phone with Christian Klee. Now he faced Congressman Jintz and Senator Lambertino and gave them a rueful smile. 'I'm sorry you had to hear that,' he said to them. 'Christian doesn't like this impeachment business, but he makes it a personal thing when it's a matter of the country's welfare.'

Senator Lambertino said, 'I advised against approaching Klee. But I thought we had a chance with you, Otto. When the President appointed you as liaison to Congress, I thought it a foolhardy thing to do, what with all our Southern colleagues who are not fully reconstructed. But I must say you have won them over in these past three years. If the President listened to you, his programs would not have gone down in Congress.'

Oddblood Gray kept his face impassive. He said in his silky voice, 'I'm glad you came to me. But I think Congress is making a big mistake with this impeachment proceeding. The Vice President hasn't signed up. Sure you've got nearly all of the Cabinet, but none of the staff. So Congress can override the express vote of the people of this country.'

Oddblood Gray got up and started pacing the room. Usually he never did this when he was negotiating. He knew the impression he made. He was too overpowering physically, and it would seem like an offensive gesture of domination. He was nearly six feet four, his clothes were beautifully tailored and his physique was that of an Olympic athlete. He had just a touch of intimidation.

'You are both men I have admired in Congress,' he said. 'We have always understood each other. You know I advised Kennedy not to go forward with his social programs until he laid a better groundwork. All three of us understand one important thing. There is no greater opening for tragedy than a stupid exercise of power. It is one of the most common mistakes in politics. But that is exactly what Congress is going to do when they impeach the President. If you succeed, you start a very dangerous precedent in our government that could lead to fatal repercussions when some President acquires excess power in the future. He may then make his first aim the emasculation of Congress. And what do you gain here in the short term? You prevent the destruction of Dak and its fifty billion dollar investment by Bert Audick, and the people of this country will despise you, for make no mistake, the people support Kennedy's action. Maybe for the wrong reasons, we all know that the electorate is too easily swayed by obvious emotions, emotions we as governors have to control and redirect. Kennedy right now can order atom bombs dropped on Sherhaben and the people of this country would approve. Stupid? OK. But that's how the masses feel. You know that. So the smart thing is for the Congress to lay back, to see if Kennedy's actions get the hostages back and the hijackers in our prisons. Then everybody's happy. If the policy fails, if the hijackers slaughter the hostages, then you can remove the President and look like heroes.'

Oddblood had tried his best pitch but he knew it was hopeless. From long experience, he had learned that even the wisest of men or women once they wished to do a thing, they would do it. No manner of persuasion could change their minds. They would do what they wanted to do, simply because it was their will.

Congressman Jintz did not disappoint him. 'You are arguing against the will of the Congress, Otto.'

Senator Lambertino said, 'Really, Otto, you're fighting a lost cause. I know your loyalty to the President. I know that if everything had gone well the President would have made you a Cabinet member. And let me tell you, the Senate would have approved. That still can happen, but not under Kennedy.'

Oddblood Gray nodded his thanks. 'I appreciate that, Senator. But I can't comply with your request. I think the President is justified in the action he's taken. I think that action will be effective. I think the hostages will be released and the criminal given into custody.'

Jintz said abruptly and crudely, 'This is all beside the point. We can't let him destroy the city of Dak.'

Senator Lambertino said softly, 'It's not just the money. Such a savage act would hurt our relationships with every country in the world. You see that, Otto.'

Oddblood Gray said, 'I don't have to worry about foreign relations. I just deal with the Congress for the President. And I can see you gentlemen don't agree with me. So let me tell you this. Unless Congress cancels its special session tomorrow, unless it withdraws the motion to impeach, the President will appeal directly to the people of the United States on television. And you know how good the President is on the tube. He will massacre Congress. And then, who knows what will happen? Especially if your plans go wrong and the hostages are killed anyway. Please present this to your fellow members.' He resisted saying, 'And to the Socrates Club.'

They parted company with those protestations of good will and affection that have been political good manners since the murder of Julius Caesar. Then Oddblood Gray went out to pick up Christian Klee for the meeting with the President.

But his last speech had shaken Congressman Jintz. Jintz had accrued a great deal of wealth during his many years in Congress. His wife was a partner or stockholder in cable television companies in his home state, his son's law firm was one of the biggest in the south. He had no material worries. But he loved his life as a Congressman, it brought him pleasures that could not be bought with mere money. The marvellous thing about being a successful politician was that old age could be as happy as your youth. Even as a doddering old man, your brain floating away in a flood of senile cells, everyone still respected you, listened to you, kissed your ass. You had the Congressional committees and subcommittees, you could wallow in the pork barrels. You could still help steer the course of the greatest country in the world. Though your body was old and feeble, young virile men trembled before you. At some time, Jintz knew, his appetite for food and drink and women would fade, but if there was still one last living cell in his brain he could enjoy power. And how can you really fear the nearness of death when your fellow man still obeys you?

And so Jintz was worried. Was it possible by some catastrophe his seat in Congress could be lost? There was no way out. His very life depended on the removal of Francis Kennedy from office. He said to Senator Lambertino, 'We can't let the President go on TV tomorrow.'

13

Matthew Gladyce, the Press Secretary to the President, knew that in the next twenty-four hours he would make the most important decisions of his professional life. It was his job to control the responses of the media to the tragic and world-shocking events of the last three days. It would be his job to inform the people of the United States just exactly what their President was doing to cope with these events, and to justify his actions. Gladyce had to be very careful.

Now on this Thursday morning after Easter, in the middle of the crisis fireball, Matthew Gladyce cut himself off from direct contact with the media. His junior assistants held the meetings in the White House Press Conference Room but were limited to handing out carefully composed press releases and ducking shouted questions.

Matthew did not answer the phones constantly ringing in his office, his secretaries screened all his calls and brushed off insistent reporters, the highest powered TV commentators trying to call in markers he owed them. It was his job to protect the President of the United States.

Matthew Gladyce knew from his long experience as a journalist that there was no ritual more revered in America than the traditional insolence of the print and TV media toward important members of the establishment. Imperious TV anchor stars shouted down affable Cabinet members, knocked chips off the shoulders of the President himself, grilled candidates for high office with the ferocity of prosecuting attorneys. The newspapers printed libelous articles in

247

the name of free speech. At one time he had been a part of all this and even admired it. He had enjoyed the inevitable hatred that every public official has for representatives of the media. But three years as Press Secretary had changed this. Like the rest of the Administration, indeed like all government figures down through history, he had come to distrust and devalue that great institution of democracy called free speech. Like all authority figures he had come to regard it as assault and battery. The media were sanctified criminals who robbed institutions and private citizens of their good name. Just to sell their newspapers and commercials to three hundred million people.

And today he would not give those bastards an inch. He was going to throw his fast ball by them.

He thought back on the last four days and all the questions he had fielded from the media. The President had cut himself off from all direct communication and Matthew Gladyce had carried the ball. On Monday it had been, 'Why haven't the hijackers made any demands? Is the kidnapping of the President's daughter linked to the killing of the Pope?' Those questions eventually answered themselves, thank God. Now it was established. They were linked. The hijackers had made their demands.

Gladyce had issued the press release under the direct supervision of the President himself. These events were a concerted attack on the prestige and worldwide authority of the United States. Then the murder of the President's daughter and the stupid fucking questions. 'How did the President react when he heard of the murder?' Here Gladyce lost his temper. 'What the fuck do you think he felt, you stupid bastard?' he told the anchor person. Then there had been another stupid question, 'Does this bring back memories of when the President's uncles were murdered?' At that moment Gladyce decided he would leave these press conferences to his juniors.

But now he had to take the stage. He would have to

defend the President's ultimatum to the Sultan of Sherhaben. He would cut out the threat to destroy the Sultanate of Sherhaben. He would say that if the hostages were released and Yabril imprisoned, the city of Dak would not be destroyed. In language to leave him an out when Dak was destroyed. But most important of all he would say that the President of the United States would go on televison in the afternoon with a major address to the nation.

He glanced out of the window of his office. The White House was surrounded by TV trucks and media correspondents from all over the world. Well fuck them, Gladyce thought. They would only know what he wanted them to know.

The envoys of the United States arrived in Sherhaben. Their plane set down on a parallel runway far away from the hostage lane commanded by Yabril and still surrounded by Sherhaben troops. Behind those troops were the hordes of TV trucks, media correspondents from all over the world and a vast crowd of onlookers who had travelled from the city of Dak.

The Ambassador of Sherhaben, Sharif Waleeb, had taken pills to sleep through most of the voyage. Bert Audick and Arthur Wix had talked, Audick trying to persuade Wix to modify the President's demands, so that they could get the release of the hostages without any drastic action.

Finally Wix told Audick, 'I have no leeway to negotiate. I have a very strict brief from the President, they've had their fun and now they are going to pay.'

Audick said grimly, 'You're the National Security Advisor, for God's sake, advise.'

Wix said stonily, 'There is nothing to advise. The President has made his decision.'

Upon arrival at the Sultan's palace, Wix and Audick were escorted to their palatial suites by armed guards. Indeed the palace seemed to be overrun with military formations.

Ambassador Waleeb was ushered into the presence of the Sultan where he formally presented the ultimatum documents.

In the ornate official conference room they formally embraced, but since they were in Western clothes they both felt awkward doing so.

The Sultan said, 'The cables and your telephone conversation with me is something I cannot believe. Surely, my dear Waleeb, it must be a bluff. It goes against everything in the American character. They will destroy their world reputation for international morality, and they will go against their own ingrained greed. If they destroy Dak they lose fifty billion. What is this threat of the most dire circumstances?'

Waleeb, a tiny man, dapper as a puppet, was so terrified that the Sultan pressed his hand to give him courage enough to speak.

'Your Highness,' Sharif Waleeb said, 'I beg of you to consider this most carefully. They have film that shows you support Yabril. It is beyond question. As for President Kennedy, he is not bluffing. The city of Dak will be destroyed. And as for the dire consequences which are in his memorandum, and which are known to his Congress and government staff, that is even worse than it appears. He gave me this message to give you personally. A message which he cleverly does not allow to be official. He swears that if you do not comply with his demands to free the hostages and give up Yabril, the state of Sherhaben will cease to exist.'

The Sultan did not believe the threat, anybody could terrify this little man. He said, 'And when Kennedy told you this, how did he appear? Is he a man who utters such wild threats merely to frighten? Would his government even support such an action? He would be gambling his whole political career on this one throw of the dice. Is it not merely a negotiating ploy?'

Waleeb rose from the gold brocaded chair in which he

had been sitting. Suddenly his tiny puppet-like figure became impressive. He had a good voice, the Sultan noted. 'Your Highness,' Waleeb said. 'Kennedy knew exactly what you would say, word for word. Within twenty-four hours after the destruction of Dak, if you do not comply with his demands, all Sherhaben will be destroyed. And that is why Dak cannot be saved. That is the only way he can convince you of his most serious intent. He also said that after Dak is destroyed you will agree to his demands but not before. He was calm, he smiled. He is no longer the man he was. He is Azazel.'

Later, the two envoys of the President of the United States were brought to a beautiful reception room that included air-conditioned terraces and a swimming pool. They were attended by male servants in Arab dress who brought them food and drinks, that were not alcoholic. Surrounded by counselors and bodyguards, the Sultan greeted them.

Ambassador Waleeb made the introductions. Bert Audick, the Sultan knew. They had been closely interlocked on past oil deals. And Audick had been his host the several times he had visited America, a discreet and obliging host. The Sultan greeted Audick warmly.

The second man was the surprise and in the stirring clutch of his heartbeat, the Sultan recognized the presence of danger and began to believe the reality of Kennedy's threat. For the second Tribune, as the Sultan thought of them, was none other than Arthur Wix, the President's National Security Advisor, and a Jew. He was by reputation the most powerful military figure in the United States and the ultimate enemy of the Arab States in their fight against Israel. The Sultan noted that Arthur Wix did not offer his hand, only bowed with cold courtesy.

The next thought in the Sultan's mind was that if the President's threat was real, why would he send such a high official into such danger? What if he took these Tribunes as hostages, would they not perish in any attack on Sherhaben? And indeed would Bert Audick come and risk a possible death? From what he knew of Audick, certainly not. So that meant there was room for negotiation and that the Kennedy threat was a bluff. Or, Kennedy was simply a madman and did not care what happened to his envoys and would carry out his threat anyway. He looked around at his reception room that served as his chamber of State. It was far more luxurious than anything in the White House. The walls were painted gold, the carpets were the most expensive in the world with exquisite patterns that could never be duplicated, the marble the purest and most intricately worked. How could all this be destroyed?

The Sultan said with quiet dignity, 'My Ambassador has given me the message from your President. I find it very hard to believe that the leader of the free world would dare to utter such a threat, much less implement it. And I am at a loss. What influence can I have over this bandit, Yabril? Is your President another Attila the Hun? Does he imagine he rules ancient Rome rather than America?'

It was Audick who spoke first. He said, 'Sultan Maurobi, I came here as your friend, to help you and your country. The President means to do as he threatens. It seems you have no alternative, you must give up this man Yabril.'

The Sultan was quiet for a long moment then turned to Arthur Wix. He said ironically, 'And what are you doing here? Can America spare an important man like yourself if I refuse to comply with your President's demands?'

'The fact you would hold us as hostages if you refused those demands was carefully discussed,' Arthur Wix said. He was absolutely impassive. He did not show the anger and hatred he was feeling for the Sultan. 'As the head of an independent country you are quite justified in your anger and in your counter threat. But that is the very reason I am here. To assure you that the necessary military orders have been given. As the Commander in Chief of American military forces, the President has that power. The city of Dak will shortly be no more. Twenty-four hours after that, if you do not comply, the country of Sherhaben will also be destroyed. All this will be no more,' he gestured around the room, 'and you will be living on the charity of the rulers of your neighboring countries. You will be a Sultan still, but you will be a Sultan of nothing'

The Sultan did not show his rage. He turned to the other American. He said, 'Do you have anything to add?'

Bert Audick said almost slyly, 'There is no question Kennedy means to carry out his threat. But there are other people in our government who disagree. This action may doom his Presidency.' He said almost apologetically to Arthur Wix, 'I think we have to bring this out in open.'

Wix looked at him grimly. He had feared this possibility. Strategically it was always possible that Audick might try to make an end run. The bastard was going to try to undermine the whole deal. Just to save his fucking fifty billion.

Arthur Wix looked venomously at Audick and said to the Sultan, 'There is no room for negotiation.'

Audick gave Wix a defiant glance and then addressed the Sultan again. 'I think it fair, based on our long relationship, to tell you there is one hope. And I feel I must do it now in front of my countryman, rather than in a private audience with you as I could easily do. The Congress of the United States is holding a special session to impeach President Kennedy. If we can announce the news that you are releasing the hostages, I guarantee Dak will not be destroyed.'

The Sultan said, 'And I will not have to give up Yabril?'

'No,' Audick said. 'But you must not insist on the release of the Pope's killer.'

The Sultan, for all his good manners, could not completely disguise the note of glee when he said, 'Mr Wix, is this not a more reasonable solution?'

'My President impeached because a terrorist murdered his

253

daughter? And then the murderer goes free?' Wix said. 'No, it is not.'

Audick said, 'We can always get that guy later.'

Wix gave him a look of such contempt and hatred, that Audick knew this man would be his enemy for life.

The Sultan said, 'In two hours we will all meet with my friend Yabril. We will dine together, and come to an agreement. I will persuade him with sweet words or force. But the hostages will go free as soon as we learn that the city of Dak is safe. Gentlemen, you have my promise as a Muslim and as the ruler of Sherhaben.'

Then the Sultan gave orders for his communications center to notify him of the congressional vote as soon as it was known. He had the American envoys escorted to their rooms to bathe and change their clothing.

The Sultan had ordered Yabril to be smuggled off the plane and brought to the palace. Yabril was made to wait in the huge reception hall and he noted that it was filled with the Sultan's uniformed security guards. There had been other signs that the palace was on an alert status. Yabril sensed immediately that he was in danger but there was nothing to be done.

When Yabril was ushered into the Sultan's reception room he was relieved that the Sultan embraced him. Then the Sultan briefed him on what had happened with the American Tribunes. The Sultan said, 'I promised them you would release the hostages without further negotiations. Now we await the decision of the American Congress.'

Yabril said, 'But that means that my friend, Romeo, has been deserted by me. It is a blow to my reputation.'

The Sultan smiled and said, 'When they try him for murder of the Pope, your cause will gain that much more publicity. And the fact that you go free after that coup and murdering the daughter of the President of the United States, *that* is glory. But what a nasty little surprise you gave me at the

254

end. To kill a young girl in cold blood. That was not to my liking and really not clever.'

'It made a certain point,' Yabril said.

'And now you must be satisfied,' the Sultan said. 'In effect you have unseated the President of the United States. Which was beyond your wildest dreams.'

The Sultan gave a command to one of his retinue. 'Go to the quarters of the American, Mr Audick, and bring him here to us.'

When Bert Audick came into the room he did not offer to shake hands with Yabril or make any gesture of acknowledgment. He simply stared. Yabril bowed his head and smiled. He was familiar with these types, these bloodsuckers of Arabian lifeblood, who made contracts with Sultans and Kings to enrich America and other foreign states.

The Sultan said, 'Mr Audick, please explain to my friend the mechanics of how your Congress will dispose of your President.'

Audick did so. He was convincing, Yabril believed him. But he asked, 'What if something goes wrong and you do not get your two-thirds vote?'

Audick said grimly, 'Then you, me and the Sultan here, are shit out of luck.'

President Francis Xavier Kennedy looked over the papers that Matthew Gladyce presented and then initialed them. He saw the look of satisfaction on Gladyce's face and knew exactly what it meant. That together they were putting one over on the American public. At another time, in other circumstances, he would have destroyed that look of smugness, but Francis Kennedy realized that this was the single most dangerous moment in his political career, and he must use every weapon available.

This evening the Congress would try to impeach him. They would use the vague wording of the Twenty-fifth Amendment to the Constitution to do so. Maybe he could

255

win the battle in the long run, but by then it would be too late. Bert Audick would arrange the release of the hostages, the escape of Yabril in return for the remaining hostages. The death of his daughter would go unavenged, the murderer of the Pope would go free. But Kennedy counted on his appeal to the nation over TV to launch such a wave of protesting telegrams as to make Congress waver. He knew the people would support his action, they were outraged at the murder of the Pope and of his daughter. They felt his heartbreak. And at that moment he felt a fierce communion with the people. They were his allies against the corrupt Congress, the pragmatic and merciless businessmen like Bert Audick.

As all through his life, he felt the tragedies of the unfortunate, the mass of people struggling through life. Early in his career he had sworn to himself that he would never be corrupted by that love of money that seemed to generate all the accomplishments of gifted men. He grew to despise the power of the rich, money used as a sword. But he had always felt, he realized now, that he was some sort of champion who was invulnerable and above the woes of his fellow man. He had always felt a part of the rich though he championed the poor. He had never before grasped the hatred that the underclass must feel. But he felt it now. Now the rich, the powerful, would bring him down, now he must win for his own sake. And now he felt the hatred.

But he refused to indulge himself. His mind must be clear in the coming crisis. Even if he were impeached, he must make sure he would return to power. And then his plans would be far-reaching. The Congress and the rich might win this battle but he saw clearly that they must lose the war. The people of the United States would not suffer humiliation gladly, there would be another election in November. This whole crisis could be in his favor even if lost; his tragedy one of his weapons. But he had to be careful to hide these long-range plans even from his staff.

Kennedy understood he was preparing himself for ultimate power. There was no other course except to submit to defeat and all its anguish and that he could never survive.

On Thursday afternoon, nine hours before the special session of Congress that would impeach the President of the United States from office, Francis Kennedy met with his advisors, his staff and Vice President Helen DuPray.

It was to be their last strategy session before the Congressional vote and they all knew the enemy had the necessary two thirds. Francis Kennedy saw immediately the mood in the room was one of depression and defeat.

He gave them all a cheerful smile and opened the meeting by thanking the CIA Chief, Theodore Tappy, for not having signed the impeachment proposal. Then he turned to the Vice President, Helen DuPray, and laughed, a genuine good-humored laugh.

'Helen,' he said with unaffected delight, 'I wouldn't be in your shoes for anything in the world. Do you realize how many enemies you made when you refused to sign the impeachment papers? You could have been the first woman President of the United States. Congress hates you because without your signature they can't get away with it. Men will hate you for being so magnanimous. Feminists will consider you a traitor. God, how did an old pro like you get in such a fix? By the way, I want to thank you for your loyalty.'

'They are wrong, Mr President,' Helen DuPray said. 'And they are wrong now to pursue it. Is there a chance for any negotiation with Congress?'

'I can't,' Francis Kennedy said. 'And they won't.' Then Kennedy said to Dazzy, 'Have my orders been followed, is the naval air fleet on its way to Dak?'

'Yes, sir,' Dazzy said, then shifted uncomfortably in his chair. 'But the Chiefs of Staff have not given the final go. They will hold back until Congress votes tonight. If the impeachment succeeds, they will send the planes home.' He

257

paused for a moment. 'They haven't disobeyed you. They have followed your orders. They just figure they can countermand everything if you lose tonight.'

Kennedy turned to Helen DuPray. His face was grave. 'If the impeachment succeeds you will be the President,' he said. 'You can order the Chiefs of Staff to proceed with the destruction of the city of Dak. Will you give that order?'

'No,' Helen DuPray said. There was a long uncomfortable silence in the room. Helen DuPray kept her face composed and spoke directly to Kennedy. 'I have proved my loyalty to you,' she said. 'As your Vice President, I supported your decision on Dak, as it was my duty to do. I resisted the demand to sign the impeachment papers. But if I become President, and I hope with all my heart I will not, then I must follow my own conscience and make my own decision.'

Francis Kennedy nodded. He smiled at her and it was a gentle smile that broke her heart. 'You are perfectly right,' he said gently. 'I asked the question merely as a point of information, not to persuade.' He addressed the others in the room. 'Now the most important thing is to get a bare bones script ready for my television speech. Eugene, have you cleared networks? Have they broadcast bulletins that I will speak tonight?'

Eugene Dazzy said cautiously, 'Lawrence Salentine is here to see you about that. It looks fishy. Shall I have him sent here? He's in my office.'

Francis Kennedy said softly, 'They wouldn't dare. They wouldn't dare to show their muscle so out in the open.' He was thoughtful for a long moment. 'Send him in.'

While they waited they discussed how long the speech would be. 'Not more than a half-hour,' Kennedy said. 'I should get the job done by then.'

And they all knew what he meant. Francis Kennedy on television could overpower any audience except Congress. It was the handsomeness of the face, the startling blue eyes, the controlled energy of his body. It was the magical speaking voice with the melodies in the lyrics of the great Irish poets. It didn't hurt that his thinking, the progress of his logic was always absolutely clear. Congress and the Socrates Club would be the villains of America. And all this backed by the magical myth of his two martyred uncles.

When Lawrence Salentine was ushered in, Kennedy spoke to him directly and without greeting. 'I hope you're not going to say what I think you're going to say.'

Salentine said coolly, 'I have no way of knowing what you're thinking. I've been chosen by the other networks to give you our decision not to give you air time tonight. For us to do so would be to interfere in the impeachment process.'

Kennedy smiled and said to him, 'Mr Salentine, the impeachment, even if successful, will only last for thirty days. And then what?'

It was not Francis Kennedy's style to be threatening. It occurred to Salentine that he and the heads of the other networks had embarked on a very dangerous game. The legal justification of the federal government to issue and review licenses for TV stations had become archaic in practical terms, but a strong President could put new teeth in it. Salentine knew he had to go very carefully.

'Mr President,' he said. 'It is because we feel our responsibility is so important that we must refuse you the air time. You are in the process of impeachment, much to my regret, and to the sorrow of all Americans. It is a very great tragedy, and you have all my sympathy. But the networks agree that letting you speak would not be in the best interests of the nation or our democratic process.' He paused for a moment. 'But after Congress votes, win or lose, we will give you air time.'

Francis Kennedy laughed angrily and said, 'You can go.'

Lawrence Salentine was escorted out by one of the Secret Service guards.

Then Kennedy said to his staff, 'Gentlemen, believe me

when I tell you this,' Kennedy's face was unsmiling, the blue of his eyes seemed to have gone from a light to heavier slatier blue, 'They have overplayed their hand. They have violated the spirit of the Constitution.'

For miles around the White House, traffic had become congested with only thin corridors to pass through official vehicles. TV cameras and their back-up trucks commanded the whole area. Congressmen on their way to Capitol Hill were unceremoniously grabbed by TV journalists and questioned on this special meeting of the Congress. Finally, an official bulletin appeared on TV networks that the Congress was convening at eleven p.m. to vote on a motion to remove President Kennedy from office.

In the White House itself, Kennedy and his staff had already done everything they could to ward off the attack. Oddblood Gray had called Senators and Congressmen, pleading with them. Eugene Dazzy had made countless calls to different members of the Socrates Club trying to enlist the support of some segments of big business. Christian Klee had sent legal briefs to the leaders of Congress stressing that without the signature of the Vice President, the removal was illegal. Congress had rejected this.

Just before eleven, Kennedy and his staff met in the Yellow Room to watch the big television screen that was wheeled in. For though the session of Congress would not be broadcast over commercial networks, it was being photographed for later use and a special cable brought it to the White House.

Congressman Jintz and Senator Lambertino had done their work well. Everything had been synchronized perfectly. Patsy Troyca and Elizabeth Stone had worked closely together to iron out administrative details. All the necessary documents had been prepared for the turnover of government.

In the Yellow Room, Francis Kennedy and his personal

staff watched the proceedings on their television. It would take Congress time to go throuh all the formalities of speeches and roll calls to vote. But they knew what the outcome would be. Congress and the Socrates Club had built a steamroller for this occasion. Kennedy said to Oddblood Gray, 'Otto, you did your best.'

At that moment, one of the White House duty officers came in and handed Dazzy a memo sheet. Dazzy looked at it, then studied it. The shock on his face was evident. He handed the memorandum to Kennedy.

On the TV screen, Congress had just voted to impeach Francis Xavier Kennedy from the Presidency.

It was eleven p.m. Thursday, Washington time, but six in the morning in Sherhaben when the Sultan had everyone summoned to the terraced reception room for an early breakfast. The Americans, Bert Audick and Arthur Wix arrived shortly. Yabril was escorted in by the Sultan. A huge table was laden with countless fruits and beverages, both hot and cold.

Sultan Maurobi was smiling broadly. He did not introduce Yabril to the Americans and there was no pretense of any courtesy.

The Sultan said, 'I am happy to announce, more than that, my heart overflows with joy, that my friend Yabril has agreed to the release of your hostages. There will be no further demands from him and I hope no further demands from your country.'

Arthur Wix, his face beaded with sweat, said, 'I cannot negotiate or change in any way the demands of my President. You must give up this murderer.'

The Sultan smiled and said, 'He is no longer your President. The American Congress has voted to impeach him. I am informed that the orders to bomb the city of Dak have already been canceled. The hostages will be freed, you have your victory. There is nothing else you can ask.'

Yabril stared into Wix's eyes and saw the hatred there.

261

This was the highest man in the mightiest army on the face of the globe and he, Yabril, had defeated him. Yabril felt a great rush of energy go through his body, he had impeached the President of the United States. For a moment his mind held the image of himself pressing the gun against the silky hair of Theresa Kennedy. He remembered again that sense of loss, of regret when he pulled the trigger, the little burn of anguish as her body tumbled away in the desert air. He bowed his head to Wix and the other men in the room.

The Sultan Maurobi motioned for the servants to bring platters of fruit and drink to his guests. Arthur Wix put down his glass and said, 'Are you sure that your information that the President has been impeached is absolutely correct?'

The Sultan said, 'I will arrange for you to speak directly to your office in the United States.' He paused. 'But first, I have my duty as a host.'

The Sultan commanded they must have one last full meal together, and insisted that the final arrangements for the release of the hostages be made over this meal. Yabril took his place at the right hand of the Sultan, Arthur Wix on the left.

They were resting on the divans along the low table when the Sultan's Prime Minister came hurrying in and begged the Sultan to come into the other room for a few moments. The Sultan was impatient until finally the Prime Minister whispered something into his ear. The Sultan raised his eyebrows in surprise and then he said to his guest, 'Something has happened quite unforeseen. All communication to the United States has been cut off, not just to us, but all over the world. Please continue your breakfast while I confer with my staff.'

But after the Sultan left, the men around the table did not speak. Only Yabril helped himself to the hot smoking dishes and fruits.

Gradually the Americans moved away from the table and gathered on the terrace. The servants brought them cool drinks. Yabril continued to eat.

On the terrace, Bert Audick said to Wix, 'I hope Kennedy hasn't done something foolish. I hope he hasn't tried to buck the constitution.'

Wix said, 'God, first his daughter, now he's lost his country. All because of that little prick in there eating like a fucking beggar.'

Bert Audick said, 'It is terrible, all of it.' Then Audick went in to the dining table inside and said to Yabril, 'Eat well, I hope you have a good place to hide in the years to come. There will be a lot of people looking for you.'

Yabril laughed. He had finished eating and was lighting a cigarette. 'Oh, yes,' he said. 'I will be a beggar in Jerusalem.'

At that moment the Sultan Maurobi came into the room. He was followed by at least fifty armed men who stationed themselves to command the room. Four of them stood behind Yabril. Four others stood behind the Americans on the terrace. There was surprise and shock on the Sultan's face. His skin seemed yellow, his eyes were wide open, the eyelids seemed to fold back. 'Gentlemen,' he said, haltingly, 'my dear sirs, this will be as incredible to you as it is to me. Congress has annulled their vote impeaching Kennedy and he has declared martial law.' He paused and let his hand rest on Yabril's shoulder. 'And gentlemen, at this moment planes from the American Sixth Fleet are destroying my city of Dak.'

Arthur Wix asked almost jubilantly, 'The city of Dak is being bombed?'

'Yes,' the Sultan said. 'A barbaric act but a convincing one.'

They were all looking at Yabril who now had four armed men very closely surrounding him. Yabril lit a cigarette and said thoughtfully, 'Finally I will see America, it has always been my dream.' He looked at the Americans but spoke to the Sultan. 'I think I would have been a great success in America.'

'Without a doubt,' the Sultan said. 'Part of the demand is

that I deliver you alive. I'm afraid I must give the necessary orders so that you do not harm yourself.'

Yabril said, 'America is a civilized country. I will go through a legal process that will be long and drawn out, since I will have the best lawyers. Why should I harm myself? It will be a new experience and who knows what can happen? The world always changes. America is too civilized for torture and besides I have endured torture under the Israelis so nothing will surprise me.' He smiled at Wix.

Arthur Wix said quietly, 'As you once observed, the world changes. You haven't succeeded. You won't be such a hero.'

Yabril laughed delightedly. His arms went up in an exuberant gesture. 'I have succeeded,' he almost shouted. 'I've torn your world off its axis. Do you think your mealy-mouthed idealism will be listened to after your planes have destroyed the city of Dak? When will the world forget my name? And do you think I will step off the stage now when the best is yet to come?'

The Sultan clapped his hands and shouted an order to the soldiers. They grabbed Yabril and put handcuffs on his wrists and rope around his neck. 'Gently, gently,' the Sultan said. When Yabril was secure he touched him gently on the forehead. He said, 'I beg your forgiveness, I have no choice. I have oil to sell and a city to rebuild. I wish you well, old friend. Good luck in America.'

As Congress impeached President Francis Xavier Kennedy, possibly illegally, as the world awaited the resolution of the terrorist crisis, there were many hundreds of thousands of people in New York who didn't give a flying fuck. They had their own lives to lead and their own problems. This Thursday night many of these thousands converged in the Times Square area of New York City, a place that once had been the very heart of the greatest city in the world, where once Great White Way, Broadway itself, ran down from Central Park to Times Square.

264

These people had varied interests. Horny, yearning, sub-
urban, middle-class men haunted the adult pornographic
book shops. *Cinéastes* surveyed miles of film of naked men,
naked women indulging themselves in the most intimate
sexual acts with varied animals in best-friend character roles.
Teenaged gangs with lethal but legal screwdrivers in their
pockets sallied forth as gallantly as the knights of old to slay
the dragons of the well-to-do, and with the irrepressible high
good spirits of the young, to have some laughs. Pimps,
prostitutes, muggers, murderers, set up shop after dark
without even having to pay overheads for the bright neon
light of what was left of the Great White Way. Tourist lambs
came bleating to see Times Square where the ball fell on
New Year's Eve and proclaimed the coming of another
joyous New Year. On most of the buildings in the area and
the slum streets leading into it were posters with a huge red
heart and inside that red heart the inscription 'I LOVE NEW
YORK'. Courtesy of Louis Inch.

On that Thursday near midnight, Blade Booker was
hanging out in the Times Square Bar and Cinema Club
looking for a client. Blade Booker was a young black man
noted for his ability to hustle. He could get you coke, he
could get you H, he could get you a wide assortment of pills.
He could also get you a gun but nothing big. Pistols,
revolvers, little .22s but after he got himself one he didn't
really get into that any more. He wasn't a pimp, but he was
very good with the ladies. He could really talk to their shit,
and he was a great listener. Many a night he spent with a
girl and listened to her dreams. Even the lowest down hooker
who would do things with men that took his breath away,
had dreams to tell. Blade Booker listened, he enjoyed listening, it made him feel good when ladies told him their dreams.
He loved their shit. Oh, they would hit the numbers, their
astrological chart showed that the coming year a man would
love them, they would have a baby, or have kids grow up to
be doctors, lawyers, college professors, be on TV; their kids

265

could sing or dance or act or do comedy as good as Richard Pryor, maybe even another Eddie Murphy.

Blade Booker was waiting for the Swedish Cinema Palace to empty out after the completion of its X-rated film. Many of the cinema lovers would stop here for a drink and a hamburger and the hopes of seeing some pussy. They would straggle in singly but you could spot them by the abstracted look in their eyes, as if they were pondering an insoluble scientific problem. Also most of them had a melancholy look on their faces. They were lonely people.

There were hookers all over the place but Blade Booker had his very own placed in a strategic corner. Men at the bar could see her at a little table that her huge red purse almost covered. She was a blonde girl from Duluth, Minnesota, big-boned, her blue eyes iced with heroin. Blade Booker had rescued her from a fate worse than death, namely a life on a farm where the cold winter would chill her tits as hard as boulders. But he was always careful with her. She had a reputation and he was one of the few who would work with her.

Her name was Kimberly Ansley and just six years ago she had chopped her pimp up with an axe while he was sleeping. Watch out for girls named Kimberly and Tiffany, Booker always said. She had been arrested and prosecuted, tried and convicted, but convicted only of manslaughter with the defense proving she had numerous bruises and had been 'not responsible' because of her heroin habit. She had been sentenced to a correctional facility, cured, declared sane and released on to the streets of New York. There she had taken up residence in the slums around Greenwich Village, supplied with an apartment in one of the housing projects built by the city which even the poor were fleeing.

Blade Booker and Kimberly were partners. He was half pimp, half roller; he took pride in that distinction. Kimberly would pick up a *cinéaste* in the Times Square Bar, and then lead her customer to a tenement hallway near Ninth Avenue for quick sexual acts. Then Blade would step from the shadows and clunk the man on the head with a New York Police Department blackjack. They would split the money in the man's wallet but Blade got the credit cards and jewelry. Not out of greed but because he didn't trust Kimberly's judgement.

The beauty of this was that the man was usually an errant husband reluctant to report the incident to the police and have to answer questions about just what he was doing in a dark hall of Ninth Avenue when his wife was waiting for him in Merrick, Long Island or Trenton, New Jersey. For safety's sake both Blade and Kim would simply avoid the Times Square Cinema Bar for a week. And Ninth Avenue. They would move to Second Avenue. In a city like New York that was like going to another black star in the galaxy. That was why Blade Booker loved New York. He was invisible, like The Shadow, The Man With a Thousand Faces. And he was like those insects and birds he saw on the TV public broadcasting channels who changed color to blend with the terrain, the insects who could burrow into the earth to escape predators. In short, unlike most citizens, Blade Booker felt safe in New York.

On Thursday night the pickings were lean. But Kimberly was beautiful in this light, her blonde hair glowing like a halo, her white powdered breasts, moonlike, rising none too shyly out of her green low-cut dress. A gentleman with sly good-humored charm only faintly overladen with lust, brought his drink to her table and politely asked her if he could sit down. Blade watched them and wondered at the ironies of the world. Here was this well-dressed man, undoubtedly some kind of hot-shot like a lawyer or professor or, who knows, some low-grade politician like a City Counselor or State Senator, sitting down with an axe-murderer, and for dessert would get a bop on the head. And just because of his cock. That was the trouble. A man walked through life with only half a brain because of his

267

cock. It was really too bad. Maybe before he bopped the guy he would let him stick it into Kimberly and get his nuts off and then bop him. He looked like a nice guy, he was really being a gentleman, lighting Kimberly's cigarette, ordering her a drink, not rushing her, though he was obviously dying to get off.

Blade finished his drink when Kim gave him the signal. He saw Kim start to get up, fussing with her red purse, rummaging in it for God knows what. Blade left the bar and went out into the street. It was a clear night of early spring and the smell of hot dogs and hamburgers and onions frying on the grills of open-air restaurants made him hungry, but he could wait until work was done. He walked up 42nd Street. There were still crowds although it was midnight, and people's faces were colored by the countless neon lights of the rows of cinemas, the open-air restaurants, the giant billboards, the cone-shaped glares of hotel searchlights. He loved the walk from Seventh Avenue to Ninth. He entered the hallway and positioned himself in the well. He could step out when Kim embraced her client. He lit a cigarette and took the blackjack out of its holster beneath the jacket.

He could hear them coming into the hall, the door clicking shut, Kim's purse clattering. And then he heard Kim's voice giving the code word. 'It's just one flight.' He waited for a couple of minutes before he stepped out of the well and hesitated because he saw such a pretty picture. There was Kim on the first step, legs apart, lovely massive white thighs uncovered and the nice man so well dressed, with his dick out and shoving it into her. Kim seemed to rise for a moment into the air and then Blade saw with horror that she was still rising, and the steps were rising with her and then he saw above her head the clear sky as if the whole top of the building had been sheared off. He tried to find a hole, he tried to change his color to match the stones falling into the hole that showed the sky. He lifted the blackjack to beg, to

268

pray, to give witness, that his life could not be over. All this happened in a fraction of a second.

Cecil Clarkson and Isabel Domaine had come out of a Broadway theater after seeing a charming musical and strolled down to 42nd Street and Times Square. They were both black, as indeed were a majority of the people to be seen on the streets here, but they were in no way similar to Blade Booker. Cecil Clarkson was nineteen years of age and took writing courses at the New School for Social Research. Isabel was eighteen and went to every Broadway and off-Broadway play because she loved the theater, and hoped to be an actress. They were in love as only teenagers can be, absolutely convinced that they were the only two people in the world. And as they walked up from Seventh Avenue to Eight the blinding neon lights bathed them in benevolent light, their beauty created a magic around them which shielded off the wino beggars, the half-crazed drug addicts, the hustlers, the pimps and the would-be muggers. And Cecil was big, obviously a strong young man who looked as if he would kill anybody who even touched Isabel's body.

They stopped at a huge frankfurter and hamburger open air grill and ate alongside the counter, they did not venture inside where the floor was filthy with discarded paper napkins and paper plates. Cecil drank a beer and Isabel a Pepsi with their hot dogs and hamburgers. They watched the surging humanity that filled the sidewalks even at this late hour. They looked with perfect equanimity at the wave of human flotsam, the dregs of the city, rolling past them and it never entered their minds that there was any danger. They felt pity for these people who did not have their promise, their future, their present and everlasting bliss. When the wave receded they went back into the street and started the walk from Seventh to Eight. Above the painted ceiling of neon lights shone a lighter sky twinkling with fainter lights. Isabel felt the spring air on her face and buried her face in

269

Cecil's shoulder, one hand at his chest, the other caressing his neck. Cecil felt a vaulting tenderness. They were both supremely happy, the young in love as billions and billions of human beings had been before them, living one of the few perfect moments in life. Then suddenly to Cecil's astonishment all the garish red and green lights blotted out and all he could see was the vault of the sky with its faint stars, and then both of them in their perfect bliss dissolved into nothing.

A group of eight tourists visiting New York City for an Easter week vacation, walked down from St Patrick's cathedral and on Fifth Avenue turned up 42nd Street and sauntered up toward where a forest of neon light beckoned. When they reached Times Square they were disappointed. They had seen it on TV when on New Year's Eve hundreds of thousands gathered to appear on television and greet the coming New Year.

It was so dirty, there was a carpet of garbage that covered the streets. The crowd seemed menacing, drunk, drugged, or driven insane by being enclosed by the great towers of steel through which they had to move. The women were garishly dressed, they matched the women in the stills outside the porno cinemas. They seemed to move through different levels of hell, the void of a sky with no stars, the street lamps a puslike spurt of yellow.

The tourists, four married couples from a small town in Ohio, their children grown, had decided to take a trip to New York as a sort of celebration. They had completed a certain duty in their lives, fulfilled a necessary destiny. They had married, they had brought up children, they had been able to make their moderately successful careers. Now there would be a new beginning for them, the start of a new kind of life. The main battle had been won.

The X cinemas didn't interest them, there were plenty in Ohio. What did interest and frighten them about Times

270

Square was that it was so ugly and the people filling the streets seemed so evil in the neon light stained on the night. The tourists all wore great big red 'I LOVE NEW YORK' buttons that they had purchased on their first day. Now one of the women took off her button and threw it into the gutter.

'Let's get out of here,' she said.

The group turned and walked back toward Sixth Avenue away from the great corridor of neon. They had almost turned the corner when they heard a distant 'boom' and then a faint rustle of wind, and then down the long Avenues from Ninth to Sixth came rushing a tornado of air filled with metal soda cans, garbage baskets and a few cars that seemed to be flying. The group with an animal instinct turned the corner of Sixth Avenue out of the path of that rushing wind, but were swept off their feet by a tumult of air. From far away they heard the crashing of buildings falling to the ground, the screams of thousands of dying people. They stood crouched low in the shelter of the corner, not knowing what had happened.

They had walked just outside the radius of destruction caused by the explosion of the nuclear bomb. They were eight survivors of the greatest calamity that had befallen a peacetime United States.

One of the men struggled to his feet and helped the others. 'Fucking New York,' he said. 'I hope all the cab drivers got killed.'

The police patrol car that moved slowly through traffic between Seventh and Eighth Avenue held two young cops, one Italian and one black. They didn't mind being stuck in traffic, it was the safest place in the precinct. They knew that down the darker side streets they could flush thieves stealing radios out of cars, low-grade pimps and muggers making menacing moves toward the peaceful pedestrians of New York, but they didn't want to get involved in those crimes.

271

Also, it was now a policy of the New York Police Department to allow petty crimes. There had spread in New York a sort of licence for the underprivileged to prey on the successful law abiding citizens of the city. After all, was it right that there were men and women who could afford fifty thousand dollar cars with radios and music systems worth a thousand dollars, while there were thousands of homeless who didn't have the price of a meal or who could not afford a sterile healthy needle for a fix? Was it right that these well-to-do, mentally fat, placid, oxlike citizens who had the effrontery to walk the streets of New York without a gun or even a lethal screwdriver in their pockets, could enjoy the fabulous sights of the greatest city on earth and not pay a certain price? After all there still was a spark in America of that ancient revolutionary spirit that could not resist such a temptation. And the courts of law, the higher echelons of the police, the editorials of the most respectable newspapers slyly endorsed the republican spirit of thievery, mugging, burglaries, rapes and even murders on the streets of New York. The poor of the city had no other recourse, their lives had been blighted by poverty, by a stultified family life, the very architecture of the city. Indeed one columnist made a case that all these crimes could be laid at the door of Louis Inch, the real estate lord who was restructuring the city of New York with mile-high condos that shielded the sun and starfilled skies with slats of steel.

The two police officers watched Blade Booker leave the Times Square Cinema restaurant, they knew him well. One officer said to the other, 'Should we follow him,' and the other said, 'A waste of time, we could catch him in the act and he'd get off.' They saw the big blonde and her john came out and take the same route up toward Ninth Avenue. 'Poor guy,' one of the cops said. 'He thinks he's going to get laid and he's gonna get rolled.' The other cop said, 'He'll have a lump on his head as big as his hard on.' They both laughed.

272

Their car still moving slowly by inches, both policemen watched the action on the street. It was midnight, their shift would soon be over and they didn't want to get into anything that would keep them out on the street. They watched the innumerable prostitutes stand in the way of pedestrians, the black drug dealers hawking their wares as bodly as a TV pitchman, the muggers and pickpockets jostling prospective victims and trying to engage tourists in conversation. Sitting in the darkness of the patrol car and gazing out on the streets lit brightly by neon sun they saw all the dregs of New York slouched toward their particular hells.

The two cops were constantly alert, afraid that some maniac would shove a gun through the window and start shooting. They saw two drug hustlers fall into step beside a well-dressed man who tried to hurry away but was restrained by four hands. The driver of the patrol car pressed the gas pedal and drew up alongside. The drug hustlers dropped their hands, the well-dressed man smiled with relief. At that moment both sides of the street caved in and buried 42nd Street from Ninth to Seventh Avenue.

All the neon lights of the Great White Way, fabulous Broadway, blotted out. The darkness was lit by fires, buildings burning, bodies on fire. Flaming cars moving like torches aimless in the night. And there was a great clanging of the bells, the countless shrieking of sirens as fire engines, ambulances and police vehicles moved into the stricken heart of New York.

These were just a few of the ten thousand or so people who were killed and the twenty thousand who were injured when the nuclear bomb planted by Gresse and Tibbot exploded in the Port Authority Building on Ninth Avenue and 42nd Street.

The explosion was a great boom of sound followed by a howling wind and then the screaming of cement and steel torn asunder. The blast did its damage with mathematical

273

precision. The area from Seventh Avenue to the Hudson River, and from 42nd Street to 45th Street was completely flattened. Outside that area, the damage was by comparison minimal. Radiation was lethal only within that area. The most valuable real estate outside of Tokyo was now worthless.

Of the dead more than seventy per cent were black or Hispanic, the other thirty per cent were white and foreign tourists. On Ninth and Tenth Avenue which had become a camping ground for the homeless, in the Port Authority Building itself in which many transients were sleeping, the bodies were charred into small logs.

Beyond the radius of complete destruction, all through the borough of Manhattan, glass windows shattered, cars in the streets were smashed by falling debris. And within an hour after the explosion the bridges of Manhattan were clogged with vehicles fleeing the city to New Jersey and Long Island.

BOOK IV

14

The White House Communications Center received news of the atom bomb explosion in New York City exactly six minutes after midnight and the Duty Officer immediately informed the President.

Francis Kennedy turned to Christian Klee and said, 'Give your order to isolate Congress. Cut all their communications. Now all of you will accompany me to Capitol Hill. Eugene, give the Communications office the order to transmit that martial law is declared.'

Twenty minutes later, he appeared before the assembled House of Representatives and Senate who had just voted to impeach him. They had received the news of the nuclear attack in New York and were in a state of shock.

President Francis Kennedy ascended the rostrum to address the Congress. He was attended by the Vice President, Helen DuPray, Oddblood Gray and Christian Klee. Eugene Dazzy had remained in the White House to handle the enormous amount of work necessary.

Kennedy was very grave. This was no time for anything but the most straightforward dialogue. He spoke to them without a trace of rancor or threat. He said, 'I come to you tonight knowing that whatever differences we have had, we are united in our devotion to our country.

'There has been a hostile nuclear explosion in New York City that has taken thousands of lives. Two suspects have been arrested and are in custody. These two suspects indicate that the terrorist, Yabril, is implicated. We must come to the

277

conclusion that there is a huge conspiracy against the United States that may be the greatest danger that this country has ever faced. I have declared martial law. This decision brings me into conflict with your vote to remove me. Let me say that this sacred legislative body is safe from any attack. You are protected by six divisions of the Secret Service and an Army Special Forces Regiment that has just moved into position.'

At this announcement of their imprisonment, the Senators and Congressmen moved uneasily in their seats. There were murmurs and whispers as Kennedy went on. 'This is no time for the Presidency and the Congress to be in conflict. This is a time for us to unite against the enemy. I therefore ask you to nullify your previous vote to remove me from my office.'

Francis Kennedy paused and smiled at them. These people, most of them, had been his bitter enemies for three years, now he had them at his mercy. He said quietly, 'I know you all will vote with conscience and judgment. I have made my decision in the same spirit. No matter what the outcome here, I must tell you that this country will still be under martial law and I will remain President until this new crisis is resolved. But I beg you to avoid this confrontation until the crisis is over.'

Senator Lambertino was the first to speak after Kennedy. He proposed that the vote be nullified and that both Houses of Congress give its full support to the President of the United States, Francis Xavier Kennedy.

Congressman Jintz rose to second the motion. He declared that events had proven Kennedy to be in the right, that it had been an honest disagreement. He implied that the President and the Congress would go forward hand in hand to preserve America against its enemies. He gave his word on that and sealed it with his famous handshake which Francis Kennedy could not avoid.

The vote was taken. The previous vote to impeach the President was nullified. Unanimously. Then another vote was taken. That the Congress had the fullest faith in Francis Xavier Kennedy and would follow unswervingly any policy he set to solve the crisis.

At noon Thursday morning, less than twelve hours later, President Francis Xavier Kennedy spoke to the nation on all TV and cable networks.

During the early hours of the morning, Christian Klee had Lawrence Salentine brought to his office and talked to him as the Attorney General of the United States under martial law.

'I don't want you to give me any bullshit,' Klee said. 'I'm going to tell you exactly what you and the other TV moguls have to do in the next twenty-four hours. I want you to listen very carefully. For your own sake.'

'In this crisis everybody is behind the President,' Salentine said.

'No bullshit, remember,' Christian said. 'Now here's the program. Dazzy laid it out but I thought it might be better if I, as the Attorney General, presented it to you, in case you find a legal problem.'

Lawrence Salentine said softly, 'No, Mr Attorney General, I don't think there will be a legal problem at this time.'

Christian Klee had an intimate knowledge of men like Salentine. He had listened in on many of the telephone conversations of the Socrates Club through his computer surveillance system. Salentine meant to convey a threat without being overt. Very well, you son of a bitch, Klee thought, you want to get tough later on, I'll be waiting for you.

So when President Kennedy went on the air at noon Eastern Standard time, all the TV media had prepared for an audience by using a spot every thirty minutes, advertising his coming speech.

The people of the United States never forgot that speech. They never forgot his authority and the physical beauty of his presence. The pallor of his face, the satiny blue eyes, the resolute voice. He was overwhelming on the TV screen and to an audience of three hundred million people, bewildered and terrified by the events of the past four days, he brought an absolute reassurance.

Francis Kennedy told them that the crisis was over. He gave a short summary of the events of Easter week. The assassination of the Pope, the hijacking of the plane by Yabril, the murder of Theresa Kennedy, and the demands of Yabril. And then finally the explosion of the atom bomb in New York.

He explained the motives of the terrorists, that all these crimes had been committed to undermine the authority and prestige of the United States. He told his audience of his ultimatum to the Sultan of Sherhaben and his threat; to destroy the Sultanate of Sherhaben if his ultimatum was defied. And that Dak was in ruins.

Suddenly the cameras shifted away from Kennedy in the Oval Office and the audience saw planes descending and landing. One plane was adorned with funeral black markings and when it landed the audience saw an honor guard of Marines surround it. A coffin was wheeled from a bay beneath the plane. A TV reporter anchor voiceover announced quietly, 'The body of Theresa Kennedy has been returned for burial in the United States.'

The cameras caught the other two planes landing. From one plane the released hostages descended. The TV announcer intoned that all the hostages, except Theresa Kennedy, were now in the United States unharmed. But to the surprise of the audience the cameras left this scene very quickly to focus on the third plane.

From this plane first descended Arthur Wix then Bert Audick. Then the camera focused on a man who had his arms shackled behind his back and who moved slowly and awkwardly because of the chains that hobbled his lower body. This man had a shield of guards which the camera pierced to focus on the face of the prisoner, Yabril.

The TV announcer told his audience that this was the leader of the hijackers, the man who murdered Theresa Kennedy and that this man would now stand trial in a United States Court.

Then the TV screen showed a huge photo of Romeo and the voiceover informed the audience that this was the man who had assassinated the Pope. This man was also in custody in the United States.

The TV screen showed photos of Gresse and Tibbot and told the audience their background and that they had been arrested as suspects in the planting of the atom bomb in New York. And that it was believed that there was some link between these two young men and Yabril.

Then the screen faded and President Francis Kennedy appeared before the people of the United States.

He spoke slowly. 'Again, I repeat, the crisis is over. All the men who have committed these crimes are in custody. Now our task is to judge and punish these criminals. It has already been decided that the terrorist Romeo will be extradited to Italy to stand trial for the killing of the Pope. That is a matter of law. But the others will be tried in the courts of the United States. It has been established by interrogation and investigation by our intelligence agencies that there is no further danger from this conspiracy. And so I declare the end of martial law.'

Everything had gone as programmed by Dazzy, Klee and Matthew Gladyce. The villains had been presented as defeated and helpless, and Francis Kennedy as triumphant and sympathetic. There was a final shot of Theresa Kennedy's coffin being wheeled off into the distance surrounded by the honor guard. And then a final shot of a safe America as symbolized by the Stars and Stripes flying over the White House.

Here the broadcast was supposed to end. So it was a

surprise to everyone when Kennedy spoke once again. He said, 'But I must tell you in conclusion that though the external dangers have been conquered, there is an internal danger. Last night Congress violated the Constitution and voted to impeach me as President of the United States because of my ultimatum to Sherhaben. When the atom bomb exploded in New York they had to nullify their vote. I have no powers to discipline the Congress but the popular vote can do so . . .'

Kennedy paused for a long moment. His eyelids closed so tight that he seemed sightless as a statue is sightless. Then the eyes were open again, sky blue sparkling with restrained tears. He resumed his speech, his voice modulated to one of compassion and pity. He told his audience to go to bed as he would tell a tired child to go to bed. 'Trust in me,' he said. 'The danger is past. Tomorrow we plan so that this country will never suffer such trauma again. Bless you all. Sleep well.'

For the Congress and members of the Socrates Country Club the speech spoke very clearly. The President of the United States had declared war upon them.

15

President Francis Kennedy, secure in power and office, his enemies defeated, contemplated his destiny. There was a final step to be taken, the final decision to be made. He had lost his wife and child, his personal life had lost all meaning. What he did have was a life entwined with the people of America. How far did he want to go with that commitment?

He announced that he would run for re-election in November, and organized his campaign. Oddblood Gray was instructed to neutralize the Reverend Foxworth. Christian Klee was ordered to put legal pressure on all the big businesses especially the media companies to keep them from interfering with the election process. Vice President Helen DuPray was mobilizing the women of America. Arthur Wix who was power in Eastern liberal circles and Eugene Dazzy, who monitored the enlightened business leaders of the country, mobilized money. But Francis Kennedy knew that in the last analysis all this was peripheral. Everything would rest on himself, on how far the people of America would be willing to go with him personally.

There was one crucial point, this time the people must elect a Congress solidly behind the President of the United States. Kennedy smiled and thought to himself that he did not have to censor his own brain. What he wanted was a Congress that would do exactly what he wanted them to do.

So now Francis Kennedy had to perceive the innermost feelings of America. It was a nation in shock. The atom bomb explosion in New York was a psychological trauma the country had never before experienced. And that the act had been committed by two of the most gifted and privileged of its citizens was bewildering. That act was the most daring extension of the philosophy of individual freedom on which the United States prided itself. The right of the individual was the most sacred right in American democracy. But Francis Kennedy sensed that the mood of the American people had now changed.

In the smaller cities and rural areas, after the shock and horror wore off there was a grim satisfaction. New York had gotten what it deserved. It was too bad that the bomb had not been bigger and blown up the whole city with its hedonistic rich, its conniving Semites, criminal blacks. There was after all a just God in heaven. He had picked the right place for this great punishment. But through the country there was also fear. That their fate, their lives, their very world and their posterity were in hostage to fellow men who were aberrant. All this Kennedy sensed.

Every Friday night Francis Kennedy made a TV report to the people. These were really thinly disguised campaign speeches but now he had no trouble getting air time.

He announced that in his second term he would be even tougher on crime. He would again fight to give every American the opportunity to buy a new home, cover their healthcare costs, and make certain they were able to get a higher education. He emphasized that this was not socialism. The costs of these programs would simply be paid for by taking a little bite out of the rich corporations of America. He declared he did not advocate socialism, that he just wanted to protect the people of America from its 'royal' rich. And he did this over and over again.

The members of the Socrates Club watched these perform-ances with a great deal of anger, and contempt. They had seen such demagogues before, the tattered political prophets from the south lands, Puritan communists from the heart of the west, all preaching a gospel to steal from the rich. These movements had always been overwhelmed by the good sense of the people of America. But now two things worried the Socrates Club. It was one thing for some politician, even a President, to promise the electorate pie in the sky, but a man like Kennedy was another matter. Francis Kennedy was the most charismatic speaker that television had ever seen. It was not so much that he was so extraordinarily a physical presence, his perfect style, the mingling of the patrician with the common. He was never condescending in his good humor. He had the cheerful frankness of a best friend, the familiarity of a favorite older brother; he made his point with a flashing wit. He enchanted the TV audiences with all of these but most of all he propounded his theories of government with a sharpness and clarity that made the people understand him and his goals.

He used certain catchphrases and little speeches that went straight to the heart.

'We will declare war on the everyday tragedies of human existence,' he said, 'not on other nations.'

He repeated the famous question used in his first campaign. 'How is it that at the end of every great war, when trillions of dollars have been spent and thrown away on death, then there is prosperity in the world? What if those trillions had been spent for the betterment of mankind?'

He joked that for the cost of one nuclear submarine the government could finance a thousand homes for the poor. For the cost of a fleet of Stealth bombers it could finance a million homes. 'We'll just make believe they got lost on maneuvers,' he said. 'Hell, it's happened before, and with valuable lives lost besides. We'll just make believe it happened.' And when critics pointed out that the defense of the United States would suffer, he said that statistical reports from the Defense Department were classified and that nobody would know. These flippant rejoinders enraged the news media far more than they did the Congress and the Socrates Club.

But what the Socrates Club viewed with more immediate alarm was Kennedy's nominations to head regulatory agencies; left-wingers who would follow Kennedy's vision of severely modifying the power of huge corporations. There was his program to limit the ownership of TV stations and newspapers and book publishing companies to separate units. No longer could one corporate umbrella shield all three divisions of the media. If you owned TV, you could only own TV, if you owned books you could only own books, if you owned newspapers you could only own newspapers, if you owned movie studios, you could only own movie studios. On this Francis Kennedy made a powerful address to the nation. He cited Lawrence Salentine as a prime example. Salentine not only owned a major network and some of the bigger cable companies, but also owned a movie studio in California, one of the major book publishing houses and a string of newspapers. Kennedy told his audience that it was against every principle of democracy that one man should control so many methods of communication. It amounted to the same thing as giving a man more than one vote.

The Congress, the Socrates Club, and nearly all the other big business interests united to oppose him. The stage was set for one of the greatest political battles in the history of the United States.

The Socrates Club decided to hold a seminar in California on how to defeat Kennedy in the November election. Lawrence Salentine was very worried. He knew that the Attorney General was preparing serious indictments on the activities of Bert Audick and mounting investigations of Martin Mutford's financial dealings. Greenwell was too clean to be in trouble, Salentine didn't worry about him. But Salentine knew his own media empire was very vulnerable. They had gotten away with murder for so many years that they had gotten careless. His publishing company, books and magazines were OK. Nobody could harm print media, the Constitutional protection was too strong. Except of course that a prick like Klee might get the postal charges raised.

But Salentine really worried about his TV empire. The airwaves, after all, belonged to the government and were doled out by them. The TV stations were only licensed. And it had always been a source of bewilderment to Salentine that the government allowed private enterprise to make so much money out of these airwaves without levying the proper tax. He shuddered at the thought of a strong Federal Communication Commissioner under Kennedy's direction. It could mean the end of the TV and cable companies as now constituted.

And Salentine also worried about Louis Inch. He was constantly annoyed at Inch's stupidity and lack of sensitivity. How could a guy so dumb get so rich? He was like one of those idiots who could mysteriously do mathematical equations. The man had a genius for real estate and a simple idiot's dream which consisted of one thought. Build vertically always, horizontal never.

And the man had no inkling of how much he was hated, even by those closest to him. But especially by the inner city people, by the slum-dwelling blacks and Hispanics and by the working-class whites in the countryside and the small cities. It seemed that all these people could smell his greed, his insensitivity to the human. The man could become a serious liability if things went really wrong. But they needed him in the coming fight against Kennedy. Louis Inch was not afraid to stick his neck out. The man had real courage. He was not afraid of bribing anybody. In a democracy or a dictatorship this was an invaluable asset.

Louis Inch, certainly the most hated man in New York City, volunteered to restore the atom-blighted area in that city.

287

The eight blocks were to be purified with marble monuments enclosed in a green woodland. He would do it at cost, take no profit and have it up in six months. Thank God the radiation had been minimal.

Everybody knew that Louis Inch got things done much better than any government agency. Of course Louis Inch knew he would still make a geat deal of money through his subsidiary companies in construction, planning commissions and advisory committees. And the publicity would be invaluable.

Louis Inch was one of the richest men in America. His father had been the usual hardnosed big city landlord, failing to keep up the heat in apartment buildings, skimping on services, forcing out tenants so as to build more expensive apartments. Bribery of building inspectors was a skill Louis Inch had learned at his father's knee. Later, armed with a university degree in business management and law, he bribed city councilmen, borough presidents and their staffs, even mayors.

It was Louis Inch who fought the rent control laws in New York, it was Louis Inch who put together the real estate deals that built skyscrapers alongside Central Park. A park that now had an awning of monstrous steel edifices to house Wall Street brokers, professors at powerhouse universities, famous writers, chic artists, the chefs of expensive restaurants.

It was charged by the Reverend Foxworth that Louis Inch was responsible for the horrible slums in the upper West Side and the Bronx, in Harlem, in Coney Island, simply by the amount of reasonable housing he had destroyed in his rebuilding of New York. Also that he was blocking the rehabilitation of the Times Square district, while secretly buying up buildings and blocks. To this Inch retorted that the Reverend Foxworth was representing people who, if you had a bag full of shit, would demand half of it.

Another Inch strategy was his support of city laws that

required landlords to rent housing space to anyone regardless of race, color or creed. He had given speeches supporting those laws, because they helped to drive the small landlord out of the market. A landlord who had only the upstairs and/or the basement of his house to rent, had to take in drunks, schizophrenics, drug hustlers, rapists, stick-up artists. Eventually these small landlords would become discouraged, sell their houses and move to the suburbs.

But Louis Inch was beyond all that now, he was stepping up in class. Millionaires were a dime a dozen, Louis Inch was one of the hundred or so billionaires in America. He owned bus systems, he owned hotels and he owned an airline. He owned one of the great hotel casinos in Atlantic City and he owned apartment buildings in Santa Monica, California. It was the Santa Monica properties that gave him the most trouble.

Louis Inch had joined the Socrates Club because he believed that its powerful members could help solve his Santa Monica real estate problems. Golf was a perfect sport to hatch conspiracies. There were the jokes, the good exercise and the agreements struck. And what could be more innocent? The most rabid investigator from Congressional Committees or the hanging judges of the press could not accuse golfers of criminal intent.

The Socrates Country Club turned out to be better than Inch suspected. He became friendly with the hundred or so men who controlled the country's economic apparatus and political machinery and it was in the Socrates Country Club that Louis Inch became a member of the Money Guild that could buy the entire Congressional delegation of a State in one deal. Of course you couldn't buy them body and soul, you were not talking abstracts here, like the devil and God, good and evil, virtue and sin. No, you were talking politics. You were talking of what was possible. There were times when a Congressman had to oppose you to win re-election. It was true that ninety-eight per cent of the Congressmen

289

were always re-elected, but there was always the two per cent that had to listen to their constituents.

Louis Inch dreamed the impossible dream. No, not to be President of the United States, he knew his landlord imprint could never be erased. His smudging the very face of New York was an architectural murder. There were a million slum dwellers in New York, Chicago, and especially Santa Monica who would fill the streets ready to put his head on a pike. No, his dream was to be the first trillionaire in the modern civilized world. A plebeian trillionaire, his fortune won with the calloused hands of a working man.

Inch lived for the day when he could say to Bert Audick, 'I have a thousand units.' It had always irritated him that Texan oil men talked in units, a 'unit' in Texas was one hundred million dollars. Audick had said about the destruction of the city of Dak, 'God, I lost 500 units there.' And Inch vowed some day to say to Audick, 'Hell, I got about a thousand units tied up in real estate,' and Audick would whistle and say, 'A hundred billion dollars.' And then Inch would say to him, 'Oh, no, a trillion dollars. Up in New York a unit is a billion dollars.' That would settle that Texas bullshit once and for all.

To make that dream come true, Louis Inch came up with the concept of 'air space'. That is, he would buy the air space above existent buildings and build on top of them. Air space could be bought for peanuts, it was a new concept as marsh lands had been when his grandfather bought them knowing that technology would solve the problem of draining the swamps and turn them into profitable building acres. In the same way Louis Inch knew that he could build over the existing buildings of the major cities. The problem was to prevent the people and their legislators from stopping him. That would take time and an enormous investment, but he was confident it could be done. True, cities like Chicago, New York, Dallas, Miami would be gigantic steel and concrete prisons but people didn't have to live there,

290

except for the elite who loved the museums, the cinemas, the theater, the music. There would of course be little boutique neighborhoods for the artists.

And of course the thing was that when Louis Inch finally succeeded, there would no longer be any slums in New York City. There would be simply no affordable rent for the criminal and the working classes. They would come in from the suburbs, on special trains, on special buses, and they would be gone by nightfall. The renters and buyers of the Inch Corporation condos and apartments could go to the theater, the discos, the expensive restaurants and not worry about the dark streets outside. They could stroll along the Avenues, even venture into the side streets, they could walk the parks, in comparative safety. And what would they pay for such a paradise? Fortunes.

Louis Inch had one weakness. He loved his wife Theodora. An opulent blonde with a social conscience and a tender heart. Inch had met her when she was student at NYU and he had given a lecture there on how the owners of real estate affected the culture of geat cities. As many money-oriented men, Louis admired women who considered money worthless itself. He liked Theodora's social conscience, her love for her fellow man and her desire to help them. He liked her good humor and easygoingness. And he was delighted by her no-nonsense healthy sexuality, that an hour or two in bed before supper was an important and constructive part of her day. Late at night she studied before going to sleep, reading, listening to instructional tapes on her headset and making notes on what she would do the next day.

They complemented each other perfectly. Louis Inch was that rarity in American society, a very rich man who was happily married, happy in work, delighted in his wife's ambitions, and so he could devote all of his dreams to becoming a trillionaire. For adventure and risk, he had the infinite air space of the geat cities to purchase.

The happiness of the Inch marriage lasted ten years. And

the first tiny break was caused by the Reverend Baxter Foxworth. Theodora Inch admired him as one of the country's great black leaders in the Martin Luther King tradition.

Theodora Inch became a leader in the society of rich women determined to give their husbands' money back to the poor and so she decided to organize a huge society ball for the homeless. The tickets were ten thousand dollars a couple and the proceeds would go to build a huge shelter for the homeless. The ball would be held in the Plaza Hotel and it would be one of the greatest social events in the history of New York. It would also prove that the Inch family had the welfare of the city at heart.

Theodora Inch asked for the help of the Reverend Baxter Foxworth to make sure the representatives of the black power elite would be at the ball. The Reverend told her with bemused amiability that there were very few black men rich enough to afford the price of a ticket. Theodora Inch assured him that there would be a block of fifty tickets set aside, free of charge. The Reverend accepted.

The newspapers were sown with intriguing items about the event, the participants would all be required to come in costume showing the different ages of the city of New York. They would wear masks of former mayors and famous politicians and robber barons. There would be a thousand people at the ball and indeed more tickets than that had been sold. All the giant corporations understood that they had to buy a block of tickets to keep the good will of the city officials and the Inch real estate empire. Wall Street firms had been especially generous, the stock brokers were tired of coming to work and stepping over drunken bums sleeping on the ornate plazas of the beautiful skyscrapers Louis Inch had built for them.

On the night of the ball everything was in place. The TV mobile units surrounded the Plaza Hotel, the long lines of limousines stretched and stacked up back to 72nd Street to roll up to the Plaza entrance on 59th. And as the limousines hit 60th Street they were greeted by swarms of homeless men and women armed with dirty rags who wiped the limousine windows and then stretched out dirty palms for a tip. And got nothing.

The TV audience did not understand that the very rich rarely carry cash; who has not met a celebrity who must borrow a dollar to tip the washroom attendant? But the TV image to America was poor people being refused by the very rich.

This was the Reverend Foxworth's little joke. The good Reverend had recruited alcoholics and drug addicts, then transported them to the Plaza Hotel in special vans to do their begging. It was his message to the Inch empire that they could not buy off opposition so easily.

Louis Inch the very next day countered this. He ordered one million 'I Love New York' buttons, huge red and white ovals, and distributed them free to everyone in his hotels and corporations.

But his wife was enchanted by this humiliating joke and the next day, meeting with the Reverend Baxter Foxworth to reproach him, she became his secret mistress.

Summoned to the meeting of the Socrates Club in California, Louis Inch began to trip across the United States to confer with great real estate corporations of the big cities. From them he exacted their promise to contribute money to defeat Kennedy. Arriving in Los Angeles a few days later, he decided to make a side trip to Santa Monica before going to the seminar.

Santa Monica is one of the most beautiful towns in America. Mainly because its citizens have successfully resisted the efforts of real estate interests to build sky-scrapers, voted laws to keep rents stable and control construc-tion. A fine apartment on Ocean Avenue, overlooking the

Pacific itself, only cost one sixth of the citizen's income. This was a situation that had driven Inch crazy for twenty years.

Louis Inch thought Santa Monica an outrage, an insult to the American spirit of free enterprise; these units under today's conditions could be rented for ten times the going rate. Louis Inch had bought up many of the apartment buildings. These were charming Spanish-style complexes, wasteful in their use of valuable real estate, with their inner courtyards and gardens, their scandalously low two-storey heights. Oh, this air space above Santa Monica was worth billions, the view of the Pacific Ocean worth more billions. Sometimes Louis Inch had crazy ideas of building vertically on the ocean itself. This made him too dizzy.

He did not of course try to directly bribe the three city counselors he invited to Michael's (the food delicious but again the restaurant a scandalous misuse of valuable real estate) but he told them his plans, he showed how everybody could become multimillionaires if certain laws were changed. He was dismayed when they showed no interest. But that was not the worst part. When Louis Inch got into his limousine, there was a shattering explosion. Glass flew all around the interior of the limo, the back window disintegrated, the windshield suddenly sprouted a large hole and spider webs in the rest of the glass.

When the police arrived they told Inch that a rifle bullet had done the damage. When they asked him if he had any enemies, Louis Inch assured them with all sincerity that he did not.

The Socrates Club's special seminar on 'Demagoguery in Democracy' commenced the next day.

Those present were Bert Audick, now under a RICO indictment; George Greenwell who looked like the old wheat stored in his gigantic Midwest silos; Louis Inch, his handsome pouting face pale from his near death the day before;

Martin 'Take me Private' Mutford wearing an Armani suit that could not hide his going to fat; and Lawrence Salentine.

Bert Audick took the floor first. 'Would somebody explain to me how Kennedy is not a communist?' he said. 'Kennedy wants to socialize medicine and home building. He has me indicted under the RICO laws and I'm not even Italian.' Nobody laughed at his little joke so he went on. 'We can dick around all we want but we have to face one central fact. He is an immense danger to everything we in this room stand for. We have to take drastic action.'

George Greenwell said quietly, 'He can get you indicted but he can't get you convicted, we still have due process in this country. Now I know you have endured great provocation. But if I hear any dangerous talk in this room I walk out. I will listen to nothing treasonous or seditious.'

Bert Audick took offense. 'I love my country better than anyone in this room,' he said. 'That's what gripes me. The indictment says I was acting in a treasonable way. Me! My ancestors were in this country when the fucking Kennedys were eating potatoes in Ireland. I was rich when they were bootleggers in Boston. Those gunners fired at American planes over Dak but not by my orders. Sure I gave the Sultan of Sherhaben a deal, but I was acting in the interest of the United States.'

Lawrence Salentine said dryly, 'We know Kennedy is the problem. We're here to discuss a solution. Which is our right and our duty.'

Martin Mutford said, 'What Kennedy's telling the country is bullshit. Where is the capital mass going to come from to support all these programs? He is talking a modified form of communism. If we can hammer that home in the media, the people will turn away from him. Every man and woman in this country thinks they'll be a millionaire some day and they're already worrying about the tax bite.'

'Then how come all the polls show Francis Kennedy will win in November?' Lawrence Salentine asked irritably. As

295

so many times before he was a little astonished by the obtuseness of powerful men. They seemed to have no awareness of Kennedy's enormous personal charm, his appeal to the mass of people, simply because they themselves were impervious to that charm.

There was a silence and then Martin Mutford spoke. 'I had a look at some of the legislation being prepared to regulate the stock market and banks. If Kennedy gets in, there will be mighty slim pickings. And if he gets his regulatory agency people in, the jails will be filled with very rich people.'

'I'll be there waiting for them,' Audick said, grinning. For some reason he seemed to be in a very good humor despite his indictment. 'I should be a trustee by then, I'll make sure you all have flowers in your cells.'

Louis Inch said impatiently, 'You'll be in one of those country club jails playing with computers that keep track of your oil tankers.'

Bert Audick had never liked Louis Inch. He didn't like a man who piled up human beings from underground to the stars, and charged a million dollars for apartments no bigger than a spittoon. Audick said, 'I'm sure my cell will have more room than one of your fancy apartments. And once I'm in, don't be too fucking sure you can get oil to heat those skyscrapers. And another thing, I'll get a better break gambling in jail than in your Atlantic City casinos.'

George Greenwell as the oldest and most experienced in dealing with the government felt he had to take charge of the conversation. 'I think we should, through our companies and other representatives, pour a great deal of money into the campaign of Kennedy's opponent. Martin, I think you should volunteer to be the campaign manager.'

Martin Mutford said, 'First let's decide what kind of money we are talking about and how it's to be contributed.'

George Greenwell said, 'How about a round sum of five hundred million dollars.'

Bert Audick said, 'Wait a minute, I've just lost fifty billion and you want me to go for another unit?'

Louis Inch said maliciously, 'That's one unit, Bert. Is the oil industry going chicken shit on us? You Texans can't spare a lousy one hundred million?'

Salentine said, 'TV time costs a lot of money. If we are going to saturate the air waves from now until November that's five whole months. That's going to be expensive.'

'And your TV network gets a big chunk of that,' Louis Inch said aggressively. He was proud of his reputation as a fierce negotiator. 'You TV guys put in your share out of one pocket and it appears like magic in your other pockets. I think that should be a factor when we contribute.'

Martin Mutford said, 'Look we are talking peanuts here,' which outraged the others. 'Take Me Private' Mutford was famous for his cavalier treatment of money. To him it was only a telex transporting some sort of spiritual substance from one ethereal body to another. It had no reality. He gave casual girlfriends a brand new Mercedes, a bit of eccentricity he had learned from rich Texans. If he had a mistress for a year he bought her an apartment house to secure her old age. Another mistress had a house in Malibu, another a castle in Italy and an apartment in Rome. He had bought an illegitimate son a piece of a casino in England. It had cost him nothing, merely slips of paper signed. And he always had a place to stay whenever he traveled. The Albanese girl owned her famous restaurant and building the same way. And there were many others. Money meant nothing to 'Private' Mutford.

Audick said aggressively, 'I paid my share with Dak.'

Mutford said, 'Bert, you're not in front of Congressional committees arguing oil depletion allowances.'

'You have no choice,' Louis Inch told Audick. 'If Kennedy gets elected and he gets his Congress, you go to jail.'

George Greenwell was wondering again whether he should disassociate himself officially from these men. After

297

all he was too old for these adventures. His grain empire stood in less danger than the fields of these other men. The oil industry too obviously blackmailed the government to make scandalous profits. His own grain business was low key, people in general did not know that only five or six privately held companies controlled the bread of the world. Greenwell feared that a rash, belligerent man like Bert Audick could get them all in really serious trouble. Yet he enjoyed the life of the Socrates Club, the week-long seminars filled with interesting discussions on the affairs of the world, the sessions of backgammon, the rubbers of bridge. But he had lost that hard desire to get the better of his fellow man.

Inch said, 'Come on, Bert, what the hell is a lousy unit to the oil industry? You guys have been sucking the public tit dry with your oil depletion allowance for the last hundred years.'

Salentine said dryly, 'And what about our friend, "Take Me Private"? He has more money than all of us put together. We can tap into the government treasury, he taps into the GNP. Banking and Wall Street will be the first to get kicked in the ass. They've been so blatant Kennedy could hang them from the lamp posts on Wall Street and citizens would celebrate with a ticker tape parade.'

Inch grinned and said, 'Private, you money guys are outrageous. That last decline in the market you engineered cost ordinary stockholders at least two hundred billion dollars.'

Martin Mutford laughed. 'Stop the bullshit,' he said. 'We are all in this together. And we will all hang together if Kennedy wins. Forget about the money and let's get down to business. Let's figure out how to attack Kennedy in this campaign. How about his failure to act on that atom bomb threat in time to stop the explosion? How about the fact that he has never had a woman in his life since his wife died? How about that maybe he's secretly screwing broads in the White House like his Uncle Jack did? How about a million

298

things? How about his personal staff? We have a lot of work to do.'

This distracted them. Audick said thoughtfully, 'He doesn't have any woman. I've already had that checked out. Maybe he's a fag.'

'So what?' Salentine said. Some of his top stars on his network were gay and he was sensitive on the subject. Audick's language offended him.

But Louis Inch unexpectedly took Audick's point. 'Come on,' he said to Salentine, 'the public doesn't mind if one of your goofy comedians is gay, but the President of the United States?'

'The time will come,' Lawrence Salentine said.

'We can't wait,' Mutford said. 'And besides the President is not gay. He was in some sort of sexual hibernation. And besides word has come to me that he is beginning to be interested in a certain young lady.'

'How young?' Louis Inch asked eagerly.

'Not young enough for our purposes,' Mutford said dryly. 'I think our best shot is to attack him through his staff.' He considered for a moment and then said, 'The Attorney General, Christan Klee, I've had some people check into him. You know he's a somewhat mysterious guy for a public figure. Very rich, much richer than people think, I've taken a sort of unofficial peek at his banking records. Doesn't spend much, he's not keeping women or into drugs, that would have showed up in his cash flow. A brilliant lawyer who doesn't really care that much for law. Not into good works. We know he is devoted to Kennedy and his protection of the President is a marvel of efficiency. But that efficiency hampers Kennedy's campaign because Klee won't let him press the flesh. All in all I'd concentrate on Klee.'

Audick said, 'Klee was CIA, high up in operations. I've heard some weird stories about him.'

'Maybe those stories could be our ammunition,' Mutford said.

'Only stories,' Audick said. 'And you'll never get anything out of the CIA files, not with that guy Tappey running the show.'

George Greenwell said casually, 'I happen to have some information that the President's Chief of Staff, that man Dazzy, has a somewhat messy personal life. His wife and he quarrel and he sees a young girl.'

Oh shit, Mutford thought, I have to get them off this. Jeralyn Albanese had told him all about Christian Klee's full weight.

'That's too minor,' he said. 'What do we gain even if we force Dazzy out? The public will never turn against the President for a staff member screwing a young girl, not unless it's rape or harassment.'

Audick said, 'So we approach the girl and give her a million bucks and have her yell rape.'

Mutford said, 'Yeah but she'd have to holler rape after three years of screwing and having her bills paid. It won't wash.'

It was George Greenwell who made the most valuable contribution. 'We should concentrate on the atom bomb explosion in New York. I think Congressman Jintz and Senator Lambertino should create investigating committees in the House and in the Senate, subpoena all the government officials. Even if they come up with nothing concrete, there will be enough coincidences so that the news media can have a field day. That's where you have to use all your influence,' he said to Salentine. 'That is our best hope. And now I suggest we all get to work.' Then he said to Mutford, 'Set up your campaign committees. I guarantee you'll get my hundred million. It is a very prudent investment.'

When the meeting broke up it was only Bert Audick who considered more radical measures.

Right after this meeting Lawrence Salentine was summoned by President Francis Kennedy. Lawrence Salentine prepared

300

for the meeting by having a conference with his fellow TV network owners. Salentine told them, 'Gentlemen, as I once gave him our bad news, he is going to give me bad news. We are all in a geat deal of trouble.'

And so it had been. Francis Kennedy told Salentine that action would be taken against the networks for unlawfully barring access to the President of the United States to the TV audience on the day Congress voted to impeach him. The charges were already being drawn up by the Attorney General. Francis Kennedy also told Lawrence Salentine that the lax regulatory policies of the past were over. All the TV networks and cable channels were carrying far too many minutes of advertising. That would be cut in half.

When Salentine told the President that Congress would not allow him to do this, Kennedy grinned at him, and said, 'Not this Congress, but we have an election in November. And I'm going to run for re-election. And I'm going to campaign for people in Congress who will support my views.'

Lawrence Salentine went back to his fellow TV station owners and gave them the bad news. 'We have two courses of action,' he said. 'We can start helping the President out by how and when we cover his actions and his policies. Or we can remain free and independent and oppose him when we feel it necessary.' He paused for a moment and said, 'This may be a very perilous time for us. Not just loss of revenue, not just regulatory restrictions, but if Kennedy goes far enough it may be even our losing our licenses.'

This was too much. It was inconceivable that the network licenses could be lost. No more than the homesteaders in early frontier days could lose their land back to the government. The granting of TV station licenses, the free access to the airwaves had always belonged to them. It seemed to them now a natural right. And so the owners made the decision that they would not truckle to the President of the United States, that they would remain free and independent.

And that they would expose President Kennedy for the dangerous menace to American democratic capitalism that he surely was. Lawrence Salentine would relay this decision to the important members of the Socrates Club.

Salentine brooded for days on how to mount a TV campaign against the President on his TV network without making it seem too obvious. After all the American public believed in fair play, they would resent an overwhelming hatchet job. The American public believed in the due process of law though they were the most criminal populace in the world.

He moved carefully. First step, he had to enlist Cassandra Chutt who had the highest-rated national news program. Of course, he couldn't be too direct, anchor people jealously guarded against overt interference. But they had not achieved their eminence without playing ball with top management. And Cassandra Chutt knew how to play ball.

Salentine had nurtured her career over the last twenty years. He had known her when she was on the early morning programs and then when she had switched to evening news. She had always been shameless in her pursuit of advancement. She had been known to collar a Secretary of State and burst into tears, shouting that if he did not give a two-minute interview she would lose her job. She had cajoled and flattered and blackmailed the celebrated into appearing on her prime time interview program and then savaged them with personal and vulgar questions. Lawrence Salentine thought Cassandra Chutt the rudest person he had ever known in the broadcasting business.

Lawrence Salentine invited her to dinner in his apartment. He enjoyed the company of rude people.

When Cassandra arrived the next evening, Salentine was editing a videotape. He brought her to his work room, which had the latest equipment in videos and TV and monitoring and cutting machines, all behatted with small computers.

Cassandra sat on a stool and said, 'Oh shit, Lawrence, do

I have to watch you make your cut of *Gone with the Wind* again?' By answer he brought her a drink from the small bar in a corner of the room.

Lawrence Salentine had a hobby. He would take a video-tape of a movie (he had a collection of what he thought were the hundred best movies ever made) and he would recut these tapes to make them better. Even in his most favorite movies there would be a scene or dialogue that he thought not well done or unnecessary and he would cut it out with editing machines. Now arrayed in the bookcase of his living room were a hundred videotapes of the best motion pictures, somewhat shorter, but perfect. There were even some movies that had their unsatisfactory endings chopped off.

While he and Cassandra Chutt ate the dinner served by a butler, they talked about her future programs. This always put Cassandra Chutt in a good mood. She told Salentine of her plans to visit the Arab states and bring them together on one program with Israel. Then a program with three Prime Ministers of Western Europe chatting with her. And then she was exuberant about going to Japan to interview the Emperor. Salentine listened patiently. Cassandra Chutt had delusions of grandeur but every once in a while she came up with a stunning coup.

Finally he interrupted her and said jokingly, 'Why don't you get President Kennedy on your program?'

Cassandra Chutt lost her good humor. 'He'll never give me a break after what we did to him.'

'It didn't turn out so well,' Lawrence Salentine said. 'But if you can't get Kennedy, then why not go to the other side of the fence? Why not get Congressman Jintz and Senator Lambertino to give their side of the story?'

Cassandra Chutt was smiling at him. 'You sneaky bastard,' she said. 'They lost. They are losers and Kennedy is going to slaughter them in the elections. Why should I have losers on my program? Who the hell wants to watch losers on TV?'

Lawrence Salentine said, 'Jintz tells me they have very important information on the atom bomb explosion, that maybe the Administration dragged its heels. That they didn't utilize properly the Nuclear Search Teams who might have located the bomb before it exploded. And they will say that on your program. You'll make headlines all over the world.'

Cassandra Chutt was stunned. Then she started to laugh. 'Oh, Christ,' she said. 'This is terrible but right after you said that, the question, the very next question I thought to ask those two losers was this, "Do you honestly think the President of the United States is responsible for the ten thousand deaths in the explosion of the nuclear bombs in New York?"'

'That's a very good question,' Lawrence Salentine said.

In the month of June, Audick traveled on his private plane to Sherhaben to discuss with the Sultan the rebuilding of Dak. The Sultan entertained him royally. There were dancing girls, fine food, and a consortium of international financiers the Sultan had assembled who would be willing to invest their money in a new Dak. Bert Audick spent a wonderful week of hard work picking their pockets for a hundred million dollar 'unit' here and a 'unit' there, but the real money would have to come from his own oil firm and the Sultan of Sherhaben.

On the final night of his stay he and the Sultan were alone together in the Sultan's palace. At the end of the meal the Sultan banished the servants and bodyguards from the room.

He smiled at Bert Audick and said, 'I think now we should get down to our real business.' He paused for a moment. 'Did you bring what I requested?'

Bert Audick said, 'I want you to understand one thing. I am not acting against my country. I just have to get rid of that Kennedy bastard or I'll wind up in jail. And he's going to track down all the ins and outs of our dealings over the past ten years. So what I am doing is very much in your interest.'

'I understand,' the Sultan said gently. 'And we are far removed from the events that will happen. Have you made sure the documents cannot be traced to you in any way?'

Bert Audick said, 'Of course.' He then handed over the leather briefcase beside him. The Sultan took it and drew out a file which contained photographs and diagrams.

The Sultan looked at them. They were photos of the White House interiors and the diagrams showed the control posts in different parts of the building. 'Are these up to date?' the Sultan asked.

'No,' Bert Audick said. 'After Kennedy took office three years ago, Christian Klee who's head of the FBI and the Secret Service changed a lot of it around. He added another floor to the White House for the Presidential Residence. I know that the fourth floor is like a steel box. Nobody knows what the set-up is. Nothing is ever published and they sure as hell don't let people know. It's all secret except to the President's closest advisors and friends.'

'Then this isn't much help,' the Sultan said.

Audick shrugged. 'I can help with money, we need fast action. Preferably, before Kennedy gets re-elected.'

'The Hundred can always use the money,' the Sultan said. 'I'll see that it gets to them. But you must understand these people act out of their own true faith. They are not hired assassins. So they will have to believe. The money comes from me as an oppressed small country.' He smiled. 'After the destruction of Dak, I believe Sherhaben qualifies.'

Bert Audick said, 'That's another matter I've come to discuss. My company lost fifty billion dollars when Dak was destroyed. I think we should reconstruct the deal we have on your oil. You were pretty rough last time.'

The Sultan laughed but in a friendly way. 'Mr Audick,' he said, 'for over fifty years the American and British oil companies raped the Arab lands of their oil. You gave

305

ignorant nomad sheiks pennies while you made billions. Really it was shameful. And now your countrymen get indignant when we want to charge what the oil is worth. As if we had anything to say about the price of your heavy equipment and your technological skills for which you charge so dearly. But now it is your turn to pay properly, it is your turn even to be exploited if you care to make such a claim. Please don't be offended but I was even thinking of asking you to "sweeten" our deal.'

They smiled at each other in a friendly fashion. They recognized in each other kindred souls, bargaining men who never missed the chance to pursue a negotiation.

'I guess the American consumer will have to pick up the bill for the crazy President they voted into office,' Audick said. 'I sure hate to do it to them.'

'But you will,' the Sultan said. 'You are a businessman after all, not a politician.'

'On my way to being a jailbird,' Audick said with a laugh. 'Unless I get lucky and Kennedy disappears. I don't want you to misunderstand me. I would do anything for my country but I sure as hell won't let the politicians push me around.'

The Sultan smiled in agreement. 'No more than I would let my parliament.' He clapped his hands for servants and then he said to Audick, 'Now I think it is time for us to enjoy ourselves. Enough of this dirty business of rule and power. Let us live life while we still have it.'

Soon they were sitting down to an elaborate dinner. Audick enjoyed Arab food, he was not squeamish like other Americans, the heads and eyeballs of sheep were mother's milk to him.

As they were eating Audick said to the Sultan, 'If you have someone in America, or anyplace else, who needs a job or some other help send me a message. And if you need money for some worthy cause I can arrange for its transfer from an untraceable source on my end. It is very important to me that we do something about Kennedy.'

'I understand completely,' the Sultan said. 'And now, no more talk of business. I have a duty as your host.'

Annee, who had been hiding out with her family in Sicily, was surprised when she was summoned to a meeting with fellow members of the first Hundred.

She met with them in Palermo. They were two young men she had known when they were all university students in Rome. The oldest, now about thirty years of age, she had always liked very much. He was tall, but stooped and he wore gold-rimmed glasses. He had been a brilliant scholar, destined for a distinguished career as a Professor of Etruscan Studies. In personal relationships he was gentle and kind. His political violence sprang from a mind that detested the cruel illogic of a capitalistic society. His name was Giancarlo.

The other member of the Hundred she knew as the firebrand of leftist parties at the University. A loudmouth, and a brilliant orator who enjoyed fanning crowds to violence but was essentially inept in action. This had been changed when he had been picked up by the Anti-Terrorist Special Police and severely interrogated. In other words, Annee thought, they had kicked the shit out of him and put him in the hospital for a month. Sallu, for that was his name, then talked less and acted more. Finally he was recognized as one of the Christs of Violence, one of the First Hundred.

Both of these men, Giancarlo and Sallu, now lived underground to elude the Italian Anti-Terrorist Security Police. And they had arranged this meeting with care. Annee had been summoned to the town of Palermo and instructed to wander and sightsee until she was contacted. And on the second day, she had encountered a woman named Livia in a boutique who had taken her to a meeting in a small restaurant in which they were the only customers. The restaurant had then closed its doors to the public, the proprietors and the single waiter were obviously cadre. Then Giancarlo and Sallu had emerged from the kitchen. Giancarlo was in chef's regalia and his eyes were twinkling with amusement. In his hands was a huge bowl of spaghetti dyed black with the ink of chopped squid. Sallu, behind him, carried the wooden basket of sesame-seeded golden bread and a bottle of wine.

The four of them, Annee, Livia, Giancarlo and Sallu, sat down to lunch. They could not see into the street because protective curtains shielded them from passers-by.

Giancarlo served them portions of spaghetti from the bowl. The waiter brought them salad and a dish of pink ham and a black and white grainy cheese.

'Just because we fight for a better world, we shouldn't starve,' Giancarlo said. He was smiling and seemed completely at ease.

'Nor die of thirst,' Sallu said as he poured the wine. But he was nervous.

The women let themselves be served; as a matter of revolutionary protocol they did not assume the stereotypic feminine role. But they were both amused. They were here to take orders from men.

As they were eating, Giancarlo opened the conference. 'You two have been very clever,' he said. 'It seems you are not under suspicion for the Easter operation. So it has been decided that we can use you for our new task. You are both extremely qualified. You have the experience but more important, you have the will. So you are being called. But I must warn you. This is more dangerous than Easter.'

Livia asked, 'Do we have to volunteer before we hear the details?'

It was Sallu who answered, and abruptly, 'Yes.'

Annee said impatiently, 'You always go through this routine and ask, "Do you volunteer?" Do we come here for this lousy spaghetti? When we come, we volunteer. So go on with it.'

Giancarlo nodded, he was amused by her. 'Of course. Of course,' he said.

Giancarlo took his time. He ate and said contemplatively, 'The spaghetti is not so bad.' They all laughed and right off that laugh he said, 'The operation is directed against the President of the United States. Mr Kennedy is linking our organization with the atom bomb explosion in his country. His government is planning Special Operations Teams to target us on a global basis. I have come from a meeting where our friends from all over the world have decided to co-operate on this operation.'

Livia said, 'In America, that's impossible for us. Where would we get the money, the lines of communication, how can we set up safe houses and recruit personnel? And above all, the necessary intelligence. We have no base in America.'

Sallu said, 'Money is no problem. We are being funded. Personnel will be infiltrated and have only limited knowledge.'

Giancarlo said, 'Livia, you will go first. We have secret support in America. Very powerful people. They will help you set up safe houses and lines of communication. You will have funds available in certain banks. And you, Annee, will go in after as Chief of Operations. So you will have the tricky part.'

Annee felt a thrill of delight. Finally she would be an operational chief. Finally she would be the equal of Romeo and Yabril.

Livia's voice broke into her thoughts. 'What are our chances?' she asked.

Sallu said reassuringly, 'Yours are very good, Livia. If they get on to us, they'll let you ride free so they can scoop up the whole operation. By the time Annee goes operational, you will be back in Italy.'

Giancarlo said to Annee, 'That's true. Annee, you will be at the greater risk.'

'I understand that,' Annee said.

'So do I,' Livia said. 'I meant what are our chances to succeed?'

'Very small,' Giancarlo said. 'But even if we fail, we gain. We state our innocence.'

They spent the rest of the afternoon going over the operational plans, the codes to be used, the plans for development of the special networks.

It was dusk when they were finished and Annee asked the question that had been unasked the whole afternoon. 'Tell me then, is the worst scenario that this could be a suicide mission?'

Sallu bowed his head. Giancarlo's gentle eyes rested on Annee and then he nodded. 'It could be,' he said, 'but that would be your decision, not ours. Romeo and Yabril are still alive, and we hope to free them. And I promise the same if you are captured.'

President Francis Kennedy instructed Oddblood Gray to contact the Reverend Baxter Foxworth, the most influential and charismatic black leader in America. The way it looked, the black vote might prove to be crucial.

The Reverend Foxworth was forty-five years old and movie-star handsome. He was lithe, his skin showed the infusion of the white blood that he so implored his fellow blacks to shed, figuratively. His hair was crinkly and grown out into a huge Afro that rejected his Caucasian appearance. When he was ushered into Oddblood Gray's office he said, 'The White House at last. Someday, Brother, you and me will be sitting in that Oval Office and handing out the shit.' His voice was as sweet as the birds in his native Louisiana.

Oddblood Gray had risen to greet the preacher and shake his hand. The Reverend always irritated him but they were on the same side, allied in the same battle. And Oddblood Gray was too intelligent not to realize that the Reverend's methods, though contrary to his own, were as necessary in the battle they fought.

Gray said to the Reverend, 'Sideass, I got no time for bullshit today. This is off the record, just you and me.'

The Reverend Foxworth never lost his cool with white folk and he considered Oddblood Gray as white as Simon Legree. He didn't take offense at the use of his nickname. If Oddblood Gray had said Reverend Sideass then there would have been big trouble, White House or cotton shack.

The name Sideass had come from the way the Reverend moved when he was one of the great dancers in New Orleans. He had the moves of a cat, feet crossing sideways over the other. In fact it had been his father who had given him the nickname. Oddblood Gray reminded Foxworth of his father. Gray and his father were both powerfully built, both scornful of religion, severely disciplined, and contemptuous of Baxter Foxworth's high-spirited rebelliousness.

Foxworth was an inflammatory issue between black and white political leaders because of his outrageousness. It was his extremeness that barred him from running for political office but he didn't want political office, or so he claimed.

At the beginning of the Francis Kennedy administration Reverend Foxworth believed that something might be done for the poor blacks of America. But that hope was gone. He had supported Kennedy and respected him. And Kennedy had tried, but Congress and the Socrates Club had been too much for him. So now Foxworth was in for the long haul, to lay down a bed of coals for the fire next time.

He fought the cause of each and every black person, right or wrong. It was the Reverend Foxworth who led marches for convicted murderers caught redhanded. It was the Reverend Foxworth who asked for indictments of police officers who shot and killed black criminals. As the Reverend himself said, in public, on television with his own special grin, 'It's all black and white to me.'

All this could be accepted, in fact, was in the fine liberal tradition and even had some logic since the police were always suspects in American society; here and there the random arrow found a sensitive mark. What made Reverend Foxworth the subject of condemning editorials, his alienation from the two major parties, was his sly anti-Semitism. He implied that Jews sweated money out of the ghettos, Jews controlled political power in the great cities. Jews scooped black maids out of their culture to clean houses and wash dishes. It was worse than the old South, the Reverend said. At least in the South they trusted the niggers with their white children. In fact the Reverend always compared the old South favorably to the modern North.

Therefore it was no surprise, not even to the Reverend himself, that he was hated by many whites in America. And he did not blame the people who hated him. After all he was shooting craps and they were fading him, he often said, the analogy deliberately one that would inflame both sides.

The Reverend Baxter Foxworth was rubbing the cancer in American society until the pain produced the cure. At the beginning of Francis Xavier Kennedy's administration he restrained himself. But when he saw all of Kennedy's social measures defeated by Congress, he shouted to the crowds that this Kennedy was like all the other Kennedys, impotent against the big money people in Congress. And he went on a rampage. All the more so because he had supported Kennedy on the urging of Oddblood Gray. So at this particular moment he was not pleased with Oddblood Gray.

'It's nice having one of the Brothers in this nice office in the White House,' Foxworth said to Gray. 'The Brothers expected you to do a lot for us but you haven't done shit. And then I'm nice enough to come at your beckoning and you call me out of my name. What can I do for you this time, Brother?'

Oddblood Gray had sat down again and the Reverend also sat down. Gray looked at the Reverend grimly. 'I told you not to fuck around. And don't call me brother. In the English language a brother means we have the same mother and father. Use English. You're like those old time leftists, those Jewish Communists you hate so much, who used to call everybody comrade. Today we talk serious business.'

The Reverend took this in good part. He said, 'Isn't the word "friend" a little cold? That white-assed Kennedy, isn't he like a brother? Or why would you support all this crazy stuff he's doing? Otto, we've known each other a long time and you can call me Sideass. But if you weren't so big and mean, your name would have been "Tightass".' The Reverend gave his great laugh. He was immensely tickled. Then he said in a conversational voice, 'How come a man as black as you got the name of Gray? You are the only black named Gray I ever heard of. We get called "White", we get called "Blue", we get called "Green", we even get called "Black". So how come you got called Gray?'

Oddblood Gray smiled. For some reason the Reverend cheered him up. It was the man's high spirits, his energy now as he roamed the office chuckling over the special honoring plaques, the White House ashtrays, even going around the desk and taking a couple of pieces of White House stationery as a joke but Oddblood Gray took them out of his hands. He didn't trust the Reverend.

A long time ago they had been close friends but they had split because of their political differences. The Reverend was too rash for Oddblood Gray, too revolutionary; Gray believed in making the black's place in the existing structure. They had argued the point many times and remained friends and sometimes allies. The Reverend himself had put the difference: 'The trouble with you, Otto,' he said, 'is that you have faith and I don't.'

And that had been the case. The Reverend had adorned himself with the holy cloth as a knight in a joust puts on armor. Nobody dared call a man of the church a liar and a thief and fornicator, not on the TV or even in the sleaziest tabloid. America and its media held the established authority of God's churches in the utmost reverence. A kind of voodoo instinct but also because the churches of every religion had

313

enormous financial clout and expensive lobbyists. Special laws exempted church revenue from taxes.

Oddblood Gray knew all this and in public he always treated the Reverend Baxter Foxworth with the utmost respect. But in private because they were such old friends, because he knew that Foxworth had not a speck of religious feeling, he could be familiar. And besides they had done each other many favors over the years, they had a basic understanding. So now they settled down after the sparring.

'Reverend,' Oddblood Gray said, 'I am going to do you a favor and ask you one. You are smart enough to know we are living in very dangerous times.'

The Reverend smiled and said, 'No shit.'

Oddblood Gray said, 'If you keep fucking around, you could be in serious trouble. The National Security is the overriding interest of the government right now and if you start any of your riots and demonstrations even the Supreme Court can't help you. Not right now. In fact the FBI and the National Security and even the CIA are asking questions, paying you close attention. So that's my favor I'm giving you. Lay low.'

The Reverend was serious now. 'I appreciate the favor, Otto,' he said. 'It's that bad, huh?'

'Yes it is,' Oddblood Gray said. 'This country is scared shitless after that atom bomb explosion. The people of this country will back any repressive actions the Government takes. They won't tolerate anything that even hints at rebellion against authority. Forget about the Constitution right now. And don't think that whitey lawyer of yours can pull one of his tricks.'

Foxworth chuckled. 'Old Whitney Cheever Number III. How I love that man. You ever see him on TV? I swear to God he looks more American than the Stars and Stripes. You print his name and face on the currency, a Shylock would take it. And smart. And sincere. He's one of the best lawyers in the country. He loves anybody breaking the law

314

especially when it's for social progress, especially if it's robbing an armored car and shooting three guards to death. He can turn the defendants into Martin Luther King and keep a straight face. That's why I love the man.'

'Don't trust him,' Oddblood Gray said. 'If things get tough he's the first guy that gets picked up.'

'Whitney Cheever III,' Foxworth said incredulously. 'It would be like locking up Abraham Lincoln.'

'Don't trust him,' Oddblood Gray said.

'Oh, I never trusted him,' Foxworth said. 'He's the worst combination there is. He's white, he's red. Now he's black before he is white. But I understand he's red before he's black.'

Oddblood Gray said, 'I want you to quiet down. I want you to co-operate with this administration. Because new thing are going to happen, that you will love. And also to save your ass.'

Foxworth said, 'Don't worry about my ass. I know enough to lay low right now. What's the favor I do you?'

Gray said, 'I'm going to be named to the Cabinet. And guess as what? The new Secretary of Health, Education and Welfare, the HEW. And I'll have a mandate. Everybody in this country, black or white, never goes hungry, never has to lack medical care, always has a home.'

Foxworth whistled and then smiled at Gray. Same old shit. 'Hundreds of thousands of new jobs. Brother, you and I are going to do great things together. We must stay in touch.'

'You bet,' Oddblood Gray said. 'But lay low.'

'I can't lay *that* low,' Foxworth said. 'And, Otto, I know basically you're on our side but why are you chickenshit and you so black? Why are you so cautious when you know things are not right? Why aren't you out on the streets with us and fighting the good fight?' He was earnest now, not mocking.

Oddblood Gray shrugged. 'Because some day I'm going to

have to save your ass. Listen, Reverend, every once in a while I have to listen to Arthur Wix go on about Israel and how we have to prop it up. How there can never be another holocaust. And I want to say to him that if concentration camps and ovens come in this country it won't be the Jews, it will be us blacks. Don't you see? If ever there is a great calamity, if we should lose a war or something else, the blacks will become the scapegoats in this country. You can see it in the movies. You can see it in the literature. Oh it's not overt, they don't come right out with it. They are not as straight as you are when you come out with your anti-whitey stuff. But that's what I'm afraid of all the time.'

The Reverend listened to him intently. Now he pushed himself against the huge desk and stared into Oddblood Gray's eyes. He said angrily, 'Let me tell you this, our brothers don't walk into those camps like the Jews did. We'll burn down the cities, we'll take them with us.'

Oddblood Gray said gently, 'You'll never know what hit you. You have no idea what a government can muster in power, in deceit, in division, in sheer unfeeling cruelty. You have no idea.'

'Sure I do,' the Reverend said. 'Guys like you will be the Judas goats. Like you're practicing for now.'

'Oh, fuck you, Sideass,' Gray said. 'I was talking about a thousand-to-one shot. Now here's the favor you do me. Kennedy runs for re-election. We need you to get him re-elected by the greatest majority vote in the history of the United States. And to get him his very own Congress.'

Whitney Cheever III was a brilliant, ultra WASP lawyer who firmly believed that the form of the United States government was wrong. He believed in Communism, he believed capitalism was now a great evil, that the pursuit of money had become a cancer in the human psyche. But he was a civilized man, that is, he enjoyed the pleasures of life, classical music, French gourmet food, literature, an exquisitely furnished home, sculpture, painting and young girls. He had been raised rich and enjoyed it but had noted, even as a very young boy, the humiliations of his family servants in their forced deferentiality and their fate resting in the hands of his mother and father. So that everything that was a pleasure in his life had the taint of blood and shit.

Whitney Cheever knew there were many kinds of lawyers. There were the fighters who loved to be in court, but these were few. There were the lawyers who believed in the sanctity of the law, who could forgive anything on this earth, except the breaking of the forms of law, and these were few. There were the workaday lawyers who hacked away at the underbrush of civilization, the guarding of estates, the selling of houses, the arbiter of divorce between husband and wife, between business partners, and many other duties. There were the criminal lawyers, prosecution and defense, a little bleary-eyed and exhausted in spirit who did not escape from the slimy pit in which they labored. There were the constitutional lawyers who aspired to a high judgeship and there were the fierce guardians of the great corporate structures of America who were as ferocious as saints. And then there were lawyers who believed that lasting and beneficial change could only be made fighting against the law. Whitney Cheever III proudly counted himself as one of these.

He was a craggy-faced, handsome man with a full mop of unruly gray hair and he wore his huge black eyeglasses on the top of his head when he was not reading. On television this gave a sort of dashing, intellectual look. He was always being attacked for being a Communist and furthering the interests of the Soviet Union under the sheep's clothing of civil libertarian. He never replied to these attacks, treating them as beneath contempt. Altogether he made a favorable impression on even the most conservative viewers. When he was attacked for defending black criminals or any criminal in which there was political subtext, he would say that it

317

was his duty as a lawyer and an American who believed in the Constitution.

Cheever was having dinner in a New York restaurant with the Reverend Baxter Foxworth and listening to the description of the events in Oddblood Gray's office. When the Reverend had finished, Whitney Cheever said, 'Didn't you bring up the brutal suppression of the demonstrations in New York after that atom bomb exploded?'

The Reverend Foxworth studied that all-American crag of a face, the eyeglasses pushed up on his hair. Is this guy for real, he thought, does Otto have the same shit with those people he works for up in Washington? 'No,' Foxworth said, 'he told me to lay low.'

'Well you and I have always co-operated in these things,' Whitney Cheever said. 'I think we should take the initiative. I think we should start an action of police brutality.'

'Mr Cheever,' Foxworth said, he was most of the time formal with this white man, preserving mutual respect, 'it wasn't the police that shot them, it was the National Guard.'

'But the police were also present,' Whitney Cheever said. 'It is their duty not only to protect against crime, it is also their duty to protect civil rights.'

With some exasperation, Foxworth realized the man was serious. Then he realized he was being argued into an untenable position. 'You're not going to do anything,' he said flatly. 'Reason number one. That was not a demonstration or a free assembly. That was looters out there taking advantage of a national disaster. If we try to exploit that situation we do ourselves more harm than good. Sure a couple of them got shot and there are hundreds in jail, so what. They deserve it. We only weaken our cause if we defend them.'

'But there were no whites shot or arrested,' Cheever said. 'Surely that tells us something.'

'What it tells us is that whites don't need the loot,' the

318

Reverend Foxworth said. 'No good, we don't go along if you do anything.'

'Very well,' Cheever said. 'I agree it may not be the time. And also I've decided on something which will keep me busy and which I know you will not want to be associated with in any way.'

'What's that?' Foxworth asked.

Cheever pushed his glasses down and pushed a little bit away from the table. 'I've decided to defend those two immature boys who set off the atom bomb. Pro bono.'

'JESUS CHRIST,' the Reverend Foxworth said.

16

Christian Klee's Special Division of the FBI ran computer surveillance on the Socrates Club, members of Congress, the Reverend Foxworth and on Whitney Cheever. Klee always started his morning going through their reports. He personally operated his desktop computer which held personal dossiers under his own secret codes.

This particular morning he called up the file of David Jatney. Klee had a fondness for his hunches and his hunch was that Jatney could be trouble. He studied the video image of the young man that appeared on his monitor, the sensitive face, the dark recessed eyes. How the face changed from handsomeness in repose to one of frightening intensity when he became emotional. Were the emotions ugly or just the structure of the face? Jatney was under a loose surveillance, it was just a hunch. But when Klee read the written reports on the computer, he felt a sense of satisfaction. The terrible insect buried in the egg of David Jatney was breaking out of its shell.

Two days after David Jatney assassinated the cardboard effigy of Kennedy, he was kicked out of Brigham Young University. Jatney did not go back to his home in Utah, to his strict Mormon parents who owned a string of dry cleaning stores. He knew his fate there, he had suffered it before. His father believed in starting his son at the bottom, handling bundles of sweaty clothes, male trousers, female dresses, male suit jackets that seemed to weigh a ton. All

320

that cloth and cotton soaked with the warmth of human flesh was agonizing to Jatney's touch.

And like many of the young, he had had quite enough of his parents. They were good, hard-working people who enjoyed their friends, the business they had built up, and the comradeship of the Mormon Church. They were to him the two most boring people in the world.

And then too they lived a happy life which irritated David Jatney. His parents had loved him when he was little, but grown he was so difficult that they joked that they had been given the wrong child in the hospital. They had videos of David Jatney at every stage, the small baby crawling on the floor, the tottering around the room on holidays, leaving him at school for the first time, his graduation from grammar school, his receiving a prize for English composition in high school, fishing with his father, hunting with his uncle.

After his fifteenth birthday he refused to let himself be photographed. He was sensitive, horrified by the banalities of his life recorded on video, an insect programmed to live a short existence in an eternity of sameness. He was determined he would never be like his parents, never realizing that this too was another banality.

Physically he was the opposite pole. Where they were tall and blonde, and then massive by middle age, David Jatney was dark-skinned, thin and wiry. His parents joked about it but predicted that with age he would grow to be more like them, which filled him with horror. By his fifteenth year he showed a coldness toward them that was impossible to ignore. Their own affection in no way lessened, but they were relieved when he went off to Brigham Young.

He grew handsome with dark hair that glowed in its blackness. His features were all-American, that is the nose without a bump, the mouth strong but not too generous, the chin protruding but not intimidatingly so. What his photos did not show was the continuing reaction of his features and of his body. In the beginning, if you knew him for only a

321

short time he seemed merely vivacious. A small motor ran his lips, his nose, his eyelids. His hands were busy when he spoke. His voice inflected sharply on an unimportant note. Then at other times he would sink into a lassitude that froze him into a sort of sullenness.

In college, his vivaciousness and intelligence made him attractive to the other students. But he was just a little too bizarre in his reactions and his earnestness; and sometimes brutally insulting, almost always condescending.

The truth was that David Jatney was in an agony of impatience to be famous, to be a hero, to have the world know he was special.

With women he had a shy confidence that won them over initially. They found him interesting and so he had his little love affairs. But they never lasted. He was off-putting, he was distant; after the first few weeks of vivaciousness and good humor he would sink into himself. Even in sex he seemed detached as if he did not want to lose control of his body. His greatest failing in the area of love was that he refused to worship the beloved, even in the courtship phase, and when he did his best to fall deeply in love it had the aura of a valet exerting himself for a generous tip.

He had always been interested in politics and the social order. Like most young men, he had contempt for authority in any form, the study of history revealed that the story of humanity was simply endless warfare between the powerful elite and the helpless multitude. He desired fame to join the powerful.

It was natural that he was voted Chief Hunter in the assassination game played every year at Brigham Young. And it was his clever planning that resulted in victory. He had also supervised the making of the effigy that so resembled Kennedy.

With the shooting of that effigy and the victory banquet afterwards, David Jatney experienced a revulsion for his student life. It was time to make a career. He had always written poetry, kept a diary in which he felt he could show his wit and intelligence. Since he was so sure he would be famous, this keeping of a diary with an eye on posterity was not necessarily immodest. And so he recorded, 'I am leaving college, I have learnt all that they can teach me. Tomorrow I drive to California to see if I can make it in the movie world.'

When David Jatney arrived in Los Angeles, he did not know a single soul. That suited him, he liked the feeling. With no responsibilities, he could concentrate on his thoughts, he could figure out the world. The first night he slept in a small motel room and then found a one-room apartment in Santa Monica that was cheaper than he had expected. He found this through the kindness of a matronly woman who was a waitress in a coffee shop where he took his first breakfast in California.

David Jatney ate frugally, a glass of orange juice, toast and coffee, and the waitress noticed him studying the rental section of the *Los Angeles Times*. She asked him if he was looking for a place to live and he said yes. She wrote down a phone number on a piece of paper and said it was just a one-room apartment but the rent was reasonable because the people in Santa Monica had fought a long battle with the real estate interests and there was a tough rent control law. And Santa Monica was beautiful and he would be only a few minutes away from the Venice beach and its board-walk and it was a lot of fun.

Jatney at first was suspicious. Why would this stranger be interested in his welfare? She looked motherly but she had a sexy air about her. Of course she was very old, she must be forty at least. But she didn't seem to be coming on to him. And she gave him a cheery goodbye when he left. He was to learn that people in California did things like this. The constant sunshine seemed to mellow them. Mellowing. That's what it was. It cost her nothing to do him the service.

Jatney had driven from Utah in the car that his parents

323

had given him for college. In it was his every worldly possession, except for a guitar that he had once tried to learn and which was back in Utah. Most important was a portable typewriter which he used to write his diary, poetry, short stories and novels. Now that he was in California he would try his first screenplay.

Everything fell into place easily. He got the apartment, a little place with a shower but no bath. It looked like a dollhouse with frilly curtains over its one window and prints of famous paintings on the wall. The apartment was in a row of two-storey houses behind Montana Avenue and he could even park his car in the alley. He had been very lucky.

He spent the next fourteen days hanging around the Venice beach and boardwalk taking rides up to Malibu to see how the rich and famous lived. He leaned against the steel link fence that cut off the Malibu Colony from the public beach and peered through. There was this long row of beach houses that stretched far to the north. Each worth three million dollars and more, and yet they looked like ordinary countrified shacks. They wouldn't cost more than twenty thousand in Utah. But they had the sand, the purple ocean, the brilliant sky, the mountains behind them across the Pacific Coast Highway. Some day he would sit on the balcony of one of those houses and gaze over the Pacific.

At night in his dollhouse he sank into long dreams of what he would do when he too was rich and famous. He would lay awake until the early hours of the morning weaving his fantasies. It was a lonely and curiously happy time.

He called his parents to give them his new address and his father gave him the number of a producer to call at the movie studio, a childhood friend named Dean Hocken. Jatney waited a week. Finally he made the call and got through to Hocken's secretary. She asked him to hold. In a few moments she came back on the phone and told him that Mr Hocken was not in. He knew it was a con, that he was being sloughed off and he felt the surge of anger at his father for being so dumb. But he gave the secretary his phone number when she asked. He was still on his daybed brooding angrily an hour later when the phone rang. It was Dean Hocken's secretary and she asked him if he was free at eleven the next morning to see Mr Hocken in his office. He said he was and she told him that she would leave a pass at the gate so that he could drive on the studio lot.

When he hung up the phone David Jatney was surprised at the gladness welling up in him. A man he had never seen had honored a schoolboy friendship. And then he was ashamed of his own debasing gratitude. Sure the guy was a big wheel, sure his time was valuable, but eleven in the morning? That meant he would not be asked to lunch. It would be one of those quick courtesy interviews so the guy wouldn't feel guilty. So that his relatives back in Utah could point out that he didn't have a big head. A mean politeness basically without value.

But the next day turned out differently than he expected. Dean Hocken's office was in a long low building on the movie lot, and impressive. There was a receptionist in a big waiting room whose walls were covered with posters of bygone movies. Two other offices behind the reception room held two more secretaries, and then a larger, grander office. This office was furnished beautifully with deep armchairs and sofas and rugs, the walls were hung with original paintings, it had a bar with a large refrigerator. In a corner was a working desk topped with leather. On the wall above the desk was a huge photograph of Dean Hocken shaking hands with President Francis Xavier Kennedy. There was a coffee table littered with magazines and bound scripts. The office was empty.

The secretary who had brought him in said, 'Mr Hocken will be with you in ten minutes. Can I get you a drink or some coffee?'

Jatney was polite in his refusal. He could see that the young secretary was giving him an appraising glance so he used his real shitkicker's voice. He knew he made a good impression. Women always liked him at first, it was only when they got to know him better that they didn't like him, he thought. But maybe that was because he didn't like them when he got to know them better.

He had to wait for fifteen minutes before Dean Hocken came into the office from a back door that was almost invisible. David Jatney was for the first time in his life really impressed. This was a man who truly looked successful and powerful, he radiated confidence and friendliness as he grabbed David Jatney's hand.

Dean Hocken was tall and David Jatney cursed his own shortness. Hocken was at least six foot two and he looked amazingly youthful, though he must be the same age as Jatney's father which was fifty-five. He wore casual clothes, but his white shirt was whiter than any Jatney had ever seen. His jacket was some sort of linen and hung beautifully on his frame. The trousers were linen also, sort of off white. Hocken's face seemed without a wrinkle and painted over with bronze ink sprayed from the sun.

Dean Hocken was as gracious as he was youthful. He diplomatically revealed a homesickness for the Utah mountains, the Mormon life, the silence and peace of rural existence, the quiet Tabernacled cities. And he also revealed that he had been suitor to the hand of David Jatney's mother.

'Your mother was my girlfriend,' Dean Hocken said. 'Your father stole her away from me. But it was for the best, those two really loved each other, made each other happy.' And Jatney thought, yes, it was true, his mother and father really loved each other and with their perfect love they had shut him out. In the long winter evenings they sought their warmth in a conjugal bed while he watched his TV. But that had been a long time ago.

He watched Dean Hocken talk and be charming and he saw the age beneath that carefully preserved outward armor of bronzed skin stretched too tight for nature. The man had no flesh beneath his chin, not a sign of the wattles that had grown on his father. He wondered why the man was being so nice to him.

'I've had four wives since I left Utah,' Dean Hocken said, 'and I would have been much happier with your mother.' Jatney watched for the usual signs of satisfaction, the hint that his mother too might have been much happier if she had stuck with the successful Dean Hocken. But he saw none. The man was still a country boy beneath that California polish.

Jatney listened politely and laughed at the jokes. He called Dean Hocken 'Sir' until the man told him to please just call him 'Hock', and then he didn't call him anything. Hocken talked an hour and then looked at his watch and said abruptly, 'It was good seeing somebody from down home, but I guess you didn't come to hear about Utah. What do you do?'

'I'm a writer,' David Jatney said. 'The usual stuff, a novel that I threw away and some screenplays, I'm still learning.' He had never written a novel.

Dean Hocken nodded approval of his modesty. 'You have to earn your dues. Here's what I can do for you right now. I can get you a spot in the reader's department on the studio payroll. You read scripts and write a summary and your opinion. Just a half page on each script you read. That's how I started. You get to meet people and learn the basics. Truth is, nobody pays much attention to the reports, but do your best. It's just a starting point. Now I'll arrange all this and one of my secretaries will get in touch with you in a few days. And soon, we'll have dinner together. Give my best to your mother and father.' And then Hock escorted David Jatney to the door. They were not going to have lunch, Jatney thought, and the promise of dinner would stretch out for ever. But at least he would get a job, he would get one foot in the door, and then when he wrote his screenplays, everything would change.

Jatney spent a month reading scripts which seemed to him utterly worthless. He wrote the short, less than half page of summary, then wrote his opinion on the same page. His opinion was supposed to be only a few sentences but he usually finished using the rest of the space on the page.

At the end of the month the office supervisor came to his desk and said, 'David, we don't have to know how witty you are. Just two sentences of opinion will be fine. And don't be so contemptuous of these people, they didn't piss on your desk, they just try to write movies.'

'But they are terrible,' Jatney said.

The supervisor said, 'Sure they are, do you think we'd let you read the good ones? We have more experienced people for that. And besides this stuff you call dreadful, every one of them has been submitted by an agent. An agent hopes to make money from them. So they have passed a very stringent test. We don't accept scripts over the transom because of lawsuits, we're not like book publishers. So no matter how lousy they are, when agents submit, we have to read them. If we don't read the agent's bad scripts they don't send us the good ones.'

Jatney said, 'I could write better screenplays.'

The supervisor laughed. 'So can we all.' He paused for a moment and then said, 'When you've written one let me read it.'

A month later David Jatney did just that. The supervisor read it in his private office. He was very kind. He said gently, 'David, it doesn't work. That doesn't mean you can't write. But you don't really understand how movies work. It shows in your summaries and critiques but your screenplay shows it too. Listen, I'm trying to be helpful. Really. So starting next week you'll be reading the novels that are published and that have been considered possible for movies.'

328

David Jatney thanked him politely but felt the familar rage. Again it was the voice of the elder, the supposedly wiser, the ones who had the power.

It was just a few days later that Dean Hocken's secretary called and asked if he was free for dinner that night with Mr Hocken. He was so surprised it took him a moment to say yes. She told him it would be at Michael's restaurant in Santa Monica at eight p.m. She started to give him directions to the restaurant but he told her he lived in Santa Monica and knew where it was, which was not strictly true.

But he had heard of Michael's restaurant. David Jatney read all the newspapers and magazines and he listened to the gossip in the office. Michael's was the restaurant of choice for the movie and music people who lived in the Malibu Colony. When he hung up the phone he asked the manager if he knew exactly where Michael's was located mentioning casually that he was having dinner there that night. He saw that the manager was impressed. He realized that he should have waited until after this dinner before submitting his screenplay. It would have then been read in a different context.

That evening when David Jatney walked into Michael's restaurant he was surprised that only the front part was under a roof, the rest of the restaurant was in a garden made beautiful with flowers and large white umbrellas that formed a secure canopy against rain. The whole area was glowingly lit. It was just beautiful, the balmy open air of April, the flowers gushing their perfume and even a gold moon over-head. What a difference from a Utah winter. It was at this moment that David Jatney decided never to go home again.

He gave his name to the receptionist and was surprised when he was led directly to one of the tables in the garden. He had planned on arriving ahead of Hocken, he knew his role and intended to play it well. He would be absolutely respectful, he would be waiting at the restaurant for good old Hock to arrive and that would be acknowledging his

329

power. He still wondered about Hocken. Was the man genuinely kind or just a Hollywood phony being condescending to the son of a woman who once rejected him and now must, of course, be regretting it?

He saw Dean Hocken at the table he was being led to and with Hocken was a man and a woman. The first thing that registered on David Jatney was that Hocken had deliberately given him a later time so that he would not have to wait, an extraordinary kindness that almost moved him to tears. For in addition to being paranoid and ascribing mysterious evil motives for other people's behavior, David Jatney could also ascribe wildly benevolent reasons.

Hocken got up from the table to give him a down-home hug and then introduced him to the man and woman. Jatney recognized the man at once. His name was Gibson Grange and he was one of the most famous actors in Hollywood. The woman's name was Rosemary Belair, a name that Jatney was surprised he didn't recognize because she was beautiful enough to be a movie star. She had glossy black hair worn long and her face was perfect in its symmetry. Her make-up was professional and she was dressed elegantly in a dinner dress over which was some sort of little jacket.

They were drinking wine, the bottle rested in a silver bucket. Hocken poured Jatney a glass.

The food was delicious, the air balmy, the garden serene, none of the cares of the world could enter here, Jatney felt. The men and women at the tables around them exuded confidence, these were the people who controlled life. Someday he would be like them.

He listened through the dinner, saying very little. He studied the people at his table. Dean Hocken, he decided was legitimate and as nice as he appeared to be. Which did not necessarily mean that he was a good person, Jatney thought. He became conscious that though this was ostensibly a social occasion, Rosemary and Hock were trying to talk Gibson Grange into doing a picture with them.

It seemed that Rosemary Belair was also a producer, in fact the most important female producer in Hollywood.

David Jatney listened and watched, he took no part in the conversation, and when he was immobile his face was handsome as his photographs. The other people at the table registered it but he did not interest them and Jatney was aware of this.

And it suited him right now. Invisible, he could study this powerful world he hoped to conquer. That Hocken had arranged this dinner to give his friend Rosemary a chance to talk Gibson Grange into doing a picture with her. But why? There was a certain easiness between Hocken and Rosemary that could not be there unless they had been through a sexual period. It was the way Hocken soothed Rosemary when she became too excited in her pursuit of Gibson Grange. At one time she said to Gibson, 'I'm a lot more fun to do a picture with than Hock.'

And Hocken laughed and said, 'We had some pretty good times didn't we, Gib?'

And the actor said, 'Nah, we were all business.' He said this without cracking a smile.

Gibson Grange was a 'bankable' star in the movie business. That is, if he agreed to do a movie, that movie was financed immediately by any studio. Which was why Rosemary was so anxiously pursuing him. He also looked exactly right. He was in the old American Gary Cooper style, lanky, with open features: he looked as Lincoln would have looked if Lincoln had been handsome. His smile was friendly and he listened to everyone intently when they spoke. He told a few good-humored anecdotes about himself that were funny. This was especially endearing. Also he dressed in the style that was more homespun than Hollywood, baggy trousers and a ratty yet obviously expensive sweater with an old suit jacket over a plain woolen shirt. And yet he magnetized everyone in the garden. Was it because his face had been seen by so many millions and shown so intimately by the camera? Were there mysterious ozone layers where his face remained for ever? Was it some physical manifestation not yet solved by science? The man was intelligent, Jatney could see that. His eyes as he listened to Rosemary were amused but not condescending and though he seemed to always agree with what she was saying, he never committed himself to anything. He was the man David Jatney dreamed to be.

They lingered over their wine. Hocken ordered dessert, wonderful French pastries, Jatney had never tasted anything so good. Both Gibson Grange and Rosemary Belair refused to touch the desserts, Rosemary with a shudder of horror and Gibson Grange with a slight smile. But it was Rosemary who would surely let herself be tempted in the future. Grange was secure, Jatney thought. Grange would never touch dessert again in his life but Rosemary's fall was inevitable.

At Hocken's urging, David Jatney ate the other desserts, and then they still lingered and talked. Hocken ordered another bottle of wine but only he and Rosemary drank from it and then Jatney noticed another undercurrent in the conversation. Rosemary was putting the make on Gibson Grange.

Rosemary had barely talked to Jatney at all during the evening and now she ignored him so completely that he was forced to chat with Hocken about the old days in Utah. But both of them finally became so entranced by the contest between Rosemary and Gibson that they fell silent.

For as the evening wore on and more wine was drunk Rosemary mounted a full seduction. It was of alarming intensity, an awesome display of sheer will. She presented her virtues. First were the movements of her body and face, somehow the front of her dress had slipped down to show more of her breasts. There were the movements of her legs which crossed and recrossed then hiked the gown higher to show a glint of thigh. Her hands moved about, touching Gibson on his face when she was carried away by what she was saying. She showed her wit, told funny anecdotes, and revealed her sensitivity. Her beautiful face was alive to show each emotion, her affection for the people she worked with, her worries about members of her immediate family, her concern about the success of her friends. She avowed her deep affection for Dean Hocken himself, how good old Hock had helped her in her career, rewarded her with advice and influence. Here good old Hock interrupted to say how much she deserved such help because of her hard work on his pictures and her loyalty to him and as he said this Rosemary gave him a long look of grateful acknowledgement. At this moment Jatney, completely enchanted, said that it must have been a great experience for both of them. But Rosemary, eager to renew her pursuit of Gibson, cut Jatney off in mid-sentence.

Jatney felt a tiny shock at her rudeness but surprisingly no resentment. She was so beautiful, so intent on gaining what she desired, and what she desired was becoming clearer and clearer. She must have Gibson Grange in her bed that night. Her desire had the purity and directness of a child, which made her rudeness almost endearing.

But what Jatney admired above all was the behavior of Gibson Grange. The actor was completely aware of what was happening. He noticed the rudeness to Jatney and tried to make up for it by saying, 'David, you'll get a chance to talk someday,' as if apologizing for the self-centeredness of the famous who have no interest in those who have not yet acquired their fame. But Rosemary cut him off too. And Gibson politely listened to her. But it was more than politeness. He had an innate charm that was part of his being. He regarded Rosemary with genuine interest. His eyes sparkled and never wandered from her eyes. When she touched him with her hands he patted her back. He made no bones about it, he liked her. His mouth too, always parted in a smile that displayed a natural sweetness which softened his craggy face into a humorous mask.

But he was obviously not responding in the proper fashion

for Rosemary. She was pounding on an anvil that gave off no sparks. She drank more wine and then played her final card. She revealed her innermost feelings.

Talking directly to Gibson, ignoring the other two men at the table. Indeed she had maneuvered her body so that it was very close to Gibson isolating them from David Jatney and Hocken.

No one could doubt the passionate sincerity in her voice. There were even tears in her eyes. She was baring her soul to Gibson. 'I want to be a real person,' she said. 'I would like to give up all this shit of make-believe, this business of movies. It doesn't satisfy me. I want to go out to make the world a better place. Like Mother Teresa, or Martin Luther King. I'm not doing anything to help make the world grow. I could be a nurse or a doctor, I could be a social worker. I hate this life, these parties, this always being on a plane for meetings with important people. Making decisions about some damned movie that won't help humanity. I want to do something real.' And then she reached out and clutched Gibson Grange's hand.

It was marvelous for David Jatney to see why Grange had become such a powerful star in the movie business, why he controlled the movies he appeared in. For Gibson Grange somehow had his hand in Rosemary's, somehow he had slid his chair away from her, somehow he had captured the central position in the tableau. Rosemary was still staring at him with an impassioned look on her face waiting for his response. He smiled at her warmly, then tilted his head downward and to the side so that he addressed Jatney and Hocken.

Gibson Grange said with affectionate approval, 'She's slick.'

Dean Hocken burst into laughter, David Jatney could not repress a smile. Rosemary looked stunned but then said in a tone of jesting reproof, 'Gib, you never take anything seriously except your lousy movies.' And to show she was not offended she held out a hand which Gibson Grange gently kissed.

David Jatney wondered at all of them. They were so sophisticated, they were so subtle. He admired Gibson Grange most of all. That he would spurn a woman as beautiful as Rosemary Belair was awe-inspiring, that he would outwit her so easily was godlike.

Jatney had been ignored by Rosemary all evening, but he acknowledged her right to do so. She was the most powerful woman in the most glamorous business in the country. She had access to men far worthier than he. She had every right to be rude. Jatney recognized that she did not do so out of malice. She simply found him non-existent.

They were all astonished that it was nearly midnight, they were the last ones in the restaurant. Hocken stood up and Gibson Grange helped Rosemary put on her jacket again, which she had taken off in the middle of her passionate discourse. When Rosemary stood up she was a little off balance, a little drunk.

'Oh, God,' she said. 'I don't dare drive myself, the police in this town are so awful. Gib, will you take me back to my hotel?'

Gibson smiled at her. 'That's in Beverley Hills. Me and Hock are going out to my house in Malibu. David will give you a ride, won't you, David?'

'Sure,' Dean Hocken said. 'You don't mind do you, David?'

'Of course not,' David Jatney said. But his mind was spinning. How the hell was this coming about? Good old Hock was looking embarrassed. Obviously Gibson Grange had lied, didn't want to take Rosemary home because he didn't want to have to keep fending the woman off. And Hock was embarrassed because he had to go along with the lie or else he would get on the wrong side of a big star, something a movie producer avoided at all costs. Then he saw Gibson give him a little smile and he could read the man's mind. And of course that was it, that was why he was such a great actor. He could make audiences read this mind just wrinkling his eyebrows, tilting his head, a dazzling smile. With just that look, without malice but celestial good humor, he was saying to David Jatney, 'The bitch ignored you all evening, she was rude as hell to you, now I have put her in your debt.' Jatney looked at Hocken and saw that he was now smiling, not embarrassed. In fact he looked pleased as if he too had read the actor's look.

Rosemary said abruptly, 'I'll drive myself.' She did not look at Jatney when she said it.

Dean Hocken said smoothly, 'I can't allow that, Rosemary, you are my guest and I did give you too much wine. If you hate the idea of David driving you then of course I'll take you back to your hotel. Then I'll order a limo to Malibu.'

It was Jatney realized, superbly done. For the first time he detected insincerity in Hocken's voice. Of course Rosemary could not accept Hocken's offer. If she did so she would be offering a grievous insult to the young friend of her mentor. She would be putting both Hocken and Gibson Grange to a great deal of inconvenience. And her primary purpose in getting Gibson to take her home would not be accomplished anyway. She was caught in an impossible situation.

Then Gibson Grange delivered the final blow. He said, 'Hell, I'll ride with you, Hock. I'll just take a nap in the back seat to keep you company to Malibu.'

Rosemary gave David a bright smile. She said, 'I hope it won't be too much trouble for you.'

'No, it won't,' David Jatney said. Hocken clapped him on the shoulder, Gibson Grange gave him a brilliant smile and a wink. And that smile and wink gave Jatney another message. These two men were standing by him as males. A lone powerful female had shamed one of their fellow males and they were punishing her. Also she had come on too strong to Gibson, it was not in a woman's place to do so

336

with a male more than equal in power. They had just administered a patriarchal blow to her ego, to keep her in her place. And it was all done with such marvelous good humor and politeness. And there was another factor. These men remembered when they had been young and powerless as Jatney was now, they had invited him to dinner to show that their success did not leave them faithless to their fellow males, a time-hallowed practice perfected over centuries to forestall any envious revenge. Rosemary had not honored this practice, had not remembered her time of powerlessness and tonight they had reminded her. And yet Jatney was on Rosemary's side, she was too beautiful to be hurt.

They walked out into the parking lot together and then when the other two men roared away in Hocken's Porsche, David Jatney led Rosemary to his old Toyota.

Rosemary said, 'Shit I can't get out at the Beverly Hills Hotel from a car like that.' She looked around and said, 'Now I have to find my car. Look, David, do you mind driving me back in my Mercedes? It's somewhere around here, and I'll have a hotel limo bring you back. That way I won't have to have my car picked up in the morning. Could we do that?' She smiled at him sweetly then reached into her pocketbook and put on spectacles. She pointed to one of the few remaining cars in the lot and said, 'There it is.' Jatney, who had spotted her car as soon as they were outside, was puzzled. Then he realized she must be extremely nearsighted. Maybe it was nearsightedness that made her ignore him at dinner.

She gave him the key to her Mercedes and he unlocked the door on her side and helped her in. He could smell the wine and perfume composted on her body and felt the heat of her bones like burning coal. Then he went to the other side of the car to get in the driver's seat and before he used the key, the door swung open, Rosemary had unlocked it from the inside to open it for him. He was surprised by this, he would have judged it not in her character.

337

It took him a few minutes to figure how the Mercedes worked. But he loved the feel of the seats, the smell of the reddish leather, was it a natural smell or did she spray the car with some sort of special leather perfume? And the car handled beautifully, for the first time he understood the acute pleasure some people took from driving.

The Mercedes seemed to just flow through the dark streets. He enjoyed driving so much that the half hour to the Beverly Hills Hotel seemed to pass in an instant. In all that time Rosemary did not speak to him. She took off her spectacles and put them back into her purse and then sat silent. Once she glanced at his profile as if appraising him. Then she just stared straight ahead. Jatney never once turned to her or spoke. He was enjoying the dream of driving a beautiful woman in a beautiful car, in the heart of the most glamorous town in the world.

When he stopped at the canopied entrance to the Beverly Hills Hotel, he took the keys out of the ignition and handed them to Rosemary. Then he got out and went around to open her door. At the same moment one of the valet parking men came down the red-carpeted runway and Rosemary handed him the keys to her car. Jatney realized he should have left them in the ignition.

Rosemary started up the red-carpeted runway to the entrance of the hotel and Jatney knew she had completely forgotten about him. He was too proud to remind her about offering a limo to take him back. He watched her. Under the green canopy, the balmy air, the golden lights, she seemed like a lost princess. Then she stopped and turned, he could see her face, and she looked so beautiful that David Jatney's heart stopped.

He thought she had remembered him, that she expected him to follow her. But she turned again and tried to go up the three steps that would bring her to the doors. At that moment she tripped, her purse went flying out of her hands and everything in that purse scattered on the ground. By that time Jatney had dashed up the red carpet runway to help her.

The contents of the purse seemed endless, it was magical in the way it continued to spill out its contents. There were solitary lipsticks, a make-up case which burst open and poured mysteries of its own, there was a ring of keys which immediately broke and scattered at least twenty keys around the carpet. There was a bottle of aspirin and prescription vials of different drugs. And a huge pink toothbrush. There was a cigarette lighter and no cigarettes, there was a tube of Binaca and a little plastic bag that held blue panties and some sort of device that looked sinister. There were innumerable coins, some paper money and a soiled white linen handkerchief. There were spectacles, gold-rimmed, spinsterish without the adornment of Rosemary's classically sculptured face.

Rosemary looked at all this with horror then burst into tears. Jatney knelt on the red carpet runway and started to sweep everything into the purse. Rosemary didn't help him. When one of the bellmen came out of the hotel, Jatney had him hold the purse with its mouth open while he shoveled the stuff into it.

Finally he had gotten everything and he took the now full purse from the bellman and gave it to Rosemary. He could see her humiliation and wondered at it. She dried her tears and said to him, 'Come up to my suite for a drink until your limo comes, I haven't had a chance to speak to you all evening.'

Jatney smiled. He was remembering Gibson Grange saying, 'She's slick.' But he was curious about the famous Beverly Hills Hotel and he wanted to stay around Rosemary.

He thought the green-painted walls were weird for a high-class hotel, dingy in fact. But when they entered the huge suite he was impressed. It was beautifully decorated and it had a large terrace, a balcony, in fact. There was also a bar in one corner. Rosemary went to it and mixed herself a drink, then, after asking him what he wanted, mixed him one. He had asked for just a plain scotch, though he rarely drank he was feeling a little nervous. She unlocked the glass sliding doors to the terrace and led him outside. There was a white glass-topped table and four white chairs. 'Sit here while I go to the bathroom,' Rosemary said, 'then we'll have a little chat.' She disappeared back into the suite.

David Jatney sat in one of the chairs and sipped his scotch. Below him were the interior gardens of the Beverly Hills Hotel. He could see the swimming pool and the tennis courts, the walks that led to the bungalows. There were trees and individual lawns, the grass greener under moonlight and the lighting glancing off the pink-painted walls of the hotel gave everything a surrealistic glow.

It was no more than ten minutes later when Rosemary reappeared. She sat in one of the chairs and sipped her drink. Now she was wearing loose white slacks and a white pullover cashmere sweater. She had pushed the sleeves of her sweater up above her elbows. She smiled at him, it was a dazzling smile. She had washed her face clean of make-up and he liked her better this way. Her lips were now not voluptuous, her eyes not so commanding. She looked younger and more vulnerable. Her voice when she spoke seemed easier, softer, less commanding.

'Hock tells me you're a screenwriter,' she said. 'Do you have anything you'd like to show me? You can send it to my office.'

'Not really,' Jatney said. He smiled back at her. He would never let himself be rejected by her.

'But Hock said you had one finished,' Rosemary said. 'I'm always looking for new writers. It's so hard to find some-thing decent.'

'No,' Jatney said. 'I wrote four or five but they were so terrible I tore them up.'

They were silent for a time, it was easy for David Jatney

to be silent, it was more comfortable for him than speech. Finally Rosemary said, 'How old are you?'

David Jatney lied and said, 'Twenty-six.'

Rosemary smiled at him. 'God, I wish I were that young again. You know when I came here I was eighteen, I wanted to be an actress, and I was a half-assed one. You know those one-line parts on TV, the salesgirl the heroine buys something from? Then I met Hock and he made me his executive assistant and taught me everything I know. He helped me set up my first picture and he helped all through the years. I love Hock, I always will. But he's so tough, like tonight. He stuck with Gibson against me.' Rosemary shook her head. 'I always wanted to be as tough as Hock,' she said. 'I modeled myself after him.'

David Jatney said, 'I think he's a very nice gentle guy.'

'But he's fond of you,' Rosemary said. 'Really, he told me so. He said you look so much like your mother and you act just like her. He says you're a really sincere person, not a hustler.' She paused for a moment and then said, 'I can see that too. You can't imagine how humiliated I felt when all that stuff spilled out of my purse. And then I saw you picking everything up and never looking at me. You were really very sweet.' She leaned over and kissed him on the cheek. He could smell a different sweeter fragrance coming from her body now.

Abruptly she stood up and sent back into the suite, he followed her. She closed the glass door of the terrace and locked it and then said, 'I'll call for your limo.' She picked up the phone. But instead of pressing the buttons she held it in her hand and looked at David Jatney. He was standing very still, standing far enough away not to be in her space. She said to him, 'David, I'm going to ask you something that might sound odd. Would you stay with me tonight? I feel lousy and I need company but I want you to promise you won't try to do anything. Could we just sleep together like friends?'

Jatney was stunned. He had never dreamed this beautiful woman would want someone like him. He was dazzled by his good fortune. But then Rosemary said sharply, 'I mean it, I just want someone nice like you to be with me tonight. You have to promise you won't do anything. If you try, I'll be very angry.'

This was so confusing to Jatney that he smiled and as if not understanding, he said, 'I'll sit on the terrace or sleep on the couch here in the living room.'

'No,' Rosemary said. 'I just want somebody to hug me and go to sleep with. I just don't want to be alone. Can you promise?'

David Jatney heard himself say, 'I don't have anything to wear. In bed I mean.'

Rosemary said briskly, 'Just take a shower and sleep naked, it won't bother me.'

There was a foyer from the living room of the suite that led to the bedroom. In this foyer was an extra bathroom in which Rosemary told David Jatney to take his shower. She did not want him to use her bathroom. Jatney showered and brushed his teeth using soap and tissues. There was a bathrobe hanging from the back of the door with blue stitching script that said elegantly 'Beverly Hills Hotel'. He went into the bedroom and found Rosemary was still in her bathroom. He stood there awkwardly not wanting to get into her bed which had already been turned down by the night maid. Finally Rosemary came out of the bathroom wearing a flannel nightgown that was so elegantly cut and printed that she looked like a doll in a toy store. 'Come on, get in,' she said. 'Do you need a Valium or a sleeping pill?' And he knew she had already taken one. She sat at the edge of the bed and then got in and finally Jatney got into the bed but kept his bathrobe on. They were lying side by side when she turned the light out on her night table. They were in darkness. 'Give me a hug,' she said and they embraced for a

342

long moment and then she rolled away to her side of the bed and said briskly, 'Pleasant dreams.'

David Jatney lay on his back staring up at the ceiling. He didn't dare take off the bathrobe, he didn't want her to think that he wanted to be naked in her bed. He wondered if he should tell Hock about this the next time they met but he understood that it would become a joke that he had slept with such a beautiful woman and nothing had happened. And maybe Hock would think he was lying. He wished he had taken the sleeping pill Rosemary had offered him. She was already asleep, she had a tiny snore just barely audible.

Jatney decided to go back to the living room and got out of bed. Rosemary came awake and said sleepily, 'Could you get me a drink of Evian water.' Jatney went into the living room and fixed two Evian waters with a little ice. He drank from his glass and refilled it. Then he went back into the bedroom. By the light in the foyer he could see Rosemary sitting up, the bedsheets tight around her. He offered a glass and she reached out a bare arm for it. In the dark room he touched her upper body before finding her hand to give her the glass, and realized she was naked. As she was drinking he slipped into the bed but he let his bathrobe fall to the floor.

He heard her put the glass on the night table and then he put out his hand and touched her flesh. He felt the bare back and the softness of her buttocks. She rolled over and into his arms and his chest was against her bare breasts. Her arms were around him and the hotness of their bodies made them kick off the covers as they kissed. They kissed for a long time, her tongue in his mouth, and then he couldn't wait any longer and he was on top of her, and her hand as smooth as satin, a permission, guided him into her. They made love almost silently as if they were being spied upon until both their bodies together arched in the flight toward climax and they lay back separate again.

Finally she whispered, 'Now go to sleep.' She kissed him gently on the side of the mouth.

He said, 'I want to see you.'

'No,' she whispered.

David Jatney reached over and turned on her table light. Rosemary closed her eyes. She was still beautiful. Even with desire sated, even though she was stripped of all the arts of beauty, the enhancements of coquetry, the artifices of special light, but it was a different beauty.

He had made love out of animal need and proximity, a natural physical expression of his body. She had made love out of a need in her heart, or some spinning need in her brain. And now in the glow of the single light, her naked body was no longer formidable. Her breasts were small with tiny nipples, her body smaller, her legs not so long, her hips not so wide, her thighs a little slender. She opened her eyes, looking directly into his and he said, 'You're so beautiful.' He kissed her breasts and as he did so she reached up and turned out the light. They made love again and then fell asleep.

When Jatney woke and reached out, she was gone. He threw on his clothes and put on his watch. It was seven in the morning. He found her out on the terrace in a red jogging suit against which her black hair seemed to char. A table had been wheeled in by room service and on it were silver coffee pitchers and silver milk jugs and an array of plates with metal covers over them to keep the food warm.

Rosemary smiled at him and said, 'I ordered for you. I was just going to wake you up. I have to get my run in before I start work.'

He sat down at the table and she poured him coffee and uncovered a dish that held eggs and sliced up bits of fruit. Then she drank her orange juice and got up. 'Take your time,' she said. 'Thanks for staying last night.'

David Jatney wanted her to have breakfast with him, he wanted her to show that she really liked him, he wanted to

344

have a chance to talk, to tell her about his life, say something that would make her interested in him. But now she was putting a white headband over her charred hair and lacing up her jogging shoes. She stood up. David Jatney said, not knowing his face was twitching with emotion, 'When will I see you again?' And as soon as he said it he knew he had made a terrible mistake.

Rosemary was on her way to the door but she stopped. 'I'm going to be awfully busy the next few weeks. I have to go to New York. When I come back I'll give you a call.' She didn't ask for his number.

Then another thought seemed to strike her. She picked up the phone and called for a limo to bring Jatney back to Santa Monica. She said to him, 'It will be put on my bill. Do you need any cash to tip the driver?'

Jatney just looked at her for a long moment. She picked up her purse, opened it and said, 'How much will you need for the tip?'

Jatney couldn't help himself. He didn't know his face was twitching with a malice and a hatred that was frightening. He said insultingly, 'You'd know that better than me.' Rosemary snapped her purse shut and went out of the suite.

He never heard from her. He waited for two months and then one day on the movie studio lot he saw her come out of Hocken's office with Gibson Grange and Dean. He waited near Hocken's parking space so that they would have to greet him. Hocken gave him a little hug and said they had to have dinner and asked how the job was going. Gibson Grange shook his hand and gave him a sly but friendly smile, the handsome face radiating its easy good humor. Rosemary looked at him without smiling. And what really hurt was that for a moment it seemed to Jatney that she had forgotten him.

David Jatney had fired his rifle at Louis Inch because of a young woman named Irene Fletcher. Irene was delighted that someone had tried to kill Inch but never knew it was her lover who fired the shot. This despite the fact that every day she beseeched him to tell her his most innermost thoughts.

They had met on Montana Avenue where she was one of the salesgirls in the famous Fioma Bake Shop, which sold the best breads in America. David Jatney went there to buy biscuits and rolls and chatted with Irene when she served him. One day she said to him, 'Would you like to go out with me tonight? We can eat Dutch.'

Jatney smiled at her. She was not one of the typical blonde California girls. She had a pretty round face with a determined look, her figure was just a little buxom and she looked like she might be just a little too old for him. She was about twenty-five or twenty-six, but her gray eyes had a lively sparkle to them and she always sounded intelligent in their conversations, so he said yes. And truth to tell he was lonely.

They started a casual, friendly love affair, Irene Fletcher did not have the time for something more serious, nor the inclination. She had a four-year-old son and lived in her mother's house and also she was very active in local politics and Eastern religions, not at all unusual for a young person in Southern California. For Jatney it was a refreshing experience. Irene often brought her young son, Campbell, to these meetings which sometimes lasted far into the night, and she simply rolled her little boy into an Indian blanket and put him to sleep on the floor as she vigorously argued her points of view on the merits of the candidate for the Santa Monica Council or the latest seer from the Far East. Sometimes Jatney went to sleep on the floor with the young boy.

To Jatney, it was a perfect match, they had nothing in common. Jatney hated religion and despised politics. Irene detested the movies and was only interested in books on exotic religions and left-wing social studies. But they kept each other company, they filled in the holes in their existence.

346

When they had sex they were both a little offhand, but were always friendly. Sometimes Irene succumbed to a tenderness during sex which she immediately made an excuse for afterwards.

It was helpful that Irene loved to talk and David Jatney loved to be silent. They would lie in bed and Irene would talk for hours and David would listen. Sometimes she was interesting and sometimes she was not. It was interesting that there was a continuous guerrilla struggle between the real estate interests and the small home owners and renters in Santa Monica. Jatney could sympathize with this. He loved Santa Monica, he loved the low skyline of two-storey houses and one-storey shops, the Spanish-looking villas, the general air of serenity, the total absence of chilling religious edifices like the Mormon tabernacles in his home state of Utah. He loved the many slitted looks at the ocean, the great Pacific lying unobscured by the cataracts of glass and stone skyscrapers. He thought Irene a heroine for fighting to preserve all this against the ogres of the real estate interests.

She talked about her current Indian gurus and played their mantras and lectures on her tapes. These gurus were far more pleasant and humorous than the stern elders of the Mormon Church he had listened to while growing up and their beliefs seemed more poetic, their miracles purer, more spiritual, more ethereal than the famous Mormon bible of gold and the Angel Moroni. But finally they were just as boring with their rejection of the pleasures of this world, the fame on earth, all of which Jatney so desperately desired.

And Irene would never stop talking, she achieved a kind of self ecstasy when she talked even of the most ordinary things. Unlike Jatney, she found her life, ordinary as it was, too meaningful.

Sometimes when she was carried away and dissected her emotions for a full hour without interruption he would feel that she was a star in the heavens growing larger and brighter and that he himself was falling into a black endless

347

hole that was the universe, falling further in that darkness while she never noticed.

He liked too that she was generous in material things but thrifty with her personal emotions. She would never really come to grief, she would never fall in that universal darkness. Her star would always expand, never lose its light. And he was grateful that this should be so. He did not want her company in the darkness.

One night they went for a walk on the beach just outside Malibu. It seemed weird to David Jatney that here was this great ocean on one side, then a row of houses and then mountains on the other. It didn't seem natural to have mountains almost bordering an ocean. Irene had brought along blankets and a pillow and her little child. They lay on the beach and the little boy, wrapped in blankets, fell asleep.

Irene and David Jatney sat on their blanket and the beauty of the night overcame them. For that little moment they were in love with each other. They watched the ocean blue-black in the moonlight, the little thin birds hopping ahead of the incoming waves. 'David,' Irene said, 'you never have told me anything really about yourself. I want to love you. You won't let me know you.'

David Jatney was only twenty-one years old and this touched him. He laughed a little nervously and then said, 'The first thing you should know about me is that I'm a Ten Mile Mormon.'

'I didn't even know you were a Mormon,' Irene said.

'If you are brought up a Mormon, you are taught that you must not booze or smoke or commit adultery,' David said. 'So when you do it you make sure you are at least ten miles from where anybody knows you.' And then he told her about his childhood. And how he hated the Mormon Church.

'They teach you that it's OK to lie if it helps the church,' David Jatney said. 'And then the hypocritical bastards give you all this shit about the Angel Moroni and some gold

348

bible. And they wear angel pants, which I have to admit my mother and father never believed in, but you could see those fucking angel pants hanging on their clotheslines. The most ridiculous thing you ever saw.'

'What's angel pants?' Irene asked. She was holding his hand to encourage him to keep speaking.

'It's sort of a robe they wear so they won't enjoy screwing,' David Jatney said. 'And they are so ignorant they don't know that Catholics in the sixteenth century had the same kind of garment, a robe that covers your whole body except for a single hole in it so you can screw without supposedly enjoying it. When I was a kid I could see angel pants hanging from the laundry lines. I'll say this for my parents, they didn't buy that shit, but because he was an elder in the church they had to fly the angel pants.' Jatney laughed and then said, 'God, what a religion.'

'It's fascinating but it sounds so primitive,' Irene said.

David Jatney thought and what the hell is so civilized in you believing all those fucking gurus who tell you that cows are sacred, that you are reincarnated, but that this life means nothing, all that voodoo karma bullshit. But she felt his tensing and wanted to keep him talking. She slid her hands inside his shirt and felt his heart beating furiously.

'Did you hate them?' she asked.

'I never hated my parents,' he said. 'They were always good to me.'

'I meant the Mormon Church,' Irene said.

David Jatney said, 'I hated the Church ever since I can remember. I hated it as a little kid. I hated the faces of the elders, I hated the way my mother and father kissed their asses. I hated their hypocrisies. If you disagree with the rulings of the church they could even have you murdered. It's a business religion, they all stick together. That's how my father got rich. But I'll tell you the thing that disgusted me the most. They have special anointments and the top

349

elders get secretly anointed and so they get to go to heaven ahead of other people. Like somebody slipping you to the head of the line while you're waiting for a taxi or a table in a popular restaurant.'

Irene said, 'Most religions are like that except the Indian religions. You just have to watch out for karma.' She paused a moment. 'That is why I try to keep myself pure of greed for money, why I can't fight my fellow human being for the possessions of this earth. I have to keep my spirit pure. We're having special meetings, there is a terrible crisis in Santa Monica right now. If we're not on the alert, the real estate interests will destroy everything we've fought for and this town will be full of skyscrapers. And they'll raise the rents and you and I will be forced out of our apartments.'

She went on and on and David Jatney listened with a feeling of peace. He could lie on his beach for ever, lost in time, lost in beauty, lost in the innocence of this girl who was so unafraid of what would happen to her in this world. She was telling him about a man named Louis Inch who was trying to bribe the city council so that they would change the building and rental laws. She seemed to know a lot about this man Inch, she had researched him. The man could be an elder in the Mormon Church. Finally Irene said, 'If it wasn't so bad for my karma, I'd kill the bastard.'

David Jatney laughed. 'I shot the President once.' And he told her about the assassination game, the Hunt, when he had been a one-day hero at Brigham Young University. 'And the Mormon elders who run the place had me thrown out,' he said.

But Irene was now busy with her small son who had a bad dream and woke up screaming into uncomprehended moonlight. She soothed him and said to Jatney, 'This guy Inch is having dinner with some of the town council tomorrow night. He's taking them to Michael's and you know what that means. He'll try to bribe them. I really would like to shoot the bastard.'

350

David Jatney said, 'I'm not worried about my karma, I'll shoot him for you.' They both laughed.

The next night David Jatney cleaned the hunting rifle he had brought from Utah and fired the shot that broke the glass in the limousine of Louis Inch. He had not really aimed to hit anyone, in fact the shot came much closer than he had intended. He was just curious to see if he could bring himself to do it.

17

It was Patsy Troyca who tricked Peter Cloot and nailed
Christian Klee. Going over testimonies to the Congressional
Committees of Inquiry into the atom bomb explosion he
noted Klee's testimony that the great international crisis of
the hijacking took precedence. But then there were glitches,
Troyca noticed that there was a time gap. Christian Klee had
disappeared from the White House scene. Where did he go?

They wouldn't find out from Klee, that was certain. But
the only thing that could have made Klee disappear during
that crisis was something terribly important. What if Klee
had gone to interrogate Gresse and Tibbot?

Troyca did not consult with his boss, Congressman Jintz;
he called Elizabeth Stone, the administrative aide to Senator
Lambertino, and arranged to meet her at an obscure restaurant for dinner. In the months since the atom bomb crisis
the two of them had formed a partnership, both in public
and private life.

On their first date, initiated by Troyca, they had come to
an understanding. Elizabeth Stone beneath her cool, impersonal beauty had a fiery sexual temperament, her mind
however was cold steel. The first thing she said was, 'Our
bosses are going to be out of their jobs in November. I think
you and I should make plans for our future.'

Patsy Troyca was astonished. Elizabeth Stone was famous
for being one of those aides who are the loyal right arms to
their Congressional chiefs.

'The fight isn't over yet,' he said.

'Of course it is,' Elizabeth Stone said. 'Our bosses tried to impeach the President. Now Kennedy is the biggest hero this country has known since Washington. And he will kick their asses.'

Troyca, was instinctively a more loyal person to his chief. Not out of a sense of honor, but because he was competitive, he didn't want to think of himself as being on a losing side.

'Oh, we can stretch it out,' Elizabeth Stone said. 'We don't want to look like the kind of people who desert a sinking ship. We'll make it look good. But I can get us both a better job.' She smiled at him mischievously and Troyca fell in love with that smile. It was a smile of gleeful temptation, a smile full of guile and yet an admission of that guile, a smile that said that if he wasn't delighted with her, he was a jerk. He smiled back.

Patsy Troyca had, even to his own way of thinking, a sort of greasy, pig-like charm which worked only on certain women, and which always surprised other men and himself. Men respected Troyca because of his cunning, his high level of energy, his ability to execute. But the fact that he could charm women so mysteriously aroused their admiration.

Now he said to Elizabeth Stone, 'If we become partners, does that mean I get to fuck you?'

'Only if you make a commitment,' Elizabeth Stone said.

There were two words Patsy Troyca hated more than any of the others in the English language. One was commitment and the other was relationship.

'You mean like we should have a real relationship, a commitment to each other, like love?' he said. 'Like the house niggers used to make to their masters down in your dear old South?'

She sighed. 'Your macho bullshit could be a problem,' she said. Then she went on. 'I can make a deal for us. I've been a big help to the Vice President in her political career. She owes me. Now you have to see reality. Jintz and Lambertino are going to be slaughtered in the November election. Helen

DuPray is reorganizing her staff and I'm going to be one of her top advisors. I have a spot for you as my aide.'

Patsy Troyca said smilingly, 'That's a demotion for me. But if you're as good in the sack as I think you are, I'll consider it.'

Elizabeth Stone said impatiently, 'It won't be a demotion since you won't have a job. And then when I go up the ladder, so do you. You'll wind up with your own staff section to the Vice President.'

She paused for a moment. 'Listen,' she said. 'We were attracted to each other in the Senator's office, not love maybe, but certainly lust at first sight. And I've heard about you screwing your aides. But I understand it. We both work so hard, we don't have time for a real social life or a real love life. And I'm tired of screwing guys just because I'm lonely a couple a times a month. I want a real relationship.'

'You're going too fast,' Patsy Troyca said. 'Now if it was on the staff of the President . . .' He shrugged and grinned to show that he was kidding.

Elizabeth Stone gave him her smile again. It was really a hardboiled sort of grin but Patsy Troyca found it charming. 'The Kennedys have always been unlucky,' she said. 'The Vice President could be the President. But please be serious. Why can't we have a partnership, if that's what you prefer to call it? Neither one of us wants to get married. Neither of us wants children. Why can't we sort of half live with each other, keep our own places of course but sort of live together? We can have companionship and sex and we can work together as a team. We can satisfy our human needs and operate at the higher point of efficiency. If it works, it could be a great arrangement. If it doesn't, we can just call it quits. We have until November.'

They went to bed that night and Elizabeth Stone was a revelation to Patsy Troyca. Like many shy reserved people, man or woman, she was genuinely ardent and tender in bed. And it helped that the act of consummation took place in her townhouse. Patsy Troyca had not known that she was independently wealthy. Like a true WASP, he thought, she had concealed that fact, where he would have flaunted it. Troyca immediately saw that the townhouse would be a perfect place for both of them to live, much better than his just adequate flat. Here with Elizabeth Stone he could set up an office. The townhouse had three servants and he would be relieved of time consuming and worrying details like sending clothes out for cleaning, shopping for food and drink.

And Elizabeth Stone, ardent feminist in politics and her social life, performed like some ancient courtesan in bed. She was a slave to his pleasure. Well it was only the first time they were like that Patsy Troyca thought. Like when they first came to be interviewed for a job, they never looked as good after that. But in the month that followed, she proved him wrong.

They built up an almost perfect relationship. It was wonderful for both of them after their long hours with Jintz and Lambertino to come home, go out for a late supper then sleep together and make love. And in the morning they would go to work together. He thought for the first time in his life about marriage. But he knew instinctively that this was something Elizabeth Stone would not want.

They lived contained lives, a cocoon of work, companionship and love, for they did come to love each other. But the best and most delicious part of their times together was their scheming on how to change the plots of their world. They both agreed that Kennedy would be re-elected to the Presidency in November. Elizabeth Stone was sure that the campaign being mounted against the President by Congress and the Socrates Club was doomed to failure. Patsy Troyca was not so sure. There were many cards to play.

Elizabeth Stone hated Francis Kennedy. It was not a personal hatred, it was that steely opposition to someone she thought of as a tyrant. 'The important thing,' she said,

355

'is that Kennedy should not be allowed to have his own Congress in the next election. That should be the battleground. It's clear from Kennedy's statements in the campaign that he will change the structure of American democracy. And that would create a very dangerous historical situation.'

'If you are so opposed to him now, how can you accept a position on the Vice President's staff after the election?' Patsy asked her.

'We're not policy makers,' Elizabeth said. 'We're administrators. We can work for anybody.'

So after a month of intimacy, Elizabeth Stone was surprised when Patsy Troyca asked that they meet in a restaurant rather than the comfort of the townhouse they now shared. But he had insisted.

In the restaurant over their first drinks, Elizabeth said, 'Why couldn't we talk at home?'

Patsy Troyca said thoughtfully, 'You know, I've been studying a lot of documents going a long way back. Our Attorney General is a very dangerous man.'

'So?' Elizabeth Stone said.

'He may have your house bugged,' Patsy said.

Elizabeth Stone laughed. 'You are paranoid,' she said.

'Yeah,' Patsy Troyca said. 'Well how about this. Christian Klee had those two kids, Gresse and Tibbot, in custody and didn't interrogate them right away. But there's a time gap. And the kids were tipped off and told to keep their mouths shut until their families supplied lawyers. And what about Yabril? Klee has him stashed, nobody can get to see or talk to him. Klee stonewalls and Kennedy backs him up. I think Klee is capable of anything.'

Elizabeth Stone said thoughtfully, 'You can get Jintz to subpoena Klee to appear before a Congressional committee. I can ask Senator Lambertino to do the same thing. We can smoke Klee out.'

'Kennedy will exercise executive privilege and forbid him

to testify,' Patsy Troyca said. 'We can wipe our asses with those subpoenas.'

Elizabeth Stone was usually amused by his vulgarities, especially in bed, but she was not amused now. 'His exercising executive privilege will damage him,' she said. 'The papers and TV will crucify him.'

'OK, we can do that,' Patsy Troyca said. 'But how about if just you and me go to see Peter Cloot and try to pin him down? We can't make him talk but maybe he will. He's a law and order nut, and maybe psychologically he's horrified at Klee's handling of the atom bomb incident. Maybe he even knows something concrete.'

Two days later they went to see Peter Cloot. He received them in his office and told them he could not give them any information, but when pressed, admitted that he had been surprised at Christian Klee's order that Tibbott and Gresse not be interrogated immediately. He also admitted that since the warning call could not be traced, it was likely placed through a phone electronically protected against tracing. He also admitted that only highly placed government officials had such phones. When asked about the time gap in which Klee had disappeared from the White House, he shrugged.

It was Elizabeth Stone who put the question to him directly. 'Did he interrogate those two young men during the time period?'

Cloot looked them in the eye. 'That whole thing bothers me,' he said. 'I can't believe that Klee would deliberately foster such a situation. Now I tell you this privately, but I will deny it, unless under oath. Klee did come back and interrogate Gresse and Tibbot. Alone for five minutes with all the listening devices turned off. No record was made of that meeting. What was said I don't know.'

Elizabeth Stone and Patsy Troyca tried to hide their excitement. Back in their offices they notified their chiefs and subpoenas were prepared for Peter Cloot to testify before a joint House and Senate Committee.

18

President Francis Kennedy pondered his problems, what countermeasures to take. He was worried about the accusations against Christian Klee. They were fabrications of course and he would have to unravel that story but not now.

Right now he had to decide what to do with Yabril and those two young professors, Adam Gresse and Henry Tibbot. The people of America would cheer if he hung them from the balcony of the White House but such power could not be exercised in a democracy. As President he could pardon them, but not execute them. Meanwhile the finest lawyers in America had been retained to defend these men. Whitney Cheever who had joined the defense of Gresse and Tibbot, pro bono, would be formidable. But Francis Kennedy knew he had reached another crossroad in his mind. He had potent cards he could play, but did he have the will to play them? Could he discard his democratic and ethical principle, so useless in this particular power struggle? Could he become as ruthless as his opponents, the Congress, the Socrates Club, the criminals presently held incommunicado by Christian Klee in the detention hospitals? Oh, he could destroy them all if he had the will. For a moment he felt despair, then he brought back the memories of his helplessness when his wife and daughter died. Again he felt as though his brain was being compressed with hatred and he thought, nothing is meaningful if I am helpless again.

He isolated the most immediate dangers to be addressed.

*

In the beginning of June Congress launched its first attack signaling the end of the short peace after the defeat of Yabril. A joint House and Senate committee was formed to investigate the circumstances of the atom bomb explosion in New York. There had already been rumors planted in the newspapers and the TV that there was some sort of negligence on the part of the Kennedy administration. The suspected planters of the bomb, Gresse and Tibbot, had been captured twenty-four hours before the explosion. Why had they not been interrogated to force them into revealing the location of the bomb? There were also reports that the two young physicists had been warned just before their arrest. Who had warned them? Had there been some sort of conspiracy in the higher reaches of government? Kennedy's worried staff had already isolated this issue as a 'wrecker' in the coming campaign for re-election.

A Congressional committee was also investigating how many people in the Secret Service were being used to protect the President. Congress claimed there were over ten thousand. Did Kennedy really need such a large army in a democracy like America?

At a special meeting with his staff, Kennedy also summoned Vice President Helen DuPray; Dr Zed Annaccone; Theodore Tappey, the CIA chief; and his press secretary, Matthew Gladyce.

Helen DuPray had long ago reasoned out the male definition of honor. Quite simply when men owed a debt to a fellow male or female, they believed paying that debt was a greater debt than the one they owed to the social contract.

Females on the other hand took too literally the social contract, that is the understanding that a human being subordinates his personal motives to the broad needs of his fellow human beings. In that sense, females, as men often insisted, did not have that sense of 'honor'. Helen DuPray, within the limits of political prudence, despised this concept of hypocritical bribery. That she classified it as a male concept did not blind her to its power and its restriction on her own political movement.

On this early May morning before the President's meeting, she decided to go for her five-mile run to clear her head. She knew she was a hero to the Senior Staff since she had refused to sign the petition to remove Kennedy. But she also knew that they thought of it as an act of 'male' honor. She would have to be careful at the coming meeting.

In her secret heart she truly believed that the only solution to the world's ills was the transfer of power from the Patriarch. She had no wild dreams that this could be done in her lifetime. She could only push it a few inches and wait for a new history to begin. Or a new 'herstory', a word ardent feminists loved to use and men hated. She smiled. History, herstory, she didn't give a damn. Her job was to make the world work. She prepared her mind for the meeting with Francis Kennedy. It was, she knew, an important and dangerous occasion.

Dr Zed Annaccone dreaded his meeting with President Kennedy and his staff. It made him slightly ill to talk science and mix it in with political and sociological targets. He would never have accepted being the President's Medical Science Advisor except for the fact that he knew it was the only way to assure the proper funding of his beloved National Brain Research Institute.

It wasn't so bad when he dealt with Francis Kennedy directly. The man was brilliant and had a flair for science though the newspaper stories that claimed the President would have made a great scientist were simply absurd. But he certainly understood the subtle values of research and how it affected all walks of life. He could also use his imagination to see the almost miraculous results of even the most far-fetched of scientific theories. Kennedy was not the problem. It was the staff and the Congress and all the bureaucratic dragons. Plus the CIA and the FBI who kept looking over his shoulder.

Until serving in Washington, Dr Zed Annaccone had not truly realized the awful gap between science and society in general. It was scandalous that the human brain had made such a great jump forward in the sciences and that political and sociological disciplines had remained almost stationary. Science had solved so many mysteries of the body and brain and yet society in general was still muddling along in the Dark Ages.

He found it incredible that mankind still waged internal war, at enormous cost and to no advantage. That individual men and women still killed each other when there were treatments that would dissipate the murderous tendencies in human beings. He found it contemptible when the science of genetic splicing was attacked by politicians and the news media as if the tampering with the spirit of mankind was a corruption of some holy spirit. Especially when it was obvious that the human race as now genetically constituted was doomed.

Dr Zed Annaccone had been briefed on what the meeting would be about. There was still some doubt about whether the exploding of the atom bomb had been part of the terrorist plot to destabilize American influences in the world, whether there was a link between the two young physics professors, Gresse and Tibbot, and the terrorist leader Yabril. He would be asked whether they should use the PET brain scan to question the prisoners and determine the truth.

Which made Dr Zed Annaccone irritable. Why hadn't they asked him to run the PET before the atom bomb exploded? Christian Klee claimed that he had been tied up in the hijacking crisis and that the bomb threat had not seemed that threatening. Typical asshole reasoning. And President Kennedy had refused Klee's request for the PET brain scan out of humanitarian reasons. Yes, if the two young men were innocent and damage was done to their brains during the scan it would be an inhuman act. But Annaccone knew that this was a politician covering his ass. He had thoroughly briefed Kennedy on the procedure and Kennedy had understood. The PET scan was almost completely safe, and it would make the subject answer truthfully. They could have located the bomb and disarmed it. There would have been time.

It was regrettable, surely, so many people killed and injured. But Dr Annaccone felt a sneaking admiration for the two young scientists. He wished he had their balls, for they had made a real point, a lunatic one, true, but a point. That as man in general became more knowledgeable, individuals causing an atomic disaster became more probable. It was also true that the greed of the individual entrepreneur or the megalomania of a political leader could do the same. But these two kids were obviously thinking of sociological controls not scientific ones. They were thinking of repressing science, halting its march forward. The real answer of course was to change the genetic structure of man so that violence would become an impossible act. To put brakes in the genes and in the brain as you put brakes on a locomotive. It was that simple.

While waiting in the Cabinet Room of the White House for the President to arrive, Dr Zed Annaccone dissociated himself from the rest of the people there by reading his stack of memoranda and articles. He always felt himself resistant to the President's staff. Christian Klee kept track of the National Brain Institute and sometimes slapped a Secrecy order on his research. Annaccone didn't like that and used evasionary tactics when he could. He was often surprised that Klee could outwit him in such matters. The other staff members, Eugene Dazzy, Oddblood Gray and Arthur Wix, were primitives with no understanding of science, immersed in those comparatively unimportant matters of sociology and statecraft.

He noted that the Vice President Helen DuPray was present, as was Theodore Tappey, the CIA Chief. He was always surprised that a woman was Vice President of the United States. He felt that science ruled against something like this. In his researches of the brain he always felt he would some day come upon a fundamental difference between the male and female brain and was amused that he did not. Amused because if he found a discrepancy the fur would fly in a delightful way.

Theodore Tappey, he always regarded as Neanderthal. Those futile machinations for a slight degree of advantage in foreign affairs against fellow members of the human race. So futile an endeavor in the long run.

Dr Zed Annaccone took some papers out of his briefcase. There was an interesting article on the hypothetical particle called the tachyon. Not one person in this room had ever heard of the work, he thought. Though his field of expertise was the brain, Dr Annaccone had a vast knowledge of all the sciences.

So now he studied the paper on tachyons. Did tachyons really exist? Physicists had been quarreling about that for the last twenty years. Tachyons, if they existed, would fracture Einstein's theories, tachyons would travel faster than the speed of light which Einstein had said was impossible. Sure there was the apology that tachyons were already moving faster than light from the beginning but what the hell was that? Also the mass of a tachyon is a negative number. Which supposedly was impossible. But the impossible in real life could be possible in the spooky world of mathematics. And then what could happen? Who knew? Who cared? Certainly nobody in this room which held the most powerful men on the planet. An irony in itself. Tachyons might change human life more than anything these men could conceive.

Finally the President made his entrance and the people in the room stood up. Dr Annaccone put away his papers. He might enjoy this meeting if he kept alert and counted the eye blinks in the room. Research showed that eye blinks could reveal whether a person was lying or not. There was going to be a lot of blinking.

Francis Kennedy came to the meeting dressed comfortably in slacks, a white shirt covered by a sleeveless blue cashmere sweater, and with a good humor extraordinary in a man beset by so many difficulties.

Vice President Helen DuPray wondered why it was that being in love made men cheerful and women distressed.

After greeting them he said, 'We have Dr Annaccone with us today so that we can settle the problem of whether the terrorist Yabril was in any way connected with the atom bomb explosion. Also to respond to the charges that have been made in the newspapers and on television that we in the administration could have found the bomb before it exploded. Now to set the record straight, Christian, is there any evidence at all to link Yabril?'

They had already discussed this many times, Christian Klee thought. Francis just wanted to put it on record at this moment and specifically with Dr Annaccone.

'No, there is no hard evidence,' Christian said.

Dr Annaccone had been scribbling mathematical equations on the memo pad in front of him.

Kennedy gave him a friendly grin and said, 'Dr Annaccone, what are your thoughts on this subject? Maybe you can help us. And as a favor to me, stop figuring out the secrets of the universe on that pad of yours. You've discovered enough to get us into trouble.'

Dr Annaccone realized that this was a rebuke in the disguise of a compliment. He said, 'I still don't understand why you didn't sign the order for the PET scan before the nuclear device exploded. You already had the two young men in custody. You had the authority under the Atomic Security Act.'

364

Christian said quickly, 'We were in the middle of what we thought was a far more important crisis if you remember. I thought it could wait another day. Gresse and Tibbot claimed they were innocent and we had only enough evidence to grab them. We didn't have enough to indict. Then Tibbot's father got tipped off and we had a bunch of very expensive lawyers threatening a lot of trouble. So we figured we'd wait until the other crisis was over and maybe we had a little more evidence.'

Vice President Helen DuPray said, 'Christian, do you have any idea how Tibbot Senior was tipped off?'

Christian said, 'We are going over all the telephone company records in Boston to check the origin of calls received by Tibbot Senior. So far no luck.'

The head of the CIA, Theodore Tappey, said, 'With all your high-tech equipment, you should have found out.'

'Helen, you've got them off on a tangent,' Kennedy said. 'Let's stick to the main point. Dr Annaccone, let me answer your question. Christian is trying to take some heat off me, which is why a President has a staff. But I made the decision not to authorize the brain probe. According to the protocols, there is some danger of damaging the brain and I didn't want to risk it. The two young men denied everything, and there was no evidence that a bomb existed except for the warning letter. What we have here is really a scurrilous attack by the news media supported by the members of Congress. I want to pose a specific question. Do we eliminate any collusion between Yabril and Professors Tibbot and Gresse by having the PET scan done on all of them? Would that solve the problem?'

Dr Annaccone said crisply, 'Yes. But now you have a different circumstance. You are using the Medical Interrogation to gather evidence in a criminal trial, not to discover the whereabouts of a nuclear device. The Security Act does not authorize PET scanning under those circumstances.'

President Kennedy gave him a cold smile. 'Doctor,' he

said, 'You know how much I admire your work in the sciences, but you are not really instructed in the law.' Kennedy seemed to stiffen, to become more erect when he added, 'Listen to me carefully. Now I want Gresse and Tibbot to undergo the brain scan. And, more important, I want Yabril to undergo the brain scan. The question they will all be asked is this. "Was there a conspiracy? And was the atom bomb explosion part of Yabril's plan?" Now if the answer is yes, the implications are enormous. There may still be a conspiracy going on. And it may involve much more than New York City. Other members of the terrorist One Hundred could plant other nuclear devices. Now do you understand?'

Dr Annaccone said, 'Mr President, do you think that is really a possibility?'

Kennedy said, 'We have to erase any doubt. I will rule that these medical interrogations of the brain are justified under the Atomic Security Act.'

Arthur Wix said, 'There will be one hell of an uproar. They'll claim we're performing a lobotomy.'

Eugene Dazzy said dryly, 'Aren't we?'

Dr Annaccone was suddenly as angry as anyone was allowed to be in the presence of the President of the United States. 'It is not a lobotomy,' he said. 'It is a brain scan with chemical intervention. The patient is completely the same after the interrogation is completed.'

'Unless there's a little slip-up,' Dazzy said.

The Press Secretary, Matthew Gladyce, said, 'Mr President, the outcome of the test will dictate what kind of announcement we make. We have to be very careful. If the test proves there was conspiracy linking Yabril, Gresse and Tibbot, we'll be in the clear. If the scan proves there is no collusion, we just make an announcement to that effect without mentioning the probe.'

Francis Kennedy said gently, 'We can't do that, Matthew. There will be a written record that I have signed the order.

Our opponents will surely unearth it in the future and that will be a terrible problem.'

'We don't have to lie about it,' Matthew Gladyce said. 'Just don't mention it.'

Kennedy said curtly, 'Let's go on to other things.'

Eugene Dazzy read from the memo in front of him. 'The Congress wants to haul Christian up in front of one of their investigation committees. Senator Lambertino and Congressman Jintz want to take a crack at him. They are claiming, and they planted it all over in the media, that Attorney General Christian Klee is the key to any funny work that went on.'

'Invoke Executive Privilege,' Kennedy said. 'As President, I order him not to appear before any Congressional Committee.'

Dr Annaccone, bored with the political discussions, said jokingly, 'Christian, why don't you volunteer for our PET scan? You can establish your innocence irrevocably. And endorse the morality of the procedure.'

'Doc,' Christian said, 'I'm not interested in establishing my innocence as you call it. Innocence is the one fucking thing your science will never be able to establish. And I'm not interested in the morality of a brain probe that will determine the veracity of another human being. We are not discussing innocence or morals here. We are discussing the employment of power to further the functioning of society. Another area in which your science is useless. As you've often said to me, don't dabble with something in which you are not expert. So go fuck yourself.'

It was rare at these staff meetings that anyone let their emotions go unrestrained. It was even rarer for vulgar language to be used when Vice President Helen DuPray was attending staff meetings. Not that the Vice President was a prudish woman. Yet the people in the Cabinet room were surprised at Christian Klee's outburst.

Dr Annaccone was taken aback. He had just made a little

joke. He liked Christian Klee, as most people did. The man was urbane and civilized and he seemed more intelligent than most lawyers. Dr Annaccone, though a great scientist, prided himself on his serene understanding of everything in the universe. He now suffered the regrettable petty human vulnerability of having his feelings hurt. So without thinking he said, 'You used to be in the CIA, Mr Klee. The CIA headquarter building has a marble tablet that reads, "Know the truth and the truth shall set you free".'

But Christian had regained his good humor. 'I didn't write it,' he said. 'And I doubt it.'

Dr Annaccone had also recovered. He had started analyzing. Why the furious response to his jocular question? Did the Attorney General, the highest law official in the land, really have something to hide? He'd dearly love to have the man on the scan's test table.

Francis Kennedy had been watching this byplay with a gravely amused eye. Now he said gently, 'Zed, when you have the brain lie detector test perfected, so it can be done without side effects, we may have to bury it. There's not a politician in this country who could live with that.'

Dr Annaccone interrupted. 'All these questions are irrelevant. The process had been discovered. Science has begun its exploration of the human brain. You can never halt that process, Luddites proved that when they tried to halt the Industrial Revolution. You couldn't outlaw the use of gunpowder as the Japanese learned when they banned firearms for hundreds of years and were overwhelmed by the Western world. Once the atom was discovered you could no longer stop the bomb. The brain lie detector test is here to stay, I assure you all.'

Christian Klee said, 'It violates the Constitution.'

President Kennedy said briskly, 'We may have to change the Constitution.'

Matthew Gladyce said, with a look of horror on his face,

368

'If the news media heard this conversation they could run us right out of town.'

President Kennedy said, 'It's your job to tell the public what we've said in the proper language, and at the proper time. Remember this. The people of America will decide. Under the Constitution. Now I think the answer to all our problems is to mount a counter attack. Christian, press the prosecution of Bert Audick under the RICO laws. His company will be charged as a criminal conspiracy with the country of Sherhaben to defraud the American public by illegally creating oil shortages to raise prices. That's number one.'

He turned to Oddblood Gray. 'Rub the Congressional nose in the news that the new Federal Communications Commissions will deny the licenses of the major network TV stations when they come up for renewal. And the new laws will control those stacked deck deals on Wall Street and by the big banks. We'll give them something to worry about, Otto.'

Helen DuPray knew that she had every right to disagree in the private meetings even though as the Vice President it was mandatory to agree with the President publicly. Yet she hesitated before she said cautiously, 'Don't you think we're making too many enemies at one time? Wouldn't it even be better to wait until we've been elected for a second term? If we do indeed get a Congress more sympathetic to our policies, why fight the present Congress? Why unnecessarily set all the business interests against us when we are not in a position of prime strength?'

'We can't wait,' Kennedy said. 'They are going to attack us no matter what we do. They are going to continue to prevent my re-election, and my Congress, no matter how conciliatory we are. By attacking them we make them reconsider. We can't let them go ahead as if they didn't have a worry in the world.'

They were all silent and then Kennedy rose and said to his

staff. 'You can work out the details and draw up the necessary memos.'

It was then that Matthew Gladyce spoke about the Congress-inspired media campaign to attack President Kennedy by highlighting how many men and how much money was spent to guard the President.

Gladyce said, 'The whole thrust of their campaign is to paint you as some kind of Caesar and your Secret Service as some sort of Imperial Palace guard. To the public, ten thousand men and one hundred million dollars to guard just one man, even the President of the United States, seems excessive. It makes a lousy public relations image.'

They were all silent. The memory of Francis Kennedy's two uncles' assassinations made this a particularly touchy issue. Also all of them being so close to Kennedy were aware that the President went in some sort of physical fear. So they were surprised when Francis Kennedy turned to the Attorney General and said, 'In this case I think our critics are right. Christian, I know I gave you the veto on any change in protection but how about if we make an announcement that we will cut the Secret Service White House Division in half. And the budget in half also. Christian, I'd like you not to use your veto on this.'

Christian smiled and said, 'Maybe I went a little over board, Mr President. I won't use my veto that you could always veto.' Everyone laughed. But Matthew Gladyce was a little worried by this seemingly easy victory.

'Mr Attorney General, you can't just say you'll do it and not do it. The Congress will be all over our budget and appropriations figures,' Gladyce said.

'OK,' Christian said. 'But when you give out the press release, make sure you emphasize it is over my strong objections and make it seem like the President is bowing to the pressure of the Congress.'

Kennedy said, 'I thank you all. Dr Annaccone, give me thirty minutes in the Yellow Room, just you and I. Dazzy,

370

the Secret Service will not be in that room, neither will you or anyone else.'

It was almost two hours later that Kennedy buzzed his Chief of Staff and said, 'Dazzy, please escort Dr Annaccone out of the White House.'

Dazzy did so. He noticed that Dr Annaccone, for the first time, seemed frightened. The President must have really socked it to him.

The Director of the White House Military Office, Colonel Henry Canoo (Retired), was the most cheerful and unflappable man in the Administration. He was cheerful because he had what he thought was the best job in the country. He was responsible to no one but the President of the United States and he controlled Presidential secret funds credited to the Pentagon that were not subject to audit except by himself and the President. Also he was strictly an administrator, he decided no questions of policy, did not even have to offer advice. He was the one who arranged for all the airplanes and helicopters and the limos for the President and his staff. He was the one who disbursed funds for the building and maintenance of buildings used by the White House that were classified secret. He ran the administration of the 'Football', the warrant officer and his briefcase that held atom bomb codes for the President. Whenever the President wanted to do something that cost money that he didn't want Congress or the news media to know about, Henry Canoo disbursed money from the Secret Fund, and stamped the fiscal sheets with the highest security classification.

So in the late May afternoon when the Attorney General Christian Klee came into his office, Henry Canoo greeted him warmly. They had done business together before, and early on in his administration the President had given Canoo instructions that the Attorney General could have anything he wanted from the Secret Fund. The first few times Canoo had checked it out with the President but not any longer.

371

'Christian,' he said jovially, 'are you looking for information or cash?'

'Both,' Christian said. 'First the money. We are going to promise publicly to cut down on the Secret Service Division fifty per cent and to cut the Security budget. I have to go through the motions. It will be a paper transfer, nothing will change. But I don't want Congress to sniff out a financial trail. So your Office of the Military Advisor will tap the Pentagon Budget for the money. Then stamp it with your top security classification.'

'Jesus,' Henry Canoo said. 'That's a lot of money. I can do it, but not for too long.'

'Just until the election in November,' Christian said. 'Then we'll either be out on our ass or in too strong for Congress to make any difference. But right now we have to look good.'

'OK,' Canoo said.

'Now the information,' Christian said. 'Have any of the Congress committees been sniffing around lately?'

'Oh, sure,' Canoo said. 'More than usual. They keep trying to find out how many helicopters the President has, how many limos, how many big aircraft, shit like that. They try to find out what the executive branch is doing. If they knew how many we really have, they'd shit.'

'What Congressman in particular?' Christian asked.

'Jintz,' Canoo said. 'He has that admin assistant, Patsy Troyca, a clever little bastard. He says he just wants to know how many copters we have and I tell him three. He says I hear you have fifteen and I say what the hell would the White House do with fifteen? But he was pretty close, we have sixteen.'

Christian Klee was surprised. 'What the hell do we do with sixteen?'

'Copters always break down,' Canoo said. 'If the President asks for a chopper, am I going to tell him no because they're in the shop? And besides somebody on the staff is always

372

asking for a chopper. You're not so bad, Christian, but Tappey at CIA and Wix sure put in a lot of chopper time. And Dazzy too, for what reason I don't know.'

'And you don't want to know,' Christian said. 'I want reports from you on any Congress snooper who tries to find out what the logistics are in supporting the Presidential mission. It has a bearing on security. Reports to me and top classifications.'

'OK,' Henry Canoo said cheerfully. 'And any time you need some work done on your personal residence we can tap the fund for that too.'

'Thanks,' Christian said, 'I have my own money.'

In the late evening of that day, President Francis Xavier Kennedy sat in the Oval Office and smoked his thin Havana cigar. He reviewed the events of the day. Everything had gone exactly as he had planned. He had showed his hand just enough to win the support of his staff.

Klee had reacted in character, as if he read his President's mind. Canoo had checked with him. Annaccone was more difficult but would come around. Helen DuPray might be a problem if he wasn't careful, but he needed her intelligence and her political base of the women's organizations.

Francis Kennedy was surprised at how well he felt. There was no longer any depression and his energy level was higher than it had ever been since his wife had died. Was it because he had finally found a woman who interested him or was it because he had at last gained control of the huge and complex political machinery of America?

19

In May Francis Kennedy, to his astonishment and even dismay, had fallen in love. This was not the time, and the woman not appropriate. She was on the legal staff of the Vice President.

Kennedy loved her charm, which was natural, her guileless smile, her brown eyes so lively and sparkling with wit. She was cuttingly sharp in argument, sometimes too much the lawyer. She had physical beauty, a lovely voice, and the body of a pocket Venus; long legs to a tiny waist and full bust, though she was not a tall woman. She could be dazzling in full regalia, but dressed so casually that most men were not aware that she was a legitimate beauty.

Lanetta Carr had that kind of naiveté and frankness that bordered sometimes on vulgarity. She had the romantic air of a Southern belle underneath a sharp intelligence that had led her to the study of law. It was as a lawyer that she had come to Washington and finally, after being on the staff of government agencies devoted to application of social programs and woman's rights, she had become a very junior member of the staff of the Vice President.

It was a courtesy extended to all the Vice Presidential staff that they were invited to at least one large Presidential reception in the White House during a four-year term. Lanetta Carr had been one of the four hundred guests to receive an invitation to a reception late in July.

Lanetta Carr was thrilled that she would be able to see Francis Kennedy in the flesh. Now, far down on the receiving line in the White House she saw President Francis Kennedy greeting his guests. To her he was the most beautiful man she had ever seen. The planes of his face had that lovely symmetry that only the Irish seem to breed. He was tall and very thin and had to stoop a little to say a few words to each of the guests. She noticed that he treated everyone with an exquisite courtesy. And then as she waited, he turned his head toward her, not yet seeing her, seemingly caught in some inward movement of isolation, and she saw the look of sadness in those cerulean eyes, his face frozen in some sort of grief. And then in an instant, he was the politician greeting her.

Vice President Helen DuPray was at Kennedy's side and she murmured that Lanetta Carr was one of her assistants. Kennedy instantly became warmer, more friendly, she was one of his more immediate official family. His two hands pressed hers and she felt so drawn to him that she said impulsively, though she had been briefed that it was a subject never to be discussed, 'Mr President, I'm so sorry about your daughter.'

She could see the slight look of disapproval on the face of Helen DuPray. But Kennedy said quietly, 'Thank you.' He released her hand and she moved on. Lanetta joined other Vice Presidential staff at the party. She had just finished drinking a glass of white wine when she was surprised to see the President and Vice President making their way slowly through the crowd, chatting briefly with the people in their way, but obviously making a path to her group.

Her companions immediately fell silent. Vice President Helen DuPray introduced the five members of the staff to the President with intimate friendly comments on the value she attached to their work. For the first time, Lanetta noticed how attractive the Vice President was as a woman, how feminine she could be. How instinctively she was sensitive to all the psychological needs of her staff and their need to be singled out to the President of the United States. How she gave off a sexual aura that had never been visible before. Lanetta divined instantly that this was stimulated not by Kennedy as a male, but as a male who had supreme power. Still she felt a strange twinge of jealousy.

The rest of the group fell into an awed silence showing only grateful smiles at the words of praise. Kennedy made a few polite comments but he was looking at Lanetta directly. So she said the first thing that occurred to her. 'Mr President, in all my years in Washington I've never been in the White House. Could I ask one of your aides to show me through? Just the public rooms of course.'

She did not really know the pretty picture she made, great eyes in a very young face for her years, an extraordinary complexion, the skin a mixture of creamy white and an exquisite pink on her cheeks and ears. President Kennedy smiled, a genuine smile not a political smile. He was delighted with just the sight of her. And her voice beguiled him. It was very soft with just a trace of Southern accent. Suddenly he realized that he had, in the last few years, missed that kind of voice. So he took her by the hand and said, 'I'll show you myself.'

He took her on the ground floor, they went through the Green Room with the white-mantled fireplace and white-bottomed chairs and settees, then the Blue Room with its wall with the blue and gold silk, through the Red Room hung in cerise silk, red and beige carpet on the floor, and then the Yellow Oval Room which he told her was his favorite, the yellow walls, the similarly colored rugs and couches seemed to relax him, he said. And all the time he was asking her questions about herself and observing her.

He noticed that she was more interested in conversation than by the awe-inspiring beauty of the rooms. That she asked intelligent questions about the historic paintings and the various antiques. She did not seem overly impressed by her awesome surroundings. Finally, he showed her the famous Oval Office of the President. 'I hate this room,'

Kennedy said. And she seemed to understand him. The Oval Office was always used for public photographs that were published in all the newspapers. The chats with visiting foreign dignitaries, the signing of important bills and treaties. It gave off an aura of insincerity.

Lanetta, though she did not show it, was thrilled by the tour and by the company of the President. She was aware that this treatment was more than an ordinary courtesy.

On the way back to the huge reception room, he asked her if she would like to come to a small dinner at the White House the following week. She said she would.

In the days that followed before the night of the dinner, Lanetta expected Vice President Helen DuPray to call her in for a chat on how to behave, to inquire about how she had gotten the President to invite her, but the Vice President never did so. In fact, she seemed not even to know about it, though this could not be true.

Lanetta Carr knew, as what woman would not, that Francis Kennedy had an interest in her that was sexual. He sure as hell wasn't thinking of her for Secretary of State.

The small informal dinner in the White House was not a success. No woman could have faulted Francis Kennedy's behavior toward her. He was unfailing in his courteous friendliness, he prompted her into conversation and kept the discussions going, nearly always taking her side when she disagreed with the members of his staff. She was not awed that these men were the most powerful in the country. Eugene Dazzy she liked despite the scandal that had appeared in the media. She wondered how his wife could bear to be with him in public afterwards, but none of the others seemed to be embarrassed. Arthur Wix was reserved but they quarreled in a civilized way when Lanetta said she thought the Defense budget should be cut in half. She found Otto Gray charming. Their wives were subdued.

Christian Klee she disliked. She could not say why.

Perhaps it was the sinister reputation he now had in Washington. But she told herself that she of all people with her training in the law should not hold such prejudice. Charges are not proof, accusations are mere hearsay without the backing of evidence, he was still innocent. What repelled her was his complete absence of interest or response to her as a woman. He seemed constantly vigilant. One of the stewards serving dinner had hovered behind Klee for a moment longer than was necessary and Klee had immediately turned his head, his body beginning to move out of his chair, the ball of his right foot sliding forward. The steward, who had merely paused to unfold a napkin, was obviously startled by Klee's look.

But what made the dinner unpleasant for Lanetta was the constant show of power. There were Secret Service men in every doorway, even in the dining room, posted at the door.

She had been brought up in the South but by no means the redneck South. She had been brought up in a cultured civilized progressive little city which prided itself on its relationship with black people. But even as a little girl she had caught the nuances of a society which believed that the two races should be separated. She had caught that tiny trace of meanness, with which even the most civilized of the privileged proclaimed their superiority to fellow men less well equipped in the human struggle for survival. And she had hated it.

She could not detect the meanness here, but she felt that it must exist when one man had so much more power than any of the others present and she was determined not to succumb to that kind of power. And so she automatically resisted Kennedy's charm without being anything less than bright and friendly.

But Kennedy had caught it. And she was astonished when he said, 'You didn't have a good time, I'm sorry.'

'Oh, I did,' she said. And then in her best and slyest

Southern Belle manner gave him his dismissal. 'I'll be bragging about this night to my kids when I'm old and gray.'

The others invited to the dinner party had already taken their leave and two aides were waiting to escort Lanetta to her car. Almost humbly Kennedy said, 'I know all this is awfully offputting. But let's give it one more chance. Why don't I cook dinner for you at your place?'

At first she really didn't get it. That the President of the United States was asking for a date. That he would come to her apartment like any other boyfriend and cook in her kitchen. The image so delighted her that she burst out laughing and Francis Kennedy was laughing too.

'OK,' she said. 'There goes the neighborhood.'

Francis Kennedy smiled gravely. 'Yes,' he said. 'Thank you. I'll call you when I'm sure I have a night free.'

From that night on, Secret Service men blanketed the area of her apartment. Two apartments were rented on her floor and in a building across the street. Christian Klee had her phone bugged. Her history was explored through documents and personal interviews with anyone she had ever worked with and with people in her home town.

Christian Klee personally supervised this exercise, deliberately not planting a bug that would record any sound in Lanetta's apartment. He didn't want his Secret Service agents listening when the President of the United States dropped his trousers.

What he found completely reassured him. Lanetta Carr had been a model of bourgeois behavior until she went to college. In college she had for some reason pursued the study of the law and on passing the bar had taken a position as a public defender in the City of New Orleans. She had defended women, mostly. She had become involved with the feminist movement but he noted with satisfaction that she had had three serious love affairs. The lovers were interviewed and the one thing they said about Lanetta Carr was that she was a stable, serious woman.

379

At the White House dinner, she had said, with anger and contempt, 'Do you know that under our system the breaching of a contract is not against the law?' Not realizing she was saying this at a table where two men, Kennedy and Klee, were considered amongst the foremost legal minds in the country.

For one moment Klee had been irritated and had said, 'So what.'

Lanetta had turned on him and said, 'The person who suffers under a breach of contract then has to go to law. It costs him a lot of money and then he usually has to settle for less than he is entitled to under his original contract. And if the plaintiff is less powerful and has less money, if he's up against a big corporation who can string the case out for years, then he has to lose something. It's gangsterism pure and simple.' She paused for a moment and then said, 'The very concept is immoral.'

Christian Klee had said, 'Law is not a moral discipline. It's a machinery that makes a society work.'

He remembered that she had turned away from him with a gesture that dismissed his explanation.

Christian Klee believed in overkill when providing security for his President. On the night of Francis Kennedy's date with Lanetta Carr, he already had his men in two apartments and he had a hundred men covering the streets, the roofs of buildings, the hallways of the apartment building itself. But he knew that the procedure had to change, that these 'dates' could not continue. That if the affair lasted, it would have to be conducted in the safety of the White House. But he was glad Francis had finally found some hint of personal happiness. He hoped everything would turn out all right. He didn't worry about how the affair would affect the election results. All the world loved a lover, especially one so handsome and doomstruck as Francis Kennedy.

On the night that the President of the United States was going to cook her dinner, Lanetta dressed with just a little extra care. She wore a floppy sweater, loose slacks, and flat-heeled shoes. Of course she tried to look pretty, the sweater was from Italy, the slacks bought in New York's Bloomingdale's. She made up her eyes very carefully and she wore a favorite bracelet. And she cleaned up her apartment.

Francis Kennedy arrived wearing a sports jacket over a loose white shirt. He wore slacks and shoes she had never seen before, dress shoes with rubber soles and heels, the tops a beautifully soft leather almost blue.

After they chatted for a few minutes Francis Kennedy began to prepare a very simple meal, roasted chicken with oven fried potatoes, and a string bean and tomato salad with raspberry vinaigrette dressing. He laughed when Lanetta offered him an apron, but stood still as a small boy when she placed it over his head and then turned him around so she could tie it around his waist.

Lanetta watched silently as he did everything with complete concentration and she smiled to herself when she realized that he actually cared about how the dinner turned out. As the soft classical music of the Pachelbel Kanon played in the background, Lanetta couldn't help but think about how unlike the other men she had gone out with this man was. Certainly, he had more power than they, but what she responded to more was some deep vulnerability that she perceived in his eyes when he wasn't paying attention.

Lanetta had observed that Francis Kennedy was not really a man to whom food was interesting. She had bought a bottle of decent wine. She was excited, as what woman would not be, but was also a little terrified. She knew he expected something from her, and she was sure she would not be able to respond. And yet how do you refuse a President? She resented the feeling of awe inside her, and feared she would accede to him because of that awe. But she was curious and excited as to what would happen and had enough self-confidence to believe it would all end happily.

It proved to be an amazingly simple evening. He helped

her clear the table in the kitchen of her apartment and then they had coffee in her living room.

Lanetta was proud of her apartment. She had furnished it slowly, with good taste. There were reproductions of famous paintings on the walls and bookcases had been fitted in all around the living room.

All through the evening Francis Kennedy did not make any of the moves of a courting male and Lanetta was not seductive. Kennedy had caught all of her signals in dress and bearing.

But as the evening wore on, they became more and more friendly to each other. He was very skillful in making her talk about herself, her family life in the South, her experiences in Washington. About her work as one of the legal advisors to the Vice President. And what she was impressed by, even more than by his unique good looks, was that he was always in good taste, that his questions were not prying questions, merely leads to let her tell what she wanted to tell him.

There is nothing more enjoyable than having dinner with someone who is eager to listen to the story of your life, your true beliefs, your hopes and your sorrows. So Lanetta had a good time and then suddenly realized that Kennedy had never said anything about himself. She had forgotten her manners.

'I've been going on about myself,' she said, 'when I have an opportunity very few people get. How is it being President of the United States? I'll bet it's awful.' She said the last with such sincerity that Kennedy laughed.

'It was terrible,' Kennedy said, 'but it's getting better.'

'You've had such bad luck,' Lanetta said.

'But my luck is changing,' Kennedy said. 'Politically and personally.' They were both embarrassed by this, by the callowness of the avowal. Kennedy went on to repair the damage. He did so in perhaps the worst possible way.

'I miss my wife, I miss my daughter, maybe you remind me of my daughter. I don't know.'

When they said good night, he leaned over, not able to resist and brushed her lips with his. She did not respond so he said, 'Can we have dinner again?' And she, liking him but not sure, just nodded her head.

She watched from the window and was surprised that her normally quiet street was so busy. When Kennedy left the building he was preceded by two men, another four men came behind him. There were two cars waiting for him, each car surrounded by four men. Kennedy got into one of the cars and it zoomed away. Far down the street a parked car pulled out and preceded Kennedy's. Then other cars in the street started up, followed, and then men who had been on foot turned corners and disappeared. To Lanetta it was an offensive display of power that one human being should be guarded so jealously. She stood at the window struggling with this feeling and then remembered how kind and caring he had been in this evening alone with her.

20

In Washington, Christian Klee turned on his computer. First he called up the file on David Jatney. Nothing happening there. Then he called up the files on the Socrates Club. He had all of them under computer surveillance. There was only one item of real interest – Bert Audick had flown to Sherhaben ostensibly to plan the rebuilding of the city of Dak. Klee was interrupted by a call from Eugene Dazzy.

President Kennedy wanted Christian Klee to come to breakfast in the White House bedroom suite. It was rare that meetings were held in Kennedy's private living quarters.

Jefferson, the President's private butler and Secret Service guard, served the large breakfast and then discreetly withdrew to the pantry room, to appear only when summoned by the buzzer.

Kennedy said casually, 'Did you know Jefferson was a great student, a great athlete? Jefferson never took shit from anybody.' Kennedy paused and said, 'How did he become a butler, Christian?'

Christian knew he had to tell the truth. 'He is also the best agent in the Secret Service. I recruited him myself and especially for this job.'

Kennedy said. 'The same question applies, why the hell would he take a Secret Service job? And as a butler?'

Christian said, 'He has a very high rank in the Secret Service.'

Kennedy said, 'Yeah, but still.'

'I organized a very elaborate screening procedure for these jobs. Jefferson was the best man and in fact he is the White House team leader.'

'Still,' Kennedy said.

'I promised him that before you left the White House I would get him an appointment in Health, Education and Welfare, a job with clout.'

'Ah, that's clever,' Kennedy said, 'but how does his resumé look from butler to clout? How the hell can we do that?'

'His resumé will read executive assistant to me,' Christian said.

Kennedy lifted the coffee mug, its white glaze adorned with stenciled eagles. 'Now don't take this wrong but I've noticed that all my immediate servants in the White House are very good at their jobs. Are they all in the Secret Service? That would be incredible.'

'A special school and a special indoctrination appealing to their professinal pride,' Christian said. 'Not all.'

Kennedy laughed out loud and said, 'Even the chefs?'

'Especially the chefs,' Christian said smiling. 'All chefs are crazy.' Like many men, Christian always used a gag line to give himself time to think. He knew Kennedy's method for preparing to go on dangerous ground, showing good humor plus a piece of knowledge he wasn't supposed to have.

They ate their breakfast, Kennedy playing what he called 'mother', passing plates and pouring. The china, except for Kennedy's special coffee mug, was beautiful, with blue Presidential seals and as fragile as an eggshell. Kennedy finally said almost casually, 'I'd like to spend an hour with Yabril. I expect you to handle it personally.' He saw the anxious look on Christian's face. 'Only for an hour and only for this one time.'

Christian said, 'What's to be gained, Francis? It could be too painful for you to bear. I worry about your health.' And indeed Francis Kennedy did not look well. He was very pale these days and seemed to have lost weight. And there were lines in his face that Christian had never noticed before.

'Oh, I can bear it,' Kennedy said.

'If the meeting leaks there will be a lot of questions,' Christian said.

'Then make sure it doesn't leak,' Kennedy said. 'There will be no written record of the meeting and the White House log won't be entered. Now when?'

'It will take a few days to make the necessary arrangements,' Christian said. 'And Jefferson has to know.'

'Anybody else?' Kennedy asked.

'Maybe six other men from my Special Division,' Christian said. 'They will have to know Yabril is in the White House but not necessarily that you're seeing him. They'll guess but they won't know.'

Kennedy said, 'If it's necessary I can go to where you're holding him.'

'Absolutely not,' Christian said. 'The White House is the best place. It should be in the early hours after midnight. I suggeest one a.m.'

Kennedy said, 'The night after tomorrow, OK.'

'Yes,' Christian said. 'You'll have to sign some papers, which will be vague, but will cover me if something goes haywire.'

Kennedy sighed as if in relief then said briskly, 'He's not a superman. Don't worry. I want to be able to talk to him freely and for him to answer lucidly and of his own free will. I don't want him drugged or coerced in any way. I want to understand how his mind works and maybe I won't hate him so much. I want to find out how people like him truly feel.'

'I must be physically present at this meeting,' Christian said awkwardly. 'I'm responsible.'

'How about you waiting outside the door with Jefferson?' Kennedy asked.

Christian, panicked by the implication of this request,

slammed the fragile blue line coffee cup and said earnestly, 'Please, Francis, I can't do that. Naturally he'll be secured, he will be physically helpless, but I still have to be between the two of you. This is one time I have to use the veto you gave me.' He tried to hide his fear of what Francis might do.

They both smiled. It had been part of their deal when Christian had guaranteed the safety of the President. That Christian as head of the Secret Service could veto any Presidential exposure to the public. 'I've never abused that power,' Christian said.

Kennedy made a grimace. 'But you've exercised it vigorously. OK, you can stay in the room but try to fade into the Colonial woodwork. And Jefferson stays outside the door.'

'I'll set everything up,' Christian said. 'But, Francis, this can't help you.'

Christian Klee prepared Yabril for the meeting with President Kennedy. There had of course been many interrogations but Yabril had smilingly refused to answer any questions. He had been very cool, very confident and was willing to make conversation in a general way; discuss politics, Marxist theory, the Palestinian problem which he called the Israeli problem; but he refused to talk about his background or his terrorist operations. Refused to talk about Romeo, his partner, or about Theresa Kennedy and her murder and his relationship with the Sultan of Sherhaben.

Yabril's prison was a small ten-bed hospital built by the FBI for the holding of dangerous prisoners and valuable informers. This hospital was staffed by Secret Service medical personnel and guarded by Christian's Secret Service Special Division agents. There were five of these detention hospitals in the United States; one in Washington DC area, another in Chicago, one in Los Angeles, one in Nevada and another on Long Island.

These hospitals were sometimes used for secret medical experiments on volunteer prison inmates. But Christian Klee

387

had cleared out the hospital in Washington DC to hold Yabril in isolation. He had also cleared out the hospital in Long Island to hold the two young scientists who had planted the atom bomb.

In the Washington hospital, Yabril had a medical suite fully equipped to abort any suicide attempt by violence or fasting. There were physical restraints and equipment for intravenous feeding.

Every inch of Yabril's body had been X-rayed, including his teeth and he was always restrained by a loose specially made jacket that only permitted him partial use of his arms and legs. He could read and write and walk with little steps, but could not make violent movements. He was also under twenty-four-hour surveillance through a two-way mirror by teams of Secret Service agents from Klee's Special Division.

After Christian left President Kennedy he went to visit Yabril, knowing that he had a problem. With two of the Secret Service agents he entered Yabril's suite. He sat on one of the comfortable sofas and had Yabril brought in from the bedroom. He pushed Yabril gently into one of the armchairs and then had his agents check the restraints.

Yabril said contemptuously, 'You're a very careful man with all your power.'

'I believe in being careful,' Christian told him gravely. 'I'm like those engineers who built bridges and buildings to withstand a hundred times more stress than possible. That's how I run my job.'

'They are not the same thing,' Yabril said. 'You cannot foresee the stress of Fate.'

'I know,' Christian said. 'But it relieves my anxieties and it serves well enough. Now the reason for my visit; I've come to ask you a favor.' At this Yabril laughed, a fine derisive laugh, a genuine mirth.

Christian stared at him and smiled. 'No, seriously, this is a favor it is in your power to grant or refuse. Now listen carefully. You've been treated well, that is my doing and

388

also the laws of this country. I know it's useless to threaten. I know you have your pride but it is a small thing I ask, one that will not compromise you in any way. And in return I promise to do everything I can so that nothing unlucky should happen. I know that you still have hope. You think your comrades of the famous First Hundred will come up with something clever so that we must set you free.'

Yabril's thin dark face lost its saturnine mirthfulness. He said, 'We tried several times to mount an action against your President Kennedy, very complicated and clever operations. They were all suddenly and mysteriously wiped out before we could even get into this country. I personally conducted an investigation into these failures and the destruction of our personnel. And the trail always led to you. And so I know we're in the same line of work. I know that you're not one of those cautious politicians. So just tell me the courtesy you want. Assume I'm intelligent enough to consider it very carefully.'

Christian leaned back on the sofa. Part of his brain noted that since Yabril had found his trail he was far too dangerous ever to be let free under any circumstances. Yabril had been foolish to let out that information. Then Christian concentrated on the business at hand. He said, 'President Kennedy is a very complicated man, he tries to understand events and people. And so he wanted to meet you face to face and ask you questions, engage in a dialogue. As one human being to another. He wants to understand what made you kill his daughter; he wants, perhaps, to absolve himself of his own feelings of guilt. Now all I ask is that you do talk to him, answer his questions. I ask you not to reject him totally. Will you do that?'

Yabril loosely locked in his steel fabric tried to raise his arms in a gesture of rejection. He totally lacked physical fear and yet the idea of meeting the father of the girl he had murdered aroused an agitation that surprised him. After all it had been a political act and a President of the United

389

States should understand that better than anyone. Still, it would be interesting to look into the eyes of the most powerful man in the world and say, 'I killed your daughter. I injured you more grievously than you can ever injure me, you with your thousand ships of war, your tens of thousands of thunderbolt aircraft.'

Yabril said, 'Yes, I will do you this little favor. But you may not thank me in the end.'

Christian Klee got up from the sofa and caressed Yabril's shoulder as Yabril shrugged him away with contempt. 'It doesn't matter,' Christian said. 'And I will be grateful.'

Two days later, an hour after midnight, President Francis Kennedy entered the Yellow Oval Room of the White House to find Yabril already seated in a chair by the fireplace. Christian was standing behind him.

On a small oval table inlaid with a shield of the Stars and Stripes was a silver platter of tiny sandwiches, a silver coffee pot and cups and saucers rimmed with gold. Jefferson poured the coffee into the three cups and then retreated to the door of the room and put his wide shoulders back against it. Kennedy could see that Yabril, who bowed his head to him, was immobilized in the chair. 'You haven't sedated him?' Kennedy said sharply.

'No, Mr President,' Christian said. 'Those are jacket and legging restraints.'

'Can't you make him more comfortable?' Kennedy said.

'No, sir,' Christian said.

Kennedy spoke directly to Yabril. 'I'm sorry but I don't have the last word in these matters. I won't keep you too long. I would just like to ask you a few questions.'

Yabril nodded. The restraints making his arm move in slow motion, he helped himself to one of the sandwiches. They were delicious. And it helped his pride in some way that his enemy could see that he was not completely helpless. Also with these motions he could study Kennedy's face. And

390

he was struck by the fact that this was a man who in other circumstances he would have instinctively respected and trusted to some degree. The face showing suffering but a powerful restraint of that suffering. It also showed a genuine interest in his discomfort, there was no condescension or false compassion, but the interest of one human being to another. And yet with all this there was a grave strength.

Yabril said softly and more politely and perhaps more humbly than he intended, 'Mr Kennedy, before we begin you must first answer me one question. Do you really believe that I am responsible for the atom bomb explosion in your country?'

'No,' Kennedy said. And Christian was relieved that he did not give any further information.

'Thank you,' Yabril said. 'How could anyone think me so stupid? And I would resent it if you tried to use that accusation as a weapon. You may ask me anything you like.'

Kennedy motioned to Jefferson to leave the room and watched him do so. Then he spoke softly to Yabril. Christian lowered his head as if not to hear. He really did not want to hear.

Kennedy said, 'We know you orchestrated the whole series of events. The murder of the Pope, the hoax of letting your accomplice be captured so that you could demand his ransom. The hijacking of the plane. And the killing of my daughter, which was planned from the very beginning. Now we know this for certain but I would like you to tell me if this is true. By the way, I can see the logic of it.'

Yabril looked at Kennedy directly. 'Yes, that is all true. But I'm amazed that you put it all together so quickly. I thought it clever.'

Kennedy said, 'I'm afraid it's nothing to be proud of. It means that basically I have the same kind of mind that you do. Or that there is not much difference in the human mind when it comes to deviousness.'

'Still it was maybe too clever,' Yabril said. 'You broke the

391

rules of the game. But of course it was not chess, the rules were not so strict. You were supposed to be a pawn with only a pawn's moves.'

Kennedy sat down and drank a bit of his coffee, a polite social gesture. Christian could see he was very tense and of course to Yabril the casualness of the President was transparent. Yabril wondered what the man's real intentions were. It was obvious that they were not malicious, there was no intent to use power to frighten or harm.

'I knew from the very beginning,' Kennedy said. 'With the hijacking of the plane, I knew you would kill my daughter. When your accomplice was captured I knew it was part of your plan. I was surprised by nothing. My advisors did not agree until later in your scenario. So what concerns me is that my mind must be something like yours. And yet it comes to this. I can't imagine myself doing such an operation. I want to avoid taking that next step and that is why I wanted to talk to you. To learn and foresee, to guard myself against myself.'

Yabril was impressed by Kennedy's courteous manner, the evenness of his speech, his seeming desire for some kind of truth.

Kennedy went on. 'What was your gain in all this? The Pope will be replaced, my daughter's death will not alter the international power structure. Where was your profit?'

Yabril thought, the old question of capitalism, it comes down to that. Yabril felt Christian's hands rest lightly on his shoulders for a moment. Then he hesitated before he said, 'America is the colossus to which the Israeli state owes its existence. This by definition oppresses my countrymen. And your capitalistic system oppresses the poor people of the world and even your own country. It is necessary to break down the fear of your strength. The Pope is part of that authority, the Catholic Church has terrorized the poor of the world for countless centuries, with hell and even heaven; how disgraceful. And it went on for two thousand years. To

392

bring about the Pope's death was more than a political satisfaction.'

Christian had wandered away from Yabril's chair but was still alert, ready to interpose himself. He opened the door to the Yellow Oval Room to whisper to Jefferson for a moment. Yabril noted all this in silence then went on.

'But all my actions against you failed. I mounted two very elaborate operations to assassinate you and they failed. You may one day ask your Mr Klee the details, they may astonish you. The Attorney General, what a benign title, I must confess it misled me at the beginning. He destroyed my operations with a ruthlessness that compelled my admiration. But then, he had so many men, so much technology. I was helpless. But your own invulnerability ensured your daughter's death, and I know how that must trouble you. I speak frankly since that is your wish.'

Christian came back to stand behind the chair and tried to avoid Kennedy's look. Yabril felt a strange tinge of fear but he went on. 'Consider,' Yabril said and tried to raise his arms to make an emphatic gesture, 'if I hijack a plane, I am a monster. If the Israelis bomb a helpless Arab town and kill hundreds they are striking a blow for freedom; more they are avenging the famous holocaust with which Arabs had nothing to do. But what are our options? We do not have the military power, we do not have the technology. Who is the more heroic? Well in both cases the innocent die. And what about justice? Israel was put in place by foreign powers, my people were thrown out into the desert. We are the new homeless, the new Jews, what an irony. Does the world expect us not to fight? What can we use except terror? What did the Jews use when they fought for the establishment of their state against the British? We learned everything about terror from the Jews of that time. And those terrorists are now heroes, those slaughterers of the innocent. One even became the Prime Minister of Israel and was accepted by the

393

heads of states as if they never smelled the blood on his hands. Am I more terrible?'

Yabril paused for a moment and tried to rise but Christian pushed him down back in his chair. Kennedy made a gesture for him to go on.

Yabril said, 'You ask what I accomplished. In one sense I failed and the proof is that I am here a prisoner. But what a blow I dealt to your authority figure in the world. America is not so great after all. It could have ended better for me, but it's still not a total loss. I exposed to the world how ruthless your supposedly humane democracy really is. You destroyed a great city, you mercilessly subdued a foreign nation to your will. I made you peel off your thunderbolts to frighten the whole world and you alienated part of the world. You are not so beloved, your America. And in your own country you have polarized your political factions. Your personal image has changed and you have become the terrible Mr Hyde to your saintly Dr Jekyll.'

Yabril paused for a moment to control the violent energy of the emotions that had passed over his face. He became more respectful, more grave.

'I come now to what you want to hear and what is painful for me to say. Your daughter's death was necessary. She was a symbol of America because she was the daughter of the most powerful man on earth. Do you know what that does to people who fear authority? It gives them hope, never mind that some may love you, that some may see you as benefactor or friend. People hate their benefactors in the long run. They see you are no more powerful than they are, they need not fear you. Of course it would have been more effective if I had gone free. How would that have been? The Pope dead, your daughter killed and then you are forced to set me free. How impotent you and America would have seemed before the world.'

Yabril leaned back in the chair to lessen the weight of restraint and smiled at Kennedy. 'I only made one mistake. I misjudged you completely. There was nothing in your history that could foretell your actions. You, the great liberal, the ethical modern man. I thought you would release my friend. I thought you would not be able to put the pieces together quickly enough and I never dreamed you would commit such a great crime.'

Kennedy said, 'There were very few casualties when the city of Dak was bombed, we dumped leaflets hours before.'

Yabril said, 'I understand that. It was a perfect terrorist response. I would have done the same myself. But I would never have done what you did to save yourself. Set off an atom bomb in one of your own cities.'

'You are mistaken,' Kennedy said. And Christian was relieved again that he did not offer more information. And he was also relieved to see that Kennedy did not take the accusation seriously. In fact Kennedy went on immediately to something else. He poured himself another cup of coffee and then said, 'Answer me this as honestly as you can. Did the fact that my name is Kennedy have any bearing on your plans?'

Both Christian and Yabril were astonished by this question. Christian for the first time stared Kennedy in the face. Kennedy seemed entirely calm. Yabril pondered this question as if he did not quite understand. Finally he answered.

'To be honest, I did think about that aspect, the martyrdom of your two uncles, the love that most of the world and your country in particular has for that tragic legend. It added to the force of the blow I intended. Yes, your name was a small part of the plan, I must confess.'

There was a long pause, Christian turned his head away and thought, I will never let this man live.

'Tell me,' Kennedy said, 'how can you justify in your own heart the things you have done, your betrayals of human trust? I've read your dossier. How can any human being say to himself, I will better the world by killing innocent men, women and children. I will raise humanity out of its despair

395

by betraying my best friend, all this without any authority given by God or your fellow beings. Compassion aside, how do you even dare to assume such power?'

Yabril waited courteously as if he expected another question. Then he said, 'The acts I committed are not so bizarre as the press and moralists claim. What about your bomber pilots who rain down destruction as if the people below them were mere ants? Those good-hearted boys with every manly virtue. But they were taught to do their duty. I think I am no different. Yet I do not have the resources to drop death from thousands of feet in the air. Or naval guns that obliterate from twenty miles away. I must dirty my hands with blood. I must have moral strength, the mental purity to shed blood directly for the cause I believe in. Well, that is all terribly obvious, an old argument and it seems cowardly to even make it. But you say how do I have courage to assume that authority without being approved by some source? That is more complicated. Let me believe that the suffering I have seen in my world has given me that authority. Let me say that the books I have read, the music I have heard, the example of far greater men than myself, have given me the strength to act on my own principles. It is more difficult for me than you who have the support of hundreds of millions and so commit your terror as a duty to them, as their instrument.'

Here Yabril paused to sip helplessly at his coffee cup. Then he went on with a calm dignity.

'I have devoted my life to revolution against the established order, the authority I despise. I will die believing what I have done is right. And as you know, there is no moral law that exists for ever.'

Finally Yabril was exhausted and leaned back in his chair, arms appearing broken from the restraints. Kennedy had listened without any sign of disapproval. He did not make any counter argument. There was a long silence and finally Kennedy said, 'I can't argue morals, basically I've done what

396

you have done. And as you say it is easier to do when one does not personally bloody one's hands. But again as you say I act from a core of social authority not of my own personal animosity.'

Yabril interrupted him. 'That is not correct. Congress did not approve your actions, neither did your Cabinet Officers. Essentially you acted as I did on your own personal authority. You are my fellow terrorist.'

Kennedy said, 'But the people of my country, the electorate, approve.'

'The mob,' Yabril said. 'They always approve. They refuse to foresee the dangers of such actions. What you did was wrong politically and morally. You acted on a desire for personal vengeance.' Yabril smiled. 'And I thought you would be above such an action. So much for morality.'

Kennedy was silent for a time as if giving careful consideration to his answer. Then he said, 'I hope you're wrong, time will tell. I want to thank you for speaking to me so frankly, especially since I understand you refused to co-operate in former interrogations. You know of course that the best law firm in the United States has been retained for you by the Sultan of Sherhaben and shortly they will be permitted to consult with you on your defense.'

Kennedy smiled and rose to leave the room. He was almost to the door when it swung open. Then as he walked through it he heard Yabril's voice. Yabril had struggled to his feet despite his restraints and fought to keep his balance. He was erect when he said, 'Mr President.'

Kennedy turned to face him.

Yabril lifted his arms slowly, ending them crookedly under the nylon and wire corset. 'Mr President,' he said again, 'you do not deceive me. I know I will never see or talk to my lawyers.'

Christian had interposed his body between the two men and Jefferson was by Kennedy's side.

Kennedy gave Yabril a cold smile. 'You have my personal

397

guarantee that you will see and talk to your lawyers,' he said. And walked out of the room.

At that moment Christian Klee felt an anguish close to nausea. He had always believed he knew Francis Kennedy but now he realized he did not. For in one clear moment he had seen a look of pure hatred on Kennedy's face that was alien to everything in his character.

BOOK V

21

Just before the Democratic Convention in August, the Socrates Club and Congress unleashed a full-scale attack against the Presidency.

The first shot was the exposure of Eugene Dazzy having an affair with a young dancer. The girl was persuaded to go public and give exclusive interviews to the more respected papers. Salentine tipped off a publisher of a literate semipornographic magazine who paid for exclusive rights and explicit photos which showed the opulent physical charms Eugene Dazzy had enjoyed. Enriched by the money and spurred by a newly inspired morality, the dancer made innumerable appearances on Salentine's TV network and on Cassandra Chutt's *Five Star Interview*, revealing how she had been seduced by an older, more powerful man. When Kennedy refused to fire Dazzy, Salentine was overjoyed.

Then Peter Cloot was subpoenaed by the Jintz and Lambertino committees and repeated the information he had given Patsy Troyca and Elizabeth Stone in their private discussion. The committees leaked this testimony to the media and it was spread over the newspapers and TV. Christian Klee issued a denial and again Kennedy supported his staff. Kennedy refused on the grounds of executive privilege to have Christian Klee testify before any Congressional Committee. Again the Socrates Club was delighted. Kennedy was digging his own grave.

Then the Congressional Committees managed to get information on Klee's deal with Canoo and the secret funds that were being used for thousands of Secret Service personnel to guard Kennedy. This was published as proof that the Kennedy administration had lied to the American Congress and the American people. Here Kennedy gave ground and personally ordered that the use of the Office of the Military Advisor funds be cut off and the Secret Service protection reduced. Canoo refused to answer any questions and hid himself behind the shield of the President. Again Kennedy refused to take action. He asserted that he would not give in to an obvious vendetta by the media and Congress. He said he might take action after the election if the facts warranted.

Then there was a big story that Kennedy would propose a Constitutional Convention and would ask that the limitation of the Presidency to only two terms be annulled. That his obvious plan was to be re-elected to a third and fourth and fifth term. This story, though unsubstantiated, was given a great deal of play by the media. Kennedy ignored it. When questioned, he said with a disarming smile, 'I'm worried about getting elected to my second term.'

But Lawrence Salentine was proudest of the special story that was run in the most widely read magazine in the country. This article was about the woman that was reputed to be Kennedy's mistress and the woman whom he expected to marry after the election. It was a completely laudatory article, she was a woman wise beyond her years, though rather young. She was witty. She was beautiful, she dressed elegantly while spending no more than the ordinary professional woman. She was modest, she was shy, yet a good conversationalist and had a knowledge of world affairs. She was well read and had a social conscience, she had no vices, she did not drink to excess, nor did she do drugs. Her sexual history was short, she was not promiscuous for a woman of twenty-eight, not married. And in a short paragraph dropped in the middle of the story was the information, given with the utmost casualness, that she was one-eighth 'Negro'.

Lawrence Salentine regarded that little paragraph as the

one drop of poison that would effectively erase a good fifteen per cent of Kennedy's popularity. This particular item was not true. It was simply one of those small-time rumors or gossip that abounded in small Southern towns. As Klee found when he sent a small army of investigators to her birthplace.

All this had its effect in the last poll before the Democratic Convention, Kennedy's strength dropped to only sixty of the electorate, a loss of twenty points.

The television talk show hostess, Cassandra Chutt, had Peter Cloot on her show, the highest-rated interview program on television. She asked him the ultimate question. 'Do you think that the Attorney General Christian Klee is responsible for the explosion of the atom bomb and the death and injury of over ten thousand people?'

And Peter Cloot answered, 'Yes.'

Then Chutt asked another question. 'Do you think that President Kennedy and Attorney General Klee are responsible to some degree for what is probably the greatest tragedy in American history?'

Here Peter Cloot was more careful. 'President Kennedy was mistaken out of some humanitarian impulse. I happen to be a strong believer in law enforcement. So I have my bias. But, yes, I think he was wrong. Strictly a matter of beliefs and judgment.'

Cassandra Chutt said, 'But you have no doubts about the Attorney General's guilt?'

Peter Cloot faced the camera squarely and sincerely. His voice was filled with anger, righteous pain. 'Attorney General Christian Klee was guilty of a criminal act. He deliberately delayed an important interrogation. I believe he is the man who made the phone call that tipped off the defendants. I believe that Christian Klee wanted that bomb to go off and so precipitated a crisis that would prevent President Kennedy from being impeached by Congress. I believe he committed the most terrible crime in American history, and I believe he should be brought to justice. President Kennedy, by protecting the Attorney General, is an accomplice.'

Then Cassandra Chutt addressed her TV audience of sixty million people and said simply, 'Our guest, Peter Cloot, was formerly Assistant and Executive Director of the FBI under Attorney General Christian Klee. He was forced to resign from that post after testifying to a Senate Committee on this matter he has discussed here with us tonight. The Kennedy administration denied all his charges and to this very day Christian Klee is still the Attorney General of the United States and the Director of the FBI.'

The program had an enormous impact and was picked up by every TV and cable company and quoted extensively in all the newspapers.

At the same time Whitney Cheever III had given a press conference on TV in which he stated that his clients, Gresse and Tibbot, were innocent, that they were the victims of a gigantic conspiracy by the government, that he would prove that a fascistic cabal had engineered the catastrophic crime to save the Presidency of Francis Kennedy.

Christian Klee was worried about many things. There were the charges by Tibbot's father that Klee had made the warning call. There was the Peter Cloot testimony. There was the leakage on the arrangement he had made with Canoo to divert funds to the Secret Service. There was the drop in Kennedy's popularity after these massive attacks. But most of all he was worried about Bert Audick's visit to the Sultan of Sherhaben. That Audick had gone to arrange the detail for the rebuilding of Dak was, to him, just a cover story.

Klee decided to take a vacation but to combine business with pleasure. He would go around the wide world. First to London, then to Rome to check on Romeo in prison and then on to Sherhaben to check on Bert Audick's visit there.

He pulled up the David Jatney file again on the computer screen and checked. Still nothing there.

In London, Christian Klee touched base with his opposite numbers in the English Security establishment. During dinner at the Ritz Hotel, they were exquisitely polite but he sensed a coldness. Cloot's charges had done their work and the English had never liked any of the Kennedys. In any case they had no information to give him.

Klee had a woman friend in England who lived in a small country house just outside of London. It was extremely rural, with roses climbing over everything and even some sheep in a nearby meadow. Christian Klee spent a long weekend there and relaxed.

The woman was the widow of a wealthy newspaper publisher and led a quiet life. She had two house servants but drove her own car. Klee loved the times he spent with her. There was nothing remotely exciting in her life. She read, she tended her garden, managed the estate and always seemed eager to receive him when he visited England. She never made any demands, never asked him questions about his work. She was a perfect hostess and she made love like a gentlewoman, as though it was a necessary courtesy.

He relaxed there for three days and then his idyll was interrupted by a special courier. A message that the terrorist named Romeo, who had been extradited to Italy, had just committed suicide in a Roman prison. Christian immediately called Franco Sebbediccio and caught the next flight for Rome. At the airport, he called his office in Washington and ordered a special suicide watch on Gresse and Tibbot. And on Yabril.

Franco Sebbediccio when a little boy in Sicily had chosen the side of law and order not only because it seemed the stronger side but because he loved the sweet consolation of living under strict rules of authority. The Mafia had been too impressionistic, the world of commerce too dicey and so he had become a policeman and thirty years later he was the head of the Italian Anti-Terrorist Division of all of Italy.

He had now had under his arrest the assassin of the Pope, a young Italian of good family named Armando Giangi, codenamed Romeo. This code name irritated Franco Sebbediccio enormously. Sebbediccio had incarcerated Romeo in the deepest cells of his Roman prison.

Under surveillance was Rita Fallicia whose code name was Annee. She had been easy to track down because she had been a troublemaker since her teens, a firebrand at the University, a pugnacious leader of demonstrations and linked in Security to the abduction of a leading banker of Milan.

The evidence had come flooding in. The 'safe houses' had been cleaned by the terrorist cadres but those poor bastards had no way of knowing the scientific resources of a national police organization. There was a towel with traces of semen that identified Romeo. One of the captured men had given evidence under severe interrogation. But Sebbediccio had not arrested Annee. She was to remain free.

Franco Sebbediccio worried that the trial of these guilty parties would glorify the Pope's murder and that they would become heroes and spend their prison sentences without too much discomfort. Italy did not have a death penalty, they could only receive life imprisonment, which was a joke. With all the reductions for good behavior and the different conditions for amnesties they would be set free at a comparatively young age.

It would have been different if Sebbediccio could have conducted the interrogation of Romeo in a more serious fashion. But because this scoundrel had killed a Pope, his rights had become a cause in the Western world. There were protesters and human rights groups from Scandinavia and England and even a stern letter from a lawyer in America named Whitney Cheever. All these proclaimed that the two

406

murderers must be handled as human beings, not subjected to torture, not ill-treated in any way. And orders had come down from the top, don't disgrace Italian justice with anything that might offend the left-wing parties in Italy. Kid gloves.

Franco Sebbediccio had gone through this before, and it was a disgrace. But the killing of a Pope was something else. And the resurgence of the terrorist groups was again something else. He had to get information and the prisoners had not co-operated. But the final straw was that just a week ago Franco Sebbediccio's Administrative Judge had been assassinated with a message to the effect that this would continue until the killers of the Pope were freed. A ridiculous request but a public relations excuse to kill a judge.

But he, Franco Sebbediccio, would cut through all the nonsense and send a message to the Red Army. Franco Sebbediccio was determined that this Romeo, this Armando Giangi, would commit suicide.

Romeo had spent his months in prison weaving a romantic dream. Alone in his cell he had chosen to fall in love with the American girl, Dorothea. He remembered her waiting for him at the airport, the tender scar on her chin. In his reveries, she seemed so beautiful, so kind. He tried to remember their conversation that last night he spent with her in the Hamptons. Now in his memory, it seemed to him that she had loved him. That her every gesture had dared him to declare his desire so that she could show her love. He remembered how she sat, so gracefully, so invitingly. How her eyes stared at him, great dark pools of blue, her white skin suffused with blushes. And now he cursed his timidity. He had never touched that skin. He remembered the long slim legs and imposed them around his neck. He imagined the kisses he would rain on her, her eyes, the length of her lithesome body.

And then Romeo dreamed of how she stood in the

sunlight, draped in chains, staring at him in reproach and despair. He weaved fantasies of the future. She would only serve a short term in prison. She would be waiting for him. And he would be freed. By amnesty or by the trading of hostages, perhaps by pure Christian mercy. And then he would find her.

There were nights that he despaired and thought of Yabril's treachery. The murder of Theresa Kennedy had never been in the plan and he believed in his heart that he would never have consented to such an act. He felt a disgust for Yabril, for his own beliefs, for his own life. Sometimes he would weep quietly in the darkness. Then he would console himself and lose himself in his fantasies of Dorothea. It was false, he knew. It was a weakness, he knew, but he could not help himself.

Romeo in his bare, smooth cell received Franco Sebbediccio with a sardonic grin. He could see the hatred in this old man's peasant eyes, could sense his bewilderment that a person from a good family who enjoyed a pleasant, luxuriant life, could also become a revolutionary. He was also aware that Sebbediccio was frustrated that the international public watch restrained him from treating his prisoner as brutally as he might wish.

Sebbediccio had himself locked in with the prisoner, the two of them alone with two guards and an observer from the governor's office watching but unable to hear from right outside the door. It was almost as if the burly older man were inviting some sort of attack. But Romeo knew that it was simply that the older man had confidence in the authority of his position. Romeo had a contempt for this kind of man, rooted in law and order, handcuffed by his beliefs and bourgeois moral standards. Therefore he was terribly surprised when Sebbediccio said to him casually, but in a very low voice, 'Giangi, you are going to make life easier for everyone. You are going to commit suicide.'

Romeo laughed. 'No, I'm not, I'll be out of jail before you die of high blood pressure and ulcers. I'll walk the streets of Rome when you're lying in your family cemetary. I'll come and sing to the angels on your tombstone. I'll be whistling when I walk away from your grave.'

Franco Sebbediccio said patiently, 'I just wanted to let you know that you and your cadre are going to commit suicide. Two of my men were killed by your friends to intimidate me and my associates. Your suicides will be my answer.'

Romeo said, 'I can't please you. I'm enjoying life too much. And with all the world watching you don't dare to even give me a good kick in the ass.'

Franco Sebbediccio gave him a benevolent smile. He had an ace in the hole.

Romeo's father, who all his life had done nothing for humanity, had done something for his son. He had shot himself. A Knight of Malta, father of the murderer of the Pope, a man who had lived his whole life for his own selfish pleasure, he had unfathomably decided to don the mantle of guilt.

When Romeo's newly widowed mother asked to visit her son in his prison cell and was refused, the newspapers took up her cause. The telling blow was struck by Romeo's defense lawyer as he was interviewed on television. 'For God's sake he just wants to see his mother.' Which struck a responsive chord, not only in Italy but all over the Western world. Every newspaper gave it a front page headline, verbatim, 'For God's sake, he just wants to see his mother.'

Which was not strictly true, Romeo's mother wanted to see him, he did not want to see her.

With pressure so great, the government was forced to allow Mother Giangi to visit her son. Franco Sebbediccio had opposed this visit, he wanted to keep Romeo in seclusion, to keep him cut off from the outside world. But the governor of the prison overrode him.

The governor had a grand palatial office and summoned

Sebbediccio to it. He said, 'My dear sir, I have my instructions, the visit is to be allowed. And not in his cell where the conversation can be monitored but in this office itself. With nobody within earshot, but recorded by cameras in the last five minutes of the hour, after all the media must be allowed to profit.'

Sebbediccio said, 'And for what reason is this allowed?'

The governor gave him the smile he reserved usually for the prisoners and the members of his staff who had become almost like the prisoners themselves. 'For a son to see his widowed mother. What could be more sacred?'

Sebbediccio hated the governor who always had observers outside the door during interrogations. He said harshly, 'A man who murders the Pope? He has to see his mother? Why didn't he talk to his mother before he shot the Pope?'

The governor shrugged. 'Those far above us have decided. Reconcile yourself. Also the defense lawyer insists that this office be swept for bugs so don't think you can plant electronic gear.'

'Ah,' Sebbediccio said. 'And how is the lawyer going to do the debugging?'

'He will hire his own electronic specialists,' the governor said. 'They will do their job in the lawyer's presence immediately before the meeting.'

Sebbediccio said, 'It is essential, it is vital that we hear that conversation between them.'

'Nonsense,' the governor said. 'His mother is your typical rich Roman matron. She knows nothing and he would never confide anything of importance to her. This is just another silly episode in the quite ridiculous drama of our times. Don't take it seriously.'

But Franco Sebbediccio did take it seriously. He considered it another mockery of justice, another scorn of authority. And he hoped Romeo might let something slip when he talked to his mother.

410

As head of the Anti-Terrorist Division for all Italy Sebbediccio had a great deal of power. The defense lawyer was already on the secret list of left-wing radicals who could be put under surveillance. Which was done, the phone tapped, the mail intercepted and read before it was delivered. And so it was easy to find the electronic company the defense would use to sweep the governor's office. Sebbediccio used a friend to set up an 'accidental' meeting in a restaurant with the owner of the electronics company.

Even without the help of force, Franco Sebbediccio could be persuasive. It was a small electronics corporation, making a living but by no means an overwhelming success. Sebbediccio pointed out that the Anti-Terrorist Division had great need of electronic sweeping equipment and personnel, that it could interpose security vetoes on the companies selected. In short that he, Sebbediccio, could make the company rich.

But there must be trust and profit on both sides. In this particular case why should the electronics company care about the murderers of the Pope, why should it jeopardize its future prosperity over such an inconsequential matter as the recording of a meeting between the mother and son? Why could not the electronics company plant the bug as it was supposedly debugging the governor's office? And who would be the wiser? And Sebbediccio himself would arrange to have the bug removed.

It was done in a very friendly way, but somewhere during the dinner Sebbediccio made it understood that if he was refused, the electronics company would run into a great deal of trouble in the coming years. Without any personal animosity, but how could his government service possibly trust people who protected the murderer of the Pope?

It was all agreed and Sebbediccio let the other man pick up the check. He was certainly not going to pay for it out of his personal funds, and to be reimbursed on his expense voucher might lead to a paper trail years later. Besides, he was going to make the man rich.

The meeting between Armando 'Romeo' Giangi and his mother was therefore fully recorded and heard only by Franco Sebbediccio and he was delighted with it. Though he took his time in removing the bug simply out of curiosity at what the snotty governor of the prison was really like but there he got nothing.

Sebbediccio took the precaution of playing the tape in his home while his wife slept. None of his colleagues must know about it. He was not a bad man and he almost wept when Mother Giangi sobbed over her son, implored him to tell the truth that he had not really killed the Pope, that he was shielding a bad companion. Sebbediccio could hear the woman's kisses as she rained them down upon the face of her murderous son and he wondered for a moment does it ever matter what anyone does in reality? But then the kissing and wails stopped and the conversation became very interesting to Franco Sebbediccio.

He heard Romeo's voice attempting to calm the mother down. And then Romeo said, 'I don't understand why your husband killed himself. He didn't care about his country or the world, and forgive me, he didn't even love his family. He lived a completely selfish and egocentric life. Why did he feel it necessary to shoot himself?'

The mother's voice came hissing from the tape. 'Out of vanity,' she said. 'All his life your father was a vain man. Every day to his barber, once a week to his tailor. At the age of forty he took singing lessons. To sing where? And he spent a fortune to become a Knight of Malta and never a man so devoid of the Holy Spirit. On Easter he had a white suit made with the palm cross woven specially into the cloth. Oh, what a grand figure in Roman society. The parties, the balls, his appointment to cultural committees whose meetings he never attended. And the father of a son graduated from the University, he was proud of your brilliance. Oh, how he promenaded on the streets of Rome. I never saw a

412

man so happy and so empty.' There was a pause on the tape. 'After what you did, your father could never appear in Roman society again. That empty life was finished and for that loss he killed himself. But he can rest easy. He looked beautiful in his coffin with his new Easter suit.'

Then came Romeo's voice on the tape saying what delighted Sebbediccio. 'My father never gave me anything in life and by his suicide he stole my option. And death was my only escape.'

Sebbediccio listened to the rest of the tape in which Romeo let his mother persuade him to see a priest and then when the TV cameras and reporters were let into the room he turned it off. He had seen the rest on TV. But he had what he wanted.

When Sebbediccio paid his next visit to Romeo, he was so delighted that when the jailer unlocked the cell he entered doing a little dance step and greeted Giangi with great joviality.

'Giangi,' he said, 'you are becoming even more famous. It is rumored that when we have a new Pope he may ask mercy for you. Show your gratitude, give me some of the information I need.'

Romeo said, 'What an ape you are.'

Sebbediccio bowed and said, 'That's your last word then?'

It was perfect. He had a recording that said Romeo was thinking of killing himself.

A week later the news was released to the world that the murderer of the Pope, Armando 'Romeo' Giangi, had committed suicide by hanging himself in his cell.

Christian Klee arrived in Rome from London to have dinner with Sebbediccio. He noted that Sebbediccio had almost twenty bodyguards, which did not seem to affect his appetite.

Sebbediccio was in high spirits. 'Wasn't it fortunate that our Pope-killer took his own life?' he said to Christian Klee.

'What a circus the trial would have been with all our left-wingers marching in support. It's too bad that fellow Yabril wouldn't do you the same favor.'

Christian Klee laughed and said ironically, 'Different systems of government. I see you're well protected.'

Sebbediccio shrugged. 'I think they are after bigger game. I have some information for you. That woman, Annee, that we've let run loose. Somehow we lost her. But we have some information that says she's now in America.'

Christian Klee felt a thrill of excitement. 'Do you know what port of embarkation? What name she is using?'

'No,' Sebbediccio said. 'But we think she is now operational.'

'Why didn't you pick her up?' Christian said.

'I have high hopes for her,' Sebbediccio said. 'She is a very determined young lady and she will go far in the terrorist movement. I want to use a big net when I take her. But you have a problem my friend. We hear rumors that there is an operation in the United States. It can only be against Kennedy. Annee, as fierce as she may be, cannot do it alone. Therefore, there must be other people involved. Knowing your security for the President, they will have to mount an operation that would require a goodly number with material and safe houses. On that I have no information. You had better set to work.'

Christian Klee didn't ask why the Italian Security Chief had not sent this information through regular channels to Washington. He knew Sebbediccio did not want his close surveillance of Annee made part of an official record in the United States, he did not trust the Freedom of Information Act in America. Also, he wanted Christian Klee in his personal debt.

In Sherhaben, Sultan Maurobi received Christian Klee with the utmost friendliness. As if there had never been the crisis of a few months before. The Sultan was affable but on guard

414

and appeared a little puzzled. 'I hope you bring me good news,' he said to Christian Klee. 'After all the regrettable unpleasantness, I am very anxious to repair relations with the United States and, of course, your President Kennedy. In fact, I hope your visit is in regard to this matter.'

Christian Klee smiled. 'I came for that very purpose,' he said. 'You are in a position, I think, to do us a service which might heal the breach.'

'Ah, I am very happy to hear that,' the Sultan said. 'You know, of course, that I was not privy to Yabril's intentions. I had no foreknowledge of what Yabril would do to the President's daughter. Of course, I have expressed this officially, but would you tell the President personally that I have grieved over this for the past months. I was powerless to avert the tragedy.'

Christian Klee believed him. The murder had not been in the original plans. And he thought how all powerful men like Sultan Maurobi and Francis Kennedy were helpless in the face of uncontrollable events, the will of other men.

But now he said to the Sultan, 'Your giving up Yabril has reassured the President on that point.' This they both knew was mere politeness. Klee paused for a moment and then went on. 'But I'm here to ask you to do me a personal service. You know I am responsible for the safety of my President. I have information that there is a plot to assassinate him. That terrorists have already infiltrated into the United States. But it would be helpful if I could get information as to their plans and to their identity and location. With your contacts I thought you might have heard something through your intelligence agencies. That you might give me some scraps of information. Let me emphasize that it will only be between the two of us. You and I. There will be no official connection.'

The Sultan seemed astonished. His intelligent face screwed up into amused disbelief. 'How can you think such a thing?' he asked. 'After all the tragedies, would I get involved in such dangerous activities? I am the ruler of a small rich country that is powerless to remain independent without the friendship of great powers. I can do nothing for you or against you.'

Christian Klee nodded his head in agreement. 'Of course that is true. However Bert Audick came to visit you and I know that had to do with the oil industry. But let me tell you that Mr Audick is in very serious trouble in the United States. He would be a very bad ally for you to have in the coming years.'

'And you would be a very good ally?' the Sultan asked, smiling.

'Yes,' Klee said. 'I am the ally that could save you. If you co-operate with me now.'

'Explain,' the Sultan said. He was obviously angered by the implied threat.

Christian Klee spoke very carefully. 'Bert Audick is under indictment for conspiracy against the United States government because his mercenaries or those of his company fired on our planes bombing your city of Dak. And there are other charges. His oil empire could be destroyed under certain of our laws. He is not a strong ally at this moment.'

The Sultan said slyly, 'Indicted but not convicted. I understand that will be more difficult.'

'That is true,' Christian Klee said. 'But in a few months Francis Kennedy will be re-elected. His popularity will bring in a Congress that will ratify his programs. He will be the most powerful President in the history of the United States. Then Audick is doomed, I can assure you. And the power structure of which he is a part will be destroyed.'

'I still fail to see how I can help you,' the Sultan said. And then more imperiously, 'Or how you can help me. I understand you are in a delicate position yourself in your own country.'

'That may or may not be true,' Christian Klee said. 'As for my position, delicate as you say, that will be resolved when Kennedy is re-elected. I am his closest friend and closest advisor and Kennedy is noted for his loyalty. As to how we can help each other, let me be direct without intending any disrespect. May I do so?'

The Sultan seemed to be impressed and even amused by this courtesy. 'By all means,' he said.

Klee said, 'First, and most importantly, here is how I can help you. I can be your ally. I have the ear of the President of the United States and I have his trust. We live in difficult times.'

The Sultan interrupted smilingly, 'I have always lived in difficult times.'

'And so you can appreciate what I am saying better than most,' Klee retorted sharply.

'And what if your Kennedy does not achieve his aims?' the Sultan said. 'Accidents befall, heaven is not always kind.'

Christian Klee was cold now as he answered. 'What you are saying is, what if the plot to kill Kennedy succeeds? I am here to tell you that it will not. I don't care how clever and daring the assassins may be. And if they try and fail and there is any trace to you, then you will be destroyed. But it doesn't have to come to that. I'm a reasonable man and I understand your position. What I propose is an exchange of information between you and myself on a personal basis. I don't know what Audick proposed to you, but I'm a better bet. If Audick and his crowd wins, you still win. He doesn't know about us. If Kennedy wins, you have me as your ally. I'm your insurance.'

The Sultan nodded and then led him into a sumptuous banquet. During the meal, the Sultan asked Klee innumerable questions about Kennedy. Then finally, almost hesitantly, he asked about Yabril.

Klee looked him directly in the eyes. 'There is no way that Yabril can escape his fate. If his fellow terrorists think they can get him released by holding even the most important of

417

hostages, tell them to forget about it. Kennedy will never let him go.'

The Sultan sighed. 'Your Kennedy has changed,' he said. 'He sounds like a man going berserk.' Klee didn't answer. The Sultan went on, very slowly. 'I think you have convinced me,' he said. 'I think you and I should become allies.'

When Christian Klee returned to the United States, the first person he went to see was the Oracle. The old man received him in his bedroom suite, sitting in his motorized wheelchair, an English tea spread on the table in front of him, a comfortable armchair waiting for Christian opposite.

The Oracle greeted him with a slight wave that he should sit down. Christian served him tea and a tiny bit of cake and a small finger sandwich. Then served himself. The Oracle took a sip of tea, crumbled the bit of cake in his mouth. They sat there for a long moment.

Then the Oracle tried to smile, a slight movement of the lips, the skin so dead it could not move. 'You've got yourself into a fine mess for your fucking friend Kennedy,' he said.

The vulgarism, spoken as if from the mouth of an innocent child, made Christian smile. Again he wondered, was it a mark of senility, a decaying of the brain, that the Oracle who had never used profanity, now was using it so freely? He waited until he had eaten one of the sandwiches and gulped down some hot tea then he answered. 'Which fix?' he said. 'I'm in a lot of them.'

'I'm talking about that atom bomb thing,' the Oracle said. 'The rest of the shit doesn't matter. But they are accusing you of being responsible for the murder of thousands of citizens of this country. They've got the goods on you it seems, but I refuse to believe you to be so stupid. Inhuman, yes, after all you're in politics. Did you really do it?' The old man's face was not judgmental, just curious.

Who else in the world was there to tell? Who else in the

world would understand. 'What I'm astonished about,' Christian Klee said, 'is how quickly they got on to me.'

'The human mind *leaps* to an understanding of evil,' the Oracle said. 'You are surprised because there is a certain innocence in the doer of an evil deed. He thinks the deed so terrible that it is inconceivable to another human being. But that is the first thing they jump at. Evil is no mystery at all, love is the mystery.' He paused for a moment, started to speak again and then relaxed back in his chair, his eyes half closed, dozing.

'You have to understand,' Christian said, 'that letting something happen is so much easier than actually doing something. There was the crisis, Francis Kennedy was going to be impeached by the Congress. And I thought just for a second, if only the atom bomb exploded it would turn things around. It was in that moment that I told Peter Cloot not to interrogate Gresse and Tibbot. That I had the time to do it. The whole thing flashed by in that one second and it was done.'

The Oracle said, 'Give me some more hot tea and another piece of cake.' He put the cake in his mouth, tiny crumbs appearing on his scar-like lips. 'What about Peter Cloot's testimony, that you came back and interrogated them. That you got the information out of them and then didn't act on it?'

Christian sighed. 'They were only kids. I squeezed them dry in five minutes. That's why I couldn't have Cloot at the interrogation. But I didn't want the bomb to explode. It just went so quick.'

The Oracle started to laugh. It was a curious laugh even in so old a man. It was a series of grunted 'heh, heh, heh's'. 'You've got it ass backwards,' the Oracle said. 'You had already made up your mind that you would let the bomb explode. Before you told Cloot not to interrogate them. It didn't go by in a second, you planned it all out.'

Christian Klee was a little startled. What the Oracle said

419

was true. Then how had he twisted it in his own mind? He said to the Oracle, 'You have to understand how it was. I wasn't sure that it all would happen. If I was sure, I would have prevented it. I was just hanging to some sort of hope that something might solve Kennedy's situation.'

'And all to save your hero, Francis Kennedy,' the Oracle said. 'The man who can do no wrong except when he sets the whole world on fire.' The Oracle had placed a box of thin Havana cigars on the table and Christian took one of them and lit it. 'You were lucky,' the Oracle said. 'Those people that were killed were mostly worthless. The drunken, the homeless, the criminal. And it's not so great a crime. Not in the history of our human race.'

'Francis really gave me the go ahead,' Christian Klee said. And that made the Oracle touch a button on his chair so that the back of it straightened to make his body upright and alert.

'Your saintly President?' the Oracle said. 'He is far too much a victim of his own hypocrisy, like all the Kennedys were. He could never be party to such an act.'

'Maybe I'm just trying to make excuses,' Christian said. 'It was nothing explicit. But remember I know Francis so intimately, we're almost like brothers. I asked him for the order so that the Medical Interrogation team would be able to do the chemical brain probe. That would have settled the whole atom bomb problem immediately. And Francis refused to sign the authorization. Sure he gave his grounds, good civil liberty and humanitarian grounds. That was in his character. But that was in his character before his daughter was killed. Not in his character afterwards. Remember, he had ordered the destruction of Dak by this time. He gave the threat that he would destroy the whole nation of Sherhaben if the hostages were not released. So his character had changed. His new character would have signed the Medical Interrogation order. And then when he refused to sign, he

420

gave me a look, I can't describe it, but it was almost as if he were telling me to let it happen.'

The Oracle was fully alive now. He spoke sharply. 'All that doesn't matter. What matters is that you save your ass. If Kennedy doesn't get re-elected, you may spend years in jail. And even if Kennedy gets re-elected, there may be some danger.'

'Kennedy will win the election,' Christian said. 'And after that, I'll be OK.' He paused for a moment. 'I know him.'

'You know the old Kennedy,' the Oracle said. Then as if he had lost interest he said, 'And how about my birthday party? I'm a hundred years old and nobody gives a shit.'

Christian laughed. 'I do. Don't worry. After the election you'll have a birthday party in the White House Rose Garden. A birthday party for a king.'

The Oracle smiled with pleasure, then said slyly, 'And your Francis Kennedy will be the king. You do know, don't you, that if he is re-elected and carries his Congressional candidates with him, he will in effect be a dictator?'

'That's highly unlikely,' Christian Klee said. 'There has never been a dictator in this country. We have safeguards, too many safeguards I think sometimes.'

'Ah,' the Oracle said. 'This is a young country yet. We have time. And the devil takes many seductive forms.'

They were silent for a long time and then Christian rose to take his leave. They always touched hands when they parted, the Oracle too fragile for a real handshake.

'Be careful,' the Oracle said. 'When a man rises to absolute power, he usually gets rid of those closest to him, those who know his secrets.'

22

Two months before the Presidential election, polls showed Francis Kennedy's margin of victory would not be enough to carry his Congressional candidates into office.

There were problems. The scandal of Eugene Dazzy's mistress, the charges that Attorney General Christian Klee had deliberately permitted the explosion of the atom bomb, the scandal of Canoo and Klee using the funds of the Office of the Military Advisor to beef up the Secret Service.

That the President of the United States was having an affair with a girl twenty years younger than himself and reputedly with a strain of Negro blood did damage and the possibility that they would marry and that she would be First Lady lost Kennedy votes.

And perhaps Francis Kennedy himself went too far. America was not ready for a brand of socialism. It was not ready to reject the corporate structure of America. The people of America did not want to be equal, they wanted to be rich. Nearly all the states had their own lottery with prizes running high up into the millions. More people bought lottery tickets than voted in the national elections.

The power of the Congressmen and Senators already in office was also overwhelming. They had their staffs paid for by the government. They had the vast sums of money contributed by the corporate structure which they used to dominate TV with brilliantly executed ads. By holding government office they could appear on special political programs on TV and in the newspapers, increasing their name-recognition factor.

Lawrence Salentine had organized the overall campaign against Kennedy so brilliantly that he was now the leader of the Socrates Club group. With the delicate precision of a Renaissance poisoner, he had dropped little references of Lanetta Carr's Negro blood on TV and in the prints. And then only in a way that praised. Salentine was counting on the fact that a part of the United States of America which prided itself on its racial tolerance was, underneath, racially biased.

On the third day of September, Christian Klee secretly went to the office of the Vice President. As an extra precaution, he gave special instructions to Helen DuPray's Secret Service detail chief before he announced himself to Helen DuPray's secretary and said his business was urgent.

The Vice President was astonished to see him, it was against all protocol that he should visit her without advance warning or even permission. For a moment, he was afraid she might take offense, but she was too intelligent to do so. She knew immediately that Christian Klee would only breach protocol for the most serious problem. In fact, what she felt was apprehension. What new terrible thing could have happened now after the past months?

Christian Klee sensed this immediately. 'There's nothing to be worried about,' he said. 'It's just that we have a security problem involving the President. As part of our coverage, we have sealed off your office. You will not answer the phone but you can deal with your immediate staff. I will remain with you the entire day, personally.'

Helen DuPray understood immediately that no matter what happened, she was not to take command of the country and that's why Klee was there. 'If the President has a security problem, why are you with me?' she said. But without waiting for an answer from Klee, she said, 'I will have to check this with the President personally.'

'He is appearing at a political luncheon in New York,' Christian Klee said.

'I know that,' Helen DuPray said.

Christian Klee looked at his watch. 'The President will be calling you in about one half hour,' he said.

When the call came, Klee watched Helen DuPray's face. She seemed to show no astonishment, only twice she asked questions. Good, Klee thought, she would be OK, he didn't have to worry about her. Then she did something that aroused Christian's admiration; he didn't think she had it in her – Vice Presidents were noted for their timidity. She asked Kennedy if she could speak to Eugene Dazzy, the President's Chief of Staff. When Dazzy came on the phone, she made a simple query about their work schedule for the next week. Then she hung up. She had been checking to see if the person on the phone had really been Kennedy, despite the fact that she recognized his voice. Of the questions she had asked, only Dazzy would recognize the reference. She was making sure that there was no voice impersonation.

She addressed him icily, she knew something was fishy, Klee thought. She said, 'The President has informed me that you will be using my office as a command post, that I will be under your instruction. I find this extraordinary. Perhaps you will give me an explanation.'

'I apologize for all this,' Christian Klee said. 'If I could have some coffee, I'll give you a full briefing. You will know as much as the President about this matter.' Which was true but a little devious. She would not know as much as Klee.

Helen DuPray was studying him very intently. She didn't trust him, Christian knew. But women didn't understand power, they didn't understand the stark efficiency of violence. He gathered up all his energy to convince her of his sincerity. When he was through almost an hour later, she seemed won over. She was a very beautiful woman and intelligent, Christian thought. Too bad that she would never become the President of the United States.

*

On this glorious summer day, President Francis Kennedy was to speak at a political luncheon held in New York City's Sheraton Hotel Convention Center which would be followed by a triumphal motorcade down Fifth Avenue. Then he would make a speech near the atom bomb destruction area. The event had been scheduled three months before and had been well publicized. It was the kind of situation that Christian Klee detested, the President too exposed. There were deranged people, even the police were a danger in Klee's eyes because they were armed and also because as a police force, they were completely demoralized by the uncontrolled crime in the city.

For these reasons Klee didn't trust the police in any of the big cities. He took his own elaborate precautions. Only his operational staff in the Secret Service knew the awesome detail and manpower that was used to protect the President in his rare public appearances.

Special Advance teams had been sent ahead. These teams patrolled and searched the area of the visit twenty-four hours a day. Two days before the visit, another thousand men were sent to become part of the crowds that greeted the President. These men formed a line on both sides of the motorcade and in the front of the motorcade and acted as part of the crowd but actually formed a sort of Maginot line. Another five hundred men manned the rooftops, constantly scanning the windows that overlooked the motorcade and these men were heavily armed. In addition to this there was the President's own special and personal detail which numbered a hundred men. And then, of course, there were the Secret Service men under deep cover who were accredited to newspapers and TV stations, who carried newspaper cameras and manned mobile TV vehicles.

And Christian Klee had other tricks up his sleeve. In the nearly four years of the Kennedy administration there had been five assassination attempts, what the more lurid newspapers commonly referred to as the 'hat trick', a reference to the expression in hockey when a man scores three goals. Meaning the assassinations of three Kennedy's. None of them had even come close. They had been crazies, of course, and were now behind bars in the toughest of Federal prisons. And Klee made sure that if they got out, he would find a reason to put them back in again. It was impossible to jail all the lunatics in the United States who made threats to kill the President of the United States: by mail, by phone, by conspiring, by shouting it in the streets. But Christian Klee had made their lives miserable for them, so that they would be too busy preserving their own safety to worry about grandiose ideas. He put them under mail surveillance, phone surveillance, personal surveillance, computer surveillance, he had their tax returns examined carefully. If they spit on the sidewalk, they were in trouble.

All these precautions, all these arrangements, were in effect this September third when President Francis Xavier Kennedy gave his speech at the political luncheon at the Sheraton Convention Center in New York. Hundreds of Secret Service men were scattered through the audience, and the building was sealed off after his entrance.

On the morning that Christian Klee went to the Vice President's office, he knew that he had the situation under control. The Sultan of Sherhaben had sent him valuable information and Sebbediccio's briefing on Annee had made the job that much easier. He had tremendous resources; unlimited manpower, technical facilities, information the terrorists did not know he had. He had Annee under surveillance, individual, computer and telephonic. He had the two assassination teams blanketed. But he did not want anyone, not even the President or Helen DuPray, to know all this. The only part he did let them know was that he had certain information that on September the third in New York City, an attempt would be made on the life of Francis Kennedy. And, he told them, this was by no means a

426

certainty, that it was only one chance in a hundred that the tip was legitimate, that he was just taking precautions for any eventuality.

The opposite was the case. He knew the attempt on the President's life would be made that day. He knew that he could crush the whole operation before it started but he wanted the attempt made. And then the whole nation would see how the President of the United States always lived in mortal danger. There would be an overwhelming tide of love for Kennedy throughout the nation. It was the kind of event that the media could not downplay, in fact, they would be swept into the very vortex of public emotion. That tide of love would carry over into the elections two months away and Francis Kennedy would sweep everything before him. Not only would he be re-elected by a vast majority, but he would carry his Congressional candidates in with him.

Congressman Jintz would be back on his farm, Senator Lambertino would be back with his law firm in New York, and Bert Audick would be in prison.

Three weeks before, Annee had received her orders. She had traveled under the name of Isabella Cesaro and was met at the airport by a married couple who took her to a luxurious apartment on the Lower East Side. There, the married couple handed over documents which gave her access to funds in the Chemical Bank branch nearby. She had been astonished to see that she had control of over five hundred thousand dollars. She also had a list of encoded phone numbers to call.

The married couple stayed with her for a week guiding her around New York in what was actually a heavy training period. Annee spoke English passably and picked up things very quickly. In that week, two furnished condos were rented and stocked with food and medicines. When all this was done, the married couple said their goodbyes and vanished.

During the next three weeks, Annee remained in place and

used telephones in public places to call the encoded numbers. She moved freely about the city, and like a true radical, she toured the black neighborhoods to marvel at their poverty and squalor with a certain amount of satisfaction. She was actually having a good time moving about in the heart of the enemy. She could not know Christian Klee's FBI was picking up her phone calls in the very air, that every move she made was covered, that the two assassination teams sent from Europe had been spotted immediately when they arrived as crewmen on one of Bert Audick's oil tankers, and that their phone calls to her in the public booths had been intercepted and read by Christian Klee.

On September third, summoned, Lanetta Carr came into the office of Vice President Helen DuPray and was astonished by two things. The first was that the large TV set was tuned into one of the networks with the sound so low that she could barely hear it; the second was that Attorney General Christian Klee was seated opposite the Vice President's desk.

Christian Klee smiled at her pleasantly and said, 'Hello, Lanetta,' and watched her carefully as she put her papers on the Vice President's desk.

Helen DuPray said in a cold voice, 'Mr Attorney General, I think you should tell Miss Carr what you told me.'

'She has no need to know,' Christian said.

'If you don't tell her, I will,' Helen DuPray said.

'That would be a breach of security,' Christian Klee said. 'Acting under the authority of the President, I forbid you to disclose any information.'

'How do you propose to stop me?' Helen DuPray said contemptuously.

There was a long moment of silence.

Then Klee said cautiously, 'Nothing may happen.'

'I don't give a damn,' Helen DuPray said. 'Do you tell her or do I?'

'Nothing may happen,' Klee repeated.

Helen DuPray said briskly to Lanetta, 'Sit down, you won't be able to leave this office after I tell you what's going on.'

Christian Klee sighed and said, 'There's only one chance in a hundred that anything will happen.' And then he briefed Lanetta as thoroughly as he had briefed the Vice President.

On that same September third, the woman terrorist named Annee went shopping on Fifth Avenue. In her three weeks in the United States, she had helped everything move into place. She had made her phone calls, had her meeting with the two assassination teams that had finally made their way to New York and moved into the two apartments prepared for them. These apartments had already been stocked with weapons procured by a special underground logistics team which had no part of the central plan.

Annee thought how strange it was that she would go shopping just four hours before what might be the end of her life.

Patsy Troyca and Elizabeth Stone were working hard together interviewing Peter Cloot on his testimony that Christian Klee could have prevented the explosion of the atom bomb. They were going to leak the story in full detail to blow up the original charges made before the Congressional committee. They were so elated by Peter Cloot's obvious hatred of Christian Klee, his sincere indignation at the monstrousness of Klee's crime and giving them the 'off the record' information about the workings of the FBI, that they decided to celebrate. Elizabeth Stone's townhouse was only a ten-minute ride away. So at lunch-time, they spent a couple of hours in bed.

Once in bed, they forgot all the stress of the day. After an hour, Elizabeth went into the bathroom to take a shower and Patsy Troyca wandered into the living room, still naked, to turn on the TV. He stood in amazement at what he was seeing. He watched for a few moments longer and then ran into the bathroom and pulled Elizabeth Stone out of the shower. She was startled and a little frightened by his brutality as he dragged her naked and dripping wet into the living room.

There, watching the TV screen, she began to weep. Patsy Troyca took her into his arms. 'Look at it this way,' he said, 'our troubles are over.'

The campaign speech in New York on September third was to be one of the most important stops in President Kennedy's bid for re-election. And it had been planned to have a great psychological effect on the nation.

First, there would be a luncheon at the Sheraton Convention Center on 58th Street. There, the President would address the most important and influential men of the city. This luncheon was sponsored oddly enough by Louis Inch, who was a backer of the Democratic party.

The luncheon was to raise funds to build the eight blocks in New York that had been leveled by the atom bomb explosion during the Easter week crisis. An architect, without a fee, had designed a great memorial for the devastated area, the rest of the acreage to be a small park with a tiny lake. The city was to buy and donate the land.

After luncheon, the Kennedy party would lead a motorcade that would begin at 125th Street and go down Seventh and Fifth Avenues to place the first symbolic wreath of marble on the rubbled heap that was what remained of Times Square.

As one of the sponsors of the luncheon, Louis Inch was seated on the dais with President Kennedy and expected to accompany him to his waiting car and so get in newspaper and TV coverage. But to his surprise, he was cut off by Secret Service men who isolated Kennedy in a human net. The President was escorted through a door at the rear of the platform. As the President disappeared, Louis Inch saw that the whole vast room had been sealed off so that all those people who had paid ten thousand dollars each to attend were now imprisoned and unable to leave.

In the streets outside, huge crowds gathered. The Secret Service had cleared the area so that there was a space of at least a hundred feet around the Presidential limousine. There were enough Secret Service men to protect the inner hundred feet with a solid phalanx. Outside that, the crowd was controlled by the police. On the edge of this perimeter were photographers and TV camera crews who immediately surged forward when the advance guard of Secret Service men came out of the hotel. And then, unaccountably, there was a fifteen-minute wait.

The figure of the President finally emerged from the hotel shielded from the TV cameras as he rushed toward his waiting car. At that very moment, the Avenue exploded into a beautifully choreographed but bloody ballet.

Six men burst through the police restraining line mowing down part of the police wall, running toward the President's armored limousine. A second later, as if to tempo, another group of six men burst through the opposite perimeter and raked the fifty Secret Service men around the armored limousine with their automatic weapons.

In the very next second eight cars swung into the open area and Secret Service men in combat gear and bulletproof vests that made them seem like inflated gigantic balloons came tumbling out with shotguns and machine pistols and caught the attackers in the rear. They shot with precision and short bursts. All twelve attackers were lying in the Avenue dead, their guns silenced. The Presidential limousine roared away from the curb, other Secret Service cars following.

At that moment, Annee, with a supreme effort of will, stepped in the path of the Presidential limousine with her two Bloomingdale shopping bags in her hand. The shopping bags were filled with explosive gel, two powerful bombs that

431

detonated as the car hit her. The Presidential car flew up into the air at least ten feet off the ground and came down a mass of flames. The force of the explosion blew everyone inside it to bits. And there was absolutely nothing left of Annee except tiny bits of gaily colored paper from the shopping bags.

The TV cameraman had the wit to swing his camera for a panoramic shot of everything that was visible. The crowd, thousands of people, had flung themselves to the ground when the firing broke out and were still lying prone as if begging some unforgiving God to remit them from an obscene terror. From that prone mass issued small brooks of blood coming from spectators that had been hit by the heavy fire from the assassination teams or killed by the explosion of the powerful bombs.

Many of the crowd suffered from concussions and when it was quiet, rose and staggered in circles. The camera caught all this for television to horrify the nation.

In the office of Vice President Helen DuPray, Christian Klee jumped out of his chair and cried out, 'That wasn't supposed to happen.' Lanetta Carr was staring wide-eyed at the screen.

Helen DuPray watched the TV screen and then said sharply to Christian Klee, 'Who was the poor bastard who took the President's place?'

'One of my Secret Service men,' Christian Klee said. 'They were not supposed to get that close.'

'You told me there was only one chance in a hundred that anything might happen.' DuPray was looking at Klee very coldly. And then she became angrier than Lanetta Carr had ever seen her. 'Why the hell didn't you cancel the whole thing?' she shouted. 'Why didn't you avert this whole tragedy? There are citizens dead out there in the streets who came to see their President. You've wasted the lives of your own men. I promise you, your actions will be questioned by

432

me to the President and to the appropriate Congressional Committee.'

'You don't know what the hell you're talking about,' Christian Klee said. 'Do you know how many tips I get, how many threats against the President are made by mail? If we listened to all of them, the President would be a prisoner in the White House.'

Helen DuPray was studying his face while he spoke. 'Why did you use a double this time?' she said. 'That is an extreme measure. And if it was *that* serious, why did you have the President go there at all?'

'When you are the President, you can ask me those questions,' Christian Klee said curtly.

Lanetta said softly, 'Where is Francis now?'

It was an inappropriate question at this moment and an inappropriate form of address. They both looked at her. Helen DuPray gave a slight shrug and waited for Klee to speak.

Christian Klee stared at her for a moment as if he would not answer. But he noticed the anguish on her face and said quietly, 'He's on his way to Washington. We don't know how extensive this plot is, so we want him here. He is very safe.'

Helen DuPray said in a sardonic voice, 'OK, now she knows he's safe. I assume you've briefed the other members of the staff, they know he's safe, you and I know he's safe, what about the people of America? When will they know he's safe?'

Christian Klee said, 'Dazzy has made all the arrangements. The President will go on television and speak to the nation as soon as he sets foot in the White House.'

'That's rather a long wait,' the Vice President said. 'Why can't you notify the media and reassure people now?'

'Because we don't know what's out there,' Christian Klee told her smoothly. 'And maybe it won't hurt the American public to worry about him a bit.'

433

In that moment, it seemed to Helen DuPray that she understood everything. She understood that Klee could have cut the whole thing off before it reached the culminating point. She felt an overwhelming contempt for the man and then, remembering the charges that he could have stopped the atom bomb explosion but didn't, she was convinced that that charge was also true.

BOOK VI

23

In November, Francis Xavier Kennedy was re-elected to the Presidency of the United States. It was a victory so overwhelming that it carried into office nearly all his handpicked candidates for the House and Senate. Finally the President controlled both houses of Congress.

In that time period before the Inauguration, from November to January, Francis Kennedy set his Administration to work drafting new laws for his captured Congress.

The release of Gresse and Tibbot created such a firestorm of public outrage that Francis Kennedy knew the time was right to rally support for his new laws. In this he was helped by the newspapers and TV who were weaving fantasies to the effect that Gresse and Tibbot were linked with Yabril and the attempted assassination of the President in one giant conspiracy. The *National Enquirer* had run a full front page headline.

Summoned, the Reverend Baxter Foxworth met with Oddblood Gray at the latter's White House office.

'Otto,' he said, 'you're on the President's staff, you're one of the men closest to him. What's this I hear about the new criminal laws that are being drawn up. And what's this I hear about these concentration camps planned up in Alaska?'

Oddblood Gray said, 'They are not concentration camps. They are prison work camps being built for habitual offenders.'

The Reverend Foxworth laughed. 'Brother,' he said. 'The least you could do was have them built in a warm climate. Most of those criminals are going to be black. They'll freeze their asses off up there. And as time goes on, who knows, you and I might be with them.'

Oddblood Gray sighed. He said softly, 'You've got a point.'

That sobered the Reverend. He was all business now. He said in a flat serious voice, 'Otto, you can see it, can't you? Your fucking Kennedy will be the first American dictator. You're not that dumb. He's laying the groundwork.'

It was not a token meeting in the Oval Office where things were done for publicity purposes. It was lunch with the President, Eugene Dazzy and Oddblood Gray.

The lunch went well. Kennedy thanked the Reverend Foxworth for his help in the election and accepted the Reverend's list of candidates for the housing and social welfare department appointments. Then Reverend Foxworth, who had been extremely courteous and showing the deference due to the office of the President of the United States, said somewhat abruptly, 'I must say to you, Mr President, that I oppose the new laws you propose to control crime in this country.'

Francis Kennedy said curtly, 'Those laws are necessary.'

'And the work camps in Alaska?' the Reverend said.

Kennedy smiled at him. 'That opponents of mine are calling concentration camps?'

'That's right,' the Reverend said.

'The only people that will go to those camps are habitual offenders,' Kennedy said. His voice was quiet, explanatory. 'They will be work camps, there is a lot of work to be done in Alaska and they need population. But it will also be a whole educational system as well. The people who go there will not be in the work camps for life. They will be trained

438

as they work. If they behave well, they will be the Alaskan population of the future.'

Thinking, shit, at least they can't make us pick cotton in Alaska, the Reverend Baxter Foxworth said, 'Mr President, my people will oppose this with all the means we have available.'

Eugene Dazzy knew that this was one of the few times he was observing pure anger in Kennedy's handsome face. There was a long silence. Finally, it seemed that Kennedy had mastered his emotion. He said to the Reverend Foxworth, 'I want you to understand one thing very clearly. This is not a racial issue, this is a criminal justice issue.'

The Reverend was in no way intimidated. 'The majority who go to your Alaska work camps will be black.'

Oddblood Gray and Eugene Dazzy had never seen Kennedy so cold. He said to Foxworth, 'Then let them stop committing criminal acts.'

The Reverend was just as cold. 'Then let your bankers and your real estate guys and your big corporations stop using blacks for cheap labor.'

'I'll give you the reality,' Francis Kennedy said. 'Trust me or trust the Socrates Club.'

'We don't trust anybody,' the Reverend said.

Kennedy seemed not to have heard. 'It's very simple,' he said. 'Black criminals will be weeded out from the black people. Thank me for that. Black people are the chief victims, though, of course, that doesn't make much of a fuss. The primary thing is that black people must not be regarded as a permanent criminal class.'

'And what about the white criminal class?' the Reverend said. 'Do they go to Alaska?' He couldn't believe what he was hearing and from the President of the United States.

The President said softly, 'Yes, they will. Let me make it more simple, Reverend. The white people in this country are afraid of the black criminal class. When we get through, the

439

great majority of middle-class blacks will be integrated with the white middle class.'

Oddblood Gray noted that for the first time, he was seeing his friend Foxworth so astonished he could not even use his rhetoric. So Oddblood said, 'Mr President, I think you should tell the Reverend the other side of the story.'

Francis Kennedy said, 'Crime is not going to run this country any more. More to the point, money is not going to run this country any more. You're worried about criminal blacks going to a work camp in Alaska? Why? The black communities will be better off. Let them go.'

'But the camps will be there,' the Reverend Foxworth said, 'for true revolutionaries. They will be there for anyone who doesn't want to live a middle-class life. They are a threat to individual freedom.'

Kennedy said, 'That is an argument, but it is no longer valid. We can't afford an excess of liberty any more. Take those two young Professors Tibbot and Gresse. They killed thousands of people and they get off. They could not even be convicted of the crime they really committed because of the technical violations of due process, and most of those dead people were black. Those two young men go free, because of our treasured due process of the law.' He paused for a moment. 'That's all going to change,' he said.

The Reverend turned to Oddblood Gray. He said, 'Otto, do you really go along with this?'

Oddblood Gray smiled back at him and said softly, 'When I don't, I'll resign.'

Kennedy said, 'In my personal life and political career, I have always supported your basic cause, Reverend. Isn't that true?'

'Yes, Mr President, but that doesn't mean you're always right,' the Reverend shot back. 'And you can't always control the administrative side down to the lowest level. Those Alaskan work camps will wind up being black concentration camps.'

440

Kennedy said, 'That's a possibility.' The Reverend was surprised by this answer. Otto Gray was not. He had known Kennedy for a long time, knew that he could see such dangers. And then Gray saw another look of Kennedy's, the one of absolute determination, an overpowering force of will that usually subdued everyone else in his presence.

'I've followed your career,' Kennedy said with a tiny smile. 'What you have done was a necessary prodding of our society. And its always a pleasure to see a man like you operate with a certain wit. And I never doubted your sincerity no matter how much you fucked around.' Odd-blood Gray was surprised by the obscenity. Kennedy went on. 'But these times are dangerous, wit will be less important. So I want you to listen to me very carefully.'

'I'm listening,' Reverend Foxworth said. His face was impassive.

Kennedy bowed his head and then lifted it. 'You must know,' he said, 'that many people of the United States hate the blacks. Out of fear. They love the athletes, they love the artists, they love the blacks who have achieved distinction in various different fields.'

'You astonish me,' the Reverend Foxworth said. He laughed.

Francis Kennedy looked at him speculatively. Then he went on. 'Then who do they hate? They certainly don't hate the truly middle-class black. Maybe hate is too strong a word, maybe dislike is a better word.'

'Either one,' the Reverend said.

'We agree so far then,' Kennedy said. 'So the object of this scorn, this dislike, this hate, is generated by the poor blacks and the criminal blacks.'

The Reverend interrupted him. 'It's not all that simple.'

'I know,' Kennedy said. 'But it will do for a start. Now I'm telling you this. My way is the way it's going to be and you might as well get on the train. Black or white, if you take to crime as a way of life, you go to Alaska.'

441

'I'll fight it,' Foxworth said.

'Let me give you the alternative scenario,' Kennedy said and his voice had an elegant courtesy. 'We go on as we are. You fight for affirmative actions on the part of government agencies, you fight against acts of racial injustice. As you pointed out, good laws are one thing, enforcing them is another. Do you think the people who run this country now will really want to give up a source of cheap labor? Do you think they really want your people to be a powerful voting influence? Do you think you'll get a better break from the Socrates Club than you will from me?'

The Reverend was looking at Kennedy intently. He took a long time before he answered. 'Mr President,' he said, 'what you're saying is that we sacrifice the next generation of blacks for what you see as a political strategy. I don't believe in that kind of thinking. That's not to say that we can't work together on other issues.'

President Kennedy said, 'Either you are with us or you are the enemy. Think it over carefully.'

The Reverend Foxworth, smiling, said, 'Are you going to talk the same way to the Socrates Club?'

For the first time Kennedy smiled back at him. 'Oh, no,' he said. 'They don't get the option.'

'If I go along,' Foxworth said, 'I want to make sure that white asses freeze with black asses.'

A Federal judge set Henry Tibbot and Adam Gresse free. In what he thought was the greatest day in his life, Whitney Cheever III appeared in court on behalf on his clients. They might go to jail or not, it didn't matter, he would be a winner. The media coverage was enormous and the Kennedy administration was playing into his hands.

The government did not contest that the arrest had been illegal. The government did not contest that there had been no warrants. Cheever exploited every legal loophole.

The fate of his clients was a minor issue, in fact, like all sophisticated clients, they had confessed their guilt to him. But Cheever was outraged by the Atomic Secrecy Act itself. Its provisions were so sweeping that they constituted an abolition of the Bill of Rights itself.

Whitney Cheever was so eloquent he was one of TV's folk heroes for two days. And when the judge sentenced Gresse and Tibbot to three years of community service and freed them, Cheever was for one day the most famous man in America.

But the realization soon dawned on him that he had been suckered. Hate mail poured in by the hundreds of thousands. The two murderers of thousands of people had gone free due to the legal cunning of a left-wing lawyer notorious for his defense of revolutionaries opposed to the legal authority of the United States. The people of America were infuriated.

Cheever was an intelligent man and when the Reverend Foxworth sent him a letter that the black movement would no longer have anything to do with him, he knew he was finished. He believed he was, in his small way, a hero, and believed that in future histories, he would rate a small asterisk as a fighter for true freedom. But now the hatred coming at him through the mails, the telephones, and even in his public political meetings was overwhelming.

Gresse and Tibbot had been, for the time being, spirited out of the country by their relatives, were in hiding some-place in Europe and all the public fury was concentrated on Cheever. But what dismayed him most was coming to the realization that his victory had been engineered by the Kennedy government. And that it had one purpose. To arouse in the public a raging contempt for the due process of law. When he heard about the new reforms that Kennedy proposed for the legal system, the work camps in Alaska, the restrictions on due process, he knew that his battle had been lost with that one victory he had achieved by getting Gresse and Tibbot free. He then had a frightening thought. Was it possible that there would come a time when he would

443

be in real danger? Was it possible that Francis Kennedy had it in him to become the first dictator of the United States of America? It might be a good idea to have a personal meeting with Attorney General Christian Klee.

President Francis Kennedy met with his staff in the Yellow Room. Also present by special invitation were Vice President Helen DuPray and Dr Zed Annaccone. Kennedy knew he had to be very careful, these were the people who knew him best, he must not let them know what he really wanted to accomplish. He said to them, 'Dr Annaccone has something to say that may astound you.'

Francis Kennedy listened abstractedly while Dr Annaccone announced that the PET Scan Verification Test had been perfected so that the ten per cent risk of cardiac arrest and complete memory loss had been reduced to one tenth of one per cent. He smiled faintly when Helen DuPray voiced her outrage at any free citizen being forced by law to take such a test. He had expected that of her. He smiled when Dr Annaccone showed his hurt feelings, too learned a man to be so thin-skinned.

He listened with less amusement when Oddblood Gray, Arthur Wix and Eugene Dazzy agreed with the Vice President. He had known that Christian Klee would not speak.

They were all watching him, waiting for him, trying to see which way he would go. He would have to convince them he was right. He began slowly. 'I know all the difficulties,' he said, 'but I am determined to make this test part of our legal system. Not totally, there is still some amount of danger, small as it is. Though Dr Annaccone has assured me that with further research even that will be reduced to zero. But this is a scientific test that will revolutionize our society. Never mind the difficulties, we will iron them out.'

Oddblood Gray said quietly, 'Even the Congress we own won't pass such a law.'

'We'll make them,' Kennedy said grimly. 'Other countries

will use it. Other intelligence agencies will use it. We have to.' He laughed and said to Dr Annaccone, 'I'll have to cut your budget. Your discoveries cause too much trouble, and put all the lawyers out of work. But with this test no innocent man will ever be found guilty.'

Very deliberately he rose and walked to the doors that looked out on to the Rose Garden. Then he said, 'I will show how much I believe in this. Our enemies constantly accuse me of being responsible for the atom bomb going off. They say that I could have stopped it. Euge, I want you to help Dr Annaccone set it up for me. I want to be the first to undergo the PET Verification Test. Immediately. Arrange for witnessing, the legal formalities.'

He smiled at Christian Klee. 'They will ask the question, "Are you in any way responsible for the explosion of the atom bomb?" And I will answer.' He paused for a moment and then said, 'I will take the test, and so will my Attorney General. Right, Chris?'

'Sure,' Christian Klee said, 'but you first.' Both knew that this was what Kennedy had been coming to all along.

At Walter Reed Hospital, the suite reserved for President Kennedy had a special conference room. In it were the President and his personal staff and a panel of three qualified physicians who would monitor and verify the results of the brain scan test. Now they listened to Dr Annaccone as he explained the procedure.

Dr Annaccone prepared his slides and turned on the projector. Then he began his lecture. He said, 'This test is, as some of you already know, an infallible lie detector test, the truth assessed by measuring the levels of activity from certain chemicals in the brain. This has been done by the refinement of positron emission tomography (PET) scans. The procedure was first shown to work in a limited way at Washington University School of Medicine in St Louis. Slides were made of human brains at work.'

445

A large slide showed on the huge white screen in front of them. Then another, and another. Brilliant colors appeared lighting up the different parts of the brain as patients read, listened or spoke. Or simply just thought about the meaning of a word. Dr Annaccone used blood and glucose to tag them with radioactive labels.

'In essence, under the PET scan,' Dr Annaccone said, 'the brain speaks in living color. A spot in back of the brain lights up during reading. In the middle of the brain against that background of dark blue, you can see an irregular white spot appear with a tiny blotch of pink and a seepage of blue. That appears during speech. In the front of the brain, a similar spot lights up during the thinking process. Over these images we have laid a magnetic resonance image of the brain's anatomy. The whole brain is now a magic lantern.'

Dr Annaccone looked around the room to see if everyone was following him. Then he went on. 'You see that spot in the middle of the brain changing? When a subject lies, there is an increase in the amount of blood flowing through the brain which then projects another image.'

Startlingly, in the center of the white spot there was now a circle of red within a larger yellow irregular field. 'The subject is lying . . .' Dr Annaccone said. 'When we test the President, that red spot within the yellow is what we must look for.' Dr Annaccone nodded to the President. 'Now we will proceed to the examining room,' he said.

Inside the lead-walled room, Francis Kennedy lay on the cold hard table. Behind him, a large long metal cylinder loomed. As Dr Annaccone strapped the plastic mask over Kennedy's forehead and across his chin, Francis Kennedy felt a momentary shiver of fear. He hated anything over his face. His arms were then tied down along his sides. Then Francis Kennedy felt Dr Annaccone slide the table into the cylinder. Inside the cylinder, it was narrower than he expected, blacker. Silent. Now Francis Kennedy was surrounded by a ring of radioactive detection crystals.

446

Kennedy heard the echo of Dr Annaccone's voice instructing him to look at the white cross directly in front of his eyes. The voice sounded hollow. 'You must keep your eyes on the cross,' the doctor repeated.

In a room five storeys below, in the basement of the hospital, a pneumatic tube held a syringe containing radioactive oxygen, a cyclotron of tagged water.

When the order came from the scanning room above, that tube flew, a lead rocket twisting through hidden tunnels behind the walls of the hospital until it reached its target.

Dr Annaccone opened the pneumatic tube and held the syringe in his hands. He walked over to the foot of the PET scanner and called in to Francis Kennedy. Again the voice was hollow, an echo, when Kennedy heard, 'The injection,' and then felt the doctor reach in to the dark and plunge the needle into his arm.

From the glass-enclosed room at the end of the scanner, the staff could see only the bottom of Kennedy's feet. When Dr Annaccone joined them again, he turned on the computer high on the wall above, so that they could all watch the workings of Kennedy's brain. They watched as the tracer circulated through Kennedy's blood, emitting positrons, particles of anti-matter which collided with electrons and produced explosions of gamma-ray energy.

They watched as the radioactive blood rushed to Kennedy's visual cortex creating streams of gamma rays immediately picked up by the ring of radioactive detectors. All the time Kennedy kept staring at the white cross as instructed.

Then, through the microphone piped directly into the scanner, Kennedy heard the question from Dr Annaccone, 'Did you in any way conspire to have the atom bomb explode in New York? Did you have any knowledge that could have prevented its explosion?'

Kennedy answered, 'No, I didn't.' And inside the black cylinder his words seemed to fall back like the wind on his face.

Dr Annaccone watched the computer screen above his head.

The computer showed the patterns form in the blue mass of the brain so elegantly formed in Kennedy's curving skull.

The staff watched apprehensively.

But no telltale yellow dot, no red circle appeared.

'He's telling the truth,' Dr Annaccone said, and he sounded exhilarated.

Christian Klee felt his knees buckling. He knew he could not pass such a test.

24

On the day after President Francis Kennedy passed his PET Scan Verification Test, Christian Klee went to visit the Oracle.

After dinner, they went to the library which was darker, more confidential. Christian was supplied with brandy and cigars, and the Oracle dozed in his padded wheelchair.

The Oracle said, 'Christian, I think you should get off your ass. Today it has been all over the TV that Kennedy passed that test, and he's innocent in the atom bomb scandal. He's sitting pretty. So when the hell am I going to have my birthday party?'

He was relentless, Christian thought. He could not tell the Oracle that everyone had forgotten about the birthday party.

'We have it all planned,' he told the Oracle. 'After the President's Inauguration next month, we'll have a great party in the Rose Garden of the White House. The Prime Minister of England will be there, his father was one of your best friends. You'll love it. Is this OK? The theme is that you are the symbol of America Past, the Grand Old Man of our country, the very incarnation of our virtues of thrift, hard work, and rise of the lowest to the highest, in short, that only in America could this happen. We get you one of those Stars and Stripes Uncle Sam hats.'

The Oracle gave his tiny cackle of heh, heh, heh's at this conceit. Christian smiled at him and emptied his brandy glass to keep up his own flow of good spirits.

'And what does your friend Kennedy get out of this?' the Oracle asked.

'Francis Kennedy will be presented as the spirit of the American future,' Christian said. 'All the people of America will have a stronger social contract, will be bound more tightly to each other. What you have planted, Kennedy nourishes to true greatness.'

The Oracle's eyes flashed in the darkness. 'Christian, how dare you bullshit me after all these years? Shove your symbolism up your ass. And what social contract? What kind of crap is that? Listen to me. You have those who govern and those who are governed. That's your social contract. The rest is negotiation.'

Christian laughed. He said, 'I'll speak to Dazzy and the Vice President. Kennedy will go along, he knows he owes you.'

'Old men have no debtors,' the Oracle said. 'Now, let's talk about you. You are in very deep shit, my boy.'

'Yes, I am,' Christian said. 'But I don't give a fuck.'

The Oracle said musingly, 'You're not even fifty years old and you don't give a fuck? That's really a very bad sign. Not giving a fuck is usually the symptom of the ignorant young. I'm a hundred, if I said I don't give a fuck, it's smart. When you're young and when you're old you don't have to give a fuck. But you, Christian, are at a very dangerous age not to give a fuck.' He was actually angry and leaned over to swipe the cigar out of Christian's hand.

At that moment Christian felt such an overwhelming affection for the old man that he was moved to tears. 'It's Francis,' he said. 'I think he's been conning me his whole life.'

'Ah,' the Oracle said. 'That lie detector test he passed. That brain scanning machine. What do they call it, the PET Scan Verification Test? The man who invented that title is a genius.'

'I don't understand how he passed it,' Christian Klee said.

The Oracle said with contempt that barely intonated because of his age, his signals, bodily and mental, fainter,

450

but still unmistakable, 'So now our civilization has an infallible test, a scientific test mind you, for determining whether a man tells the truth. And they think they can solve the darkest riddles of innocence and guilt. What a laugh. Men and women deceive themselves continually. I'm a hundred years old and I still don't know whether my life was a truth or a lie. I really don't know.'

Christian had retrieved his cigar from the Oracle and now he lit it and that small circle of fire made the Oracle's face a mask in a museum.

'I let that atom bomb go off,' Christian said. 'I'm responsible for that. And when I take that PET Scan I will know the truth and so will the scanner. But I thought I understood Kennedy better than anybody. I could always read him. He wanted me *not* to interrogate Gresse and Tibbot. He wanted that explosion to happen. Then how the hell did he pass that test?'

'If the brain were that simple, we would be too simple to understand it,' the Oracle said. 'That was the wit of your Dr Annaccone and I suggest that is your answer. Kennedy's brain refused to acknowledge his guilt. Therefore, the computer in the scanner says he is innocent. You and I know better, for I believe what you say. But he will be forever innocent even in his own heart. Now let me ask you, you are scheduled to undergo the test next week, do you think that you can also trick the test? After all, it is a sin of omission.'

'No,' Christian said. 'Unlike Kennedy, I am forever guilty.'

'Cheer up,' the Oracle said. 'You only killed ten or was it twenty thousand people? Your only hope is to refuse to take the test.'

'I promised Francis,' Christian said. 'And the media will crucify me for refusing.'

'Then why the hell did you agree to take it?' the Oracle said.

'I thought Francis was bluffing,' Christian said. 'I thought he couldn't afford to take the test and that he would back down. That's why I insisted he take it first.'

The Oracle showed his impatience by running the motor on his wheelechair. 'Climb up on the Statue of Liberty,' he said. 'Claim your civil rights and your human dignity. You'll get away with it. Nobody wants to see such infernal science become a legal instrument.'

'Sure,' Christian said. 'That's what I have to do. But Francis will know I'm guilty.'

The Oracle said, 'Christian, if that test asked you whether you were a villain, what would you answer, in all truthfulness?'

Christian laughed, genuinely laughed. 'I would answer that no, I wasn't a villain. And I'd pass. That's really funny.' Gratefully he pressed the Oracle's shoulder. 'I won't forget about your birthday party,' he said.

When Christian Klee told President Francis Kennedy and the assembled staff that he would not take the PET Scan Verification Test, they did not seem surprised. Klee cited his belief that such a test was a gross infringement of human rights. He promised that if a law were passed making the test legal but not mandatory he would volunteer again.

Christian Klee was reassured that his refusal to take the test was apparently received well. So much so that he was encouraged to ask Eugene Dazzy about the postponed birthday party for the Oracle.

'Shit,' Dazzy said. 'Francis never really liked the old guy. Maybe we should just forget it.'

'Bullshit,' Christian said. 'You and Kennedy don't like him because he's part of the Socrates Club. Christ, Eugene, how can you hold a grudge against a guy who is over a hundred years old?'

Dazzy smiled at him. 'So even a tough guy like you has a soft spot. When do you want this party?'

'Time is short,' Christian said dryly. 'He's a hundred.'
'OK,' Dazzy said. 'After the Inauguration.'

Just two days before his Inauguration President Francis Kennedy stunned the nation on his weekly television broadcast with three announcements.

First he announced he had conditionally pardoned Yabril. He explained that it had been vital to the nation to learn whether Yabril was linked to the atom bomb explosion and the attempt to assassinate him. He explained that by law neither Yabril nor Gresse and Tibbot could be forced to take the PET Verification Test. But that Yabril had agreed to take the test, on the urgings of the President, with the provision that if it proved he was not connected, he would be released after serving a five-year sentence in prison.

Yabril had passed the test. He was not linked to Gresse and Tibbot or to the assassination attempt.

Secondly, Francis Kennedy announced that after his Inauguration, he would do everything in his power to call a Constitutional Convention to amend the Constitution. Primarily to amend the sacred document. He cited the release of Gresse and Tibbot, after their great crime, as due to the faults in the Bill of Rights. He wanted the Constitution amended so that the important issues before the public would be decided not by the Congress or the President, but by the direct will of the people. That is, by referendum, a vote on the ballot.

Thirdly, on a minor note, he announced that to quiet the whole uproar about who was responsible for the explosion of the atom bomb, Attorney General Christian Klee would leave government service one month after the Inauguration. Kennedy reminded the audience that he himself had passed the PET Scan on that matter; and that he himself could vouch for Christian Klee's innocence, but that it was in the best interest of the country for Klee to resign. Now with these actions, the whole controversy would be resolved.

Kennedy promised that Gresse and Tibbot would be brought to justice. That once the Constitutional Convention revised the Bill of Rights, those criminals would be forced to take the PET Verification Scan.

Only the media controlled by the Socrates Club attacked this speech. It was pointed out that the President had used poor reasoning. That if Gresse and Tibbot had to be forced to take this test, why not Christian Klee? And then a more serious point was made. A Constitutional Convention had never once been called since the Constitution had been written. It would open up a Pandora's box. The media declared that one of the suggested amendments would be that a President could serve more than eight years in office.

It had not been easy for President Francis Kennedy to arrange these events and indeed to call a Constitutional Convention was a complicated task, but he had laid the groundwork and was sure of success. To persuade Yabril to take the brain test had been even more complicated. And to tell the man he loved most, Christian Klee, that he must resign as Attorney General, was the most painful. But it had been the struggle in his own mind that had been most difficult.

The Constitutional Convention he had planned meticulously. It would be necessary to consolidate his power, to give him the weapons he would need to make his dreams for America come true. That was settled.

He had planned with Christian that the case against Gresse and Tibbot would be weak and that they would be released. That made it ever harder to force Klee's resignation. But Kennedy knew that the critics would demand that the Attorney General take the brain test. With Klee out of the government, Kennedy knew he could keep it from being pursued.

It was the decision about Yabril that had given Kennedy the most trouble. It would be very tricky. First he had to convince Yabril to take the test voluntarily. Then he had to justify it to the American public. And then he had to struggle with himself about letting Yabril escape his punishment. Finally, he justified to himself the course of action he must take.

President Francis Kennedy summoned Theodore Tappey, the Central Intelligence Director, to a private meeting in the Yellow Oval Room. He excluded everyone, he wanted no witnesses, no recording.

He had to be careful with Theodore Tappey. The man had come up through the ranks, had been an operational chief, he was familiar with every strain of treachery. He had practiced long and hard in that business of betraying fellow human beings for the sake of his country. His patriotism was not in doubt. But there might be a line he would not cross.

Kennedy wasted no time on civilities. There was no window dressing of a leisurely tea. He spoke curtly to Tappey. 'Theo, we have a big problem that only you and I understand. And only you and I can solve.'

'I'll do my best, Mr President,' Tappey said. And Kennedy saw the feral look in his eyes. He scented blood.

'Everything we say here has the highest security classification, it has executive privilege,' Kennedy said. 'You are not to repeat this to anyone, not even members of my staff.' That was when Tappey knew the matter was extremely sensitive. Kennedy cut his staff in on everything.

'It's Yabril,' Kennedy said. 'I'm sure,' he smiled, 'I'm positive, you've thought this all out. Yabril will go on trial. That will rake up all the resentments against America. He will get convicted and sentenced to life imprisonment. But somewhere down the line there will be a terrorist action that takes important hostages. One demand will be to release Yabril. By that time, I won't be President and so Yabril will go free. Still a dangerous man.'

455

Kennedy had caught the scepticism in Tappey. The sign was no sign, Tappey was too experienced in deception. His face simply lost all expression, all animation in the eyes, the contour of the lips. He had made himself a blank so as not to be read.

But now Tappey smiled. 'You must have read the internal memos my counter Intelligence Chief has been giving me. That's exactly what he says.'

'So how do we prevent all this?' Kennedy asked. But it was a rhetorical question and Tappey did not answer. 'We still have a big question that hangs like a cloud over this administration. Is Yabril linked with Gresse and Tibbot? And is that link still an atomic danger? I'll be frank with you. We know they are not linked but we must make believers out of everyone.'

'You've lost me, Mr President,' Tappey said.

Kennedy decided the time had come. 'I will persuade Yabril to take the test. He knows once he goes to trial he's sure to be convicted. I'll tell him this, "Take the PET Scan. If the test proves you have no link to Gresse and Tibbot, or the assassination attempt, you will be sentenced to only five years in prison and then you'll be released." His lawyers will be overjoyed with such a deal. And here is how Yabril will think: "I know I can pass the test so why not take it? Only five years in prison and during that five years my fellow terrorists may get me released." He'll go for it.'

For the very first time in their relationship, Kennedy saw Tappey looking at him with the shrewd appraising eye of an opponent. He knew that Tappey thought things out far ahead but not necessarily in the same direction, as how could he? He let Tappey interrupt him.

Tappey said, and his words were not so much a question as a probing, 'So Yabril goes free after five years? That's not it. Is Christian in on this? He used to be very good when we were in Operations together. Does he do something?'

Francis Kennedy sighed, he was a little disappointed. He

had hoped Tappey would help him, would see a little further. This was difficult for him. And this was not even the hardest part. He said slowly, 'Christian doesn't do anything. Christian is going to resign. You and I have to do it because we are the only ones who see this problem clearly. Now listen very carefully. It must be proven that there is no link between those two boys and Yabril. The nation must know that. It needs the relief. Also, in a funny way it takes the pressure off Christian. OK. That can only happen if Yabril takes the test and proves he has no part in it. So we do that. But the problem remains. When Yabril is released he is still dangerous. That we can't allow'.

Now Tappey was on target. Tappey was with him. Tappey understood. Tappey was now looking at Kennedy as a servant might look at a master who was about to ask him a service which would bind them together for ever.

'I guess I don't get anything in writing,' Tappey said.

'No,' Kennedy said. 'I am going to give you specific instructions right now.'

'Be very specific,' Theodore Tappey said, 'if you will, Mr President.'

Kennedy smiled at the coolness of the response. 'Dr Annaccone would never do it,' he said. 'A year ago I myself would never have dreamed of doing it.'

'I understand, Mr President,' Tappey said.

Kennedy knew there could be no further hesitation. 'After Yabril agrees to take the test, I switch him to your CIA medical section. Your medical team does the scan. They give the test.' He could see the look in Tappey's eyes, the waver of doubt, not of moral outrage, but doubt of feasibility.

'We're not talking murder here,' Kennedy said impatiently. 'I'm not that stupid or that immoral. And if I wanted that done, I'd be talking to Christian.'

Tappey was waiting.

Kennedy knew he had to say the fatal words. 'I swear that I ask this for the protection of our country. When Yabril is

457

released after five years, he must no longer be a danger. I want your medical team to go to the extreme limit of the test. According to Dr Annaccone, it was under that protocol that the side effects occurred. And complete memory was erased. A man without memory, without beliefs and convictions, is harmless. He will live a peaceful life.'

Kennedy recognized the look in Tappey's eyes, it was the look of one predator who has discovered another strange species its equal in ferocity.

'Can you assemble a team that will do that?' Kennedy asked.

'When I explain the situation to them,' Tappey said. 'They would never have been recruited if they were not devoted to their country.' He paused for a moment and then said thoughtfully, 'And after five years in prison, we'll just say Yabril's mind deteriorated. Maybe we'll even give him an early release.'

'Of course,' Kennedy said.

In the dark hours of that night, Christian Klee escorted Yabril to Francis Kennedy's quarters. Again the meeting was short and Kennedy was all business. There was no tea, there were no civilities. Kennedy began immediately, he presented his proposal.

Yabril was silent. He looked wary.

Kennedy said, 'I see you have some doubts.'

Yabril shrugged and said, 'I find your offer too generous.'

Kennedy summoned all his strength to do what he had to do. He rememberd Yabril charming his daughter Theresa before putting a gun to her neck. Such charm would not work with Yabril. He could only persuade this man by convincing him of his own strict morality.

'I am doing this to erase fear from the mind of my country,' Kennedy said. 'That is my greatest concern. My pleasure would be to have you remain in prison for ever. So I make this offer out of my sense of duty.'

'Then why are you taking such pains to convince me?' Yabril asked.

'It's not in my nature to perform my duty as a matter of form,' Kennedy said and he could see that Yabril believed in this, believed that he was a moral man and could be trusted within that morality. Again he summoned the image of Theresa and her belief in Yabril's kindness. Then he said to Yabril, 'You were outraged at the suggestion that your people engineered the explosion of an atom bomb. Here is the chance to clear your name and the name of your comrades. Why not take it? Do you fear you will not pass the test? That is always a possibility, it occurs to me now though I don't really believe it.'

Yabril looked directly into Kennedy's eyes. 'I don't believe that any man can forgive what I have done to you,' he said.

Kennedy sighed. 'I don't forgive you. But I understand your actions. I understand you feel you did what you did to help our world. As I do what I do now. And it is within my powers. We are different men, I cannot do what you do, and you, I mean you no disrespect, cannot do what I am doing now. To let you go free.'

Almost with sorrow, he saw that he had convinced Yabril. He continued his persuasion, he used all his wit, all his charm, his appearance of integrity. He projected all the images of what he had once been, of what Yabril had known him to be, before he forfeited the whole of himself to convince Yabril. He knew he was finally successful when he saw the smile on Yabril's face was one of pity and contempt. He knew then that he had won Yabril's trust.

Four days later, after Yabril's PET medical interrogation, after he had been transferred back to FBI custody, he received two visitors. They were Francis Kennedy and Christian Klee.

Yabril was completely unrestrained, unshackled.

The three men spent a quiet hour drinking tea and eating

little sandwiches. Kennedy studied Yabril. The man's face seemed to have changed. It was a sensitive face, the eyes were slightly melancholy but good-humored. He spoke little but studied Kennedy and Klee as though trying to solve some mystery.

He seemed content. He seemed to know who he was. And he seemed to radiate such purity of soul that Kennedy could not bear to look at him and finally took his leave.

The decision about Christian Klee was even more painful to Francis Kennedy. It had been an unexpected surprise for Christian. Kennedy asked him into the Yellow Room for a private meeting, not even Eugene Dazzy was present.

But Francis Kennedy opened the meeting quietly by saying, 'Christian, I've been closer to you than anybody outside my family. I think we know each other better than anyone else knows us. So you will understand that I have to ask for your resignation to be effective after the Inauguration, at a time when I decide to accept it.'

Klee looked at that handsome face with its gentle smile. He could not believe that Kennedy was firing him without any explanation. He said quietly, 'I know I've cut a few corners here and there. But my ultimate aim was always to keep you from harm.'

'And you have done that job very well,' Francis Kennedy said. 'I would never have run for President if you hadn't made that promise to keep me safe. But I'm not afraid of that any more. I don't know why. I remember how scared I was in those old days and now I don't have that feeling.'

'Then why am I being fired?' Christian asked. He was feeling a little nauseous, he had never expected this blow, not from his friend, not from the man he admired more than anyone else in the world.

Kennedy smiled sadly. 'That atom bomb thing. I understand you did it for me, but I can't live with your doing it.'

Christian Klee said, 'You wanted me to do that.'

460

It was Kennedy's turn to be surprised. He said, 'Chris, you've known me almost thirty years. When have I been so immoral? You've always told me that you admired me and valued me because of my integrity. How could you think I would want you to do such a terrible thing?'

'Will we still be buddies?' Christian Klee asked jokingly.

'Of course,' Francis Kennedy said. And Christian knew that he would never be friends with Kennedy again.

The Socrates Club was summoned by the Oracle, and as rich and powerful as they were, they dared not refuse. Also their invitations indicated that the Oracle himself might solve their problem with Francis Kennedy.

The Oracle received them in his huge living room and despite his age was very lively. His motions seemed to be quicker, his motorized wheelchair scooted among them, he shook hands firmly, his eyes seemed to sparkle. He was impressive in his animation. But this animation, so unseemly in so old a man, was pleasing only because he was the richest man among them. The Oracle had percentages of all their empires.

George Greenwell was envious of the old man, to be so spry at a hundred years of age. Greenwell at eighty, in good health, wondered if he too could attain such blessed longevity. There was still plenty of life to enjoy, Greenwell thought, but he had to be careful.

The Oracle used the long table in his dining room for the conference. Servants were banished from the room but there was a stocked bar available and platters of English-tea sandwiches.

The Oracle addressed the meeting from the head of the table. But first he greeted each man by name. To George Greenwell he said with what was meant to be a humorous cackle, as one ancient to another, 'Well we're both still here.'

To Bert Audick, he said, 'You're out of arrest again?

461

Never mind, at the height of my career they indicted me five times and I never spent a day in jail.'

With Louis Inch, Martin Mutford, and Lawrence Salentine he merely said their names. Then he spoke to all of them. He spoke haltingly, as if the synapses of his brain, the deterioration of its neurotransmitters, caused a static in his vocalization, but his message was clear. 'Gentlemen,' he said, 'I hereby resign from the Socrates Club. And it is my duty to advise you, I will sell all of my holdings in all of your companies. We can make a pretty penny from that.' He gave one of his heh, heh, heh laughs. 'But most important of all I want to warn you, from all my long experience, that you must protect yourselves. Kennedy will destroy us all.'

In two days Lawrence Salentine had an appointment with President Francis Kennedy. The meeting was short and to the point. Kennedy informed him that no deal could be made for the others, that the whole structure of American society was to be changed. But Kennedy said that a deal could be made for Salentine and his people who owned the majority of media, newspapers, magazines, radio and TV in America. He needed their help to present his programs properly.

Salentine pointed out that the media could not really be controlled to an extreme degree. There were writers who followed their own ideas, there were TV newsmen who prided themselves on their independence in presenting the news. Many of these would criticize the legal reforms and amendments of the Bill of Rights that the President had on the drawing boards and were no secret. And that despite the power of the people who owned the media outlets, these independent working media people could not be controlled.

Kennedy assured him that he understood this. What he wanted was the overall support of the owners of the media.

Salentine finally agreed to the deal. In the spirit of free American enterprise, the others would have to look after themselves.

25

Christian Klee started making arrangements to leave government service. One of the most important things was to erase any traces of his circumventing the law in his protection of the President. He had to erase all the illegal computer surveillances of the members of the Socrates Club.

Sitting at his massive desk in the Attorney General's office, Christian Klee used his personal computer to erase incriminating files. Finally, he called up the file on David Jatney. He had been right on this guy, Klee thought, this guy was the joker in the deck. That darkly handsome face had the lopsided look of a mind unbalanced. Jatney's eyes were bright with the scattered electricity of a neural system at war with itself. And the latest information showed that he was on his way to Washington. Klee felt the thrill of a hunter closing in. This guy could be trouble. Then he remembered the Oracle's advice. He thought about it for a long time. And then he thought, let fate decide.

He pressed the delete key of the computer and David Jatney disappeared without trace from all government files. Whatever happened, he, Christian Klee, could not be blamed.

Just two weeks before President Francis Kennedy's Inauguration, David Jatney had become restless. He wanted to escape the eternal sunshine of California, the rich friendly voices everywhere, the moonlit balmy beaches. He felt himself drowning in the brown, syrupy air of its society, and

463

yet he did not want to go back home to Utah and be the daily witness to his father and mother's happiness.

Irene had moved in with him. She wanted to save on rent money, to go on a trip to India and study with a guru there. A group of her friends were pooling their resources to charter a plane and she wanted to join them with her little son, Campbell.

David Jatney was astonished when she told him her plans. She did not ask him if she could move in with him, she merely asserted her right to do so. That right was based on the fact that they now saw each other three times a week for a movie and to have sex. She had put it to him as one buddy to another, as if he were one of her California friends who routinely moved in with each other for periods of a week or more. It was done not as a cunning preliminary to marriage but as a casual act of comradeship. She had no sense of imposing, that his life would be disrupted with a strange woman and strange child made part of the daily fabric of his life.

Irene struck him as extraordinarily single-minded, in every facet of her life. She was politically to the left, she was untiring in her work for the Santa Monica Tenant League, she was immersed in the Eastern religions, passionate on making the trip to India and studying under her guru. With sex she was also direct and imperious, there was no foreplay, it had to be done and gotten over with and after the act she would pick up a book of Indian philosophy and begin to read.

What horrified David Jatney most of all was that she planned to bring her little boy with her to India. Irene was a woman who had absolute confidence that she could make her way in any world; certain that the fates would be good to her, that no calamity could befall her. David Jatney had visions of the little boy sleeping in the streets of Calcutta with the thousands of the diseased poor of that city. In a moment of anger he once told her he could not understand anyone believing in a religion that spawned the hundreds of millions who were the most desperately poverty-stricken in the world. She had answered that what happened in this world was unimportant since what happened in the next life would be so much more interesting and so much more rewarding. David Jatney didn't see the logic of that. Where was the logic? If you were reincarnated, why wouldn't you be reincarnated in exactly the same miserable life that you had left?

Jatney was fascinated by Irene and how she treated her son. She often carried little Campbell to her political meetings because she could not always get her mother to babysit and was too proud to ask too often. At these political and spiritual meetings she put Campbell in a little sleeping bag at her feet. She took him with her sometimes even to work, when the special kindergarten he attended was closed for some reason.

There was no question that she was a devoted mother. But to David Jatney her attitude towards motherhood was bewildering. She did not have the usual concern to protect her child or worry about the psychological influences that could harm him. She treated him as one would treat a beloved pet, a dog or a cat. She seemed to care nothing for what the child thought or felt. She was determined that being the mother of a child would not limit her life in any way, that she would not make motherhood a bondage, that she would maintain her freedom. David thought she was a little crazy.

But she was a pretty girl, and when she concentrated on sex, she could be compellingly ardent. David enjoyed being with her. She was competent in the everyday details of her life and was really no trouble. And so he let her move in.

Two consequences were completely unforeseen by him. He became impotent. And he became fond of the little boy, Campbell.

He prepared for their moving in by buying a huge trunk

465

to lock up his guns, the cleaning materials and the ammo. He didn't want a four-year-old kid accidentally getting his hands on weapons. And by now, somehow, David Jatney had enough guns to deck out a superhero bandit; two rifles, a machine pistol and a collection of handguns. One, a very small twenty-two caliber handgun, he carried in his jacket pocket in a little leather case that was more like a glove. At night he usually put it beneath his bed. When Irene and Campbell moved in, he locked the .22 in the trunk with the other guns. He put a good padlock on the trunk. Even if the little kid found it open, there was no way he could figure out how to load it. Irene was another story. Not that he didn't trust her, but she was a little weird, and weirdness and guns didn't mix.

On the day they moved in, Jatney bought a few toys for Campbell so he wouldn't be too disorientated. That first night, when Irene was ready to go to bed, she arranged pillows and a blanket on the sofa for the little boy, undressed him in the bathroom and put him into pajamas. Jatney saw the little boy looking at him. There was in that look an old wariness, a glint of fear and very faintly what seemed to be a habitual bewilderment. In a flash Jatney translated that look to himself. As a little boy he knew his father and mother would desert him to make love in their room.

He said to Irene, 'Listen, I'll sleep on the sofa and the kid can sleep with you.'

'That's silly,' Irene said. 'He doesn't mind, do you Campbell?'

The boy shook his head. He rarely spoke.

Irene said proudly, 'He's a brave boy, aren't you Campbell?'

At that moment, David Jatney felt a moment of pure hatred for her. He repressed it and said, 'I have to do some writing and I'll be up late. I think he should sleep with you the first few nights.'

'If you have to work, OK,' Irene said cheerfully.

She held out her hand to Campbell and the little boy jumped off the sofa and ran into her arms. He hid his head in her breast. She said to him, 'Aren't you going to say goodnight to your Uncle Jat?' And she smiled brilliantly at David Jatney, a smile that made her beautiful. And he understood it was her own little joke, an honest joke, a way of telling him that this had been the mode of her address and introduction for her child when she lived with other lovers, delicate, fearful moments in her life, and that she was grateful to him for his thoughtfulness, her faith in the universe sustained.

The boy kept his head buried in her breasts and David Jatney patted him gently and said, 'Good night, Campbell.' The boy looked up and stared into Jatney's eyes. It was the peculiar questioning look of small children, the regard of an object that is absolutely unknown to their universe.

David Jatney was stricken by that look. As if he could be a source of danger. He saw that the boy had an unusually elegant face for one so young. A broad forehead, luminous gray eyes, a firm, almost stern mouth.

Campbell smiled at Jatney and the effect was miraculous. His whole face beamed with trust. He reached out a hand and touched Jatney's face. And then Irene took him with her into the bedroom.

A few minutes later she came out again and gave him a kiss. 'Thanks for being so thoughtful,' she said. 'We can have a quick screw before I go back in.' She made no seductive movement when she said this. It was simply a friendly offer.

David Jatney thought of the little boy behind the bedroom door waiting for his mother. 'No,' he said.

'OK,' she said cheerfully and went back into the bedroom.

For the next few weeks, Irene was furiously busy. She had taken an additional job for very little pay and long hours at night, to help in the re-election campaign, she was an ardent partisan of Francis Kennedy. She would talk about the social

467

programs he favored, his fight against the rich in America, his struggle to reform the legal system. David thought she was in love with Kennedy's physical appearance, the magic of his voice. He believed that she worked at campaign headquarters because of infatuation rather than political belief.

Three days after she moved in, he dropped by campaign headquarters in Santa Monica and found her working on a computer with little Campbell at her feet. The boy was in a sleeping bag but was wide awake. Jatney could see his open eyes.

'I'll take him home and put him to bed,' David Jatney said.

'He's OK,' Irene said. 'I don't want to take advantage of you.'

Jatney pulled Campbell out of the sleeping bag, the boy was fully clothed except for his shoes. Jatney took him by the hand and he felt warm, soft skin, and for a moment he was happy.

'I'll take him for a pizza and ice cream first, is that OK?' Jatney said to Irene.

She was busy with her computer. 'Don't spoil him,' she said. 'When you're gone he gets health yogurt out of the fridge.' She took a moment to smile at him and then gave Campbell a kiss.

'Should I wait up for you?' he asked.

'What for?' she said quickly. Then added, 'I'll be late.' He went out, leading the little boy by the hand. He drove to Montana Avenue and stopped at a little Italian restaurant that made pizza on the side. He watched Campbell eat. One slice and he mangled that more than he ate it. But he was interested in eating and that made David Jatney happy. The kid really polished off the ice cream and when they left Jatney had the rest of the pizza in a doggie box.

In the apartment he put the pizza in the fridge and noted that the box of yogurt was encrusted with ice. He put

Campbell to bed, letting him wash and change into his pajamas by himself. He made his bed on the sofa, put on the TV very low and watched.

There was a lot of political talk on the air and interviews on the news programs. Francis Kennedy seemed to descend out of all the galaxies of cable. And Jatney had to admit that the man was overpowering on TV. Jatney dreamed of being a victorious hero like Kennedy. How the people of America loved him. What power he had. You could see the Secret Service men with their stone faces hovering in the background. How safe he was, how rich he was, how loved he was. Often David Jatney dreamed of being Francis Kennedy. How Rosemary would be in love with him. And he thought about Hock and Gibson Grange. And they would all be eating in the White House and they would all talk to him and Rosemary would talk to him in her excited way, touching his knee, telling him her innermost feelings.

He thought about Irene and what he felt about her. And he realized he was more bewildered than entranced. It seemed to him that with all her openness she was really completely closed to him. He could never really love her. He thought of Campbell, who had been named after the writer Joseph Campbell, famous for his books about myths, the boy so open and guileless with such an elegant innocence of countenance.

David Jatney did not have that adult desire to charm little children. But he felt it a comfort to the little boy to take him for drives through the Malibu canyons, both silent in the car, Campbell sometimes pointing out a coyote slinking away, observing and pondering, as children do. It was better than having Irene with him who talked so much he could barely resist putting his hands around her throat. He enjoyed stopping in a little café to feed the child. It was so simple. You put a hamburger in front of him with French fries and a glass of malted milk and he ate what he wanted and mashed the rest.

469

And sometimes David Jatney would take Campbell by the hand to walk along the public beaches of Malibu, up to the wire fence that walled off the Malibu Colony of the rich and powerful from the rest of the population, and they would peer through at the people who were loved by the gods. Where Rosemary Belair lived. He always looked hard to see if she was on the beach and once he thought he saw her far away.

After a few days, Campbell started calling him Uncle Jat and always put a little hand in his. Jatney accepted. He loved the innocent touches of affection the boy gave him that Irene never did. And it was during this two weeks that this extension of feeling to another human being sustained him.

David Jatney became impotent with Irene. It now became a permanent arrangement that he would sleep on the sofa and Campbell and Irene would sleep in the bedroom. From her constant chatter on every subject under the sun, she made clear that his impotence was a bourgeois hang-up because the little boy was living with them, she was in no way to blame. He thought that might be true, but he also thought that her lack of tenderness to him might have something to do with it. He would have left her, but he was worried about Campbell, he would miss Campbell.

And then he lost his job at the studio. He would have been in a jam if it had not been for Hock, his 'Uncle' Hock. When he was fired there was a message for him to come by Hock's office and because he thought that Campbell would enjoy visiting a movie studio, he brought the child. The boy was bewildered and delighted by the pictures shooting on the lot, the cameras, the shouted orders, the actors and actresses playing scenes, but Jatney saw that his sense of reality was distorted, that he could not tell apart the reality of the people on the sets acting, the everyday encounters of the people on the lot or the relationships of the people he knew from watching television. Finally Jatney held his hand and led him to Hock's office.

When Hock greeted him, David Jatney felt his overwhelming love for the man, Hock was so warm. Hock sent one of his secretaries immediately to the commissary to get ice cream for the little boy and then showed Campbell some props on his desk that would be used in the movie he was currently producing.

Campbell was enchanted by all this, and Jatney felt a twinge of jealousy that Hock was so charmed by the child. But then he could see it was Hock's way of clearing away an obstacle in their meeting. With Campbell busy playing with the props, Hock shook Jatney's hand and said, 'I'm sorry you got fired. They are cutting down the story-reading department and the others had seniority. But stay in touch, I'll get something for you.'

'I'll be OK,' David Jatney said.

Hock was studying him closely. 'You look awfully thin, David. Maybe you should go back home and visit a while. That good Utah air, that relaxing Mormon life. Is this kid your girlfriend's?'

'Yeah,' Jatney said. 'She's not exactly my girl, she's my friend. We live together but she's trying to save money on rent so she can make a trip to India.'

Hock frowned for a moment and started to say something. It was the first time he had ever seen a frown on Hock's face.

'If you financed every California girl who wanted to go to India you'd be broke,' Hock said, but cheerfully. 'And they all seem to have kids.'

He sat down at his desk, took a huge checkbook out of his drawer and wrote on it. He ripped a piece out of the book, and handed it to Jatney. 'This is for all the birthday presents and graduation presents I never had the time to send you.' He smiled at Jatney. Jatney looked at the check. He was astonished to see it was for five thousand dollars.

'Ah, c'mon, Hock, I can't take this,' he said. He felt tears

471

coming into this eyes, tears of gratitude, humiliation and hatred.

'Sure you can,' Hock said. 'Listen, I want you to get some rest and have a good time. Maybe give this girl her air fare to India so she can get what she wants and you'll be free to do what you want. The trouble with being friends with a girl is that you get all the troubles of a lover and none of the advantages of a friend. But that's quite a little boy she has. I might have something for him some time if I ever have the balls to make a kid picture.'

Jatney pocketed the check. He understood everything that Hock had said. 'Yeah, he's a nice-looking kid.'

'It's more than that,' Hock said. 'Look, he has that elegant face, just made for tragedy. You look at him and you feel like crying.'

And Jatney thought how smart his friend Hock was for that was just what he felt. Elegant was just right and yet so odd to describe Campbell's face. Irene was an elemental force, like God she had constructed a future tragedy.

Hock hugged him and said, 'David, stay in touch. I mean it. Keep yourself together, times always get better when you're young.' He gave Campbell one of the props, a beautiful miniature futuristic airplane, and Campbell hugged it to him and said, 'Uncle Jat, can I keep it?' And Jatney saw a smile on Hock's face.

'Say hello to Rosemary for me,' David Jatney said. He had been trying to say this all through the meeting.

Hock gave him a startled look. 'I will,' he said. 'We've been invited to Kennedy's Inauguration in January, me and Gibson and Rosemary. I'll tell her then.'

And suddenly David Jatney felt he had been flung off a spinning world. Here were people he knew – he had had dinner with them, he had slept with Rosemary, no he had fucked her – and they were going to ascend the highest thrones of power without him. He took Campbell by the hand, the silken skin reassuring him.

472

'Thanks for everything, Hock,' he said. 'I'll keep in close touch. And maybe I will go back to Utah for a few weeks. For Christmas.'

'That's great,' Hock said warmly. 'You should call them more often. Kids don't know how much their mother and father miss them.'

And as Hock ushered them out of his office with repeated reassuring taps on Jatney's shoulder, Jatney thought with a sudden fury, what the hell does he know? He never had any kids.

Now lying on the sofa, waiting for Irene to come home, dawn showing its smoky light through the living room window, Jatney thought of Rosemary Belair. How she had turned to him in bed and lost herself in his body. He remembered the smell of her perfume, the curious heaviness, perhaps caused by the sleeping pills traumatizing the muscles in her flesh. He thought of her in the morning in her jogging clothes, her assurance and her assumption of power, how she had dismissed him. He lived over that moment when she offered to give him cash to tip the limo driver and how he had refused to take the money. But why had he insulted her, why had he said she knew better than him how much was needed, implying that she too had been sent home in such a fashion and in such a circumstance?

He found himself falling asleep in little short gaps of time, listening for Campbell, listening for Irene. He thought of his parents back in Utah, he knew they forgot about him, secure in their own happiness, their hypocritical angel pants flutter-ing outside as they joyfully and unceasingly fornicated in their bare skins. If he called them they would have to part.

David Jatney dreamed of how he would meet Rosemary Belair. How he would tell her he loved her. Listen, he would say, think if you had cancer. I would take your cancer from you into my own body. Listen, he would say, if some great star fell from the sky I would cover your body. Listen, he

473

would say, if someone tried to kill you I would stop the blade with my heart, the bullet with my body. Listen, he would say, if I had one drop from the fountain of youth that would keep me young for ever and you were growing old, I would give you that drop so that you would never grow old.

And he perhaps understood that his memory of Rosemary Belair was haloed by her power. That he was praying to a God to make him something more than a common piece of clay. That he begged for power, unlimited riches, for beauty, for any and all the achievements so that his fellow man would mark his presence on this earth, and so he would not drown silently in the vast ocean that passed for man.

When he showed Hock's check to Irene, it was to impress her, to prove to her that someone cared enough about him to give him such a vast amount of money as a casual gift. She was not impressed, in her experience it was a commonplace that friends shared with each other and she even said that a man of Hock's vast wealth could have easily given away a bigger amount. When David Jatney offered to give her half the amount of the check so that she could go to India immediately, she refused. 'I always use my own money, I work for a living,' she said. 'If I took money from you, you would feel you have rights over me. Besides, you really want to do it for Campbell, not me.'

He was astounded by her refusal and her statement of his interest in Campbell. He had simply wanted to be rid of both of them. He wanted to be alone again to live with his dreams of the future.

Then she asked him what he would do if she took half the money and went to India, what would he do with his half. He noticed she did not suggest he go to India with her. He also noted that she had said 'your half of the money', so that in her mind she was accepting his offer.

Then he made the mistake of telling her what he would do with his twenty-five hundred.

'I want to see the country and I want to see Kennedy's

Inauguration,' he said. 'I thought it might be fun, something different. You know, take my car and drive through the whole country. See the whole United States. I even want to see the snow and ice and feel real cold.'

Irene seemed lost in thought for a moment. Then she went striding briskly through the apartment as if counting her possessions in it. 'That's a great idea,' she said. 'I want to see Kennedy too. I want to see him in person or I'll never really be able to know his karma. I'll put in for my vacation, they owe me tons of days. And it will be good for Campbell to see the country, all the different states. We'll take my van and save on motel bills.'

Irene owned a small van which she had fitted out with shelves to hold books and a small bunk for Campbell. The van was invaluable to her because even when Campbell was a little infant she had taken trips up and down the state of California to attend meetings and seminars on Eastern religions.

David Jatney felt trapped as they started off on their trip. Irene was driving, she liked to drive. Campbell was between them, one little hand in David Jatney's hand. Jatney had deposited half the check in Irene's bank account for her trip to India and now his twenty-five hundred would have to be used for three of them instead of only one. The only thing that comforted him was the .22 caliber handgun nestling in its leather glove, the glove in his jacket pocket. The East of America had too many robbers and muggers and he had Irene and Campbell to protect.

To Jatney's surprise they had a wonderful time the first four days of leisurely driving. Campbell and Irene slept in the van and he slept outside in the open fields until they hit cold weather in Arkansas; they had swung south to avoid the cold as long as possible. Then for a couple of nights they used a motel room, any motel on the route. It was in Kentucky that they first ran into trouble and in a way that surprised Jatney.

475

The weather had turned cold and they decided to go into a motel for the night. The next morning they drove into town for breakfast in a café newspaper store.

The counterman was about Jatney's age and very alert. In her egalitarian California way, Irene struck up a conversation with him. She did so because she was impressed by his quickness and efficiency. She often said it was such a pleasure to watch someone who was truly expert at the work they did, no matter how menial. She said this was a sign of good karma. Jatney never really understood the word karma.

But the counterman did. He too was a follower of the Eastern religions and he and Irene got into a long and involved discussion. Campbell became restless so Jatney paid the bill and took him outside to wait. It was a good fifteen minutes before Irene came out.

'He's a really sweet guy,' Irene said. 'His name is Christopher but he calls himself Krish.'

Jatney was annoyed by the wait but said nothing. On the walk back to the motel Irene said, 'I think we should stay here for a day. Campbell needs a rest. And it looks like a nice town to shop for Christmas presents. We might not have time to shop in Washington.'

'OK,' Jatney said. That had been the peculiar thing about their trip so far, how all the villages had been decorated for Christmas, colored lights across the main streets. A chain across America.

They spent the rest of the morning and afternoon shopping, though Irene bought very little. They had a very early supper in a Chinese restaurant. The plan was to go to bed early so that they could travel east before dark.

But they had only been in their motel room for a few hours, when Irene, who had been too restless to play checkers with Campbell, suddenly said she was going to take a little drive through town and maybe pick up a bite to eat. She left and David Jatney played checkers with the little boy

476

who beat him in every game. The boy was an amazing checker player, Irene had taught him when he was only two years old. At one point Campbell raised his elegant head with the broad brow and said, 'Uncle Jat, don't you like to play checkers?'

It was nearly midnight before Irene returned. The motel was on a little high ground and Jatney and the boy Campbell were looking out the window when the familiar van pulled into the parking lot, followed by another car.

Jatney was surprised to see Irene get out of the passenger side, since she always insisted on driving. From the driver's side the young counterman called Krish emerged and gave her the car keys. She gave a sisterly kiss in return. Two young men got out of the other car and she gave them sisterly little pecks. Irene started walking toward the motel entrance and the three young men put their arms around each other and serenaded her. 'Goodnight, Irene,' they sang, 'Goodnight, Irene.' When Irene entered the motel room and heard them still singing, she gave David Jatney a brilliant smile.

'They were so interesting to talk to I just forgot the time,' Irene said, and she went to the window to wave to them.

'I guess I'll have to go and tell them to stop,' David Jatney said. Through his mind ran flashes of him firing the handgun in his pocket. He could see the bullets flying through the night into their brains. 'Those guys are much less interesting when they sing.'

'Oh, you couldn't stop them,' Irene said. She picked up Campbell. Holding him in her arms she bowed to acknowledge their homage and then pointed to the child. The singing stopped immediately. And then David Jatney could hear the car moving out of the parking lot.

Irene never drank. But she sometimes took recreational drugs. Jatney could always tell. She had such a lovely brilliant smile on drugs. She had smiled that way one night when he had been waiting up for her in Santa Monica. In

477

that dawn light he had accused her of being in someone else's bed. She had replied calmly, 'Somebody had to fuck me, you won't.' And he had accepted the justice of that remark.

Christmas Eve they were still on the road and slept in another motel. It was cold now. They would not celebrate the Christmas season, Irene said that Christmas was false to the true spirit of religion. David Jatney did not want to bring back memories of an earlier, more innocent life. But he did buy Campbell a crystal ball with snow flurries, over the objections of Irene. Early Christmas morning he rose and watched the two of them sleep. He carried the handgun in his jacket always now and he touched the soft leather of its glove. How easy and kind it would be to kill them both now, he thought.

Three days later they were in the nation's capital. They only had to wait a short time until the Inauguration. David Jatney made up the itinerary of all the sights they would see. And then he made a map of the inaugural parade. They would all go see Francis Kennedy take the oath of office as President of the United States.

26

On Inauguration Day, the President of the United States, Francis Xavier Kennedy, was awakened at dawn by Jefferson to be groomed and dressed. The gray light of breaking day was actually cheery because a snow storm had begun. Huge white flakes pasted the city of Washington and in the bulletproofed tinted windows of his dressing room, Francis Kennedy saw himself imprisoned in those snowflakes, as if he were imprisoned in a glass ball. He said to Jefferson, 'Will you be in the parade?'

'No, Mr President,' Jefferson said. 'I have to hold the fort here in the White House.' He adjusted Kennedy's tie. 'Everybody is waiting for you downstairs in the Red Room.'

When Kennedy was ready, he shook Jefferson's hand. 'Wish me luck,' he said. And Jefferson went with him to the elevator. Two Secret Service men took him down to the ground floor.

In the Red Room they were all waiting for him. The Vice President, Helen DuPray, was stunningly regal in white satin, Lanetta Carr softly beautiful in pink. The President's staff were reflections of the President, all in white and black tuxedos, so startling against the walls and sofas of the Red Room. Arthur Wix, Oddblood Gray, Eugene Dazzy and Christian Klee formed their own little circle, solemn and tense with the importance of the day. Francis Kennedy smiled at them. The two women, these four men, were his family. It was amazing to him that he was a man in love, and that he would have a wife in the White House. That Lanetta Carr had agreed to marry him.

After his first dinner with Lanetta Carr, the dinner he had cooked so efficiently, Francis Kennedy had sunk into depression. The girl had so obviously not wanted him to woo her, had so desperately dreaded any amorous advance. He had invited her to other White House dinners, social occasions, where she would not have to worry that he would pursue a personal relationship.

He understood perfectly what she was feeling, that she was put off by his mantle of power. He had tried to allay that fear by going to her apartment dressed so casually and cooking her dinner with an apron tied around his waist. To disarm her; and it had partially succeeded. But it was only after she had seen the Presidential limousine blown up that she had weakened. That same night she had called Eugene Dazzy to ask when she could see the President. She had used those words. Dazzy had waited until the next morning to tell him of the call. Francis Kennedy still remembered the smile on Dazzy's face. It was the smile of an older brother fondly amused that his kid brother was finally being rewarded for a courtship. Francis Kennedy had called Lanetta Carr immediately.

There had been an awkward stilted conversation. Kennedy had invited her to have dinner with him in the White House, just the two of them. He explained that he could not leave, could not expose himself, that he would no longer be permitted to do so. And she had said that she would come to the White House whenever he wanted her to come. He told her to come that very night.

They had dinner in the residential apartment on the new fourth floor. Jefferson served them. They were very subdued while eating. And there was a moment as they left the dining room when Lanetta took his hand and he was startled by the warmth of her flesh. Blinded by long deprivation, by the lockings of his brain, he felt the different shape of her fingers, the shivery sleekness of her nails. And then he touched her shoulders and her neck, he felt a throbbing pulse and blindly touched the silken softness of her hair. Blindly he kissed her cheek, the corners of her eyes, all the warm flesh beneath the perfect skin. Transformed, delivered, his brain and body unlocked, he kissed her unshielded lips.

It was only when she responded that he dared to look at her face. It struck him to the heart, with amazement, with delight, with sorrow. She was so beautiful and her eyes surrendered her beauty to him out of love and her desire to make him happy. It was a look of trust, of belief in his humanity despite his trappings of power. He kissed her lips again and felt himself surrender, without compromise. Then almost as if in wonder, almost as if he had never discovered such strange land, he touched her breasts, the electric mysterious zones of her body beneath her dress. Remembered, cherished, he gave up his mind and body to her. And all the long years of dread and terror fled.

They became lovers and now Francis Kennedy had company when he roamed the rooms of the White House in the early hours of the morning when he could not sleep. And gradually he slept again through the night, eased into dreams by requited love. The nights he could not sleep, he drowsed happily, watched Lanetta Carr's sleeping face and nestled in her body. The nights became thoughts of joy rather than of dread. And like all true lovers he planned all the different ways to make his true love happy. And all the many ways he could make the people of America happy. And he thought how lucky he was that he was one of the few men in the world who could dream such dreams.

Two days before the Inauguration, Francis Kennedy and Lanetta agreed to marry. The wedding would take place the following April when the city of Washington would be celebrating spring.

*

Now that it was finally Inauguration Day, Francis Kennedy and his family emerged from the White House into a Washington made beautiful by great flakes of snow tinted gold by a cold winter sun.

Christian Klee watched Lanetta Carr and Francis Kennedy, the love on their faces. Christian thought there was no dignity in love, as there was no honor in politics, as there was no mercy in the struggles to rule this world. And what was mercy, after all, but a psychological insurance against total defeat? A subtle quid pro quo. He looked at the other men he had known so intimately for so many years. Eugene Dazzy, the President's Chief of Staff, Oddblood Gray, and Arthur Wix. They had, all of them, fought the battle for Francis Kennedy because it was their duty and he was their friend.

Then there was Theodore Tappey who dealt with evil on its own terms. Trick for trick, betrayal for betrayal. A simpler loyalty.

Dr Zed Annaccone was different from all of them. The star he followed shone clearly in the heavens. The irrevocable, unswerving truth of science, the only hope for man. He spurned evil, would have no truck with it. He would never coerce, never betray, he was bound in the immaculate conception of science. And good luck to him. As far as humanity was concerned he has his head, marvelous brain and all, stuck up his ass.

Or so Christian Klee thought as the Presidential party prepared to leave the White House for the swearing in of President Kennedy and the ride in the inaugural parade.

When President Francis Xavier Kennedy stepped out of the White House, he was astonished to see a vast sea of humanity that filled every thoroughfare, that seemed to blot out all the majestic buildings, overflowed all the TV vans and media people behind their special ropes and marked grounds. He had never seen anything like it and he called to Eugene Dazzy, 'How many are out there?'

Dazzy said, 'A hell of a lot more than we figured. Maybe we need a battalion of Marines from the Naval Base to help us control traffic.'

'No,' the President said. He was surprised that Dazzy had responded to his question as if the multitudes were a danger. He thought it a triumph, a vindication of everything he had done since the tragedies of last Easter Sunday.

Francis Kennedy had never felt surer of himself. He had foreseen everything that would happen, the tragedies and the triumphs. He had made the right decisions and won his victory. He had vanquished his enemies. He looked over at the sea of humanity and felt an overwhelming love for the people of America. He would deliver them from their suffering, cleanse the earth itself.

Never had Francis Kennedy felt his mind so clear, his instincts so true. He had conquered his grief over the death of his wife, the murder of his daughter. The sorrow that had fogged his brain had cleared away. He was almost happy now.

It seemed to Francis Kennedy that he had conquered fate, suffered through its worst blows, and by his own perseverance and judgments had made possible this present glorious future. He stepped out in the snow-filled air to be sworn in, then lead the inaugural parade through Washington and start on his road to glory.

David Jatney had registered himself and Irene and Campbell in a motel a little over twenty miles from Washington DC. The capital itself was jammed. The day before the Inauguration, they drove into Washington to see the monuments, the White House, the Lincoln Memorial and all the other sights of the capital. David Jatney also scouted the route of the inaugural parade to discover the best place to stand.

On the great day, they rose at dawn and had breakfast at

a roadside diner. Then they went back to the motel to dress in their best clothes. Irene was uncharacteristically careful brushing and setting her hair. She wore her best faded jeans, a red shirt and a green floppy sweater over it that David Jatney had never seen before. Had she kept it hidden or had she bought it here in Washington, he wondered. She had gone off by herself for a few hours leaving Campbell with Jatney.

It had snowed all night and the ground was covered white. Big flakes were lazily drifting through the air. In California there was no need for winter clothing, but on the trip East they had bought windbreakers, a bright red one for Campbell because Irene claimed she could easily find him if he strayed, Jatney a serviceable bright blue, and Irene a creamy white which made her look very pretty. She also wore a knitted cap of white wool and a tasseled cap for Campbell in bright red. Jatney was bareheaded, he hated any kind of covering.

On this Inauguration morning, they had time to spare so they went out into the field behind the motel to build Campbell a snowman. Irene had a spasm of giddy happiness and threw snowballs at Campbell and Jatney. They both very gravely received her missiles but did not throw any back. Jatney wondered at this happiness in her. Could seeing Kennedy in the coming parade have caused it? Or was it the snow, so strange and magical to her California senses.

Campbell was entranced by the snow. He sifted it through his fingers watching it disappear and melt in the sunshine. Then he began cautiously destroying the snowman with his fists, punching tiny holes in it, knocking off the head. Jatney and Irene stood a little distance away, watching him. Irene took Jatney's hand in hers, an unusual physical intimacy on her part.

'I have to tell you something,' she said. 'I've visited some people here in Washington, my friends in California told me to look them up. And these people are going to India and

I'm going with them, me and Campbell. I've arranged to sell the van but I'll give you money out of it so you can fly back to Los Angeles.'

David Jatney let her hand go and put his hands in the pockets of his windbreaker. His right hand touched the leather glove which held the .22 handgun and for a moment he could see Irene lying on the ground, her blood eating up the snow.

When the anger came he was puzzled by it. After all he had decided to come to Washington in the pitiful hope that he might see Rosemary, or meet her and Hock and Gibson Grange. He had dreamed these past days that he might even be invited to another dinner with them. That his life might change, that he would get a foot in the door that opened into power and glory. So wasn't it natural for Irene to want to go to India to open the door into a world she yearned for, to make herself something more than an ordinary woman with a small child working at jobs that could never lead to anything? Let her go, he thought.

Irene said, 'Don't be mad. You don't even like me any more. You would have ditched me if it wasn't for Campbell.' She was smiling, a little mockingly but with a touch of sadness.

'That's right,' David Jatney said. 'You shouldn't take the little kid to wherever the hell you feel like going. You can barely look out for him here.'

That made her angry. 'Campbell is my child,' she said. 'I'll bring him up as I please. And I'll take him to the North Pole if I want to.'

She paused for a moment and then said, 'You don't know anything about it. And I think you're getting a little queer about Campbell.'

Again he saw the snow stained with her blood, little flashing rivers, a prickling of red dots. But he said with complete control, 'What exactly do you mean?'

'You're a little weird, you know,' Irene said. 'That's why

485

I liked you in the beginning. But I don't know exactly how weird you are. I worry about leaving Campbell with you sometimes.'

'You thought that, and then you left him with me anyway?' Jatney said.

'Oh, I know you wouldn't harm him,' Irene said. 'But I just thought me and Campbell should split and go on to India.'

'It's OK,' David Jatney said.

They let Campbell completely destroy the snowman, then they all got into the van and started the twenty-mile drive into Washington. When they pulled into the Interstate, they were astonished to see it full of cars and buses as far as the eye could see. They managed to inch into the traffic but it took four hours before the endless monstrous steel caterpillar spilled them into the capital.

The inaugural parade wound through the broad avenues of Washington, led by the Presidential cavalcade of limousines. It progressed slowly, the enormous crowd overflowing the police barricades at spots and impeding progress. The wall of uniformed police began to crumble under the millions of people who pushed against them.

Three cars full of Secret Service men preceded Kennedy's limousine with its bulletproof glass bubble. Inside that glass bubble Kennedy stood so that he could acknowledge the multitude as he rode through Washington. Little wavelets of people surged up to the limousine itself then were driven back by the inner circle of Secret Service men outside the car. But each little wavelet of frantic worshippers seemed to lap closer and closer. The inner circle of guards was pressed back against the Presidential limousine.

The car directly behind Francis Kennedy held more Secret Service men armed with heavy automatic weapons and other Secret Service men on foot ran alongside it. The next limousine carried Christian Klee, Oddblood Gray, Arthur

Wix and Eugene Dazzy. Also in this car was the Reverend Baxter Foxworth who had been given this place of honor on the urging of Oddblood Gray. The argument being that Foxworth had delivered the black vote, more than half the population in Washington was black and it was presumed that blacks would make up a good part of the inaugural crowd. Foxworth's presence signaled that the new Kennedy administration respected the black movement. Also, Oddblood Gray worried that the Reverend Baxter Foxworth might fight the Alaskan work camps. This gesture of riding in a place of honor might give him pause.

The Reverend Foxworth was well aware of all this reasoning and rejoiced in the fact that he was going to launch an all out attack on the Alaska work camps the very next day. He had observed that the crowd had a great many blacks in it but they were overwhelmed by the influx of people all over the United States who had come to worship Francis Kennedy on this great day. Foxworth observed everything very carefully but since the cavalcade was inching along so slowly he passed the time by needling Arthur Wix, the National Security Advisor.

'I've looked up the history,' Foxworth said. 'And you are the first Jew ever to boss the military forces of America. Do you realize what that tells us? Finally the Jews no longer need feel they are a minority group, or outside the political power structure. You give us blacks some hope.'

Arthur Wix found the Reverend Foxworth unamusing. He said coldly, 'The National Security Advisor does not control the armed forces.'

The Reverend Foxworth said amiably, 'But you know your appointment was very symbolic. Maybe President Kennedy will appoint a black man to head the FBI when Attorney General Klee takes off both his hats.' He grinned at Klee.

Christian Klee had always had a sneaking admiration for the Reverend Foxworth and also knew he was not the target.

He said, 'I hope so, Reverend. As you say it would be a great symbolic appointment. I'll mention it to the President.'

Eugene Dazzy had brought a briefcase of papers with him, the case locked to his wrist with a steel cuff. He looked up for a moment and said, 'When Christian resigns Peter Cloot will be reinstated. The FBI slot will likely go to him.'

They were all silent. Christian Klee was lost in admiration at Francis Kennedy's finesse. The appointment would shut Cloot up about the atom bomb thing and then Kennedy himself would sweep everything under the rug.

The limousine was barely moving, the broad avenue was becoming awash with the crowd, stopping the advance of the cavalcade.

The Reverend Foxworth said to Wix, 'You know Israel could use your talents. But then I guess you co-operate with them pretty much even now.' He was tickled at how red Wix's face got.

Arthur Wix rose to the bait but more cold-bloodedly than Foxworth wished. Wix said, 'My record shows that I have given Israel less influence in our foreign policy than any other National Security Advisor. But I understand your implication which is essentially why don't I go back where I came from? That eternal question put to minorities. The answer is, that I come from America. What is your answer when someone puts that question to you?'

The Reverend Foxworth laughed and said, 'I just tell them you took me out of Africa, you figure out where I should go back. But I don't mean to quarrel. After all we represent the two most important minority groups in America.' He paused for a moment then added, 'Of course your people are no longer treated with any prejudice in this country. But we hope to get there someday.' It was just for a moment but Foxworth saw it. Arthur Wix held him in absolute contempt. And what made it worse was that it was not the contempt of a white man for a black man, it was the contempt of a civilized man for a primitive.

At that moment the car came to a complete stop and Oddblood Gray looked out the window. 'Oh shit, the President is getting out and walking,' he said.

Eugene Dazzy put the papers in the briefcase and snapped shut the lock. Then he unlocked the briefcase from his wrist and handed it to the Secret Service man sitting beside the driver in the front seat. 'If *he's* walking we have to walk with him,' Eugene said.

Oddblood Gray looked at Christian Klee, and said, 'Chris, you have to stop him. Use that veto of yours.'

'I haven't got it any more,' Christian Klee said.

Arthur Wix said, 'I think you'd better call a whole lot more Secret Service men down here.'

They all got out of the car and formed a wall to march behind the President.

President Francis Kennedy decided to walk the last five hundred yards to the reviewing stand. For the first time he wanted to touch physically the people who loved him, who had stood in the snow for many hours just to see him in the mechanized bulletproof glass bubble. For the first time he believed he had nothing to fear from them. And he wanted, on this great day, to show that he trusted them.

The large snowflakes were still swirling in the air, but they felt no more substantial on the body of Francis Kennedy than the communion wafer had felt on the roof of his mouth when he was a child. He walked up the avenue and shook the hands of those people who pierced the police-manned barriers and then the ring of Secret Service men assembled around him. Every so often a tiny wave of spectators managed to wash through, pushed on by the mass of a million spectators behind them. They crested over the Secret Service men who had tried to form a wider circle around their President. Francis Kennedy shook the hands of these men and women and kept this pace. Far down the avenue he could see the specially erected viewing stand where Lanetta was waiting for him. He could feel his hair getting wet from the snow but the cold air exhilarated him as did the devotion of the crowd. He was not conscious of any tiredness, of any discomfort, though there was an alarming deadness in his right arm, his right hand swollen from being gripped so often and so harshly. Secret Service men were literally tearing the lucky spectators away from their President. A young pretty woman in a creamy windbreaker had tried to keep holding his hand and he had to wrench it back to safety.

David Jatney pushed out a space in the crowd that would shelter himself and Irene who held Campbell in her arms. The crowd kept shifting in waves like an ocean and Campbell would have been trampled otherwise.

They were no more than four hundred yards from the viewing stands when the Presidential limousine came into their line of sight. It was followed by official cars holding dignitaries. Behind them was the endless crowd that would pass before the viewing stand in the inaugural parade. David Jatney estimated that the Presidential limousine was a little more than the length of a football field away from his vantage point. Then he noticed that parts of the crowd lining the avenue had surged out into the avenue itself and forced the cavalcade to halt.

Irene screamed, 'He's getting out. He's walking. Oh, my God, I have to touch him.' She slung Campbell into Jatney's arms and tried to duck under the barrier but one of the long line of uniformed police stopped her. She ran along the curb and was through the initial picket line of policemen only to be stopped by the inner barrier of Secret Service men. David Jatney watched her, thinking, if only Irene was smarter she would have kept Campbell in her arms. The Secret Service men would have recognized that she was not a threat and she might have slipped through while they were thrusting back the others. He could see her being swept back to the curb and then another wave of people swept her up again

490

and she was one of the few people who managed to slip through and shake the President's hand and then was kissing the President on the cheek before she was roughly pulled away.

David Jatney could see that Irene would never make it back to him and Campbell. She was just a tiny dot in the mass of people that was now threatening to engulf the broad expanse of the avenue. More and more people were pressing against the outer security rim of uniformed police and more and more were hitting up against the inner rim of Secret Service men. Both rims were showing cracks. Campbell was beginning to cry so Jatney reached into the pocket of his windbreaker for one of the candy bars he usually carried for the boy. His fingers felt the leather glove and inside it the cold steel of the .22.

And then David Jatney felt a suffusion of warmth through his body. He thought of the past few days in Washington, the sight of the many buildings erected to establish the authority of the state. The marble columns of the court and the memorials, the stately splendor of the façades; indestructible, irremovable. He thought of Hock's office in its splendor, guarded by his secretaries, he thought of the Mormon Church in Utah with its temples blessed by special and particularly discovered angels. All these to designate certain men as superior to their fellows. To keep ordinary men like himself in their place. And to direct all love on to themselves. Presidents, gurus, Mormon elders built their intimidating edifices to wall themselves away from the rest of humanity and, knowing well the envy of the world, guarded themselves against hate. Jatney remembered his glorious victory in the 'hunts' of the university, he had been a hero then, that one time in his life. Now he patted Campbell soothingly to make him stop crying. In his pocket, underneath the gun, his hand found the candy bar and gave it to Campbell. Then still holding the boy in his arms he stepped from the curb and ducked under the barriers.

*

491

The Reverend Baxter Foxworth didn't really like the idea of being on foot behind President Kennedy as they trudged up the avenue. It was boring, despite the multitude that cheered. He didn't like the wet snowflakes dropping, wetting and wrinkling his suit. But when members of the crowd broke through the two protecting rims, he quickened his step so that he would be beside the President. He shook the hands of the people who broke the barriers, trying to deflect them from Kennedy. He did this for two reasons. Primarily he wanted to be in the center of the TV coverage, secondly, he was worried about Kennedy. He prided himself on being streetwise, and this was a dangerous situation. But what the hell, he knew he would be walking near Kennedy, shaking hands, being hailed by the black brothers who recognized him. His spirits rose, this was one hell of a fine day. Then he saw running toward him a man with a small boy in his arms. He reached out to shake his hand.

David Jatney was filled with wonder and then a fierce elation. It would be easy. More of the crowd were overflowing the outer rim of uniformed police, more of those were piercing the inner rim of Secret Service agents and getting to shake the President's hand. Those two barriers were crumbling, the invaders marching alongside Kennedy and waving their arms to show their devotion. The street of the avenue looked like a marble floor covered with black insects. Jatney ran toward the oncoming President, a wave of spectators piercing the wooden barriers carrying him along. Now he was just outside the ring of Secret Service men who were trying to keep everyone away from the President. But there no longer were enough of them. And with a sort of glee he saw that they had discounted him. Cradling Campbell in his left arm, he put his right hand in the windbreaker, felt the leather glove, his fingers moved on to the trigger. At that moment the ring of Secret Service men crumbled and he was inside the magic circle. Just ten feet away he saw Francis

Kennedy shaking hands with a wild-looking ecstatic teenager. Kennedy seemed very slim, very tall, and older than he appeared on television. Still holding Campbell in his arms, Jatney took a step toward Kennedy.

At that moment a very handsome black man blocked him off. His hand was extended. For a frantic moment Jatney thought he had seen the gun in this pocket and was demanding it. Then he realized that the man looked familiar and that he was just offering a handshake. They stared at each other for a long moment, Jatney looked down at the extended black hand, the black face smiling above it. And then he saw the man's eyes gleam with suspicion, the hand suddenly withdrawn. Jatney with a convulsive wrenching of all his bodily muscles threw Campbell at the black man and drew his gun from the windbreaker.

The Reverend Baxter Foxworth had in that moment when Jatney stared into his face known that something terrible was going to happen. He let the boy fall to the ground and then with a quick shift of feet put his body in front of the slowly advancing Francis Kennedy. He saw the gun appear in Jatney's hand.

Christian Klee, walking to the right and a little behind Francis Kennedy, was using the cellular phone to call for more Secret Service men to help clear the crowd out of the President's path. He saw the man holding the child approach the phalanx guarding Kennedy. And then for just one second, he saw the man's face clearly.

It was some vague nightmare coming through, the reality did not sink in. The face he had called up on his computer screen these past nine months, the life he had monitored with computer and surveillance teams had suddenly sprung out of that shadowy jungle of mythology into the real world.

He saw the face, not in the repose of surveillance photos but in the throes of exalted emotion. And he was struck by how the handsome face became so ugly, as if seen through some distorted glass.

Christian Klee was already moving quickly toward Jatney, still not believing the image, trying to certify his nightmare, when he saw the Reverend Foxworth stretch out his hand. And Christian felt a tremendous feeling of relief. The man could not be Jatney, he was just a guy holding his kid and trying to touch a piece of history.

But then he saw the child in his red windbreaker and little woolen hat being hurled through the air. He saw the gun in Jatney's hand. And he saw Foxworth fall.

Unbelieving, he realized that he, himself, Christian Klee, had improperly directed fate by wiping David Jatney off the computer screen and canceling the surveillance. And in that same moment he saw that he, not Francis, must be sacrificed. Suddenly Christian Klee, in the sheer terror of his crime, ran towards Jatney and took the second bullet in the face. The bullet traveled thorugh his palate, making him choke on the blood, then there was a blinding pain in his left eye. He was still conscious when he fell. He tried to cry out but his mouth was full of shattered teeth and crumbled flesh. And he felt a great sense of loss and helplessness. In his shattered brain, his last neurons flashed with thoughts of Francis Kennedy, he wanted to warn him of death, to ask his forgiveness. Christian's brain then flicked out and his head with its deflowered eye socket came to rest in a light powdery pillow of snow.

In that same moment Francis Kennedy turned full toward David Jatney and heard the crack of the gun. He saw Foxworth fall. Then Klee. And in that moment, all his nightmares, all his memories of different death, all his terrors of malignant fate crystalized into a paralyzed astonishment and resignation. And in that moment he heard a tremendous vibration in the world, felt for a tiny fraction of a second only the explosion of steel in his brain. He fell.

David Jatney could not believe it all had happened. The black man lay where he had fallen. The white man alongside. The President of the United States was crumpling before his

494

eyes, legs bent outward, arms flying up into the air as his knees finally hit the ground. David Jatney kept firing. Hands were tearing at his gun, at his body. He tried to run, and as he ran he saw the multitude rise and swarm like a great wave toward him and countless hands reached out to him. His face covered with blood, he felt his ear being ripped off the side of his head and saw it in one of the hands. Suddenly something happened to his eyes and he could not see. His body was racked with pain for one single moment and then he felt nothing.

The TV cameraman, his all-seeing eye on his shoulder, had recorded everything for the people of the world. When the gun flashed into sight, he had backed away just enough so that everyone would be included in the frame. He caught David Jatney raising the gun, he caught the Reverend Baxter Foxworth making his amazing supple jump in front of the President and go down, and then Klee receiving a bullet in his face and going down. He caught Francis Kennedy making his turn to face the killer and the killer firing, the bullet twisting Kennedy's head as if he were in a hammerlock. He caught Jatney's look of stern determination as Francis Kennedy fell and the Secret Service men frozen in that terrible moment, all their training for immediate response wiped out in shock. And then he saw Jatney trying to run and being overwhelmed by the multitude. But the cameraman did not get the final shot, which he would regret for the rest of his life. The crowd tearing David Jatney to pieces.

Over the city, washing through the marble buildings and the monuments of power, rose the great wail of millions of worshippers who had lost their dreams.

27

President Helen DuPray held the Oracle's one hundredth birthday party in the White House on Palm Sunday three months after the death of Francis Kennedy.

Dressed to understate her beauty, she stood in the Rose Garden, and surveyed her guests. Among them there were the former staff members of the Kennedy administration. Eugene Dazzy was chatting with Elizabeth Stone and Patsy Troyca.

Eugene Dazzy had already been told he was fired to take effect the next month. Helen DuPray had never really liked the man. And it had nothing to do with the fact that Eugene Dazzy had young mistresses and was indeed already being excessively charming to Elizabeth Stone.

President Helen DuPray had appointed Elizabeth Stone to her staff, Patsy Troyca came with the package. But Elizabeth was exactly what she needed. A woman with extraordinary energy, a brilliant administrator, and a feminist who understood political realities. And Patsy Troyca was not so bad, indeed he was a fortifying element with his knowledge of the trickeries of Congress, his lower branch of cunning which could sometimes be so valuable to more sophisticated intelligences such as Elizabeth Stone's and indeed, thought Helen DuPray, her own.

After Helen DuPray assumed the Presidency she had been briefed by Kennedy's staff and other insiders of the administration. She had studied all the proposed legislation that the new Congress would consider. She had ordered all the secret memos be assembled for her, all the detailed plans, including the now infamous Alaska work camps.

After a month of study it became horrifyingly clear to her that Francis Kennedy, with the purest of motives, to better the lot of the people of the United States, would have, she believed, been the first dictator in American history.

From where she stood in the Rose Garden, the trees not yet in full leaf, President Helen DuPray could see the faraway Lincoln Memorial and the arching white of the Washington Monument, reminders of that city of massive stone and marble that was the capital of America. Here in the garden were all the representatives of America, at her special invitation. She had made peace with the enemies of the Kennedy administration.

Present were Louis Inch, a man she despised, but whose help she would need; George Greenwell; Martin Mutford and Bert Audick and Lawrence Salentine. The infamous Socrates Club. She would have to come to terms with all of them. Which was why she had invited them to the White House for the Oracle's birthday party. She would at least give them the option of helping build a new America, as Kennedy had not.

But Helen DuPray knew that America could not be rebuilt without accommodations on all sides. Also she knew that in a few years there would be a more conservative Congress elected. She could not hope to persuade the nation as Kennedy, with his charisma and personal romantic history, had done.

She saw Dr Zed Annaccone seated beside the Oracle's wheelchair. The doctor was probably trying to get the old man to donate his brain to science. And Dr Zed Annaccone was another problem. His PET Scan Verification Test was already being published in various scientific papers. Helen DuPray had always seen its virtues and its dangers. She felt it was a problem that should be carefully considered over a long period of time. A government with the capacity to find out the infallible truth could be very dangerous. True such a test would root out crime, political corruption, could reform the whole legal structure of society. But there were complicated truths, there were status quo truths and then was it not true that at certain moments in history, truth could bring a halt to certain evolutionary changes. And what about the psyche of a people who knew the various truths about themselves could be exposed?

She glanced at the corner of the Rose Garden where Oddblood Gray and the Reverend Foxworth were sitting in wicker chairs and talking animatedly. The Reverend Foxworth was wearing a flamboyant scarf bandage to remind people that he had miraculously recovered from the bullet that had torn his throat.

The Reverend Baxter Foxworth now spoke in a hoarse voice, but it was still vivacious, still enthusiastic about life in general and his own particular problems and ambitions. Helen DuPray could hear him distinctly.

'Otto, why the hell did I do it?' he said. 'I took that bullet for a white man. I didn't even think about it. I made my famous sideass move to get in front of Kennedy. He wasn't even a brother. Why, tell me why?'

Oddblood Gray, who was now seeing a psychiatrist every day for depression, said to him, 'Because you're a fucking born hero, Sideass.' The psychiatrist had told Gray that after the events of the past year it was perfectly normal for him to be suffering from depression. So why the hell was he going to a psychiatrist?

Foxworth contemplated the idea of being a hero. He said, 'I'm too competitive, that's all it was. And now that I'm going to run for Senator those fucking wishy-washy white niggers are calling me the ultimate Uncle Tom. They say only an Uncle Tom black man would take a bullet meant for a white man. How do you like that shit?'

'What do you care?' Oddblood Gray said. 'You'll be the

first black Senator from the state of New York. You can run their asses out of town.'

'The Ultimate Uncle Tom. Me,' Reverend Foxworth said. 'I broke the white man's balls for twenty years while they were combing out their Afros.' But he was smiling. 'What about you, Otto? Did the President ask for your resignation too?'

'No,' Otto gray said. 'I'm going to be a Cabinet Minister. HEW. Me and you will still be doing business.'

The Reverend Foxworth said. 'That's good. You know, Otto, now that a woman is President that sets a precedent. There's a chance for a black man to be Number One. If I were you, I'd stop going to that psychiatrist. You don't want that on your record if some day it happens you run for the highest office in the land. You can't be black and crazy both and expect to be elected President of the United States.'

In the Rose Garden, the Oracle was now the center of attraction. The birthday cake was being presented to him, a huge cake that covered the entire garden table. On the top, lettered in red, white and blue spun sugar, was the Stars and Stripes. The TV cameras moved in, they caught for the nation the sight of the Oracle blowing out the hundred birthday candles. And blowing with him were President Helen DuPray, Oddblood Gray, Eugene Dazzy, Arthur Wix and the members of the Socrates Club.

The Oracle accepted a piece of cake and then allowed himself to be interviewed by Cassandra Chutt who had managed this coup with the help of Lawrence Salentine. Cassandra Chutt had alrady made her introductory remarks while the candles were being blown out. Now she asked, 'How does it feel to be one hundred years old?'

The Oracle glared at her malevolently and at that moment he looked so evil that Cassandra Chutt was glad that this show was being taped for the evening. God the man was ugly, his head a mass of liver spots, the scaly skin as shiny

499

as scar tissue, the mouth almost disappeared. For a moment she was afraid that he was deaf or ga ga so she repeated herself. She said, 'How does it feel to be a century old?'

The Oracle smiled, his face cracked into countless wrinkles. 'Are you a fucking idiot?' he said. He caught sight of his face in one of the TV monitors, and it broke his heart. Suddenly he hated his birthday party. He looked directly into the camera and said, 'Where's Christian?'

President Helen Dupray sat by the Oracle's wheelchair and held his hand. The Oracle was asleep, the very light sleep of old men waiting for death. The party in the Rose Garden went on without him.

Helen DuPray remembered herself as a young woman, one of the protégés of the Oracle. She had admired him so much. He had an intellectual grace, a turn of wit, a natural vivacity and joy in life that was everything she wanted herself to be. And of course not to be left out, to be honest, his extraordinary achievements in life, uncommon even in America.

Did in matter that he always tried to form a sexual liaison? She remembered the years before and how hurt she had been when his friendship had turned into lechery. She ran her fingers over the scaly skin of his withered hand. She had followed the destiny of power, most women followed the destiny of love, like poor Lanetta Carr who had returned to her native Louisiana. Were the victories of love sweeter?

Helen DuPray thought of her own destiny and that of America. She was still astonished that after all the terrible events of the past year, the country had settled down so peacefully. True, she had been partly responsible for that, her skill and intelligence had blanketed the fire in the country. But still.

She had wept at the death of Kennedy, in a small way she had loved him. She had loved the tragedy written into the bones of his beautifully planed face. She had loved his idealism, his vision of what America could be. She had loved his personal integrity, his purity and selflessness, his disinterest in material things. And yet despite all this she had come to know that he was a dangerous man.

Helen DuPray realized that now she had to guard against the belief in her own righteousness. She believed that in a world of such peril, humankind could not solve its problems with strife but only with a never-ending patience. She would do the best she could, and in her heart try not to feel hatred for her enemies.

At that moment the Oracle opened his eyes and smiled. He pressed her hand and began to speak. His voice was very low and she bent her head close to his wrinkled mouth. 'Don't worry,' the Oracle said. 'You will be a great President.'

Helen DuPray for a moment felt a desire to weep as a child might when praised, for fear of failure. She looked about her in the Rose Garden filled with the most powerful men and women of America. She would have their help, most of them, some she would have to guard herself against. But most of all she would have to guard against herself.

She thought again of Francis Kennedy. He lay now with his two famous uncles, loved as they had been. Well, Helen DuPray thought, I will be the best of what he was, I will do the best of what he hoped to do. And then, holding tightly to the Oracle's hand, she pondered on the simplicities of evil and the dangerous deviousness of good.